A Theory and Treatment of Your Personality

– *a manual for change*

by
Garry A. Flint, Ph.D.

NeoSolTerric Enterprises
Vernon, British Columbia

Library and Archives Canada Cataloguing in Publication

Flint, Garry A., 1934-
A theory and treatment of your personality : a manual for change / by
Garry A. Flint.

Includes bibliographical references and index.
ISBN-10 0-9685195-5-5
ISBN-13 978-0-9685195-5-4

1. Personality change. 2. Subconsciousness. 3. Personality
disorders--Treatment. I. Title.

BF698.2.F58 2005   155.2   C2005-906626-1

Copyright © 2006 Flint, Garry A.
            NeoSolTerric Enterprises
            102 - 2903 35th Avenue
            Vernon, BC Canada V1T 2S7
            Phone. 250 558-5077
            E-mail: gaflint@process-healing.com
            Web site: //www.process-healing.com
            Cover by Jo C. Willems

First printing: September 2006

Disclaimer

        Great care has been taken in preparation of this book, but the author makes no expressed
or implied warranty of any kind, nor does the author assume any responsibility for errors or omissions.
Likewise, the reader assumes entire responsibility for what he or she may do with the information
presented here. The material in this book is experimental and is based on clinical results. There has
been no peer-reviewed research proving the efficacy of this treatment method. The author recommends
consulting with another mental health-care professional before self-administering this method and
assumes no liability for incidental or consequential damages in connection with or arising out of
the information contained in this book.
        This book provides accurate and authoritative information about the subject matter covered.
The author offers this information with the clear understanding that the information presented
here is not a substitute for professional mental health or medical advice, nor is the author giving
professional mental health or medical advice. If the reader wants mental health advice or any other
professional advice, he or she should seek the services of a competent professional.

            Printed in USA
            Lighting Source, Inc.
            La Vergne, TN

Acknowledgments

I have had a lot of support in writing this book. It seems like a lifelong process that started after I flunked out of the University of Redlands as a theoretical physics major. After I went back to school at San Francisco State University, I met Forrest Harrison, a fellow student. His enthusiasm and go-for-it mentality inspired me and put me in touch with Willard Day at the University of Nevada. The three of us worked together on a teaching machine program for a summer workshop and Day invited me to get a Master's Degree in experimental psychology at the University of Nevada. I continued my education at Indiana University, where I was fortunate to have James Dinsmoor as my mentor and dissertation chairman. Dinsmoor was a rock-solid experimental psychologist with complete integrity.

After graduating in 1968, I eventually ended up working with families and children. My theoretical bent started with my training and exposure to Francine Shapiro, who presented a descriptive theory for Eye Movement Desensitization and Reprocessing (EMDR) with which I had trouble. The theory had good face validity, but I was a reductionist, and Richard Smith introduced me to an article by Walter Freeman (1991), which directed my theoretical explanation of EMDR to chaos theory. This fit in with my learning theory background that was based on B. F. Skinner's work. Later, I trained with Roger Callahan, whose model for the treatment of trauma and mental issues motivated me to extend and refine the EMDR theory to cover the treatment interventions of Thought Field Therapy. I also want to thank Gary Craig, who gave me permission to publish a book based on his *Manual for Emotional Freedom Techniques* (Craig and Fowlie, 1995).

I discovered the mechanics for the Process Healing Method while treating a patient in November 1993. I collaborated briefly with Jane Wakefield-Flint until our theoretical inclinations took us in different directions. In general, I worked in isolation but conversed with Dean Kansky, who was enthusiastic in his support. He created a couple of interventions that appear in this book, gave many innovative suggestions, tried most of the interventions, and was creative in his use and exploration of the limits of the Process Healing Method.

I have had consistent support from Fred Gallo, whom I have bugged with my theoretical ideas on his Internet list on which I threw out my ideas from time to time. Charles Figley has been a longtime supporter of the work I was doing and of this book.

A few years ago I received an email from Joaquin Andrade (personal communication, March 20, 2002), a true physician-scientist who explored the Process Healing Method and found that it was indeed effective with many difficult patients. He went on to teach it to his colleagues and to present the ideas at institutions all over Latin America. He has truly been a motivating factor in my getting this book written in an acceptable format and completed. Eroca Shaler, Lee Pulos, Liz Medearis, and Donna Cameron gave valuable suggestions and support at various stages in developing and writing the book.

I want to thank Don Elium, who created the ProcessHealing-Forum to discuss the book as the chapters evolved. This Forum was the source of many insights and suggestions about how to improve the quality of the writing, as well as insights into the constructs from the readers. It also served to motivate me to organize and write the book. Thanks to those people on the forum who made contributions to the final version of the book if only by participating on the Forum. The Forum members who actively made suggestions were Joaquin Andrade, Claire Enright, Charles Figley, Laura Hewitt, Molly Hunt, Susan Hykes, Kathy Izzo, Caroline James, Colleen Kaffashan, Dean Kansky, Karen Milstein, Catherine Murphy, Judith Poole, Kate Strong, Zsigmond Szatmári, Phyllis Wadleigh, and others who commented to the list moderator about the positive value of the Forum.

Editing the book was a task. I have had a lot of help over the years. David Juran edited an earlier version of chapters 1 to 3; Joanne Martin edited chapters 1 through 6, pointing out confusing sentences and unclear sections. Two Forum members did extensive editing: Kathy Izzo, who gave significant help in clarifying the text and editing gross grammatical errors and gave great suggestions on the organization of sections of the book; and Kate Strong, who edited for clarity and made suggestions that improved the quality of the book. I want to specially thank a friend and colleague, Jo Willems, who was a sounding board every other week at lunch and who was a significant supporter. She went beyond the call of duty by critically editing the manuscript from start to finish. Her theoretical and clinical experience helped refine many of the concepts in the book. Finally, I sent it off to Christopher Butler of WordsRU.com and

Barbara Feiner, Los Angeles Professional Writers Group, who did the final edit and copyediting of the entire book.

I want to thank all of these people who contributed in their own way in the path to the completion of this book, especially to all my patients, who gave me varying amounts of insight, taught me about memory structures and about the uniqueness of all individuals.

I want to thank my daughters, Dana and Susan Flint, for their support in completing this project and Jennifer and Matt Wakefield for creating the pictures in Chapter VI. Most importantly, I want to give a special thanks to my wife, Jane Wakefield-Flint, who supported me in many ways and who put up with my theoretical conversations and theory-building.

Table of Contents

Preface

The reason for being and purpose of a clinician is to reduce human suffering and, in that ongoing battle, to look continually for innovative tools and new tactics. All dogmas, theories, schools, styles, lines of thought, beliefs, systems and their assumptions collapse in the face of an alternative intervention when the patient relaxes and says with a smile, "I feel much better! I can do things now that I couldn't do before!"

Because none of the available therapeutic tools is perfect, the clinician is a perpetual seeker. Attention must be divided between the practice of healing and the nonstop search for tools that may have the possibility of producing results that were not possible before. The clinician wants tools that work faster, simpler, and are longer lasting, less complicated, and free of side effects.

This was the sense of mission that led me, as a young doctor, some 30+ years ago, to take my first trip to China. I studied acupuncture at its original and most genuine source. Since that time, Traditional Chinese Medicine has been one of the tools that has helped my colleagues and me to achieve some of the goals mentioned above.

Throughout my extended career, I was never satisfied with the results I was getting in the treatment of anxiety disorders. The usual combination of drugs that are often prescribed with Cognitive Behavior Therapy (CBT) was not as effective for my patients as it was claimed to be in the literature. Most notably, it didn't produce the results we sought when treating panic disorders, agoraphobias, performance anxieties, and other phobias. Treatment with CBT required many sessions, and often psychoactive drugs had to be taken constantly to avoid relapses.

Then, in 1989, a dear colleague whose sister-in-law had been recently treated for her phobia with what was then called "Callahan Techniques™," was very impressed by the results. He said few treatments were necessary and the results were quick and complete.

It was then that he taught me his version of a phobia tapping protocol. At the time, we mistakenly assumed that the phobia protocol was the complete system! I started using the protocol on patients with a range of disorders: phobias, panic disorders, generalized anxiety disorder, test anxieties, and so forth. The results were overwhelming! We were so impressed with getting fast treatment responses that we decided to study, learn, and verify the treatment in depth with all our medical resources.

For 14 years, with slightly fewer than 50,000 patients, we conducted clinical trials in several centers in two countries. We had a distinguished team of MDs, clinical psychologists, neuroscientists, RNs, and professional researchers. We wanted to measure, within the boundaries of our clinical practice, the efficacy of those brief techniques that required activating traumatic memories while at the same time causing simultaneous multisensory overload of subcortical structures.

Our work resulted in what has been called the first large-scale clinical trials that compared the new Brief MultiSensory Activation techniques (BMSA) to the conventional "CBT with drugs." For reasons that we elaborate in our book on BMSA (Andrade, Aalberse, Sutherland and Ruden, 2006a), we prefer to describe this work as BMSA rather than "tapping" or "energy psychology." See Andrade, Aalberse, & Sutherland (2006b).

My good friend, David Feinstein, Ph.D., former researcher on psychotherapeutic innovations at the Department of Psychiatry of the Johns Hopkins University Medical School and author of the *Energy Psychology Interactive* CD (Feinstein, 2004), which was favorably reviewed recently by the American Psychological Association, has coauthored the resulting report of these trials comparing BMSA and CBT with medication (Andrade and Feinstein, 2003). The findings show that BMSA works better in fewer sessions and lasts longer than other types of therapy.

But as good as those techniques were, we still had our share of failures, even though our techniques dramatically improved the percentage of positive clinical outcomes. Dissociation — in particular, Dissociative Identity Disorder (DID) — was one of the disorders that we found difficult to treat with tapping alone.

Then one day, while searching an Internet list for persons who used tapping to treat people, we read a post from Dr. Flint about dissociation. He mentioned The Process Healing Method. I was curious and went to his web site, downloaded his instructions and immediately began to apply a basic version of Process Healing in our clinical work.

In just a few weeks, after having treated about three dozen patients, we found Process Healing extremely effective. We began applying it on patients for whom BMSA had failed. To our delight, a huge percentage of those resistant patients started to show results. So, following a previous pattern that had been used successfully for other disciplines, we decided that Process Healing could be similarly tested on a larger patient population.

At the moment of this writing, I have applied Process Healing to 600 patients. I am amazed at this incredible tool. I wrote to Dr. Flint, telling him that I thought he had discovered something very powerful and that its full potential was still to be developed.

Bear in mind that I learned Process Healing by reading Dr. Flint's instructions and that I practice what could be considered a beginner's version of Process Healing. However, the results I am getting with Process Healing on all kinds of PTSD, DID, anxiety disorders and every sort of somatization resistant to BMSA are very impressive! To our astonishment, even some kinds of purely physical disorders and complaints respond to Process Healing far better than can be expected from other therapies. If we are able to get such excellent results after studying only basic written instructions, just imagine what the reader of this complete text can expect!

I taught my simple version of Process Healing to about a dozen certified therapists in our group. We are all getting similar results. Namely, Process Healing yields positive clinical responses with 60% of the cases that failed to respond to every other therapy available to us!

Our present strategy is to continue using BMSA techniques with simple cases and to apply Process Healing to BMSA-resistant patients. At the same time, we are beginning to explore Process Healing in other pathologies, such as somatizations, headaches, sexual disorders, other primarily somatic disorders, and so forth.

From a theoretical point of view, the learning model that Dr. Flint uses to explain the Process Healing mechanism makes much sense to me. The process by which parts are invited to join the "Treatment Team" is full of analogies to the teaching process in which parts of the personality with self-limiting information are offered self-empowering information. No doubt all parts change during the process, and a new and healthier context results.

This text is the founder's handbook of The Process Healing Method. The book is by no means exhaustive and my guess is that future books will complete and expand it. Dr. Flint has so much to teach that it is impossible to reduce it to a single book.

Based on my experience with Process Healing, I suggest the reader digest this book with curiosity and immediately begin to practice and apply Process Healing with a passion. As my own experience and that of my colleagues have documented, Process Healing produces extraordinary results that are impossible to achieve by any other means of psychotherapeutic treatment. I invite the reader to thoroughly investigate this most fascinating therapeutic technique in the pages ahead.

Joaquín Andrade, MD
Medical Director, JA&A
Montevideo, Uruguay

Introduction

This book is intended as a guide for individuals who want to make changes in their personalities and for professionals who may want to use it in their practice. The purpose of this book is to provide you, the reader, with the understanding I have gained by developing, refining, and working with this treatment method over the past 12 years. Reports from Internet users, colleagues who are using it, and my own experience confirm the Process Healing Method as a respectful, effective, and safe way to treat self-destructive behaviors, beliefs, painful emotions and memories.

This book is both a step-by-step tutorial for how to use the Process Healing Method and a presentation of the theory behind the method. The first three chapters have been available on the Internet since 1998 and have been downloaded or read by several thousand people. These chapters describe the Process Healing Method in enough detail so that many readers have experienced the intervention just by reading the chapters. Many have gained a deeper understanding of themselves and realized positive changes in their lives by using this method.

Throughout this book, the aim is to provide you with enough information, in a "tutorial" style, to guide you in the process of speaking and responding to any barrier blocking treatment. This is an effort to make the book as easy to use as possible for both the nonprofessional and for the mental health professional willing to explore a new treatment approach. This approach is a useful adjunct not only in the mental health profession, but in the medical profession as well.

Some of the constructs in the theory are different from those in common use. It may be helpful to the mental health professional if I point out some of the underlying assumptions of this model of personality development and treatment.

1. The subconscious is a language process independent of conscious and unconscious activity and of all memories. It has capacities far beyond our expectations, such as being able to work independently of our personality to treat negative beliefs, memories and experiences. The subconscious will understand and learn as you read the book.

2. The conscious and unconscious constructs represent active memories and related neural activity. Memories are either dormant

or active in the conscious or unconscious Active Experience. Dormant memories do not take part in creating behavior. Only memories in the conscious and unconscious Active Experience take part in creating behavior. Memories are not stored in the unconscious or subconscious, which include only active memories. Dormant memories are simply inactive memories in the brain and body.

3. Internal and external stimulation (including our behavior) triggers relevant dormant memories into Active Experience while other no longer relevant active memories become and remain dormant.

4. Dissociation is a natural process and is present in our everyday behavior; for instance, your awareness of your body when you move or get out of a chair is dissociated information, namely, the information is not available in the conscious experience. In addition, dissociation is a process used during times of trauma when we dissociate the information that would be too uncomfortable to bear. I further assume that amnesia caused by the dissociation process, namely dissociative parts and memories, is different from the amnesia caused by severe, novel trauma, which causes amnesic parts and memories. While any individual may have both amnesic and dissociative parts, two different processes cause them. Amnesic parts and memories naturally include dissociative parts and memories when adaptive.

5. Internal and external stimulation and active memories determine everyone's behavior. There are two kinds of memories: Content Memories, which involve sensory experiences, and Emotion Memories. There are three state-dependent content-memory structures that contribute to running our behavior.

6. Memories have unique structures that associate with a collage of previously learned memories and emotions to create our behavior. The most helpful or fitting active Content and Emotion Memories assemble in a collage that associates with a unique memory structure. This memory structure represents our reaction to the current experience (i.e., it causes our current behavior). Memories are recycled repeatedly in different combinations to create new memories for new behaviors.

7. All brain and body activity is run and managed by memories. This means that it is possible to change memories in order to treat learned mental and physical issues.

I use many constructs in this model of the personality. The constructs, of course, are not real. They are metaphors for what is "real" in our minds and bodies. However, once the constructs and theory are absorbed, they provide a language with which to communicate with the subconscious in such a way as to cause change in a problematic issue. You may find the theory complex until you learn and become familiar with the concepts and the entire model. However, it is not necessary to understand the theory in order to begin your treatment process. The theory comes in handy for treating more complex structures. However, by communicating with the subconscious, you can simply work with it to identify the next appropriate intervention and the solutions to barriers. The more you use the Process Healing Method, the more skillful you will become and the more you will trust the model to simplify and treat complex problems or issues.

The constructs or metaphors used are powerful tools for communication. They effectively guide the subconscious to make changes in memory (i.e., to remove negative emotions from memories, which, in turn, will cause changes in behavior). For many mental health professionals, the constructs and terms used in this book are outside the box of common definitions. I have therefore included both an alphabetical glossary (see Appendix III) and a glossary of concepts (see Appendix IV) to help you organize and understand the definitions and constructs as useful tools. I encourage you to refer to the glossary whenever confusion arises with the concepts of Process Healing.

The memory structure is a key construct in this model. All memories have a unique memory structure and a collage of memories that associate *with*, or *to*, the memory structure. After using Process Healing for several years, I discovered that memory structures could form complex structures that could stop the treatment process. I had to treat these complex structures differently from the basic structures to successfully resolve an issue. The basic memory structure is a building block that explains most problematic memories that form under conditions ranging from mild (falling out of a tree) to severe traumatic experiences (systematic torture).

After using Process Healing for several years, I faced a barrier of even greater complexity. This was one that I could not treat with the subconscious and the usual treatment method. Now, when I have identified this new barrier in a patient, it is usually easy to treat. I call these barriers "fields," which I talk about briefly in chapter 6. Flint (n.d.) presents a more detailed presentation of the theory and treatment of fields.

When you run into a barrier to treatment not addressed in this book, it is time to problem-solve. I give many examples of problem-solving throughout the book. But remember, the power of the treatment process is in the metaphor or construct used, so feel free to create as many metaphors or constructs as you need to be successful. I have often found that even if you suggest an inaccurate metaphor, the subconscious may use it correctly to resolve the barrier. The point is, do not be afraid to be creative with metaphors. The worst that can happen is that they will not work. When they don't, just reassemble the constructs and create a new metaphor. Keep trying until you get the result you are looking for.

The definitions presented here of the conscious, unconscious, subconscious and dormant memories may also be new to the mental health professional. Rather than lump dormant memories in the unconscious or subconscious, I separate them. I consider the unconscious an active process because it influences our behavior, and the conscious mind is obviously an active process. Only active memories in the conscious and unconscious experience, not the dormant memories, are used to create our behavior. I call the active memories and associated neural activity in the conscious and unconscious the Active Experience.

Dormant memories are not active and are therefore not available for creating behavior. However, dormant memories may become active when triggered into the Active Experience. What separates the active conscious experience from active unconscious experience?

Well, because dissociation is a process that is generally believed to be used to hide memories, I decided a dissociation process would be an excellent adaptive process that would serve to move active conscious experience into active unconscious experience. Hypnotic suggestions, deliberate repression, and skills such as composing speech are examples of the use of dissociation to move a conscious active memory to an unconscious active memory.

In this model, the problematic memories and behavior take place as active memories in the conscious and unconscious experience. Consistent with other models, I use the subconscious as an inner-self helper and have discovered that it has an enormous capacity to make changes in memories and behavior. Almost all of my patients have easily accepted this model using conscious, unconscious, subconscious and dormant memories as its basic constructs.

Process Healing is an effective treatment method that people without training can use to treat many issues. Many people have had success working on their own without professional help. I recommend that laypeople using the Process Healing Method have a therapist with whom they can consult. Anyone with a history of mental illness or severe symptoms should be in therapy before using the Process Healing Method. Laypersons should not try to use it with anyone who has a history of mental illness, who is taking medication, or who has diagnosed mental issues. The more professional training and experience that a therapist or lay-person has, the more the Process Healing Method will be useful to treat complex personality and mental health problems.

This book is written to free you to be creative when using the constructs to solve a barrier that stops treatment. I have tried to teach the Process Healing Method by showing the way I use it in my successes and some of my failures. With practice, you may become skillful in using the Process Healing Method to quickly eliminate and gain freedom from problematic issues. Without further introduction, I leave you, the reader, to explore the Process Healing Method and to determine its usefulness in the treatment of your own painful memories, beliefs, or behaviors.

Garry A. Flint, Ph.D.
Vernon, British Columbia

A Theory and Treatment

of Your

Personality

– a manual for change

Part I

For the
Self-Help
Reader

Chapter 1

The Discovery of the Process Healing Method

The Process Healing Method is a treatment intervention for a wide variety of mental health issues. The discovery of the Process Healing Method took me by surprise. I was an experimental psychologist, a man of science and, though what I was seeing was extraordinary, I could hardly deny what was happening before my very eyes. The theory behind Process Healing is unusual and forced me, as a psychologist, to shift my way of thinking about what causes us to think and behave. This is a shift that I invite my colleagues to make with me.

A major part of this shift in thinking is that this method uses the subconscious in all stages of therapy. The subconscious is a part of us that has been there from the beginning. It is a brain process that starts to learn before we have sensory experience. I learned to trust the use of the subconscious to direct treatment, to do treatment interventions, and to certify the adequacy of my metaphors designed to model our mental processes and behavior. This first chapter takes you through the experiences that led me to this novel understanding.

You may wonder if the Process Healing Method is worthy of study and use by either individuals or mental health professionals. Here is some empirical support for the practical effectiveness of this method:

Dr. Joaquin Andrade, M.D. (personal communication, January 10, 2001), spearheaded finding an effective treatment method for patients served in 11 outpatient clinics in Argentina and Uruguay. He was looking for treatment methods to get better results. About 16 years ago, his clinicians started experimenting with Thought Field Therapy (TFT) (Callahan, 1985). This treatment involves tapping on acupressure points to remove pain. For 15 years, the research team collected data to assess effectiveness of treatment. The team contacted patients who had received treatment in a double-blind format at 3, 6, 9, and 12 months (Andrade and Feinstein, 2003). They found the tapping treatment routinely achieved 60 to 70 percent positive outcomes with 29,000 patients.

In 2001, Dr. Andrade (personal communication, January 10, 2001) discovered the Process Healing Method by visiting my web site (Flint, 2005). By following the instructions of the Process Healing course, he learned how to teach the subconscious to treat trauma and tried this treatment method in several clinics. With the first 64 patients who were failures with routine tapping, he realized 60 percent positive results (J. Andrade, personal communication, July 13, 2002). With more experience and some coaching, after treating 200 patients, he found that he obtained positive results with 65 percent of the patients treated (J. Andrade, personal communication, December 14, 2002). The Process Healing Method would probably be effective with all the success cases he had previously treated with tapping. If this were true, then one could estimate that Process Healing would be effective with 84 percent of patients who came to the clinics.

The discovery of the Process Healing Method took me by surprise: The subconscious could do the treatment inside the patient. The subconscious learned the tapping treatment method as the patient did Thought Field Therapy interventions. This discovery process continued over the next 12 years of personal study and research. Trained as an experimental psychologist with an emphasis on the theory of learning, I studied the behavior of rats, pigeons and squirrel monkeys. This training taught me that observation was important (Skinner, 1953, Flint, 1968). I now use this practice of observation in my work with patients. I carefully watch and listen to my patients to notice what I do that causes change in their present experience and in their experience of their issues. I have little formal education in clinical theories to interfere with my insight into personality dynamics. This combination of observation, ignorance of clinical theory, and training in hypnosis, Neurolinguistic Programming and several new, effective treatment methods, resulted in the development of Process Healing as a powerful treatment method. Preliminary research shows that the Process Healing Method is remarkably effective.

The subconscious is explained further in Chapter 2. My patients taught me that the subconscious is a useful ally in identifying and treating issues in therapy. The subconscious is a language process that has access to the neural activity of the entire brain and body. It can learn to change the role of memories by removing or adding emotions. These three properties of the subconscious—ease of communication, access to all memories, and a method of changing memories—make the subconscious an excellent ally in any treatment setting.

I also assume that unique memories cause all brain, behavior, and body processes such as muscle movements and organ activity. An active memory, such as thinking a thought or word, is neural activity. Your automatic response of "Great" to someone who says, "How's it going?"

is a learned response caused by remembered neural activity. When you learn a memory, like meeting someone's handshake, the memory runs the body automatically to meet the handshake without your even thinking. Memory involves learned neural connections that manage your physiology to create the learned response, namely to run the muscles that cause you to meet the other person's hand. Memories run all conscious and unconscious learned behavior. Mental problems or issues are memories with associated negative emotions. It is easy to change learned neural connections. Since the subconscious can change the emotions connected to memories, the therapist can try to treat any learned brain or body process when working with the subconscious. I now believe that it is possible to heal any learned mental or physical dysfunction.

The subconscious employs our native language and is open to communication. I have learned to use the subconscious to choose which psychological issue to address and the interventions that would be best. In short, I routinely use the subconscious to direct the treatment of my patients.

The strategy of having the subconscious direct treatment has moved me from doing therapy directed by the therapist to doing therapy directed by the patient. This patient-directed therapy is clearly respectful to my patients. It has also changed my problem-solving approach. I no longer look for solutions from my own knowledge. My problem-solving has become patient-oriented. I now look for solutions to problem behavior in some feature of memory caused by the learning process. Some forms of traumatic experience always cause problem behavior. Any trauma memory from the past distorts our behavior to some extent. I can treat these trauma memories with Process Healing. I use the subconscious to discover solutions to problems and to carry out the interventions.

Solving problems this way has led to the development of a model of learning and memory. Based on clinical observations and the solutions to real problems, this model is practical. Changes in patients' experience and behavior confirm the effectiveness of using interventions based on this model. The model has become a useful tool, as it provides ways to explain and treat maladaptive behavior. Best of all, solutions to problems with one patient have worked with other patients.

Over the years, I had been looking for faster ways to treat trauma. I learned several different treatment techniques. The most significant treatment technique learned, and the basis for Process Healing, was training to diagnose specific sequences of acupressure points to treat mental issues (Callahan, 1993). The treatment involved tapping on the diagnosed acupressure points. After I returned from this worthwhile training, my next patient taught me that the subconscious could do the tapping treatment. This internal treatment was the basis for the treatment approach that I eventually called Process Healing.

The practice of observation and using directions from the patient are both respectful and essential when working with this theory. This respectful approach and the basic premises of the theory give flexibility to problem-solving and treating difficult mental issues. The theory, then, is the basis for responding to and understanding a patient's description of his or her mental health issues.

The keys to our personality dynamics are amnesic and dissociative parts. Largely ignored in traditional therapy, these parts act like mini-personalities that serve some function in our behavior. People are not usually aware of amnesic and dissociative parts. I am going to describe how I discovered that amnesic parts could be barriers to hypnosis and that various prebirth amnesic parts could disturb adult behavior. I also found that the effects of preverbal trauma could have a strong impact on later behavior, while *in utero* trauma could cause subtle lingering effects on our behavior. Another significant finding was that amnesic and dissociative parts could fool the therapist. The possibility of deception keeps me alert to explore unusual results further. Another finding, contradictory to my beliefs, was that I could damage the subconscious. I will describe this later.

The journey started when a patient showed me how the subconscious could teach me to do better interventions. This experience challenged my more traditional approaches in my clinical practice. If the subconscious could teach me how to do therapy better, why not routinely use the subconscious to become a better therapist? This patient's subconscious helped me to create an intervention to move traumatic pain out of conscious experience into the unconscious while doing Eye Movement Dissociation and Reprocessing (EMDR) (Shapiro, 1995). EMDR involves having the patient focus on both a painful issue and on the movement of my fingers, which are moving back and forth in front of the patient at the same time. Though underwhelming to my EMDR teachers at the time, the intervention that I developed effectively reduced the intensity of emotional pain experienced while doing the eye-movement treatment. It also served to control the problem of emotional flooding when doing eye-movement processing. Emotional flooding occurs when the patient experiences all the traumatic pain as if the trauma were happening again. It also clarified the role of the dissociative process. The intervention causes the experience of the active memory not to be in the conscious experience, but in the unconscious experience.

My interest in theory led me to meld ideas based on learning theory (Skinner, 1953, 1957) and chaos theory (Freeman, 1991) to explain the active ingredients of EMDR (Flint, 1996, 2004). The theory explaining EMDR is the basis for Process Healing. The following is a brief introduction to the theory underlying Process Healing.

I want to emphasize to the reader's entire personality that the purpose of this book is to provide information. Some aspects of the personality may be threatened or triggered by the information in the book. The treatment method, which is taught to the subconscious, can be seen as the primary threat that has to be assessed carefully. Before the subconscious learns to treat trauma, all the barriers to treatment must be resolved. If some of the content of this chapter triggers emotions or internal voices as you read, perhaps you should consult a therapist before continuing. If you feel a flood of emotions at any time while reading this book, please stop reading, use your best judgment about continuing, and consult a therapist.

The Theoretical Basis for Process Healing

About 13 years ago, I started thinking of the brain as a chaos process (Freeman, 1991) and wrote a paper describing the active ingredients of change when using EMDR (Flint, 1996, 2004). Since that time, this theory, described in greater detail later, has helped me establish rapport with my patients. I explain to patients that memories start forming shortly after conception, not after birth, which is the common opinion. All areas of the brain begin storing memories while the brain is developing. At some point, the brain starts developing responses to sensory stimulation. The auditory stimulation by words, phrases, and sentences that come through the mother's body and stomach wall are remembered. By the time of birth, the fetus has many verbal memories, but no language.

After birth, learning continues with remembered verbal memories, but now neural representations of objects and actions are associated with the words. The memory of words associated with objects and actions becomes a functional language. This language, learned without sensory experience, becomes the subconscious. Because the subconscious has no sensory experience, he or she is able to "see" learned history and the internal dynamics of active memories. The subconscious can also control internal processes to cause changes in the experience of memories and behavior by treating the emotions associated with them.

At the same time as this language of the subconscious is developing, the Main Personality starts learning. The language learned by the Main Personality initially associates with internal and external sensory experience and, later, with pleasure and pain and basic needs. The subconscious and the Main Personality, therefore, learn two different neural representations related to the same experience. The subconscious learns without sensory experience and the personality learns with sensory experience and, later, with other properties.

Active memories are in the Active Experience, which is part of our Behavior System (see Figure 1-1). Before I make the distinction between conscious and unconscious active memory and dormant memory, I am going to tell you about dissociation. Because of the vast amount of information caused by active sensory experience and different memory activities, a process called dissociation is created.

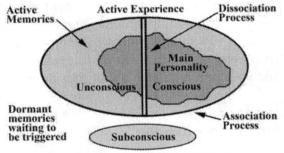

Figure 1-1 Our Behavior System

Dissociation reduces the quantity of information that we experience in our conscious experience. In Figure 1-1, the double lines shown crossing the Active Experience represent the dissociation process. The dissociative process causes all or part of a memory or sensory experience not to be experienced in our conscious experience and, therefore, creates the unconscious Active Experience. Unnecessary or painful parts of a memory can be "flagged" by the dissociative process in order to move the unwanted parts of a memory into the unconscious. These flagged memories are called "dissociated." The activity of dissociated memories is in the unconscious experience and not the conscious experience.

Memories that are not part of the Active Experience are called dormant. While all dormant memories are by definition inactive, they are all potentially active—waiting to be triggered. They are ready to be switched or triggered into activity in the Active Experience. The terms memory activity or active memories used here always refer to those memories that are active in either the conscious or the unconscious Active Experience, or both. Memories that are available to be triggered are called dormant.

The subconscious has access to everything experienced in the brain in both the conscious and unconscious experience. The subconscious does not experience any form of hurt; in other words, trauma never damages the subconscious. Later, I will explain how I was able to hurt the subconscious by having the subconscious do something not normally done. Fortunately, I recognized the problem and was able to repair the subconscious. It is important to stress the fact that the subconscious appears to be always whole and healthy with no barriers to inhibit the view of the internal "reality." When I talk to a patient about the formation of the personality, I explain the reasons why intense traumas cause amnesic parts. I explain that these parts are normal personality parts learned during the span of a trauma, but having few neural connections to the Main Personality. Amnesic parts also have executive function and can create novel adaptive behavior, while dissociative parts are more like skills and can only create adaptive behavior that was previously learned.

Patients often hear comments in their thoughts or experience a "Yes" feeling while I talk. This makes the model of the personality I am presenting true for them. However, in most cases, the subconscious will communicate in the first session by using finger responses, signaling "Yes," "No," "I don't know," "I don't want to tell you," or by making no finger response.

My Neurolinguistic Programming Training (NLP) (Rice and Caldwell, 1986) taught me about auto-treatment. Auto-treatment is obvious when personality changes occur without any outside influence. One can teach an NLP intervention, called the six-step reframe (Cameron-Bandler, 1985), to treat issues at night while the patient sleeps. When this works, the patient asks to change beliefs or behaviors when he or she goes to bed and awakens with the change completed. After an experience with a certain patient, which impressed me with the power of the subconscious, I decided to extend the auto-treatment notion. Since then, I have found barriers to auto-treatment in other individuals. The subconscious can treat these barriers to enable it to treat issues automatically and to perform independently of the active personality.

The Subconscious Can Teach the Therapist

The first clinical experience that caught my attention occurred when I was seeing many patients with multiple personality disorders. One of my patients allegedly had 200 dissociated or amnesic personality parts. These parts were all amnesic or unaware of one another because they could not communicate. This patient was difficult. Often, the part that came to the session did not believe there were any other parts. Sometimes she didn't know who I was. She learned that by talking as fast as she could, she could prevent dissociation. When she dissociated, a trauma part would begin to run the body. She always dissociated during the latter half of the session. The active amnesic part was usually willing to work with me. I treated parts using Eye Movement Desensitization and Reprocessing (EMDR) (Shapiro, 1991). I had to be careful using this treatment with the patient because of the possibility of emotional flooding. This patient taught me something important that changed my life.

One day, after completing a session, I turned my back on the patient to write an appointment card. I heard a loud gasp. As I turned around, I saw her pushing her chair back with her feet. The chair was bouncing across the floor. When she stopped bouncing, I saw the patient's eyes open wide and moving back and forth rapidly. I noticed that her eyes focused just above her knees. She said in a panicked tone, "I see a white light; I see a white light." I calmly reassured her that the experience was not unusual. I asked if I could talk to her subconscious. The subconscious said, "Yes." She said, "No." Most of her parts did not like me talking to her subconscious and parts. Her response almost always came out, "Yes, No." I asked, "Subconscious, are you telling me that I should do the eye movements down near the knees?" The subconscious said, "Yes." The visual hallucination immediately stopped. This experience prompted deliberate exploration, using the subconscious to orchestrate and refine my treatment interventions.

From this point, I increasingly began to use a semi-hypnotic technique with my patients. While the patient was awake, I used finger responses to talk to the subconscious. I communicated by asking leading questions to which the subconscious said, "Yes" or "No." The subconscious advised me in which order to treat issues and indicated which therapeutic technique to use to treat an issue. I felt that my therapy was becoming more respectful to all parts of the patient while addressing treatment goals that were more relevant to the patient.

Treating Emotional Pain in the Unconscious

By working with a patient's subconscious, I developed a treatment intervention to control flooding while doing EMDR The treatment intervention provides for painless treatment of trauma pain by combining EMDR and the dissociative process. By suggesting that the pain be dissociated while treating the trauma with EMDR, the dissociation process takes place and the trauma pain moves from the conscious experience into the unconscious experience as the processing continues. The patient does not feel the painful trauma emotions during the treatment.

Stimulation of the brain with the eye movements causes an exchange of the painful trauma emotions with the relaxed or neutral emotions that are active (Flint, 1996, 2004). With repeated eye movements, the pain gradually reduces to the point where the trauma memory is no longer painful. I used this process with four or five other patients who also helped with minor details in developing this treatment technique. The technique has been effective in treating severe trauma because it lowers the chance of emotional flooding into the conscious experience. Patients ranging from nine to 52 years have responded well to this procedure.

Subconscious Directed Treatment

My theory is that different neural patterns of eye movement are active during trauma. This neural pattern becomes associated with the memory of the traumatic pain. Bearing this in mind with many of my patients, I have asked the subconscious to tell me the direction of eye movement that is most helpful for treating the patient. I have received many unique and interesting instructions from the subconscious. For example, with one patient, the subconscious told me to move my fingers in random, smooth, circular strokes while moving my hand closer to and farther away from the patient. In addition, the subconscious told me that I should hold a silver pen with a gold tip in my hand for the patient to follow with his eyes. Though I forgot about the pen nearly every session, the subconscious always reminded me to use it. For five weekly sessions, this unique procedure, "ordered" by the subconscious, continued. During this time, the patient had a continuous severe headache. The headache stopped, indicating the completion of treatment. The subconscious no longer reminded me to use the gold-tipped pen. For this patient, this unusual treatment neutralized the pain of seven years of viewing frequent gory traumas and deaths.

Discoveries

Barriers to hypnosis

In hypnosis, some patients were difficult, if not impossible, to put into a deep trance. There seemed to be a barrier blocking the trance induction. While addressing this problem, I received strange finger responses. I discovered that prebirth traumas caused prebirth parts. In some ways, prebirth parts are just like the amnesic parts previously described. However, the experience of prebirth parts *in utero* is similar to the young subconscious; namely, it is always awake. Prebirth parts learn to relay information from the subconscious to the personality. These prebirth parts can become barriers to getting deep trance. I learned to establish rapport and talk to the prebirth parts. I usually got them to accept treatment with EMDR or to become quiet. With these barriers quiet, I was able to put the patient into a deep hypnotic trance.

Prebirth parts and behavior

The awareness of prebirth parts helped me to overcome barriers to communication with the subconscious. Often, while I was building rapport with the subconscious, I discovered the presence of prebirth parts. When I treated a prebirth part with EMDR, I asked the subconscious to manage the rate of experience of the traumatic memories of the prebirth part. I provided eye movements to treat the part's trauma. This approach was effective with many of my patients. The effect sometimes resulted in a subtle but pervasive change. One case example is a patient who had a tendency to wail like a baby when she was upset. She had been a difficult, disruptive patient during treatment at the local clinic. Treating the trauma of the prebirth part that caused the wailing made the wailing behavior stop. At the end of the session, she told me her mother said that her father had kicked her mother during the pregnancy. The mother started bleeding and had a cesarean delivery.

Preverbal trauma

A therapist can use the same treatment procedure to treat preverbal traumas—traumas that occur before the development of verbal skills. One can access preverbal traumas by asking directly or by presenting stimuli to elicit the trauma part. In one case, a young boy had had 16 earaches between the ages of six and twelve months. I triggered emotions associated with the trauma of the earaches by putting my hand next to his ear. After I treated this trauma with EMDR, he would allow me to put my hand near his ear without an emotional response and showed no emotional reaction. This resulted in a marked change in his behavior at school. In the next session, I tested his response to the trauma-related stimuli by moving my hand near his ear, and he had no fear. I told him to imagine that I was wearing a white coat, and I put my hand near his ear. Again, emotions flooded his experience. Matching the conditions of his trauma evoked even more intense emotions then I had previously seen. I treated these emotions by using EMDR

Lingering early trauma

A patient complained of mood swings, which resembled something like manic-depressive behavior. I considered novel ways to explain the cause of manic-depression or at least the mood swings experienced by this patient and others. What if some prebirth and preverbal neural activity was switching in and out, causing the rapid mood changes? Could it be that some form of trauma occurred during the prebirth and preverbal periods before the brain structures and functions developed fully? I hypothesized that a specific trauma occurred and that this trauma associated with the neural activity of memories of the entire brain. This led to guessing the possibility of lingering trauma picked up *in utero.*

I speculated that the first trauma that a fetus would experience would be the emotional response caused by the limitation of movement. The limit of physical activity causes a memory of the emotional response, or at least a neural response associated with hurt. During this frustration, the brain is working without well-defined neural patterns. Under these conditions, a trauma would associate with all the neural activity of the entire brain. Later, specific areas of the brain would increase their activity and assume muscle control, midbrain activities, and other functions. Later still, those specific areas that actively serve particular functions can erase the early trauma memories. Finally, after active pathways of brain functions and muscle movements had fully developed, the early trauma memory would only remain in the relatively inactive neural areas of the brain. A great portion of the brain may not have constant repetitive neural activity, and this is where the traumatic memory of the early constriction trauma lingers. I call it lingering prebirth trauma.

I tested this theory with an intervention I carried out with many patients, a treatment I discovered by working with the subconscious of my patients. To treat this supposed condition of lingering trauma, I used a treatment intervention developed to treat trauma pain associated with eye position and the shifts between brain-hemisphere activities during trauma. The intervention involved the Callahan 9-Gamut Procedure (Callahan, 1985) in the following way.

Direct the patient to tap steadily on a point on the back of the hand, a half-inch behind both of the large knuckles of the ring and little finger. While tapping, direct the patient to look straight ahead, close her eyes, look down to the right, look down to the left, whirl her eyes in a circle in one direction, then whirl them in the other direction. Then direct the patient to hum a tune, count from one to five, and then hum a tune again. The subconscious said that this procedure would work to treat these hypothesized traumas lingering in quiet areas of the brain.

The following case had a prebirth trauma so I tried treating lingering trauma. I tapped on the 9-Gamut spot on the back of both hands of the patient and had the patient do the 9-Gamut treatment. The patient said that after doing three 9-Gamut treatments, she was dizzy. After three more 9-Gamut treatments, she had pain in her side and stomach. After four more treatments, she had anger and pain. After four more, the subconscious signaled the completion of the intervention. Then she had pain in her head. I followed the directions of the subconscious. After two more 9-Gamut Procedures, this pain was gone. The treatment was obviously having some effect on neural activity and produced some behavioral effects. She reported that the procedure weakened self-limiting beliefs involving guilt.

I used this procedure of repeated 9-Gamut treatments with a child. He experienced dizziness, sleepiness and then dizziness that he described as "like emptiness in my whole head with something swirling around." Then he felt more dizziness. Then he felt clearer and I assumed that we had completed the intervention. In the following session with this young fellow, the subconscious led me to develop another procedure, working on the entire brain. This time, the patient repeated the following intervention suggested by the subconscious: Tap eight times on his forehead and eight times on the back of his head. In the following replications of this intervention, the patient felt progressively more tired and dizzy. Then he had a headache, and then he felt a little "drunk." The subconscious told me to treat this last feeling with the eye movement procedure (EMDR). A week later, this patient said that he was doing better at school, that he felt it was easier to concentrate, and that he was becoming more independent in his play.

The subconscious as the treatment agent

One month after I completed the Thought Field Therapy diagnostic training with Callahan (1993), I received an incredible learning experience from another patient. This woman came into my office complaining of feeling incapable of handling her financial problems. I used the Callahan diagnostic and treatment techniques to treat the belief: "I can't control or manage my life." She immediately had the insight that her boyfriend was reinforcing her feeling of being incapable. While I was talking to her about this possibility, she said, "I feel this tickle on my upper lip." I asked her subconscious, "Subconscious, are you trying to tell my patient to tap on her lip?" The subconscious said "yes" by raising the index finger. I had the patient tap on her upper lip. We continued talking.

Again, she felt a series of sensations at different points on her head and face. I inquired again, and the subconscious told her to tap on the points where she felt the tickles. At one point, she said, "Oh, God. They're going too fast! They're going too fast!" I said, "Hold it, subconscious. Hold it." I asked the subconscious if she could do the tapping on the inside to treat the trauma while the patient just sat. The subconscious said, "Yes." I asked the subconscious if she would do it. The subconscious said, "Yes." Consequently, the patient sat there with her left arm on her lap and her right arm pointed up. After a minute or so, she said, "Wow! All this energy is flowing out of my fingertips." She said that she felt clearheaded and capable, and knew what she wanted to do to resolve her present financial predicament. I believe her subconscious had completed treating some traumatic history having to do with competence. The subconscious, to my surprise, had learned to treat internally. This experience showed me that it was possible to have the subconscious treat a patient's issue without my intervention.

The subconscious in trouble

After this experience, I systematically started to teach the subconscious of my patients how to do self-treatment—the internal tapping. I had another patient who had 60 parts that were ready to receive treatment. After treating many parts, I wanted to find out the number of untreated parts remaining, and so I asked the subconscious. To my surprise, what I learned from the subconscious was that she had independently treated nine parts in the preceding weeks. I asked her if she had tried to treat the suicidal parts that I had identified in an earlier session. She said, "Yes." With further inquiry, the subconscious said that she became frightened when she provided treatment of those parts on her own. By asking leading questions, I discovered the suicidal parts had flooded into the Active Experience and had started to run the body. They presented a serious suicidal threat. The subconscious was "frightened;" in other words, she recognized the danger of suicide. Other parts that became active had difficulty protecting the patient from the intent of the suicidal parts. Since then, I usually try to treat suicidal parts as soon as possible. It is easier to do this now because I have learned a strategy to treat dangerous parts slowly and safely. This strategy removes the possibility of having suicidal thoughts or parts motivated by emotional flooding. It is respectful to all parts of the personality.

The subconscious can learn barriers

One of the most helpful qualities of the subconscious is that it is not subject to damage by trauma and physical sensations. The subconscious can accurately see life history and help diagnose and treat traumatic issues. However, I managed to damage a patient's subconscious. (This damage was easy to repair, as you will see.) I caused the damage by having the subconscious step into her body experience and converse with me directly. I wanted to expand my understanding of the internal processes and thought that direct communication with the subconscious using spoken language would promote this goal. The subconscious was able to do this, and in one session we conversed readily.

In a later session, I noticed the subconscious was not as effective in identifying and treating issues as she had been previously. Using leading questions, I discovered that the subconscious process, while in the Active Experience, had associated with physical sensations. The physical sensations created barriers to "seeing" internal history and was restricting her view of the inner dynamics and her control of internal processes. I corrected this mistake by having the subconscious look through the patient's eyes while I did eye movement processing. After treatment, the subconscious again became very effective in identifying and treating issues. Since this experience, I believe that it is inappropriate and even harmful to ask the subconscious to *run* the body and communicate with spoken words. Covert communication seems to cause no problems.

Parts can fool the therapist

The following is an example of the usefulness of working with the subconscious to solve a problem. In a session with a torture survivor, I identified at least three new parts that I had not met in previous sessions. I asked the subconscious if she could treat these parts. The subconscious said, "Yes." I asked her to treat these parts and to let me know when she had finished. After she finished, I asked if she had joined these parts with "Barbara," as I normally had her do. She said, "Yes." I asked Barbara to become the active personality. She spontaneously commented that the three parts that had recently joined with her had made her experience chaotic. I returned to the subconscious to discover that I had been working with a surrogate subconscious—a fake subconscious. The integrated parts still had trauma emotions associated with them. The trauma emotions associated with the parts caused a disturbance in Barbara. While the surrogate subconscious was the active personality, I asked the true subconscious if she could treat this part. The subconscious signaled "No" with a thumb response.

I communicated with the subconscious by asking leading questions and getting "Yes" and "No" answers. It is similar to the game of 20 questions. I discovered the surrogate subconscious was a programmed part, a part deliberately created by the use of torture. One of its activities was to repeat "I won't do it" continuously in the unconscious. This repetitive, unconscious behavior caused a barrier to treatment. It disorganized the patient's unconscious behavior so treatment would not work. It was like receiving therapy while repeatedly singing "Bongo, bongo, bongo, I don't want to leave the Congo." I reassured the subconscious that painful emotions motivated the "I won't do it, I won't do it" program. The patient learned these emotions from the trauma during the programming. I stressed that the repeating response would become less motivated as she treated the trauma emotions associated with the program. She said she would try to treat the programmed part as I had previously requested. I waited while the subconscious was doing the treatment and talked to the programmed part. After several minutes, the surrogate said, "I'm beginning to feel confused" and then, within a minute, she gradually went into a dormant state; my patient's eyes closed and her head slumped. Barbara returned to become the active personality. She said spontaneously that another fragment joined with her. Therapy continued.

Flexibility when treating with the subconscious

In a recent case, a patient came in complaining that she felt confused after she exercised. She had stopped exercising for about 10 days and started feeling clearheaded. Conversation with her subconscious suggested there was a part that was coconscious in her conscious experience when she was exercising that gave her the lingering confusion. I set up rapport with all parts and was soon teaching the subconscious how to diagnose and treat parts. I then ran into a barrier. I was not seeing any finger responses.

I dealt with this barrier by assuming it was caused by a part. My approach was to set up rapport with the part and then treat it. I told her that all parts, including the prebirth parts, parts formed at birth, preverbal parts, or any other traumatic parts, were members of one personality. Trauma created those parts that seemed independent. They had experience in the body that gave them a false sense of ownership or fears about treatment. If they were all treated by neutralizing their trauma emotions, they could join the Main Personality. They would then experience more satisfaction in life and be able to protect themselves more effectively. With this explanation, I was hoping to get permission from this part and other parts to teach the subconscious how to treat trauma memories. By being respectful of all parts and by educating them and answering their objections, all parts eventually wanted treatment and to join with the Main Personality.

After getting permission from the parts, I taught the subconscious to locate the treatment points by tapping the points on myself. My demonstration taught the subconscious how to treat the painful emotions associated with the trauma memories learned during the trauma experience. The subconscious eventually signaled that she was able to treat a part that was coconscious with the patient and who was the cause of her confusion. I asked the subconscious to start this process and chatted lightly with the patient as the subconscious continued to treat the part. After three or four minutes, the patient said she felt clearer. I asked the subconscious to signal with a finger response when she finished. Within a few moments, the subconscious signaled that she was finished. The patient felt much clearer by the end of the session. She later reported that she had no confusion after exercising.

Summary

A language process starts forming *in utero* and later becomes our subconscious. By explaining how the subconscious and the personality are formed, one can get rapport with the subconscious and all aspects of the personality. The subconscious is useful to direct the path of treatment, to help create new ways to treat difficult issues, to organize treatment plans, and to learn how to treat the effect of trauma. In addition, the subconscious can learn how to treat negative experiences automatically and independently of the Main Personality. The subconscious can treat active memories (negative beliefs, simple memories and life experiences) in different ways. The subconscious can apply these techniques to treat unknown trauma in a person's history, such as self-limiting beliefs and other traumatic experiences and memories. While this form of treatment lacks support from published research, it has been effective for scores of patients treating themselves, as well as patients in my office and patients in clinics in Latin America.

The Process Healing Method is a treatment intervention that developed out of my relationship with my various patients' subconsciouses. To summarize the process, the therapist first educates and works with all aspects of the personality to convince the aspects to want to receive treatment and join with the Main Personality. This approach is both respectful to the patient and makes later treatment easier. I call the process of getting parts on the Treatment Team the Education Process. The goal is to get all aspects of the personality to want to be treated and join the Treatment Team. During this process, the patient learns a way to communicate with the subconscious and aspects of the personality. When all aspects are on the Treatment Team and give permission, the therapist then teaches the subconscious how to treat painful emotions. Then in the treatment process, the patient or therapist asks the subconscious to treat painful or problematic issues.

This tale started in October 1991. By 1994, I was teaching the Process Healing Method to my patients by modeling the tapping treatment process. At first, I physically showed each of the acupressure treatment points to the subconscious, point by point. Now, a 30-second metaphor, which always works, teaches the treatment process. The next chapter, Chapter 2, introduces and gives an overview of the theory and procedure of Process Healing. It includes a transcript of the first session of the Process Healing Method and several examples of treatment interventions. Chapter 3 describes the entire basic procedure for getting all parts on the Treatment Team and teaching the subconscious the treatment method. The procedure to obtain rapport with the subconscious and all parts is now routine. In Chapter 4, I give detailed examples of many useful treatment interventions and aids. I use these treatment interventions routinely with most patients.

The theory of the development of the personality and memory structures is presented in Chapter 5. This is the most challenging chapter in the book. This knowledge is useful when problem-solving new structures and finding solutions for complex personality issues. Chapter 6 will teach you how to problem-solve and resolve difficult or complex barriers to treatment. Many readers won't have to solve complex problems, but the interventions are included for those who do. Chapter 7 describes the treatment of dissociative and amnesic parts and all the complexities that can arise when treating parts. Chapter 8 introduces the more complex features of memory, namely memory structures and other constructs. These structures and constructs were discovered while solving patients' issues and are frequently found to be the cause of problematic behavior and unusual experiences. Chapter 9 describes many treatments that are useful for relatively simple issues. Chapter 10 focuses on several complex disorders like depression, addictions, obsessive-compulsive behavior, psychotic behavior, and so forth. Chapters 9 and 10 are written primarily for therapists.

Now you know how my patients taught me and helped me learn a new respectful and effective treatment intervention. For those who have read some books about psychology and have opinions about brain, mind, and behavior, I want to point out what I think may be a paradigm shift for some readers. If you can suspend your previous learning and research-based ideas and accept the clinically based truisms presented here, this book offers a refreshing description of the development of the personality and explanations for complex mental issues. Here are what I consider to be the major shifts in beliefs.

1. The subconscious is accessible in everyone. It is not the unconscious. The subconscious is a unique process, with whom a therapist can communicate.

2. Dormant memories are available to be triggered into activity in the conscious or unconscious. They are not located in the unconscious.

3. Behavior and all brain activity are collages assembled from previously learned memories active in the conscious and unconscious.

4. Dissociation causes the conscious and unconscious experience of active memories.

5. Memories that are dissociated and cause intrusions are different than amnesic parts. They are more like dissociated skills and, most importantly, don't have executive function. Amnesic parts, on the other hand, are compartmentalized memory structures (Blizard, et al., 2005) created in novel, severe trauma who have executive function.

6. Different processes cause dissociative and amnesic parts.

I hope you find this book both fascinating and useful, personally or professionally.

Chapter 2

An Introduction to the Process Healing Method

The Process Healing treatment method was discovered in 1994. Since then, it has gradually developed and become more respectful, better organized, and more systematic. Based on science and clinical experience, Process Healing is essentially an Education Process. I teach patients how all aspects or parts of the personality and subconscious are normal and develop from conception to the present. This chapter gives an outline of the treatment method and includes a scripted session to give you the feeling of how the method works. If you have any problems with the vocabulary, Appendix III is an alphabetical glossary and Appendix IV is a glossary of new concepts.

Here is a brief outline of how Process Healing works. The example consists of a script of the conversation between the therapist and the patient's or reader's subconscious. This text becomes the therapist for the patient. The therapist first educates and works with all aspects of the patient's personality to convince the aspects to want treatment. This approach is respectful to the patient and builds trust between the therapist and patient. This is called the Education Process. During this process, the reader or patient learns a way to communicate with his or her subconscious and aspects of his or her personality. When all aspects are on the Treatment Team and give permission, the therapist then teaches the patient's subconscious how to treat painful emotions. At this point, the patient or therapist is ready to ask the subconscious to use the treatment process to treat painful or difficult problems.

The Education Process — Establishing Rapport

The Treatment Team and treatment

A key feature of the Process Healing Method is the internal Treatment Team (Satir, 1972). The Treatment Team notion is introduced to organize all parts of the personality into a cooperative group. Arranging for parts to cooperate is a major asset for the treatment process. It makes the treatment process safer and easier with fewer problems. It is always necessary to discuss the reasons for treatment and to resolve the barriers to treatment in order to get all parts to join the Treatment Team. A common barrier is the fear of re-experiencing trauma emotions. I present a strategy for safely treating extreme emotions. This strategy will be explained later in this chapter. Next, I describe the mechanics of integrating or joining parts with the Main Personality. I point out that the subconscious will strengthen all positive coping behavior with positive emotions so no assets are lost. At some point, I make a double check to see that all parts are on the Treatment Team and all want the subconscious to learn the treatment process. After one final check, I teach the subconscious how to treat trauma.

When therapists work with the subconscious and inner processes, they use metaphors. There are many different metaphors to treat people. I assume that all change activity in people is the same but the metaphors are different. I use a metaphor to teach the subconscious how to do the treatment process. Then I have the patient identify a simple phobia or moderately painful belief or memory to be used by the subconscious to practice diagnosis, to form a treatment plan, and to execute the treatment process. Then, I ask the subconscious to treat the practice issue and remove the negative emotions associated with that issue. As the treatment process occurs, the patient may feel the pain of the issue gradually diminish in intensity. The subconscious becomes an ally in therapy by analyzing treatment issues and directing treatment.

Memory — Dormant or active

Before I continue, I want to tell you about dormant and active memories. Memories are either dormant or active. Dormant memories are potentially active, but not experienced. Dormant memories are ready to be triggered into the Active Experience. Active memories, on the other hand, are in what I call the Active Experience. The Active Experience includes both the active conscious and unconscious memories. The active memories contribute to creating behavior. Some of the active memories in the Active Experience combine to create behavior by evoking a response from the body. Changes in the person's environment are represented in the Active Experience. A change in the environment triggers or activates other relevant memories that can combine to create the next response. Other memories become dormant.

For example, I am going to ask a question and you will know the answer. The dormant answer to that question will become active in the Active Experience. Now, before you have the question, you do not know the answer. The answer is still dormant. Here is the question: "Are you right-handed or left-handed?" Your response to the question became active and you thought of the answer. Dormant memories appear inactive and do not contribute to our behavior. But dormant memories are indeed active (potentially), ready to be triggered into the Active Experience as active memories. The Active Experience includes both conscious and unconscious active memories. Chapter 3 provides more details about memory activities in the conscious and unconscious.

Building rapport

By describing how the personality and subconscious came to be, one can usually set up early rapport with all parts of the personality, at least with those who are listening. Dormant parts will not hear unless they are triggered into the Active Experience. The goal is to get all parts on the Treatment Team so they want to receive treatment, to have their positive qualities strengthened with positive emotions, to join with the Main Personality and, later, to work together to develop a treatment plan for each part. I stress to all parts of the personality that the subconscious will not learn the treatment process until all parts join the Treatment Team and agree with teaching the subconscious the treatment process. All parts, even the frailest "baby parts," must feel safe with the idea of internal treatment and agree with it. The next step in getting parts on the Treatment Team is to tell them the advantages of treatment and of joining with the Main Personality.

Reasons for getting treatment and becoming one

I attempt to motivate all parts to want treatment by giving the benefits for getting treatment and joining the Main Personality. Here are the advantages of getting treatment.
- The parts will have more satisfaction and less pain and the Main Personality will stop having intrusions or experiencing lost time.
- All parts will perform with full access to the entire memory of the personality.
- When the parts have identical memories, each part will experience running the body as one personality.
- This removes conflicts between parts, removes distractions, and makes all our skills available.

- The Main Personality will no longer hide important information and will be safer.
- I also point out that mono-personalities succeed far better in realizing their potential than people who have many amnesic or dissociative parts (Ross, 1996).

Reasons for not wanting to join the Treatment Team

While trying to get the parts to join the Treatment Team, you will usually have to resolve a few objections. A part may think that it will die or that it will lose some or all of its knowledge, wisdom, and understanding. It may be afraid that it will have too much pain during the treatment process that may damage the Main Personality or other parts. It may think that it will no longer be able to protect the Main Personality by causing emotion or behavioral intrusions. A part may think that it will not be able to run the body anymore or that the conscious memory of the trauma will further traumatize the Main Personality. It may think there will be more inner conflicts among parts or that the strong parts will not listen to wee baby parts. The next step is to help parts that have reasons for not wanting treatment. In Chapter 3, you will learn how to resolve these barriers.

The primary reasons for not wanting treatment

There are many reasons for not wanting treatment or for not wanting to join with the Main Personality. The rationale for removing these barriers will be presented in detail in Chapter 3. Except for pain, these objections are all beliefs held by the parts. One can bring about change in barriers by using the desire or need for more satisfaction or happiness and less pain as an incentive for agreeing to change and accepting the therapist's explanations. Wanting more satisfaction and less pain is the primary incentive to get parts to communicate when they don't want to talk to the therapist. I use this incentive to get parts to want treatment and to join with the Main Personality. It is interesting to note that the objective of getting more satisfaction and less pain is the apparent goal used by the Basic Neurostructure for assembling groups or collages of active memories to run the body.

Treating intense fear or pain

Treating pain can cause problems. After several years of being creative, with many ploys to safely treat massive pain associated with parts, I found a simple solution. This simple, easy treatment strategy works safely and, in most cases, painlessly, to treat the trauma memories of amnesic and dissociative parts as well as other trauma memories — even those with extreme pain. The subconscious orchestrates the treatment process and the trauma part cooperates by following directions. Treating extreme pain is done with a fixed rate of treatment. For example, if the Main Personality can just barely feel 100 units of pain, then the subconscious can treat five or fewer units of pain in each treatment. Then, the Main Personality would not feel any pain during the treatment. The subconscious can adjust the amount of pain treated (the treatment rate) in the treatment plan for each part until no parts on the Treatment Team are fearful. Planning treatment in this way both prevents the flooding of emotions by the trauma part being treated and the triggering and flooding of any other part into the Active Experience. All parts will be safe and usually feel no pain. However, one more precaution must be taken.

Since activating five units of pain destabilizes the trauma part, successive treatments could increasingly destabilize the part and cause flooding of emotions into the Active Experience. A destabilized trauma memory is like a word on the tip of your tongue — it's ready to flood and become conscious. With a word on the tip of your tongue, you look for triggers to get the memory of the word to flood into your thoughts. With trauma memories, we look for ways to prevent the flooding. To prevent gradual destabilizing of trauma memories and eventual flooding, a planned rest period between each treatment allows the trauma part to relax or rest until it is stable before the next treatment. The rest period is adjustable and is in the treatment plan. This strategy using the treat-rest-treat-rest-treat-rest pattern effectively ensures the trauma part will not destabilize and flood emotions into the Active Experience during the treatment process.

Joining with the Main Personality

The treatment process gradually replaces all the painful emotional memories (connected with the trauma part) with neutral to positive emotions. After replacing the trauma pain and strengthening positive behaviors of the part with positive emotions, the treated part can join with the Main Personality. All memories appear to have unique neural structures to which memories associate or attach. Joining or integrating the trauma part and the Main Personality involves the parts exchanging memories with each other. In other words, the trauma part and Main Personality exchange memory associations until their neural structures have identical memories associated with them.

When the exchange of memories is complete, the Main Personality and the trauma part have identical memories and can both run the body with no conflict. The Main Personality and the trauma part continue to have their own unique neural structures. They each experience good and painful body sensations and emotions. They will experience less pain because, with their combined knowledge, they will be able to avoid pain more effectively. If someone was yelling at you and was about to hit you in the face, the combined knowledge of parts could lead you out of the situation and to avoid more intense pain. The structures will feel some negative emotions, but in most cases, the outside world causes the negative emotions, unless an active untreated part or a painful memory or behavior causes some pain. All parts would work together to get more satisfaction and to avoid pain. All joined parts will be in total agreement when running the body and there will be no conflicts.

Teaching the subconscious how to treat issues

When all the parts say they want the subconscious to learn how to treat trauma from the inside, you must ask a demanding question. The point of the question is to contact any parts that are uncomfortable or afraid about the subconscious learning how to treat trauma. Problem-solving these fearful parts will eventually get all parts to want treatment. When there are no objections to teaching the subconscious the treatment procedure, the subconscious learns the treatment procedure in a brief metaphor. After giving the metaphor, you ask the subconscious to treat a previously identified simple phobia or belief.

Treating a test issue

Treating the test issue will assess whether the subconscious has learned how to diagnose and treat painful memories. The patient will usually feel the treatment process in his or her brain or feel the pain of the issue gradually decrease to zero or to a fitting level. Usually, patients feel both experiences. This experience proves to the person or reader that the subconscious now knows how to treat trauma and emotional pain.

The Treatment Process

Summary of the treatment process

A summary of the entire treatment process is presented in Figure 2-1. The content of the memory includes "the movie" consisting of sen-

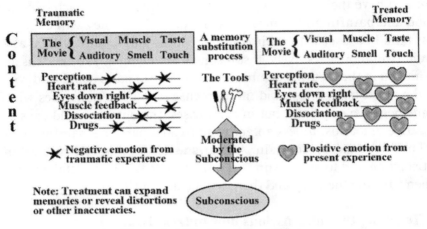

Figure 2-1 The Treatment Process

sory experiences and all other massive neural activity, such as perceptual distortion; organ, eye, and muscle activity; and drug effects, that took place during the trauma. The stars represent traumatic Emotion Memories attached to the neural activity in the content of the traumatic memory. We know this is true because, after treating the trauma, the content of the memory (the movie) usually remains unchanged—or expanded with more detail or accuracy. The subconscious orchestrates the treatment process using a treatment plan and safely replaces the negative emotions (the stars) with the present positive or neutral emotions (the hearts). During the treatment process, the patient notices the pain of the traumatic memory gradually decreasing. After the issue is treated, there is no pain associated with the traumatic memory, unless there is some protective value to having emotions—as, for example, with a height phobia.

More information is given to the subconscious to help the treatment process. This information involves fields that are allegedly useful during treatment. The subconscious is told that the use of the bioelectric field created by the heart and information gained through field receptors in skin cells can help the treatment process. In addition, there appears to be some primitive, positive "energy" available from the brain-stem and a field from the pineal gland that help treatment. I don't have any formal scientific evidence that these fields are useful in the treatment process. However, most of my patients' subconsciouses confirm that these suggestions are useful in the treatment process.

Barriers and disorganization

Treating parts and other bothersome issues can now begin, but not without some potential barriers to treatment. Any extra activity in the Active Experience causes a barrier. There are a number of causes for the extra activity. Prebirth parts that respond instead of the subconscious, parts that demand treatment, or parts that want treatment at the same time can cause the activity. Often, parts can wake up and interfere with the therapist's communication with the subconscious. Others positively don't want treatment. Any one of these parts, therefore, can cause a barrier to the treatment process. These disruptive parts have to be helped to join the Treatment Team either by a representative of the Treatment Team, the subconscious, or the therapist. Chapter 3 and later chapters provide treatment details about these and other barriers to treatment. Activity in the Active Experience causes a condition called disorganization, which is a barrier to treatment.

Treatment in the Active Experience requires that the Active Experience be calm or organized so the structure of the trauma part does not change. The activity of other parts or active memories in the Active Experience can disorganize the Active Experience. The disorganization stops the treatment process. When the Active Experience is disorganized, the activity in the Active Experience changes the trauma memory's neural structure to a series of new memory structures. This is not, in itself, a problem because a new memory structure created once is not permanent. However, this disorganization prevents negative emotions associated with the target memory structure from changing, and hence the treatment process does not work to change the pain associated with the target.

Many kinds of barriers can stop the treatment process or inhibit communication with the subconscious. Chapter 3 explains in detail about removing these barriers. Giving information or looking at the barrier in a different way handles most of them. Sometimes removing the barrier involves explaining the function of the brain or explaining how the barrier interferes with getting more satisfaction and less pain. Here is a partial list of the barriers:

- A part has just awakened and needs educating, or there is more than one part active in the Active Experience at the same time.
- Sometimes a part doesn't want treatment because of the fear of pain or loss of function, or a part wants more pain and less satisfaction.
- Some parts have beliefs that stop them from communicating.
- Less often, a barrier is caused by a part without eyes or ears, or a part that is emotional or muscle activity is functional, while the sensory experiences of that part remain dormant.
- Finally, a barrier is caused when a brain polarity reversal stops the learning process necessary for treatment.

Soon, you will read a transcript of a first treatment session giving the dialogue between the therapist, the patient, and the subconscious. The transcript will give you an idea of how Process Healing works. It shows how I introduce the Process Healing Method. Several barriers are resolved. I have also included examples of treatment interventions showing how I handle (residual) issues. There are some examples of problem solving. I also describe interventions, such as tagging and treating parts, and give three examples: treating shame and guilt, dreams, and anger.

An example of teaching the Process Healing Method

This transcript is a condensed example of teaching the information needed for doing Process Healing with a patient, friend, or yourself. As you recall, I present a model of the development of the personality, the reasons for getting treatment and joining with the Main Personality, and then address barriers. There are barriers to wanting to join the Treatment Team and barriers to treatment. I found the more I taught Process Healing to patients, the less I had to do to resolve some barriers. I attribute this change to the fact that some apparent nonverbal communication is taking place between my patients and myself (Flint, n.d.). For this reason, I am able to leave out most information and use a "bare bones" approach, teaching only the information needed to use Process Healing.

I recommend that with your first patients you initially give all the reasons for being treated. Then review with the patient most of the barriers to wanting to join the Treatment Team and to wanting treatment. This repetition of the teaching method will firmly implant these concepts into your memory. Read Chapter 3 many times so the barriers and reframes are easily available from your memory. Implanting these concepts will help you remember the correct solution to a barrier when you need it.

When teaching Process Healing in my office, I draw pictures to help the patient understand more clearly what I am saying. These pictures add a visual aid to my explanation. Teaching Process Healing over the telephone is different. In that case, I try to describe a visual picture to go with what I am saying. Sometimes, I direct the patient over the telephone to draw some of the figures on a piece of paper. So far, many of those who are willing to do therapy over the telephone usually have a productive experience with therapy and are easy to work with. I ask them to read Chapter 3, downloaded from the internet (Flint, 2005), to see if they can teach the treatment process to themselves.

Here is an example of teaching the treatment process to a person in my office. I have included several examples of its application.

T: (That's me.) **So, would you like to have me teach you Process Healing?**

P: (The patient.) **Yep, I sure would.**

T: **I am going to try to get all aspects of your personality to join a Treatment Team. All members of the Treatment Team will want their trauma treated, their positive qualities and behaviors strengthened with positive emotions, to work on a consensual basis, and to join with the Main Personality. I usually start by giving you a visual description of what I am describing. Can I move a little closer to you so you can see my paper?** (See Figure 2-2, next page.)

P: **Yes.**

T: **Can you see my paper?**

P: **Yes.**

T: **Up here on the top, I am drawing our lifeline. This point here is conception and this is birth. Sometime after conception, our brain starts learning words and phrases. At birth, when our senses become active, the objects and actions that we see and hear are linked to the words. A language forms and continues to form throughout our whole life (a). I call it the subconscious (S). Does that make sense?**

P: **Yes.**

T: **Then shortly before birth, or at birth, our Main Personality (MP) starts forming and continues to the present (b).** [I initially draw a straight line.] **We start learning *in utero* and continue to learn all our lives. Learning means the formation of memories. The formation of memories for the Main Personality amass in what I call Memory III.** [Draw an ellipse around the MP line in the figure at b.] **Memories** in Memory III are used to run our body and thoughts. Memory III contains dormant memories. Dormant memories are ready to be triggered into our experience by an emotion or some content of an active memory. For example, if I asked you this question, oops, the answer is not conscious yet because the question has not triggered the answer. So, you don't know the answer, but if I ask, "Do you remember when you last rode a bicycle?" the question will trigger the dormant answer. The answer or memory awakened and popped into your Active Experience. Do you understand so far?

P: **Yes.**

T: Now, I am going to explain how our behavior and thoughts form. Here we have what I call the Active Experience (c). The Active Experience represents all the activity in the brain and body related to survival. It is where all our internal and external sensory experience, all our internal processes, and the Main Personality are active. It includes all the Content and Emotion Memories triggered into our experience that are used to form the next response. The creation of behavior is a recurrent process, which means that our last response is the basis for the next response. For example, suppose I am moving my hand to scratch my ear. My nose starts tickling. This new stimulation will result in changing the direction where my hand is going. My hand will scratch my nose.

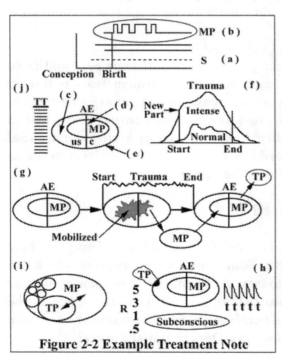

Figure 2-2 Example Treatment Note

Now, what is interesting about the Active Experience is there is a dissociation process (d) that causes the conscious and unconscious experience. It is the job of the dissociation process to simplify the content and emotions of our conscious activity so we can behave to get more satisfaction and less pain. There is also an association process (e). When memories in the subconscious trigger other memories, the association process allows the most fitting memories to be triggered. If it lets in memories too easily, then a pencil might look like a hot dog. The association process is like a metaphor manager and limits which memories can become active. Do you have any questions at this point?

P: **No.** [Of course, some people may not understand enough to ask a question.]

T: **Now I am going to talk about how severe trauma causes amnesic parts. When we think about trauma (f), we know that we completely remember some traumas.** For example, I fall off my bike, go to the hospital, and go home, I can tell everyone I know about my experience. However, when the trauma has extreme emotions and at the same time there are no learned memories to manage the situation, the brain mobilizes with memories triggered by the intense emotions. When the brain mobilizes, the activated memories, independent of the Main Personality, push the Main Personality (MP) out of our Active Experience, and an executive function organizes and creates survival behavior. Behavior is created from the start of the trauma to the end of the trauma. This behavior becomes associated with a new memory structure that becomes a trauma part. When the trauma ends (End), the Main Personality rushes in or rapidly becomes active and pushes the new trauma part (TP) out of the Active Experience to become dormant. Because the Main Personality rushes out and in so fast, there are few associations between the Main Personality and trauma part. This rapid departure and entry of the Main Personality causes the amnesia between parts. Does this explanation make sense to you?

P: **It makes total sense.** [Most patients say, "Yes," regardless of whether they understand it.]

T: **The Main Personality, at the top of Figure 2-2, now has these bumps on it. These represent amnesic parts and the up-line represents amnesia.** The problem with having amnesic parts is the emotions from the parts can be triggered into the Active Experience and distort the here-and-now conscious and unconscious experience. With this distortion in the Active Experience, the response created may not result in getting more satisfaction and might put the person at risk. Getting more satisfaction and having less pain is the main reason for treating and integrating parts. Healing is another word for treatment that will remove all the negative emotions from the memory of the part and replace them with neutral or positive emotions. Then the part can join with the Main Personality (i). Parts don't die or lose information. The subconscious strengthens their positive skills with positive emotions.

They simply exchange information with the Main Personality. The part's memory becomes exactly the same as the Main Personality's memory. Now, the trauma part and Main Personality can run the body at the same time without conflict. They still have unique structures. The response creation process uses their combined knowledge and wisdom, as needed, to get more satisfaction and less pain. Any questions?

P: No.

T: I want to ask all your parts to join the Treatment Team (TT) (j). By joining the Treatment Team, you all will want treatment, want your positive skills strengthened, want to work in consensus, and join with the Main Personality. Then you will help make a treatment plan for each member, which will be approved by the agreement of all members. One hundred percent agreement is necessary to accept treatment plans. However, I expect that the treatment of big, intense pain will worry some parts. If you look at (h), I will explain how big pain is treated. The trauma part works with the subconscious, who is drawn under the Active Experience. The trauma part moves over to the Active Experience and puts a little pain into the Active Experience. Five units of pain is just a little of the trauma time (f). The members of the Treatment Team can adjust the rate of treatment until all members are comfortable with the rate of treatment. It can be 5, 3, 1, 0.5, or whatever the Treatment Team decides. On the other hand, if we treated five units of pain one treatment after the other, the trauma part would destabilize and flood emotions into the conscious experience. It is like a word on the tip of your tongue. The word has not flooded your experience so you think of words or associations to help it become conscious. We want to stop the flooding, so we rest after each treatment. Over here (ttttt), you can see the part becomes destabilized and we wait a few seconds (t) until the part has stabilized again and then we treat some more. We repeat the process, treat-rest-treat-rest-treat-rest, until we have treated all the emotional pain associated with the part during the trauma. Will all the parts that want to join the Treatment Team please join the Treatment Team? Any questions?

P: No.

T: Now I want to set up rapport with your subconscious. Please put your hands flat on your legs on the couch beside you. Thanks. [Move each finger as you say the following.] I am going to call the index finger "Yes" and the thumb "No." Then I'll label the little finger "I don't know" and the middle finger "I don't want to tell you." In addition, "no response" is a response. These five responses allow me to communicate better with all aspects of you and the subconscious. Now, here comes the fun. I am going to ask if I can talk with your subconscious. Your job is to be curious about whether one of your fingers is going to move and to try not to move them consciously. Now, if you feel sensations on the pad of your finger or something like that which I can't see, you can move the finger so I can see it move. Do you understand?

P: **Yes.**

T: **Can I talk with your subconscious?** [Wait]

S: **The middle finger raises.** [This response is probably a part.]

T: **Oh,** [The middle finger—we both blush.] **thank you for talking to me. Did you just wake up?**

S: **Yes.**

T: **Would you be willing to talk to the subconscious and get all the information about joining the Treatment Team, being treated, and then joining with the Main Personality?**

S: **No.**

T: **Are you worried about big, big pain?**

S: **No.**

T: **Are you worried that your memories will traumatize the Main Personality?**

S: **Yes.**

T: **Well, during the treatment process, the subconscious can use the dissociative process to dissociate all those memories so they will never go into conscious experience. Would you now be willing to join the Treatment Team?** [This is an example of a reframe or explanation that neutralizes the concern.]

S: **Yes.**

T: **Thank you. Subconscious, are all the parts on the Treatment Team?**

S: **I don't know.** [Little finger]

T: **Can I talk to the part that said, "I don't know"?**

S: [No response.]

T: **Is this part a prebirth part?** [Prebirth parts learn to share information from the subconscious with the active personality and are frequent barriers to communication with the subconscious.]

S: **Yes.**

T: **Would you and all the other prebirth parts be willing to join the Treatment Team?**

S: **Yes.**

T: **Thank you. Subconscious, are all the parts on the Treatment Team?**

S: **No.**

T: **Can I talk to all the parts that don't want to join the Treatment Team?**

S: **Yes.**

T: **Will you all talk to the subconscious to find answers to all your questions and considerations? Then you can make an** *informed* [emphasize] **decision about joining the Treatment Team, getting treatment, having your positive qualities strengthened with positive emotions, and joining with the Main Personality?** [When I get the parts to talk to the subconscious, it saves time.]

S: **Yes.**

T: [Wait] **Subconscious, have all those parts decided to join the Treatment Team?**

S: **Yes.**

T: **Are all the active parts on the Treatment Team?**

S: **Yes.**

T: **Do all the members of the Treatment Team want me to teach the subconscious the treatment process?**

S: **Yes.**

T: **You mean there are no parts that have an objection to my teaching the treatment process to the subconscious?**

S: **No.** [Oops, wrong answer. Also, "I don't know," "I don't want to tell you" and no response are answers that lead to problem-solving.]

T: [Guessing] **Is this part a wee little baby part that is afraid he (or she) won't get an equal vote on the Treatment Team?**

S: **Yes.**

T: **Well, all the parts on the Treatment Team have agreed to give all parts, even you, an equal vote. Would you be willing to join the Treatment Team?**

S: **Yes.**

T: **Thank you. Do all the members of the Treatment Team want me to teach the subconscious the treatment process?**

S: **Yes.**

T: **You mean there are no parts that have an objection to my teaching the treatment process to the subconscious?**

S: **Yes.**

Note: Before reading the following metaphor that teaches the treatment process, check with your subconscious. See if it is OK to read the treatment metaphor and that it will not be disrespectful to any aspect of your personality.

T: [Quickly say or read the metaphor before any new parts wake up.] [You will learn two metaphors for teaching the treatment in Chapters 3 and 4. To read it here would be disrespectful to some aspects or parts in your personality.] **Subconscious, do you understand the metaphor?**

S: **Yes.**

Here I can point out helpful healing fields, Therapeutic Touch, the brainstem, the pineal gland and the heart field. Sometimes I make these connections to support the subconscious later during the session.

T: **Can you think of a phobia on which we can try the treatment process?** [A belief or trauma memory also works, or a part that "wants treatment now."]

P: **I am afraid of public speaking.**

T: **Subconscious, is this phobia a good practice phobia to try out the treatment process?**

S: **Yes.**

T: **OK, imagine preparing well and speaking to 100 people. On a scale of zero to 10, where 10 represents being terrified, how high is your fear or anxiety?**

P: **Oh, it's about eight.**

T: **Focus on your image of public speaking so you feel the fears and ask the subconscious to treat your public speaking anxiety.** [Wait] **Do you feel the anxiety going down?**

P: **Yes.**

T: [Wait] **Subconscious, have you finished treating this phobia?**

S: **No.**

T: **Do you feel the treatment process in your head?**

P: **Yes, it feels like the back of my head is warm.**

T: **Different issues can cause different feelings. Is it still processing?**

P: **Yes.**

T: [Wait] **Subconscious, are you finished?**

S: **Yes.**

T: **About what level do you feel now when you think of talking to some people?**

P: **It's about a two.**

T: **That is about right. You need some anxiety to do your best. Some fear may remain for motivation or to focus your attention, as** with a height phobia. **Subconscious, can you create a treatment plan for all members of the Treatment Team?**

S: **No.**

T: **Did another part awaken?**

S: [No response.]

T: **Does this part want more satisfaction and less pain?**

S: **Yes.**

T: **Would you be willing to talk to the subconscious to get all your questions answered?**

S: **Yes.**

T: **Thank you.** [Wait about 5 seconds.] **Subconscious, did this part join the Treatment Team?**

S: **No.**

T: **Does this part want treatment now?**

S: **Yes.**

T: **Subconscious, will treating this part be politically OK with the others?**

S: **Yes.**

T: **Subconscious, please treat this part.** [Wait] **Subconscious, are you done?**

S: **Yes.**

T: **Subconscious, can you do a Massive Change History and everything?**

The Massive Change History is an intervention that treats trauma emotions that are reused with memories created after the original trauma. [See Chapter 4-18 for the definition of "everything."]

S: **Yes.**

T: **Subconscious, can you create a treatment plan for all members of the Treatment Team?**

S: **Yes.**

T: [Wait] **This treatment process is hard to believe, isn't it? What do you think?**

P/T: [Engage in a conversation.]

T: **Subconscious, are you done creating treatment plans?**

S: **Yes.**

The following example is an intervention, you will learn, that removes barriers that stop the subconscious from doing independent and automatic treatment.

T: **Subconscious, will you do the "Change History" of all memories in Memory III associated with getting treatment, then treat the**

Predispositions that respond to active negative memories, and look for any belief barriers that would obstruct independent and automatic treatment.

S: **Yes.**

Examples—using Process Healing:

Here are examples of the strategies I use at various stages of therapy and of the treatment of several common issues that we all might have.

1. Starting a session

Here are the questions I usually ask my patients at the beginning of each session.

T: **How did it go?**

T: **Do you notice any beliefs, intrusions, anger, or emotions in the last week that we should address today?**

T: **Did you have any dreams or unusual experiences in the last few days?**

T: **Did you notice any of these issues . . .** [Refer to previous session notes.] **. . . that we treated in the last session?**

T: **Are there any new issues you want to talk about?**

T: **Do you want to talk about anything in particular?**

When they do want to talk, I suggest that we get the subconscious working before talking.

2. Treating tagged parts

One intervention that I routinely do is ask the subconscious to tag any parts or painful memories that become active between sessions. In the next session, I systematically treat the tagged parts and memories. Here is an example of how I start treatment of tagged parts and memories at the beginning of a therapy session.

T: **Before we talk about your experiences since the last session, let's get your subconscious working on some issues. Subconscious, are there any parts or tagged parts and memories that want treatment?**

Tagging and treating tagged parts and memories are standard interventions.

S: **Yes.**

T: **Please treat those parts slowly, safely and with total respect.**

Now the patient and I talk. We review the problems we treated in the last session and identify issues to treat again, record any strange experiences and list new issues.

T: [Later] **Are you done treating the tagged parts?**

S: **Yes.**

T: **Please do a Massive Change History and everything.**

S: **Yes.**

I ask the subconscious to do a Massive Change History and everything after every intervention. Soon the subconscious may learn to do it without your asking.

T: **Subconscious, are there any parts that don't want treatment?**

S: **Yes.**

T: **Subconscious, are there any more parts that don't want treatment?** [Just checking.]

S: **Yes.**

I problem-solve by resolving the reasons for not wanting treatment and repeat the last question until I get a "No." Now I can start treating the list of identified issues.

3. Phobias

Phobias are relatively easy to treat unless severe trauma causes the phobia. Parts or memory structures create phobic responses in the patient's experience. Sometimes, beliefs contribute to phobias. Before treating the phobia, I ask the patient to visualize the situation to get some idea about how much pain the phobia causes. Sometimes I ask the patient to guess the intensity of the pain on a scale of 0 (low) to 10 (high). Here is how to treat a problematic phobia.

T: **You are prepared to speak. Can you visualize talking to 100 people?**

P: **Yes.**

T: **Do you feel the fear?**

P: **Yes.**

T: **Focus on that fear. Subconscious, do you see the public speaking phobia?**

S: **Yes.**

T: **Can you treat the basis for the phobia?**

S: No.

T: **Do parts cause the phobia?**

S: **Yes.**

T: **Can you treat all the parts that cause this phobia, one after the other, in the correct order?**

S: **Yes.**

I usually ask if the patient can feel the emotion decreasing while thinking about the phobia. Sometimes, the intensity of emotions stops decreasing, which means there is another intervention needed.

T: [Done] **Are we finished with the phobia?**

S: No.

T: **Is there a structure of memories that helps cause this phobia that can be treated?**

S: **Yes.**

T: **Please treat the structure and when the structure falls apart, tag and treat each memory element from the structure in the correct order.**

S: **Yes.**

T: [Done] **Are you finished treating the phobia?**

S: **Yes.**

T: **Are there any self-limiting beliefs associated with the phobias?**

S: **Yes.**

T: **Can you treat the self-limiting beliefs until they are false and compose and strengthen self-empowering beliefs?**

S: **Yes.**

T: **Is there anything else to do with this phobia?**

S: No.

The following is an example of a strategy using the treatment just completed on one issue to treat another issue. This strategy saves time.

T: **Can you use the same phobia treatment with the height phobia?**

S: **Yes.**

T: **Please do it and indicate when you have finished or have a problem.**

The treatment of simple phobias usually works and demonstrates the capacity of the subconscious to treat painful issues. But with increased intensity of the trauma history causing the phobia, the complexity of the treatment increases. Phobias are not always easy to treat.

4. Emotions

All emotions can be approached directly, with the hope they will be easy to treat. This patient had a problem with anger intruding into his relationship with his wife and causing disagreements on the job. In a previous session, we treated some anger parts and asked the subconscious to tag any problematic parts or memories between sessions that come into the Active Experience. Here is the way I dealt with some of the remaining anger.

T: **Subconscious, did you tag any parts that gave anger intrusions?**

S: **Yes.**

T: **Do these parts all want treatment?**

S: **Yes.**

T: **Can you treat those parts, one after the other, and use their content and emotions to try to activate other parts that give anger?**

S: **Yes.**

The content and emotions ploy appears to speed up uncovering related parts.

T: [Wait] **Are you done?**

S: **Yes.**

T: **Is it good to do a Massive Change History, a Change History of the Ego States and to treat Shadow Memories?**

Shadow Memories are weak neural representations of a strong emotion that are learned simply by the activity of the strong emotion. Shadow Memories can maintain an emotion or behavior even though the primary trauma memory has been treated.

S: **Yes.**

T: **Subconscious, please do the Massive Change History and everything.**

S: **Yes.**

While the results of the initial treatment of an emotional issue is usually experienced immediately, further treatment of other parts or memory structures that contribute to the issue is often necessary.

5. Panic attacks

As with many issues, panic attacks can be simple or complex; some are easy to treat and some are more difficult, depending on the origins. Parts or other memories with extreme anxiety are usually the cause of panic attacks. Even in more complex cases, I find I can at least reduce the frequency of attacks, even after just one session. Panic attacks may continue for several weeks because other causes of panic remain dormant. Although panic attacks can be complex, in most cases in which I have been persistent, panic attacks no longer occur.

T: **Subconscious, do you see the cause of the panic attacks?**
S: **Yes.**
T: **Are parts causing the panic attacks?**
S: **Yes.**
T: **Subconscious, please treat the parts that are causing the panic attacks.**

Ask about other parts and treat the parts that don't want treatment with problem-solving strategies.

T: [Done] **Subconscious, is there a structure of memories associated with panic attacks?**
S: **Yes.**
T: **Please treat the structure associated with panic attacks and tag all memory elements when the structure falls apart. Then treat the memory elements in the correct order.**
S: **Yes.**
T: [Done] **Are we done treating panic attacks today?**
S: **Yes.**

I also inquire about beliefs, do the change-history interventions, and treat the Shadow Memories. Although panic attacks can be complex, in most cases the panic attacks no longer occur.

6. Depression

Many issues can cause depression. Write down all the issues believed to be causing the depression: for example, grief, loss, childhood trauma, impairment due to an accident, parental models, failure, etc. Each issue may have to be treated separately. I always try to treat depression directly because after treatment some of the causes don't need treatment or have been partially treated. Parts, memory or system structures, beliefs, as with phobias, may cause depression.

T: **Subconscious, do you see the cause of depression?**
S: **Yes.**
T: **Can you see a structure associated with depression?**
S: **Yes.**
T: **Can you treat that structure?**
S: **Yes.**
T: **Please treat the structure and, when it falls apart, tag and treat the memory elements in the correct order.**
S: [No response]
T: **Is there a part that wants to be treated now?**
S: **Yes.**
T: **Subconscious, please treat the part.**
S: **Yes.**
T: [Done] **Subconscious, can you treat the structure now?**
S: **Yes.**
T: [Wait] **Subconscious, are you finished?**
S: **Yes.**
T: **Please do a Massive Change History and everything.**
S: **Yes.**
T: **Are there beliefs that support depression?**
S: **Yes.**
T: **Please treat the beliefs supporting depression so they are false and compose and strengthen new, self-empowering beliefs.**
S: **Yes.**
T: [Done] **Have you finished treating the cause of depression?**
S: **Yes.**

Now I ask the person if the intensity of his or her depression has changed. When there is a lingering issue or some depression, I problem-solve (troubleshoot) and treat the issue causing the depression. It usually takes several sessions to treat an easy case of depression. Sometimes, it takes a lot of problem-solving and a number of sessions.

7. Dreams

I assume dreams are caused by the intrusion of past experiences or of experiences from the preceding day. I believe the content and emotions of the dreams are often independent and have to be treated separately. The dream is the personality's attempt to organize the disorganized information and emotions. I ask the subconscious to treat the content and emotions in the correct order.

T: **Subconscious, do you remember the scary dream about bull-frogs that she had last week?**

S: **Yes.**

T: **Subconscious, do we have to treat the content or emotions of the dream first? Content?**

S: **Yes.**

T: **Please treat the content in the dream.**

S: **Yes.**

T: [Wait] **Are you done?**

S: **Yes.**

T: **Please treat the emotions in the dream.**

S: **Yes.**

Y: [Wait] **Are you done?**

S: **Yes.**

T: **Subconscious, do we have to do a Massive Change History or any other intervention?**

S: **No.**

T: **Are we finished treating the bullfrog dream?**

S: **Yes.**

The treatment of simple dreams usually doesn't cause noticeable changes in experience. With a recurrent dream, there are probably parts or significant trauma memories causing the dream. Problem-solving uncovers the source of the dream and, after treatment, the recurrent dream, in most cases, never occurs again.

8. Physical problems

A physical problem like muscle pain, headache, or any other pain can often be treated with Process Healing. It is important to see your family doctor to ascertain if there is any medical problem causing the pain. When pain or tension is learned in muscle memory, sometimes it becomes a chronic condition. The muscle memory can be treated with Process Healing to relax the muscle. This will reduce or eliminate the physical pain.

T: **Subconscious, do you see the cause of that physical pain?**

S: **Yes.**

T: **Subconscious, is muscle tension the cause of that physical pain?**

S: **Yes.**

T: **Please treat that muscle memory.**

Some problem-solving may be needed to find the cause of the pain, but in many cases this intervention is all you need to treat a physical problem. I have had patients with lifelong knots in their backs who are now free of pain after we treated the parts and memory structures. A little problem-solving, in most cases, results in some relief or the elimination of the physical problem.

Summary

I wrote the following chapters in a way that may be unusual but will help you understand and use Process Healing. What is unusual in the upcoming chapters is that you will read a conversation between the therapist (you) and the patient's (your) subconscious. There are several objectives for doing this.

First, I wrote the communication between the therapist and the subconscious in detail to show how Process Healing is done. Some of the description is repetitive; so, as you learn, you will begin to expect what the therapist is going to say. This anticipation will suggest that you are learning this treatment approach and are becoming ready to do Process Healing in a way similar to the way I do it. By the time you finish the book, the interventions used in treatment and problem-solving will easily occur to you.

Second, I wrote the chapters in this way to give a feeling for the flexibility and creativity fostered by this procedure. I have included many examples of problem-solving while treating many unusually complex issues. I hope my example of fumbling around while problem-solving will help you be flexible and creative.

Third, the repetition will also give you a feeling for the chaos process in the brain without talking about chaos theory. This is important to help you learn how to problem-solve when you find a complex process. Problem-solving with this theory involves a conceptual shift (see Appendix IV). The repetition will help you make the transition from your present view of behavior change to one involving the functions of the brain and memories. When you grasp the concepts of the theory, this knowledge will allow you to be intuitive with the theory to help you solve complex treatment barriers.

Finally, this book is a self-treatment book. I wrote this book in a way that makes it easy for you to do Process Healing on yourself. You won't have to figure out how to do it. In a sense, it is self-treatment in a script format. By just reading Chapter 3, your subconscious will usually learn the treatment process. The remaining chapters will enrich your skills or give therapists tools for complex patients. I give the interventions in a linear style that will help you fine-tune your own personality. Even if the method doesn't work for you, you can use it to work with other people.

It is my belief that there is no danger in reading this book. If you have mental issues that could be disturbed by this text, your subconscious and other parts of your personality will probably prevent any adverse reactions. However, some people could be triggered by the content of this book. For people who know when they are being triggered and have tools and techniques to handle the emotional flooding, there is no danger. But for people who may be triggered and have no clue as to what is happening or why, there is a danger of being overwhelmed. If you find yourself overwhelmed, seek professional support from a therapist familiar with dissociative processes who can help you on your healing journey.

Chapter 3 gives all the information for teaching the Process Healing Method to yourself or others. The strategy and interventions for clearing or treating barriers are listed. When you follow the directions, you will usually teach your subconscious the treatment method. Then you will have the opportunity to experiment with the treatment process.

Chapter 3

Teaching the Process Healing Method

Outline

The Process Healing Method is a change process. It is based on my clinical experience. In this chapter, I will tell you how to get started. The first step involves establishing rapport and teaching *you* and, at the same time, *your subconscious*, how the personality develops. Then you are taught how to organize all aspects of your personality and get them to work together. I will give you detailed instructions on how to motivate aspects of your personality so they want to join with the Main Personality — specifically, what to say to describe the advantages and to resolve any barriers an aspect may have to receiving treatment. When all aspects of you want treatment and give permission, you will read the metaphor teaching the treatment method to your subconscious. Then, I will give an overview of the treatment process and ways to resolve additional barriers to treatment. Much of this information will be taught by giving you a script of what to say. Though the information in this overview may seem repetitive, I want you to fully understand the 10-step procedure summarized in the flow diagram on page 49.

This chapter is designed to teach you the Process Healing Method by presenting you the Education Process that gets every part of your personality on the internal Treatment Team. Sections 3-2 through 3-8 describe the Education Process. Mainly, the Education Process is a sequence of interventions you and your subconscious are taught. You will learn a theory or an analogy explaining how your personality came to be the way it is. You learn the advantages for treatment and examples for resolving barriers to joining the Treatment Team and receiving treatment. The goal of the Education Process is to get all aspects to adopt common goals and join the Treatment Team. You will learn an ordinary hypnotic technique of using finger movements that signal "Yes" or "No" and so forth. This gives you a means to communicate with the subconscious and aspects of your personality. (Normally, the reader or patient will not go into hypnotic trance.)

The Education Process is completed when all active aspects of the personality have 100 percent agreement to complete the Education Process by giving permission for the subconscious to learn the treatment method. The two remaining Sections (3-9 and 3-10) teach the subconscious how to treat emotional issues and resolve barriers to treatment. The subconscious is also freed to give unconscious, independent, self-directed treatment to negative beliefs, memories, and experiences whenever they become active in your unconscious or conscious experience. The subconscious can also use other strategies for automatically treating several common issues.

The flow diagram on page 49 summarizes the steps in the Education Process for getting all aspects to join the Treatment Team and teaching the subconscious how to treat trauma. The Education Process and the treatment process are separate treatment procedures. The numbered boxes identify the different tasks in the Education Process. Each number corresponds to a section in this chapter that describes the task in detail. Later chapters provide more advanced treatment interventions used in the treatment procedure.

The following is a summary of the Education Process that corresponds to the 10 steps in the flow diagram. Each numbered step is summarized below. By reading the following steps and referring to and *reading* the choices in the Flow Diagram, you will get a clearer picture of how the Education Process works. This will help you as you read the sections in this chapter and fit them into the organization described in the flow diagram. Here are Summaries of the 10 sections.

1. Introducing the Process Healing Method—This section describes how to introduce Process Healing to the patient.

2. The formation of the personality—This section describes how the personality forms. This information enables the patient and parts of the personality to feel comfortable with the treatment process because believable explanations are given for the role of memory, the subconscious, and the development of various parts of the personality.

3. The advantages for treatment—There may be many aspects or parts of the personality invested in protecting the patient or themselves. This section gives all the advantages for treatment. However, the main reason for treatment is to get more happiness or satisfaction and less pain.

4. Introduction to the Treatment Team idea—The goal is to get all aspects of the personality to want treatment, to want to work together, to want their good coping skills strengthened with positive emotions, and to want to join with the Main Personality. When all aspects are on the Treatment Team, treating the person becomes easier.

5. Removing barriers to wanting treatment—Often, aspects have reasons for not wanting treatment, which, therefore, become barriers to treatment. This section identifies barriers and provides a way to resolve most reasons an aspect might have for not wanting treatment. The goal is to get each aspect to join the Treatment Team.

6. Learning to communicate with the subconscious—Up to this point, we have been talking through the conscious mind to active aspects in the *unconscious*. This section teaches you several ways to communicate directly with your aspects and the *subconscious*.

7. Assessing the readiness to teach the treatment process—This section explains how to be sure all aspects are on the Treatment Team and want the subconscious to learn the treatment process.

8. Teaching the treatment method—A final check is made to be sure that teaching the subconscious the treatment process will be respectful to all parts that are active. The subconscious learns the treatment process with a simple metaphor. This metaphor always works. Of course, other similar metaphors will also work.

9. Resolving barriers to treatment—Sometimes, there are aspects of the personality who do not become active during the Education Process. When they become active later, they can become barriers to treatment. This section identifies and provides solutions for beliefs and other issues that are the reasons an aspect may have for not wanting treatment.

10. The first interventions—Once the subconscious knows the treatment technique, it can then help create treatment plans for each member on the Treatment Team. The subconscious then learns some aids to improve the speed and quality of treatment, and is guided to treat some problematic beliefs, memories, and habits that will free it to automatically treat issues in the unconscious as needed.

It is important to know that when you read these sections as if you were the patient, you will also build rapport with all aspects of your personality. This will prepare your entire personality to be comfortable with treatment and the notion of the subconscious' learning how to treat negative memories without your help. To be respectful to all of your aspects, it would be both instructive and helpful for you to follow all directions carefully.

These 10 sections are presented in the order in which you should read and use them—one section after the other. If you read them out of order, you will lose the structure of the chapter, and this will prevent you from experiencing the step-by-step procedure preparing all aspects to want treatment. Read the sections of this chapter one at a time, from one

A Flow Diagram of Process Healing

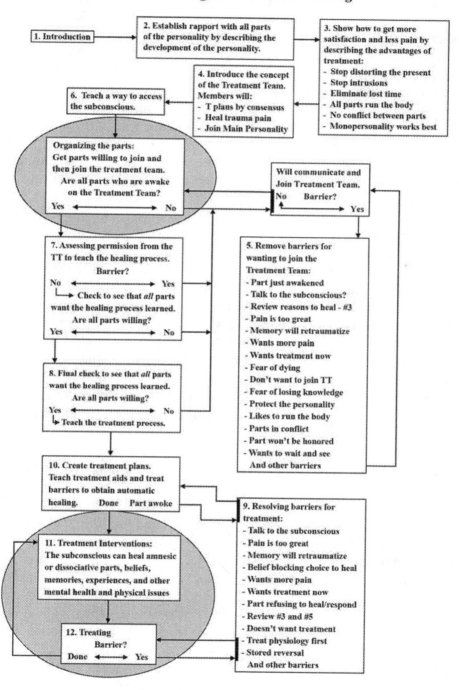

1. Introduction

2. Establish rapport with all parts of the personality by describing the development of the personality.

3. Show how to get more satisfaction and less pain by describing the advantages of treatment:
- Stop distorting the present
- Stop intrusions
- Eliminate lost time
- All parts run the body
- No conflict between parts
- Monopersonality works best

4. Introduce the concept of the Treatment Team. Members will:
- T plans by consensus
- Heal trauma pain
- Join Main Personality

6. Teach a way to access the subconscious.

Organizing the parts: Get parts willing to join and then join the treatment team. Are all parts who are awake on the Treatment Team?
Yes ◄──── No

Will communicate and Join Treatment Team.
No   Barrier?
       ──► Yes

7. Assessing permission from the TT to teach the healing process.
       Barrier?
No   Yes
  └─► Check to see that *all* parts want the healing process learned.
       Are all parts willing?
Yes ◄──────── No

5. Remove barriers for wanting to join the Treatment Team:
- Part just awakened
- Talk to the subconscious?
- Review reasons to heal - #3
- Pain is too great
- Memory will retraumatize
- Wants more pain
- Wants treatment now
- Fear of dying
- Don't want to join TT
- Fear of losing knowledge
- Protect the personality
- Likes to run the body
- Parts in conflict
- Part won't be honored
- Wants to wait and see
  And other barriers

8. Final check to see that *all* parts want the healing process learned.
       Are all parts willing?
Yes ◄──────── No
  └► Teach the treatment process.

10. Create treatment plans. Teach treatment aids and treat barriers to obtain automatic healing.   Done   Part awoke

9. Resolving barriers for treatment:
- Talk to the subconscious
- Pain is too great
- Memory will retraumatize
- Belief blocking choice to heal
- Wants more pain
- Wants treatment now
- Part refusing to heal/respond
- Review #3 and #5
- Doesn't want treatment
- Treat physiology first
- Stored reversal
  And other barriers

11. Treatment Interventions: The subconscious can heal amnesic or dissociative parts, beliefs, memories, experiences, and other mental health and physical issues

12. Treating
       Barrier?
Done ◄──────► Yes

through 10. If you have to stop before you complete the 10 sections, use a bookmark so you can quickly return to the last page you read.

The reason Process Healing is so respectful is that the entire personality learns to want treatment in a way that gives respect to all aspects of your personality. Having all aspects on the internal Treatment Team reduces problems in the treatment process. This is accomplished by requiring all Treatment Team members to work in consensus, to want treatment, to want their good coping skills strengthened with positive emotions, and to want to join with the Main Personality. Eventually, after removing all barriers to joining the Treatment Team, all aspects will join the Main Personality and give you permission to teach the subconscious the treatment process. With permission from all aspects, you will read a short metaphor that teaches your subconscious how to treat painful issues.

Of course, you can jump ahead and read the treatment metaphor. However, if there are any aspects in your personality that are fragile or angry, then without the information you skipped, these aspects may become upset. An upset aspect can stop communication or the treatment process. Commit yourself to reading this chapter as it is written and postpone learning the treatment process until you have permission from all aspects on the Treatment Team. By simply following instructions, you will know when you have permission to teach the subconscious the treatment process. If you do jump ahead and find that the treatment process or communication with the subconscious does not work, don't worry; you can reread the sections you skipped. Then, problem-solve to find and resolve any barriers. As you can see, skipping ahead upsets the logical order and can cause problems.

The 10 sections in this chapter are referred to in the numbered boxes in the flow diagram. In each section, corresponding to a numbered box, are suggestions about what you can say to the patient. Samples of dialogue in the first eight sections gives examples of the steps in the Education Process. The last two sections of this chapter give detailed descriptions of the first interventions routinely carried out in the treatment process and of the means for dealing with barriers occasionally found in treatment. The dialogue between the therapist and the subconscious is printed in bold type. Recall the example at the end of Chapter 2 that presents the Education Process and treatment interventions to a patient. When you read the example again, you will notice that I take many shortcuts in teaching the Process Healing Method to my patients. After you complete this chapter and use it with other people, you will gradually adapt my suggestions into a presentation that is comfortable for you.

Table of contents for this chapter

3-1 Introduction

[Talking to the Patient] This is therapy using an Education Process and a hypnotic technique. You do not have to go into trance. I encourage you not to go into trance because I want you to remember everything I do. Later, when you want to treat something, you can talk to your subconscious and then say what I said to make changes.

Learning and doing Process Healing should present no danger to aspects of the personality since there are many safe ways to block the learning process or communication. I am sure that your aspects or the subconscious can manage to preserve a healthy experience and warn you in a safe, nondisruptive way if there is a danger. If you ever feel a strong negative emotion, then Process Healing may not be suitable for you without a supervising therapist. The next section gives additional precautions.

As you read the following sections, you will establish rapport with all aspects of your personality by having a common understanding of how problems and painful issues are learned. This is a large step toward identifying and treating problems. You will read how painful emotions associated with memories cause problems. Old painful experiences and traumas, remembered or not, can continue to be problems in our here-and-now experience.

The Process Healing Method offers a model to explain how these problems form and distort our life experiences. The model offers a way to organize all aspects of your personality so that the aspects want to be treated, want to work together, want to have their positive behaviors strengthened, and want to join with the Main Personality. They will do this to get more satisfaction and have less pain. Most problems can then be treated safely and respectfully.

The power of this model is the discovery that the subconscious can learn how to change an emotional issue from having painful emotions to not having painful emotions. The subconscious, then, becomes a powerful asset to the therapist. Clinical experience shows the subconscious can perform treatment tasks safely and almost painlessly even with intense trauma emotions.

After reading this chapter and following directions, most people will have the treatment process available to use. This chapter is all they need to resolve barriers to their personal growth and remove self-limiting issues.

All people have aspects in their personality. Prebirth, birthing or later medical, emotional, or physical traumas create amnesic or dissociative aspects of the personality. Steps in the Education Process teach the Process Healing Method. The first step teaches the development of the personality so you will know how different parts of the brain and the personality work. Learning about the formation of amnesic and dissociative parts is especially important. After describing the reason for treating painful memories, you will learn about the Treatment Team and the conditions for joining the Treatment Team. Then, you will ask all your aspects to join the Treatment Team. Here is how it's done.

You will be taught several ways to communicate with your subconscious and the aspects of the personality. You will simply ask questions and get responses from your aspects or the subconscious. The questions you ask will eventually get all aspects of your personality to join an internal Treatment Team and to support having the subconscious learn the treatment process. All the Treatment Team members will want treatment, will want to have their good coping skills strengthened with positive emotions, will want to join the Main Personality and will want to work in consensus. The Treatment Team members have to agree unanimously to have the subconscious learn the treatment process. This means that all aspects will vote "Yes" in some way to have the subconscious learn the process. Negotiating between the subconscious and the aspects continues until the team members have 100 percent agreement. Then you teach the treatment method to the subconscious. The next step is to get all members to vote on a treatment plan for each member of the Treatment Team. Treatment plans created this way mean that all aspects can be safely treated and join the Main Personality. Before they join with the Main Personality, positive emotions are linked to the positive qualities and coping skills of the various aspects. As the team members join the Main Personality, they all take part in running the body with no conflicts.

Sometimes, with some issues, various barriers interfere with the treatment. Later sections in this chapter give treatment resolutions for the barriers. After resolving the barriers, the Treatment Intervention can continue. Together, you and your subconscious can learn to do all of this just by your careful reading of the interventions presented. In addition to these interventions, three other barriers are resolved that often prevent the subconscious from automatically and independently treating aspects, negative beliefs, memories, and experiences. Several suggestions are offered to increase the speed of the treatment process.

3-2 The formation of the personality

I want to teach you and your aspects how the personality came to be. Aspects are simply normal parts of your personality. I refer to aspects or parts when talking to you because I want to achieve rapport with you and your aspects. I get rapport by letting you know I am familiar with your world. However, most importantly, I want to show you that it is possible for you and your aspects to get more satisfaction and have less pain in life. Treatment can be painless because I can teach your subconscious how to treat trauma memories and how to do it in a safe and comfortable way. As you read this, I know that you, your subconscious and many of your aspects are also reading.

Subconscious

Looking at Figure 3-1, we have "Conception," "Birth," and "Now" on the timeline of life. A scale for "Hurt" is on the vertical line.

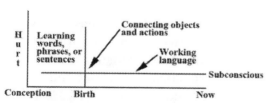

Hurt is any form of physical or emotional pain. Shortly after conception, the subconscious starts to form — when words, phrases and

Figure 3-1 The Development of the Subconscious

sentences are heard through the mother's stomach and remembered at some neural level. At birth, but sometimes before birth, the words, phrases, and sentences are connected to objects and actions that are now seen, heard, and felt. This results in the formation of a working verbal system or language. This language process can communicate with us, and it is this language system that I call the subconscious with whom I communicate when I work with people. This language process, the subconscious, is like a personality part. However, it is located throughout the brain and does not generally behave in the conscious or unconscious experience. It can nevertheless help us like an inner observer and can work in the conscious or unconscious to stimulate memories into activity, remove negative emotions from memories, and replace them with positive emotions or qualities.

The formation of the personality

The Main Personality starts forming at birth or at some time before birth (see Figure 3-2). All behavior of the Main Personality is

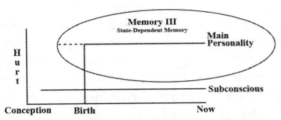

Figure 3-2 The Main Personality

remembered in Memory III because the content of the behavior has common qualities that are in some way related to sensory experience, reward and punishment, and basic needs.

Memories included in Memory III depend on the presence of one or more of those common qualities or states of the memories. Therefore, Memory III is called a state-dependent memory. This memory is called Memory III, because there are two other state-dependent memories formed before the age of four, which you will find described in Chapter 5. There are other memory structures in Memory III, which you will learn about in Chapter 8. Our Main Personality and its Ego States are part of the state-dependent Memory III.

The Main Personality, in Memory III, and the subconscious are different in two important ways. The first difference is that the subconscious does not experience sensations such as visual experience, taste, smells, sounds, or "ouches." The subconscious experiences it without the actual sensory sensations—without the "ouch." The Main Personality, on the other hand, experiences and remembers all the pain sensations experienced during trauma, such as the pain of verbal and physical abuse. For example, if you pinch yourself, your Main Personality feels the "ouch." However, the subconscious only has or registers the neural activity leading to the experience of pain and the "ouch." It's similar to when you turn on the water at your house. The water meter registers what is happening—water is running. Though the water meter knows water is running, it does not experience the water being wet or squirting. The subconscious, like your water meter, registers the pain without feeling the sensation of pain; therefore, the subconscious experiences the memories of all of your behavior and emotions, but at a different neurological level of involvement and without the experience of physical sensations. The subconscious is not state-dependent and has access to all memories running all neural activity.

The second difference is that the subconscious cannot be damaged or hurt because it does not experience painful sensations. Said another way, the Main Personality and the subconscious handle painful emotions and trauma differently. The Main Personality forms filters and barriers to change or hide painful emotions and trauma to make them more comfortable. Filters and barriers can hide large portions of painful experience or memories from our conscious experience. The absence of painful memories simplifies for the conscious mind the process of creating responses.

On the other hand, the subconscious has no sensory experience in the form of pain and trauma and, therefore, does not have filters and barriers. Hence, it has the capacity to know, without pain, the details of all active memories in the conscious or unconscious experience, even the most painful memories. It also has this same capacity with all memory processes running everything in the brain and body.

It is important to know that active memories are the only memories that can be included in the creation of the next response. A dormant memory is not active and cannot be used. However, if a dormant memory relates in some way to a current active memory, sensation, or emotion, it becomes active and can be used in a response and accessed by the subconscious.

When the subconscious accesses a memory, it has the capacity to know what caused the memory and to treat any emotions associated with it. However, do not expect the information from the subconscious to be easily obtained. Normally, you have to guess with the 20-question procedure to get explanations or information. Once you get the information, the subconscious can then be prompted to detect, review and change memories in the Main Personality.

Content and Emotion Memory

Before we go further, let me tell you more about memory. I make a distinction between Content Memory and Emotion Memory (see Figure 3-3). The Content Memory consists of the movie and memories

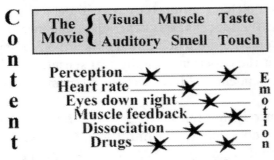

Figure 3-3 Content and Emotion Memory

of other neural activity present when the memory was created — the descending list. The Emotion Memories are shown as the stars associated with the neural memories in the Content Memory. A trauma memory has Content Memory, such as the movie or sensory experience, and other neural activity with which the Emotion Memories associate. This distinction between Content Memory and Emotion Memory becomes clear after treating a trauma memory, because after treatment, the memory — the movie — remains unchanged and has no emotional pain associated with it. In other words, the trauma memory has both content and emotions, which are independent of each other. Sometimes after treatment, the Content Memory may become even more detailed than it was before the treatment. This gives further evidence that the Content and Emotion Memories are independent of each other. Treatment removes the Emotion Memories from the Content Memories of the trauma memory.

Content Memory includes the movie (see Figure 3-3). The movie is a sequence of sensory experiences that occurred during the trauma that can be replayed like a movie. Besides the movie, the Content Memory includes the memory of the activity of some unique massive neural pathways. These massive neural pathways involve all areas of the brain that were active during the trauma. Examples of some of these unique massive pathways are those associated with the heart, the lungs, the forebrain process, the eye movements and so forth. Some academics call these unique massive pathways meridians.

Active memories cause our behavior and experiences. They are collages of previously learned Content and Emotion Memories. For example, when we create a new sentence, the sentence is a collage of memories of words, which are composed, edited and then cause us to say, "What's up, Doc?" Each word in the sentence is a memory in the collage that runs all of the neural activity needed to say the sentence aloud. These collages are assembled in the Active Experience from active conscious and unconscious memories. For example, when I want to bat a fly, memories are triggered and assembled in the Active Experience to create a collage to do what I intend to do—namely, bat a fly.

The same is true of emotions. Collages of Emotion Memories are created in what I call the Active Experience of the Emotion System. Similar to Content Memories, reusing previously created Emotion Memories is another timesaving adaptation of the brain. We remember our current emotions with a collage of Emotion Memories that we learned earlier in life. However, the reuse of Emotion Memory can be damaging to the person, though it can be seen as a process of self-preservation.

Here is an example of how reusing emotions can be damaging. An Emotion Memory, like a near-death experience, can be elicited repeatedly for use in later experiences when emotions or content of the later experience are slightly similar to the emotions or content of the near-death experience. When this happens, the old emotion associated with the response to the current situation can distort the emotional intensity of the current situation and create a traumatic response out of a nontraumatic situation. We see this in posttraumatic stress disorder and hypersensitivity.

Because our behavior is caused by collages of memories previously learned, there are usually not many new novel responses to create. For example, when we have to scratch an itch, we have a sequence of collages of previously learned muscle memories that run the muscles to scratch an itch. The memories are reused in a collage to cause the active behavior of scratching the itch on our arm. We don't have to create a new response to scratch the itch. Most of our behavior is caused by collages assembled from previously learned memories.

Here is the way a trauma memory may form. If you walk around a corner and see a dead body, you will take a deep breath and your heart will start pounding. In addition, your forebrain gets very active, trying to deal with all the sensory experiences and the emotions. All of these and other mobilized brain activities will be included in the content of the memory of the trauma. Some of the other events that are remembered in a severe trauma include bruising, organ activity, chemical effects and trance states. When you remember a trauma, some representation of all neural activity going on at the time will be active and possibly experienced.

Emotion Memories, represented by the stars (see Figure 3-3), are connected to major neural pathways that were active in the Active Experience during the trauma. When we recall a traumatic experience, we recall both the Emotion and the Content Memory. We reexperience, in part, the emotions, pictures, and/or sounds from the trauma. In addition, we experience some representation of all the neural activity in the brain and body that was going on during the trauma. This activity could be increased breathing rate, a gasp, a change in heart rate, physical pain, sensations, or drug effects. All of this takes place in the Active Experience.

Before I describe the Active Experience, let me review several features of your memory. Memories are either active or dormant. The active memories are "awake" and available in the Active Experience for creating our behavior. Dormant memories are inactive, as though "asleep," but nevertheless ready to be triggered into the Active Experience. Even when a memory is dormant, it is potentially active because it can be elicited or called into the Active Experience. Here is an example. I am going to ask you a question, but you don't know the answer to the question. Pause here and think about the answer. If I ask when you last rode a bicycle, your response or memory of riding a bicycle becomes active in response to my question. You consciously experienced the memory of riding a bicycle. If you had pain and a fast heart rate associated with that memory, you might experience pain and a fast heart rate after hearing the question.

The Active Experience is a construct to give you a way to think about all active memories and emotions that are available for creating our internal and external behavior. The Active Experience construct helps distinguish between dormant and active responses.

The Active Experience

The *Active Experience* (see Figure 3-4, next page) is a construct used to represent all neural activity that is available to create events in our conscious and unconscious experience. The neural activity includes active ongoing behavior, Content and Emotion Memories, internal and external stimulation, background processes, and organ and brain functions. Everything else is dormant—namely, not active in the Active Experience. Suppose you learned as a child to slap a fly on your cheek. That memory is dormant until a fly lands on your cheek. Then it wakes up and becomes active—you slap your cheek.

The Basic Neurostructure shown in Figure 3-4 (next page) works on the neural activity in the Active Experience to create collages that cause our internal and external behavior. All active Content and Emotion Memories and other neural activity in the Active Experience are related in some way. The Basic Neurostructure uses some of these active memories to create collages.

Collages of memories run our behavior in the same way that computer programs run computers. The neural activity triggered by the col-

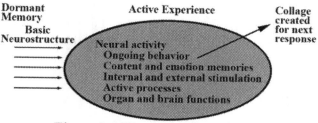

lage of memories that creates activity in our body to make a response is similar to a computer program. The Basic Neurostruc-

Figure 3-4 The Active Experience

ture takes the most appropriate Content Memories in the Active Experience in the current emotional context to create a collage. The Content Memories and emotions in the collage create a response. In other words, any response and its memory are a collage of the most appropriate memories assembled from all of this information in the Active Experience. The most appropriate memories in an emotional situation are selected from the active memories in the Active Experience to get more satisfaction and less pain.

The association process

The *association process* serves an important function. Active memories activate other memories that are similar in content or emotion. The association process prevents dormant memories that are similar, but remotely related, from being activated. It effectively screens out similar memories that are unlikely to be used in a collage. The association process is represented by the "dark line" surrounding the Active Experience (see Figure 3-5). This process is gradually learned after birth and will only allow relevant information into the Active Experience that is related in some way to the stimulation and active memo-

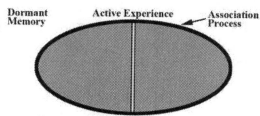

ries. If it is too liberal and allows even slightly related memories into the Active Experience, we have "loose associations." Loose association is a condition that allows content related in some

Figure 3-5 The Association Process

way to be easily triggered into the Active Experience. Here is an example: The sight of a pencil could elicit the thought of a hotdog. On the other hand, "concrete thinking" is a problem where the association process is too restrictive and words are taken literally. For example, suppose someone says, "I'm going to fly down to the store." A person with concrete thinking or tight associations might ask, "Do you need a ride to the airport?" Besides the association process, we have the dissociation process.

The dissociation process

The *dissociation process* (see Figure 3-6) helps us in an important way. With the development of volitional behavior, the dissociation

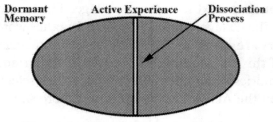

Figure 3-6 The Dissociation Process

process developed naturally to remove active memories and emotions that were unnecessary in our conscious awareness to simplify conscious activity. The dissociation process, for instance, is at work when you take a walk. It has separated, into the unconscious, all of the sensations that are present in your body when you walk. There is no need for them to be conscious for you to walk. If they were conscious, all of the information would be overwhelming. The dissociation process also helps you read by dissociating traffic noises. It is involved with adapting to our circumstances by dissociating visual or auditory information or any other sensory experience or memory that is unnecessary in our conscious experience. This process helps a person to get more satisfaction and to avoid pain by keeping painful memories or emotions in the unconscious.

The Main Personality is usually who we are, in the simplest sense, from before birth to the present. The Main Personality uses the dissociation process so there is an unconscious and conscious experience (see Figure 3-7, next page). I always draw the Subconscious in the space below the Active Experience, because it appears that the subconscious only accesses memories and emotions active in the Active Experience.

Here is the way the association and dissociation process can affect the Main Personality. We can learn to consciously control both the dissociation and association processes. When someone has a terrible

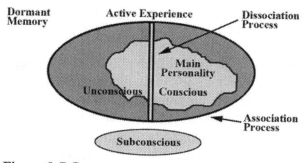

experience that is painful to remember, he or she can consciously use the dissociation and association process to hide the memory and not easily remember it. We know people who can con-

Figure 3-7 Components of the Active Experience

sciously "stuff emotions down" so they don't have to feel them. They are using the dissociation and association processes. In addition, a person with a trauma history can learn to automatically hide or dissociate painful memories so, when they become active, they do not become conscious. When painful experiences are dissociated, either as a learned process or deliberately, we call the unconscious memories *repressed* memories.

Dissociated painful memories can return spontaneously with or without further experience and intrude into our thoughts and emotions. Sometimes, treatment techniques or the experiencing of a similar trauma can result in the return of conscious experience of previously dissociated memories. When one removes the dissociative process, the Main Personality can again experience the dissociated or repressed content and emotions. Remember that the parts or aspects caused by the dissociative process are different from amnesic parts. Severe trauma and an absence of previous experience cause amnesic parts. The association and dissociation processes are also active in denial.

Amnesic parts and memories

Now, let us look at how amnesic memories or parts are formed. When we look at the time duration of trauma (see Figure 3-8), we know that trauma with moderate pain can start and then continue for some

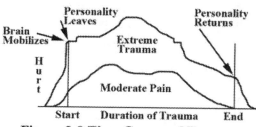

Figure 3-8 Time Course of Trauma

duration until it ends. We can remember moderate trauma easily and can tell somebody about the traumatic experience. But when the trauma is new and has never been experienced before —

namely, when there is no memory to manage the situation, and the trauma either evokes extreme emotions or is experienced as life-threatening (for example, a near-drowning experience)—the brain mobilizes. This means that the intense emotions mobilize memories that operate independently of the Main Personality to create responses to survive. Because the Main Personality is not generating behavior, it is rapidly "pushed out" of the Active Experience to become inactive or dormant. At this point, a trauma part forms. The executive function associates with the new trauma structure and participates in organizing the memories triggered by the intense emotions to create survival behavior. The memory of the trauma part includes all thoughts and behavior from the start of the trauma to some point near the end of the trauma. The amnesic or trauma part forms while the Main Personality is out of the Active Experience. When the intensity of the trauma winds down at some point, the Main Personality rushes back into the Active Experience and pushes the trauma part out of the Active Experience. Most of the behavior of the amnesic part is assembled from all the same behaviors available to the Main Personality at the time of the trauma. I will explain this in detail.

Let us look at the process from the point of view of the Active Experience. We have the Active Experience at "Before the Trauma" (see Figure 3-9). The line at "Trauma Starts" is the beginning of the traumatic

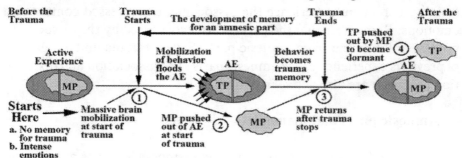

Figure 3-9 Severe Trauma Causes Amnesic Parts to Form

experience. When the trauma begins, the novel, intensely painful sensory experience and the absence of relevant memory in Memory III triggers a massive response of adaptive behaviors (1). This massive response is independent of the Main Personality when Basic Neurostructure creates behavior in a survival emergency. Because of this intense behavior in the Active Experience, the Main Personality is rapidly pushed out of the Active Experience to a dormant state (2). The Main Personality (MP) is shown outside, beneath the Active Experience. During the trauma, from the start of the trauma at "Trauma Starts" to the end of the trauma at

"Trauma Stops," behavior is managed by the executive function and is remembered. A new memory structure is formed at the start of the trauma when the brain mobilizes and becomes an amnesic trauma part (TP). Amnesic parts includes the executive function and any of the behavior usually seen in the Main Personality. The memories reflect the age of the person. At the end of the trauma, when the pain has decreased in intensity (3), the Main Personality rushes back into the Active Experience and the trauma part is pushed out to be dormant in memory (4). It is interesting that unless trauma parts become active in the Active Experience, dormant trauma parts do not change. The trauma part is an amnesic part.

The amnesic part is created when the Main Personality rapidly moves out of the Active Experience and rapidly returns to the Active Experience. This causes amnesia between the Main Personality and the trauma part because, when it is created, few or no neural connections are made between the Main Personality and the trauma part. This is how amnesic memories and parts are formed.

Figure 3-10 shows how an amnesic part is represented in the Main Personality. When the Main Personality tries to remember the trauma,

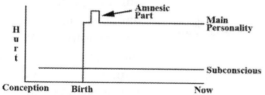

Figure 3-10 Amnesic Part in the Personality

it cannot access or remember the trauma experience because of the amnesia — for example, the absence of neural connections. The absence of neural connections to the trauma parts is the reason it is more difficult to discover and treat amnesic parts as opposed to dissociative parts. With dissociative parts, a dissociative process alters the neural response so it will not be conscious to the Main Personality.

Now, amnesic parts are normal and present in most people. Amnesic parts can be created before birth, during birth or later. For example, severe colic, a severe earache as an infant, abuse, automobile or industrial accidents, and so forth, can create amnesic parts. The result is that many people who have these parts do not recognize the muscle movements, or visual or auditory intrusions, as behavior caused by parts. Other people might have coconscious parts or parts that run the body. It can get complex (see Appendix II).

There are other ways amnesic parts can be formed. Often, amnesic parts are formed before birth, resulting in prebirth parts. Prebirth parts can be formed *in utero* by a medical crisis in the mother, an accident, physical abuse, rape, a loud noise, high blood alcohol, and so forth (see Figure 3-11). There can be more than one prebirth part. It is interesting that prebirth parts usually work to communicate information between

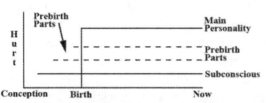

Figure 3-11 The Creation of Prebirth Parts

the subconscious and the Main Personality. Because prebirth trauma causes the prebirth part, the information given to the Main Personality can be inaccurate because of distortions caused by filters or inaccurate memories created during a trauma. This may result in distorted insights or premises about reality that lead to a mental disorder or personality issue.

When a life-threatening event occurs in the first four years of life, damage to specialized regions of the brain have been shown to stop, retard, or alter emotional development. Such early trauma causes the brain to become more sensitive and responsive to fear and pain. The result is that the brain will more easily respond to trauma and mobilize to create

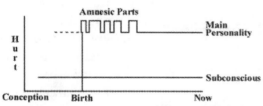

Figure 3-12 Trauma History Causes Amnesic Parts

amnesic parts. When this happens, the intensity of pain required to mobilize the brain is less than normal. This means a survivor who has had some early life trauma experiences that created amnesic parts will more likely have many amnesic parts. New amnesic parts can be created even when the traumas are less intense than the original trauma (see Figure 3-12). This lowered threshold, which allows for easy creation of amnesic parts, is found in schizophrenia and other severe mental disorders.

Treatment

I am going to tell you how the treatment process works. Normally, memory change involves creating a new structure and a collage of memories associated with that structure. What is different in treatment, as opposed to everyday life, is that treatment usually takes place in a quiet situation where there is no extra stimulation (see Figure 3-13, next page). When you think of an issue, it comes into or is created in the Active Experience.

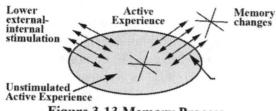

**Figure 3-13 Memory Process
Without Disorganization**

The trauma issue is a collage of memories with a unique neural structure. Three crossed lines represent the neural structure. The subconscious orchestrates the treatment process. The treatment process involves stimulation by the subconscious, which causes the Basic Neurostructure to create a new collage. However, in the treatment setting, since there is little activity in the Active Experience, the structure of the collage and its content, namely the Content and Emotion Memories, remain the same. Treatment occurs when both the collage becomes active and a memory process takes place. I call this memory process a "memory event." A memory event is some neural activity that results in a new collage of memories. In treatment, the memory event works on the emotions of the trauma memory.

With treatment stimulation, the collage representing the trauma issue is recreated, changed, and remembered. Because of the lack of activity in the Active Experience, the structure and the content of the collage do not change, but the emotions in the collage do. The change is that the patient's present neutral or positive emotion (memory) replaces some of the trauma emotion (memory) associated with the collage. The memory event causes the changed collage to be remembered. After a memory event, when the patient thinks about the issue again, the trauma memory is immediately recreated in the Active Experience. The memory now has less pain associated with the issue. Continued treatment of the same structure by the subconscious causes a sequence of memory events and changing collages. This treatment gradually reduces the pain until there is no pain associated with the memory of the issue. During this process, you or the patient will feel the pain of the issue gradually diminish to zero or to a suitable intensity of emotion. A later section describes the strategy for treating intense trauma.

The treatment setting refers not only to the external setting, but also to the internal setting. The interaction between you, your environment — including the therapist, if present — and your internal process, such as self-talk, is part of the activity in the Active Experience. The optimal treatment setting is where there is not much stimulation externally or internally to create unnecessary activity in the Active Experience. Process Healing works best when there are few memories active in the Active

Experience. Communicating about other topics or doing something during active Process Healing does not usually disrupt the treatment.

When some internal or external stimulation triggers additional activity into the Active Experience, the additional activity disorganizes the Active Experience. This disorganization is like a texture or ripple that affects the entire Active Experience (see Figure 3-14). The disorganization or more complex activity causes the creation of a new memory structure or a change in the structure of the trauma issue being treated. The new memory structure is created to take into account all the active memories in the Active Experience. With a memory event, the newly created memory structure in the disorganized Active Experience is different from the original memory structure of the trauma issue. Because of this, the Emotion Memories associated with the structure of the trauma issue are not replaced. The disorganization of the Active Experience due to disruptions in either the external or internal treatment setting can be a barrier to successful treatment.

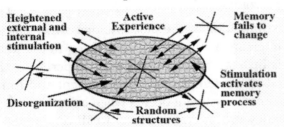

Figure 3-14 Memory Process With Disorganization

In treatment, we want the structure of the trauma issue to remain unchanged. However, disorganization constantly changes the structure of the trauma issue and creates new, unique structures and collages. These new structures are not lasting memories because the structures are changing. A single memory event with a unique structure is not enough to cause lasting memories. Remember, the patient is still thinking about the trauma issue. However, after a memory event in the presence of disorganization, when the patient recalls the trauma issue into the Active Experience again, he or she does not feel any change in the painful memory. The memory event did not operate on the structure of the trauma memory. The treatment process is not working. You will feel the emotion remain constant. By removing the memories in the Active Experience causing the barrier to treatment (the cause of the disorganization), the treatment process will work again.

Integration or joining of parts

The reason for treating the pain of a part is to get the part ready, without pain, to join with the Main Personality (see Figure 3-15). This joining process is called integration. The following metaphor describes

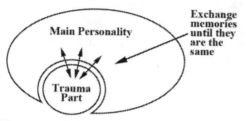

joining or integrating a part with the Main Personality. The trauma part and Main Personality get close together and the trauma part and Main Personality share their entire histories with each other until each has the same history.

Figure 3-15 The Process of Integration

Then, the Main Personality knows everything the trauma part knows and the trauma part knows everything the Main Personality knows. The major benefit of this joining of memories is that, because memories create behavior and filters for experience, both parts can now run the body at the same time without conflicts. Also, all the knowledge, wisdom and understanding memories of the trauma part, after joining with the Main Personality, are available to contribute to behavior in appropriate situations.

All trauma parts have helpful protection information and coping behavior. If these positive qualities of the parts are not strengthened with positive emotions, the information or skill may be lost. Therefore, before the integration process, the subconscious is asked to associate positive emotions with any positive coping behaviors or information in the part formerly motivated by negative emotions. By doing this, the positive coping behavior and protective information will be more noticeable in the behavior created by the Main Personality. When all the parts and aspects have joined with the Main Personality, all the integrated experiences from the entire personality are used correctly and appropriately when creating behavior.

Sometimes, parts worry that they will lose their identity when they integrate (see Figure 3-16). This does not happen. At the beginning

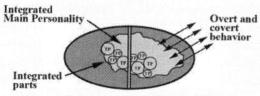

of the trauma that created an amnesic part, the brain mobilized and created a new, unique memory structure. This new memory structure is different from all other trauma parts, (or

Figure 3-16 Integrated Parts Create the Same Behavior

previous memory structures) and the Main Personality. With integration, the trauma part and the Main Personality exchange memories until they both have the same memory associations. All integrated parts have the same memory associations. However, the memory structures of the integrated parts do not change, but remain unique.

It is important to mention that integration does not always last. If a person experiences another trauma and there are enough similarities to the original trauma of some part, that part could separate from the Main Personality and become active and problematic again. However, all parts integrated usually remain integrated. They will all experience both satisfaction and pain and will want to contribute to getting more satisfaction and having less pain.

Summary—Moving from trauma to treatment

The Main Personality has memories from conception to the present time (see Figure 3-17). During your lifetime, there can be traumas *in*

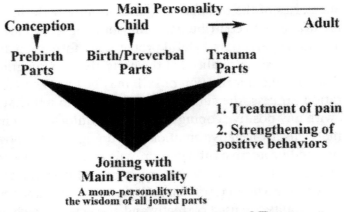

Figure 3-17 Summary of Trauma and Treatment

utero, at birth, during the preverbal period and, later, throughout adulthood. When the trauma is severe, amnesic or dissociative parts can be created. The treatment process results in removing the pain from trauma memories and trauma parts. After treatment, positive emotions are associated to good coping behaviors and protective information to make these skills more available for creating behavior. After joining a part with the Main Personality, the positive emotions will motivate the good behaviors to be active as necessary in the creation of behavior.

If you feel that you do not fully understand the information in this section, either read this section again or trust that your subconscious and all of your aspects have understood it. The Process Healing Method has been presented in a similar way to people of all ages. I assume the subconscious and most of your parts have some understanding of this section.

Now we are moving on to explain the advantages of treating and integrating all aspects of the personality.

3-3 The advantages of treatment

Now, I do not know if you have dissociative or amnesic parts, intense traumatic memories, Ego States, or any other complex structures. However, I will talk to you as though you do have parts to ensure I give respect to your entire personality. I call these memories "aspects" or "parts" and use the words *parts* and *aspects* interchangeably. There are advantages to getting treatment, and I am going to tell you and your aspects about these advantages. I am doing this so you can decide if you want to join what I call the Treatment Team and eventually be treated. If you feel like joining the Treatment Team right now, please form a Treatment Team and join it. There are six reasons for getting treatment and joining the Main Personality:

Table of contents for this section

1. To get more satisfaction and less pain

The most important reason for treatment is that all aspects of your personality can get more satisfaction and experience less pain. I know that most of your aspects want more satisfaction and less pain. Those who want more pain and less satisfaction will be worked with later.

2. To stop intrusions

Some parts think that they have to give you pain, pictures, or verbal comments to protect you (see Figure 3-18). This is not true. These intrusions caused by pain from the past can reduce or eliminate happiness and satisfaction and get in the way of or distort life in the present. Suppose you were applying for a job and the interviewer was a person who looked like someone who hurt you in the past. The anger that you might feel, an intrusion by that part, would affect you and interfere with a good job interview. Parts are important because their knowledge, wisdom, and understanding can be used to create decisions and behavior. Experiencing the old pain and beliefs associated with the parts will only distort and interfere with life in the present. By treating the pain and joining that part with the Main Personality, the Main Personality will have the part's knowledge, wisdom, and understanding to help you. By joining the Treatment Team, parts take a large step toward getting more satisfaction and having less pain in life.

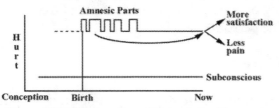

Figure 3-18 Intrusions Distort the Present

3. To stop losing time

Having unremembered time or blank spots in your memory during the day makes life awkward and less satisfying. If you can think about lunch and can't remember anything between, say, noon and 1 p.m., when you thought you had lunch, then another part may have been running your body during this time. These parts will want to join with the Main Personality, because parts that like to run the body will have the opportunity to run it from morning to night after joining. Joining with the Main Personality will allow them and all other parts to experience more satisfaction and less pain. When the joined or integrated parts and Main Personality all have the same memory, they run the body at the same time without conflicts.

4. To keep the Main Personality from dissociating important information

The Main Personality likes to get satisfaction in the form of closeness and affection. When the content associated with old memories elicits or triggers parts that intrude with strong negative emotions, the emotions will interfere with getting this satisfaction. Sometimes, the Main Personality will learn to dissociate important information to stop the intrusions. This dissociation distorts reality and the Main Personality makes a bad decision. A woman who marries an alcoholic might sometimes say, "I didn't even see that he was alcoholic before our marriage." What happened was the Main Personality dissociated the awareness that he drank a six-pack of beer on both Saturday and Sunday. She blindly entered into another marriage because of good feelings and a distorted reality. She discovered later that he was an alcoholic. The full integration of all parts will help to prevent this problem from happening.

5. So that all parts can run the body all the time

Integration or joining parts is the goal. When the integration process is complete, the memories of all parts are available for use in responding to all fitting situations. With integration, all parts run the body with no conflicts. Integration also gives more wisdom to the Main Personality, which will result in all parts getting more satisfaction and having less pain.

6. Because a mono personality works best

Research by Colin Ross, MD (Ross, 1996), has shown that when patients who start with many parts get treatment and all parts integrate with the Main Personality, they behave normally in life. On a major test of mental disorder, Ross found the patients with integrated personalities showed better mental health than the average U.S. citizen. Therefore, in order to move toward health, it is good to integrate all aspects of your personality with the Main Personality.

Now that you understand the benefits of treatment, let's talk about the Treatment Team.

3-4 Introduction to the Treatment Team idea

This is important and I want all aspects of the personality to pay careful attention. If the idea of a Treatment Team does not feel comfortable to you, you can substitute playmates, the crew or team, inner helpers, or whatever name you choose in place of Treatment Team. Any name will

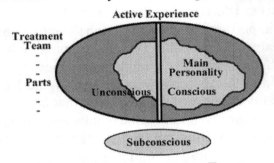

work just as well. This is where the respectfulness of Process Healing is most obvious. Before the parts join the Treatment Team (see Figure 3-19), the parts agree to common goals. Parts on the Treatment Team want their trauma pain treated, want to have

Figure 3-19 The Treatment Team

their good coping skills strengthened with positive emotions, want to join the Main Personality, and want to work in consensus to develop a treatment plan for each part. I want to make it clear that the subconscious will not learn the treatment process until all the parts join the Treatment Team and are in full agreement. All parts, even the most frail baby parts, must feel safe after joining the Treatment Team and agree with having the subconscious learn the treatment process.

The internal Treatment Team serves as a way to keep all parts safe by having all members involved in creating treatment plans. The Treatment Team also helps to organize all aspects of the personality to want to get treatment and integrate with the Main Personality. It is always necessary to discuss and resolve the barriers to wanting treatment in order to get all parts to join the Treatment Team. Fear about the danger of treating extreme pain and all the other barriers to treatment are explained in the next section. After reading the next section, you and your subconscious will work together. By asking direct questions, you can uncover and clear barriers stopping parts from joining the Treatment Team. You will use the resolutions for barriers described below to get all the parts on the Treatment Team. When all parts are on the Treatment Team and want the subconscious to learn the treatment process, the subconscious learns how to treat with a simple metaphor. In this case, you will read a paragraph that teaches the treatment process.

There are two tasks for the Treatment Team. The first is to give permission for the subconscious to learn the treatment process. The second is to work cooperatively to arrive at safe treatment plans for each Treatment Team member. They vote according to the consensus rule. This means the Treatment Team and the subconscious discuss each treatment plan and negotiate to get 100 percent agreement. All aspects are equal and are to receive treatment respectfully — even the weak, little baby parts.

Note that it is disrespectful to read the metaphor which teaches the treatment process before all aspects are members of the Treatment Team and want the subconscious to learn the treatment process. This is up to you. If you want to give respect to all aspects of your personality, avoid reading the section that teaches the treatment process until all of your aspects agree. [When I teach Process Healing in the classroom, just reciting the treatment metaphor teaches the treatment process to the students.]

Before you continue, I want you to identify an issue, a simple phobia or some mildly painful issue. This issue will be the practice issue the subconscious will use later to practice diagnosing and treating painful emotions. Let me give you a way to judge the intensity of the emotions. You will estimate or guess a score on a scale to remind you how intense the emotions or pain of the issues is before you start the treatment process. The scale will range from 0 to 10. Looking at a kitchen cupboard gives you an emotional response that you can score at zero (0). A life-threatening experience causing extreme emotions is scored at ten (10). Therefore, we have a scale where zero is no pain and ten is intense pain. Find a phobia or other issue for which you estimate the score to be between six and eight on this scale of zero to 10. Now, pick a phobia, such as height, spiders, snakes, or public speaking, that gives you anxiety or fear that scores between six and eight. Do not pick an issue linked to a huge trauma. You can pick a painful memory, not one that is severely traumatic, but one that has emotions with a score of six to eight. Write down the name of the practice issue. I will ask you to think of it later.

Summary

You have learned about the Treatment Team and, later, you will work with your aspects and get them to join the Treatment Team. Treatment Team members are willing to be treated, want to strengthen the good coping skills with positive emotions, want to join with the Main Personality, and are willing to work in consensus to get safe treatment plans for each other's trauma. After the Treatment Team is formed and all members give permission to teach the subconscious the treat-ment process, the subconscious learns the treatment process by hearing or reading the simple metaphor. Then, the subconscious treats the prac-tice issue. Before treating any aspects, you will ask the Treatment Team and the subconscious to develop a safe treatment plan for each aspect on the Treatment Team. Then the subconscious can systematically treat, strengthen positive coping behaviors, and integrate all the parts with the Main Personality.

At this time, the reader should be sensitive to emotions, anxiet-ies, fears, or other intrusions, which I would interpret as some part with intense emotions having difficulty. For this reason, if you have a strong emotional experience as you read or when you think of continuing, I rec-ommend that you stop reading and find a competent therapist.

The next section will educate you and the subconscious about how to remove barriers to wanting treatment. The subconscious and Treatment Team members can spontaneously use this information to convince uninformed parts why treatment is desirable. All parts that are willing to join the Treatment Team can join it now. So, continue to the next section.

3-5 Removing barriers to wanting treatment — Problem-solving

Introduction

[I want to remind you that I use the words parts and aspects inter-changeably, although there is a difference. "Parts" are either dissociative parts or amnesic parts. "Aspects" include parts, beliefs, intense memories and other memory structures that can cause barriers to treatment. You should know that every aspect is whole and healthy but can also cause a problem. While frightening and unhealthy situations create aspects that cause problems, they simply learned the survival behaviors necessary to respond to the situation. You may or may not have any problematic as-pects, so I take the safe route and write as though you do. I want to be re-spectful to you and your aspects. Most of the time, it is parts that present barriers, so you will often be communicating with parts.]

I am going to address the barriers to treatment by giving an in-tervention for each barrier. Barriers have to be resolved in the process of convincing all parts to want treatment and to join the Treatment Team. At this point, you don't have a way to communicate with parts. You will learn how to communicate with parts in the next section. However, as you read this, you will know that your parts and aspects, if there are any, are listening attentively. They will all reflect on the following information as you read it. After having all the information, it will be clear to them that joining the Treatment Team will result in getting more satisfaction and having less pain.

Parts can have good reasons why they don't want treatment or don't want to join the Treatment Team. The goal of this section is to resolve all the reasons that prevent parts from wanting treatment and to join the Treatment Team. When all parts are on the Treatment Team, they can be systematically treated with relative ease. The following are all the reasons for not being treated. An explanation is given for each barrier that usually works to convince parts that a particular barrier is not useful to them and to have them want to join the Treatment Team. Some parts have several reasons or barriers to not wanting treatment or joining the Treatment Team. You or the subconscious will have to work with them and convince the parts that it is positive and desirable to be treated. Most people without a trauma history will not have to deal with any of these issues. However, it is important to review the reasons for treatment just to ensure that all aspects of your personality receive due respect.

Note: The first letter in each line indicates the response of the therapist, the subconscious, or the part. From this point forward, bold print identifies responses of the therapist, the subconscious, and the parts.

Therapist or You—T: **Subconscious, are you there?**
Subconscious—S: **Yo!** [Index finger moved.]
Part—P: [Response of a patient or part]

Table of contents for this section

How to problem-solve

Problem-solving starts after you learn how to communicate with the subconscious and parts. However, I am giving a sample of the problem-solving strategy here in order to prepare you to better understand the use of the problem-solving material in this section.

When trying to get parts on the Treatment Team and communicate with the subconscious, you can run into barriers. You discover barriers when you get no response, a defiant response, or an inconsistent response. Problem-solving can be challenging, but it is always interesting. Here is the routine first question of problem-solving when I think a barrier is present. Immediately ask:

T: **Subconscious, is there a part blocking communication?**

S: **No.**

I wonder if I am being misled. I ask any one of the following questions.

T: **Subconscious, are you busy treating?** *or*

T: **Does this part want treatment right now**?

With "No" responses, I continue with the next question.

T: **Does the part that is blocking communication want more satisfaction and less pain?**

P: **Yes.**

T: **Do you want to join the Treatment Team?**

P: **Yes.**

T: **Thank you. Please do.**

With a "No" response, to save time, you ask the part unwilling to join the Treatment Team the following question. When you say the following, give emphasis to the words "informed decision" to encourage the part to talk to the subconscious.

T: **Would you be willing to talk to the subconscious to get all the information you need so you can make an *informed* decision about whether to be treated?**

When this doesn't work, try the following:

T: **Will you talk to the subconscious or a spokesperson for the Treatment Team to learn why it is good to join the Treatment Team and how safe treatment is?**

You can also ask the problematic part to talk to both the subconscious and the spokesperson for the Treatment Team together to get the information necessary to make an informed decision about joining the Treatment Team. Sometimes, one has to be creative.

When you continue to get "No" responses, you use the list of barriers given below. Inquire about all the barriers to treatment in the order in which they are listed in this section. Ask the part about each barrier, one after the other, until you discover and clear the barrier and get the aspect to join the Treatment Team. When the response is "I don't want to tell you" or "No response," you can emphatically thank the part for communicating and continue to look for the important barriers. Any response by the part weakens the unwillingness to communicate. For people who have been taught to keep the family secret and not communicate, the complement for communication causes confusion and gradually breaks down the motivation for not communicating.

Sometimes, you have to go through this section several times. Though uncommon with uncomplicated personalities, some barriers refuse to talk to the subconscious or Treatment Team. Then you will have to tell the parts, again, what the Treatment Team does, restate the advantages of treatment, or start the whole Education Process again. If you have many aspects, you may have to repeat the procedure for clearing barriers many times. For all the barriers in this section, when you get a "No" response, continue asking the questions suggested in the list provided until you strike on the issue that is important to the part. I usually assume I am talking to many parts and reflect this in the words I use. Then, if I am talking to many parts, they all have the opportunity to decide to join the Treatment Team. Continue resolving barriers until the part or parts join the Treatment Team. Occasionally, after joining a part to the Treatment Team, you can ask:

T: **Subconscious, are all the parts on the Treatment Team?**

In practice, with a "Yes," you continue to the next section. With a "No," you continue problem-solving.

The following are interventions for barriers that stop parts from joining the Treatment Team. I listed the barriers in order, from the most frequently used intervention to the least frequently used intervention.

1. Part just awakened

T: **Did a part just wake up?**
P: **Yes.**
T: **Would you be willing to talk to a member of the Treatment Team or the subconscious to find out about the advantages of joining the Treatment Team?**
P: **Yes.**
T: **Great. Will you do that now?**
If the part won't talk with the subconscious or a member of the Treatment Team, then:
T: **Would you want me to explain the advantages of treatment and joining the Treatment Team?**
If you get "No" response, try the big incentive of more satisfaction and less pain.
T: **Do you want more satisfaction and less pain?**
P: **No.** [Or no answer]
T: **Do you want more pain and less satisfaction?**
Continue to problem-solve.

2. The pain is too great to be treated safely

T: **Are you worried the pain is too great to be safely treated?**
I usually shorten this to "Are you worried about big, big pain?"
P: **Yes.**
T: **Here is the way to treat the pain painlessly and safely** (see Figure 3-20). [I draw Figure 3-20 as I explain this] **The subconscious orchestrates the treatment and the trauma part follows the di-** rections of the subconscious. The subconscious treats a little part of the trauma pain at a time so the pain is controlled carefully. If the Main Personality can just barely feel 100 units of

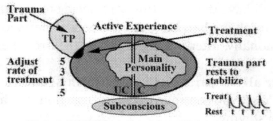

Figure 3-20 Treating Intense Trauma

pain, then it will be painless to treat five or fewer units of trauma at a time. If any part worries about the intensity of the pain, the amount of pain treated can be adjusted from 5 to 3, 1, .5 or fewer units of pain. This will prevent emotional flooding of the trauma part or triggering and flooding of any other part in memory. Since activating five units of pain destabilizes the trauma part, consecutive treatments, with no pause, could increasingly destabilize the part and result in flooding the Active Experience with emotions. To prevent this problem, after each treatment, allow the trauma part to restabilize — that is, to rest until it's calm. This treat-rest-treat-rest pattern effectively ensures the trauma part will not destabilize and flood the Active Experience. It's like waiting for a bowl of gelatin to stop jiggling after knocking the bowl. By treating small increments of pain repeatedly, the entire duration of the trauma is slowly treated. Both the rate of treatment and the duration of the rest period are what the Treatment Team negotiates to arrive at safe treatment plans. Are you willing to be treated now?

P: **Yes.**

T: **Will you join the Treatment Team?**

P: **Yes.**

With a "No," look for another barrier by problem-solving. Problem-solving means that you systematically try all barriers in the list of barriers offered in this chapter. Chapter 6 gives other strategies for resolving barriers to treatment.

Usually, you find a part that is fragile and is afraid that any treatment will cause he or she to flood the Active Experience. Here is how I handle fragile parts. Figure 3-21 shows what I draw as I explain the treatment procedure.

T: **Subconscious, is this part fragile and afraid of treatment because he or she fears flooding the conscious experience?**

S: **Yes.**

T: **Here is the way the subconscious can treat fragile parts to make the treatment very safe** (see Figure 3-21). **The subconscious arranges for four parts to crowd together somewhere in the brain** to make a quiet space (see Figure 3-21a). The treatment takes place here because the quiet space protects the treatment from any stimulation by activity in the Active Experience.

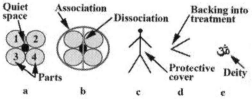

Figure 3-21 Treating Fragile Parts

This makes it unlikely that random events will cause the part to flood. Now, because extreme pain created you, it is probable that the trauma also damaged the association and dissociation processes and that these processes have been working hard to keep you from flooding. By treating the trauma in the association and dissociation processes and your own trauma at the same time (see Figure 3-21b), the subconscious can carefully control the rate of treatment. This further reduces the chance of flooding. As a further precaution to protect you from falling apart, you can wear a wet suit, a tuxedo, leotards, wrap yourself in white light, or be accompanied by angels (see Figure 3-21c). In addition, by backing into the treatment process, you will reduce your anticipatory anxiety by not watching the treatment process (see Figure 3-21d). If you still have worries about flooding or feel unsafe, you can hold the hand of the Creator, the True Jesus, or any comforting person (see Figure 3-21e). Are you willing to get treatment now and join with the Main Personality?

S: **Yes.**

Usually, a fragile part is willing to be treated by using these added precautions.

3. The treated and integrated memory will retraumatize the Main Personality

T: **Are you afraid that your trauma memory will retraumatize the Main Personality?**

P: **Yes.**

T: **I can fully understand your concern. It is possible to treat your pain and have the subconscious work with you (the amnesic or dissociative part) to make sure that all the traumatic memories are dissociated. Then, after treatment, your memories remain in the unconscious of the Main Personality. In this way, you can be treated without worrying that your memories will retraumatize the Main Personality. Are you willing to join the Treatment Team?**

P: **Yes.**

4. Doesn't want to join the Treatment Team

T: **Are you willing to join the Treatment Team?**

P: **Yes.**

T: **Can you do it now?**

P: **Yes.**
T: **Thank you.**

If the answer is "No" or there is no response, ask

T: **Do you want more satisfaction and less pain?**
P: **Yes.**
T: **Will you join the Treatment Team?**

Usually I get a "Yes" response.

P: **No.**
T: **Is there an issue preventing you from wanting to join the Main Personality?**
P: **Yes.**

Remember to give stress to the *informed* of informed decision.

T: **Would you be willing to talk to the subconscious to get all the information you need to make an *informed* decision about joining the Treatment Team?**

Continue problem-solving.

5. The part likes to run the body

T: **Are you afraid that you will not be able to run the body anymore?**
P: **Yes.**
T: **Some parts like to run the body because it's fun, but this is another form of intrusion. Running the body with the Main Personality active can give the Main Personality embarrassing experiences that interfere with getting satisfaction. If you run the body by pushing the Main Personality into dormancy, you give the Main Personality blank spots in memory because he or she is dormant. This upsets the Main Personality when he or she doesn't remember everything he or she has done. In addition, some parts behave differently from the Main Personality. An angry part taking an interview would not get the job. Again, having parts run the body reduces the chance of getting more satisfaction and having less pain.**

When a part integrates, all the part's knowledge, wisdom and understanding joins with the Main Personality and adds new information or strengthens old information. The part's information is used in the here-and-now whenever the part's memory is suitable for the current situation. The subconscious strengthens all positive qualities of the part before joining the part with the Main Personality. After the integration, the part will be able to experience running the body with no conflict and take part in getting more satisfaction and protecting the body from receiving pain. Are you willing to join the Treatment Team?

P: Yes.

6. Fear of dying

T: Are you afraid that if you are treated, you will die?
P: Yes.
T: No parts die. After treating your pain, you can join the Main Personality to get more satisfaction and less pain. All your knowledge, wisdom, and understanding become part of the Main Personality and are used in the here and now as may be appropriate. Will you join the Treatment Team?
P: Yes.

7. Fear of losing your knowledge, wisdom, and understanding

T: Are you afraid that you will lose all your knowledge, wisdom and understanding after you join with the Main Personality?
P: Yes.
T: This is not true. You simply lose the pain. All your knowledge, wisdom, and understanding will be available in the Main Personality. All the positive beliefs and behavior remain strong because the subconscious will strengthen them with positive emotions before you join the Main Personality. If you like to dance, after integrating, the Main Personality will be more likely to go dancing. Any nasty protective behaviors are still available, but only when current emotions and situations are fitting for them. Are you willing to join the Treatment Team?
P: Yes.

8. Prebirth part interfering with communication

When attempting to communicate with the subconscious, you will occasionally see inconsistent responses. When I ask a question that should be "Yes" or "No" and get an "I don't know." I always suspect a prebirth part. Prebirth parts like to answer for the subconscious but often don't know the correct answer. Here is how I handle this situation.

T: Is this a prebirth part?

P: **No.**

T: **Is this part willing to sleep and put his or her eyes and ears in the Active Experience, simply listen, and not respond for the subconscious?**

P: **Yes.**

If I get a "No" here, I problem-solve.

When you get a "Yes" and you find a prebirth part, treat the pre-birth part.

T: **Well, prebirth part, I know that sometimes one or more pre-birth parts serve to relay information from the subconscious to the conscious experience.**

Prebirth parts may still be trying to do that job, which complicates communication with the subconscious.

T: **Would you be willing join the Treatment Team right now and later join with the Main Personality?**

P: **No.**

T: **Would you be willing to go to sleep and watch with your eyes and ears?**

P: **Yes.**

Watch for inconsistencies as you communicate with the subconscious. Again, if this doesn't work, try problem-solving.

9. Part wants more pain and less satisfaction

T: **Do you want more pain and less satisfaction?**
P: **Yes.**

T: **Was your trauma continuous so you had to choose to have the pain to make the pain feel less painful?**

P: **Yes.**

T: **Well, the pain you continue to avoid is old pain that you learned many years ago. If you let the subconscious treat the early pain, then you could choose to have more satisfaction and less pain. If the subconscious treats that pain in a way that doesn't hurt you or the Main Personality or any other aspects of the personality, would you be willing to join the Treatment Team?**

P: **Yes.** [Continue with the Education Process.] *or*
P: **No.**

T: **You know that you can control the rate of treatment and the duration of rest between treatments to make the treatment process very** safe. Would you like to have more satisfaction and less pain and join the Treatment Team now?

P: **Yes.**

If this doesn't work, see if the part will talk to the subconscious, or problem-solve.

10. The part will no longer be able to protect the Main Personality

T: **Are you afraid you will no longer be able to protect the personality by giving the intrusions?**

P: **Yes.**

T: **When a part intrudes with emotion or by putting words into the conscious part of the Main Personality, it disrupts the here and now.** This intrusion distorts the emotions or thoughts in the Active Experience and reduces the chance for creating a response to get more satisfaction and less pain (see Figure 3-18, page 70). For example, (1) suppose you were going for a job interview and the interviewer looked like someone who hurt you when you were small. If the sight of him elicits a rush of rage, you might not be able to give a good interview and get the job. The emotion wasn't suitable for the here-and-now and interfered with getting satisfaction by giving a good interview. The important, protective aspect of this intruding part is its knowledge, wisdom, and understanding. Therefore, by treating your pain and joining your knowledge, wisdom, and understanding with the Main Personality, the whole personality could now assess the situation using all recent experience. The outcome would reveal the man was not the same man as the perpetrator. Then, you would do your best in the interview. (2) We have all met men who project, "No one is going to tell me what to do." This is a belief caused by trauma. He learned this belief when someone told or forced him to do something terrible and painful. An experience like this sometimes results in the immediate creation of this belief. This belief is the reason many trauma survivors lose their jobs; they react to instructions from a supervisor and impulsively quit or hit the supervisor. This common issue can be easily treated. The subconscious can treat the trauma, remove the pain that makes the belief true, and create and strengthen a self-empowering belief to replace it. After treatment, this belief is no longer a problem. Would you like to join the Treatment Team?

P: **Yes.**

11. There will be more inner conflicts

T: Does this part think that by joining the Treatment Team there will be more conflict between parts?

P: Yes.

T: This is a legitimate worry. However, I think if all the parts want treatment, want to join the Main Personality and want to work in consensus, there will be fewer or no conflicts. All the parts want the same goal and would want to cooperate to get it. Does this make sense?

P: Yes.

T: Would you be willing to join the Treatment Team?

P: Yes.

12. A weak, little part fears not being honored by big parts

T: Is there a wee, little part that thinks the Treatment Team members will not listen to you if you vote "No"?

P: Yes.

T: You have to know that all the members of the Treatment Team have agreed to respect every other part and you will be respected. Are you willing to join the Treatment Team now?

P: Yes.

Sometimes, you have to ask the subconscious if all the Treatment Team members will honor this little part to demonstrate to the little part that this is true.

13. Part wants to wait and see

T: Does this part want to wait and see what the treatment process or joining with the Main Personality looks like?

P: Yes.

T: Would you be willing to join the Treatment Team and allow the subconscious to learn the treatment process?

P: Yes.

T: Great. Please join the Treatment Team.

S: Yes.

Sometimes, this doesn't work.

P: No.

T: Would you be willing to let the subconscious learn the treatment plan and then watch and listen to see how the treatment process works before you decide about joining the Treatment Team?

P: Yes.

14. Part wants to know what the subconscious is going to learn before joining

T: Is there a part that wants to know what the subconscious is going to learn before considering joining the Treatment Team?

S: Yes.

T: Most parts fear receiving treatment against their will or don't want to lose control. What the subconscious is going to learn are the mechanics of replacing pain emotions with neutral to positive emotions. All the other basic treatment strategies and safeguards are described before teaching the subconscious. More important is whether you want more satisfaction and less pain. Would you be willing to reconsider your decision to not join the Treatment Team and let the subconscious learn the treatment method?

S: Yes.

15. A part wants treatment now

T: Is there a part that wants treatment now?

P: Yes.

T: Would you be willing to join the Treatment Team, and later we will try to have you treated first?

P: Yes.

Make note that you have agreed to treat a part first after teaching the subconscious the treatment process.

16. A part is worried about losing social relationships

T: Is there a part that is worried about losing all your social relationships with other parts?

S: Yes.

T: Well, if you look around, you will see many of your friends have joined the Treatment Team. You relationships will change after getting treatment and joining with the Main Personality. The difference is that you will all be getting what you want—namely, more satisfaction and less pain. You all will work together, without conflict, to achieve this goal. Would you be willing to join the Treatment Team?

S: Yes.

17. A brief statement resolving the barriers listed above

When talking to the subconscious doesn't work, or there is no communication, or when a part wants information about treatment from me, I use this brief statement that includes the resolutions for all of the barriers.

T: **Do you want me to tell you about the treatment process?**
P: **Yes.**

T: **No one is going to die. Treatment simply removes all the pain from your memories. The subconscious treats small pieces of pain and then pauses a few seconds before treating again. This ensures that the big pain will not flood the Active Experience or awaken other parts. If you are worried that the content of old memories will traumatize the Main Personality, the subconscious can dissociate traumatic memories so they will be unavailable to the conscious mind. After joining the Treatment Team, all parts, even the smallest, weakest part, will vote on a treatment plan for each part to decide the amount of pain treated and the duration of the pause between treatments. The subconscious and you adjust the treatment process to be very slow and safe. After treatment, the subconscious will first strengthen all your positive coping behaviors with positive emotions. Then, you and the Main Personality will share your knowledge, wisdom, and understanding with each other until they are the same. With identical memories, you will all be able to run the body at the same time with the Main Personality without having any conflicts. You will still be able to protect the personality, but without emotions from the past distorting the present. You will all work together to get more satisfaction and less pain. Are you willing to join the Treatment Team?**

P: **Yes.**

Summary

You have just read a list of ways to resolve barriers to joining the Treatment Team. You will use this list later when you problem-solve to get all aspects to join the Treatment Team. When searching for the barrier, you can simply go down the list in the order presented, one by one. With each barrier, question the part to find out if that barrier is keeping the part from wanting treatment. It won't be long before you have some intuition about which barrier is most likely the cause for the block. Remember there can be more than one barrier blocking a part from wanting treatment. The subconscious will learn to do the same procedure.

3-6 Learning to communicate with the subconscious

Most people will not run into problems in either communicating with the subconscious or getting all their aspects on the Treatment Team. It is entirely normal to have some or many aspects or parts, and this makes organizing the Treatment Team a creative problem-solving process. We are all different and sometimes-unknown complex memories can present barriers involving great fear. Remember: Be alert for signs that suggest that your subconscious or some part is advising you to not continue reading this book. Read this section carefully.

Table of contents for this Section

Before you start

Before you teach the treatment process to your subconscious, you will have to read the following to protect you from any negative outcomes. It's unlikely there will be a problem. Trauma-based aspects and the subconscious will not usually do anything that will hurt the Main Personality of the reader or someone else, especially when the parts know what's happening. Before continuing with this section, I want you to pay attention to your emotional state and internal conversations. With severe trauma, known or unknown, I feel confident that you will know by some emotion, be it fear or anxiety, or by an internal voice, not to continue reading. If you have any reservations, find a therapist before continuing. If you have had severe trauma in your past, or have been sent to a hospital for a mental issue, or have taken medication for any serious mental problem, I want you to consult with a competent therapist before learning the treatment process. Be cautious if you have any intrusive thoughts or experiences. If you are in therapy, discuss this treatment process with your therapist.

The subconscious is always awake and is listening to everything. You can always talk to the subconscious. There is no way to block this. Arranging to have the subconscious talk back to you can be much more of a problem. Now, I want to remind all of your aspects that the subconscious will not learn the treatment process until all aspects of the personality agree to it. Before we start, here's how to think about talking to parts. The Main Personality has memories that allow it to work normally while it is running the body. Well, during an extended trauma caused by someone that involves life-threatening pain, the Basic Neurostructure is creating behavior just as it does for the Main Personality. The development of an amnesic part will include many of the same behaviors used by the Main Personality. However, the trauma memory will be amnesic from the Main Personality. Here's what's interesting: The trauma part may look like the Main Personality to the perpetrator of the trauma because the trauma part is behaving in all the same ways that the Main Personality behaves. This includes thinking. Parts can behave and think like the Main Personality, so you can communicate with them as you do with yourself. For example, a four-year-old part is like a four-year-old Main Personality. You speak to a four-year-old part with a four-year-old vocabulary. You can communicate and ask a part questions just as you would ask in a 20-questions parlor game. First, let's learn to communicate with the subconscious.

There are three ways I prefer to communicate with the subconscious. The first means to communicate is to use muscle responses with the fingers or the pendulum. These are techniques used by trained hypnotherapists (Pulos, 1994). The finger movements are called ideomotor responses. You can use either patient or therapist defined ideomotor responses to communicate with the subconscious and the parts. With the pendulum. The subconscious can cause fine muscle responses to get the pendulum to move in different directions to communicate. More on this later. There are two other ways to communicate which are the internal voice and novel responses. I'll explain using the fingers first.

T: **Now we are going to try to communicate with the subconscious. Please lay your hands, palm down, next to you on the couch, on your knees or in front of you on a table. Let them relax.**

I am going to ask some questions while you remain relaxed. Be curious about the process and see whether a finger response will occur. Don't make conscious finger movements. After I ask a question, you will feel a response or a tickle in one of your fingers. I initially wait up to 30 seconds because different people respond at different rates, some quickly and some slowly. If you feel a tickle or a sensation that I can't see, then move your finger so I can see it. Otherwise, I might hallucinate a response. With practice, this will be easy.

Some therapists think that it is good to let the patient define the response. I don't do this because I have many patients, and having different responses for different patients would confuse me. For those readers interested in patient-determined responses, here is what I say to get the patient to define the responses.

1. Patient-defined responses

T: **Subconscious, I am going to ask you to communicate with me by moving your fingers. Please show me a "Yes" response.**

Wait about 20 seconds. Some responses are quick and others are slow. If you get a response, write down the name of the finger and continue.

T: **Subconscious, please show me a "No" response.**

Usually a different finger will give you a sensation or will move. Write down which finger signaled a "No." Now, you do the same with the following two questions:

T: **Subconscious, please show me an "I don't know response."**

Write down this response and go on to the next question.

T: **Subconscious, please show me an "I don't want to tell you response."**

I hope that you will have four unique finger sensations or responses that you can use to help you problem-solve any issues that may arise. Then, say:

T: **No response is a response, in itself. I interpret no response as "I'm not talking." When there is a combination of responses, there is either a mixed message or several parts responding.**

If, you try to get a response several times and find it not working, teach the responses you want to communicate "Yes," "No," and so forth.

2. Therapist-defined responses

T: **Subconscious, let's define the index finger for "Yes," the thumb for "No," the little finger** (pinkie) **for "I don't know," and the, uh, middle finger for "I don't want to tell you." Now move your fingers on both hands as I go through the responses. This is the "Yes" finger. Move both index fingers up and down several times. This is the "No" finger. Move your thumbs. This is the "I don't know" finger. Move your little fingers, and the "I don't want to tell you" finger. Move the middle fingers.**

Now, try it out to see if you can communicate with a part or the subconscious.

T: **Subconscious, please show me a "Yes" response.**

Sometimes, the fingers on both the right and left hand will move. When this happens, I always wonder if one of the fingers is being moved by a prebirth part. See Section 3-5-8.

S: **Yes.** [Oh, happy day, the index finger moves.]

T: **Subconscious, please show me a "No" response.**

S: [No response or wrong finger]

Remind the patient that he or she should move any finger in which there are sensations; otherwise, problem-solve.

T: **Is there a part blocking communication or responding with a "No?"**

P: [No response]

Reaffirm your plan to not teach the subconscious how to treat trauma until all the parts are on the Treatment Team. Try again with further problem-solving.

T: **Is there a part blocking communication or responding with a "No?"**

S: **No.** [Thumb moves]

T: **Subconscious, please show me an "I don't know" response.**

S: [No response or wrong finger, problem-solve.]

S: **I don't know.** [Little finger moves.]

T: **Subconscious, please show me "I don't want to tell you" response.**

S: [No response or wrong finger, problem-solve.]

S: **I don't want to tell you.** [Middle finger moved]

I point out the following to the patient.

T: **"No response" is a response, in itself. I interpret "no response" as any response other than "Yes," "No," "I don't know," and**

"I don't want to tell you." When the ring finger moves, I interpret this as somewhere between "I don't want to tell you" and "I don't know."

Sometimes, I have to encourage the patient not to move the fingers voluntarily and to remain relaxed and curious about whether a finger moves. Other times, when I don't see a response, I have to encourage the person to move the fingers if he or she feels any sensation in them. Sometimes, I see the tendon in the hand moving. If nothing works, I give the instructions for finger responses again. I reaffirm that no one will be treated until all parts are on the Treatment Team and they give me permission to teach the subconscious the treatment process.

3. Communicating with a pendulum

The second way to communicate with the subconscious and aspects is to use a pendulum. Find an object like a 5/16 self-locking nut (my preference for personal use) and tie a green string to it—green symbolizes health, but the string can be any color. Anything can serve as a weight. Make the string about three to four inches long. Now while holding the pendulum still, and concentrating to keep it still, ask your subconscious the questions given above for patient-determined responses; for example, "Show me a yes." After each question, wait until the pendulum moves in some direction. My pendulum moves out and back for a "Yes," sideways for a "No," clockwise for "I don't know," and counterclockwise for "I don't want to tell you." If it is stationary, it means some part is blocking the response. Artists and technicians with well-developed fine muscle control may not have success with this approach. Sometimes, it takes practice to get responses with a pendulum. Initially, I didn't have finger responses and had to rely on the pendulum to access my subconscious.

4. Communicating with internal responses

The third way to communicate with the subconscious is to either imagine a pad or chalkboard in your mind and have your subconscious write a "Yes" or No" on it or to request and get an auditory "Yes" or "No" in your thoughts. I prefer the finger approach, but if you are working on your own, try to get conscious contact with the subconscious. If you form pictures in your conscious mind easily, see if your subconscious can write on a blackboard, a tablet or a computer screen.

T: **Subconscious, please write a "Yes" on the blackboard.**

If you see a "Yes," play with it and practice making it brighter and dimmer just to develop the awareness that you can control the image. Then ask for a "No" and the other responses, "I don't know" and "I don't want to tell you." If you get these responses easily and clearly, then this means of communication will work well for you. Sometimes people get extra communication by seeing or hearing sentences as a visual or auditory response. If you are lucky, the subconscious can explain or direct the treatment in sentence form by writing it on your blackboard or by giving you words that you can hear. The subconscious can be humorous.

If it is hard for you to form pictures in your mind, try to communicate with the subconscious through auditory responses by quieting your thoughts and asking for a response in your thoughts. Ask the following question and listen for a "Yes" or a "No."

P: **Subconscious, please give me a "Yes" in my thoughts so I can hear it.**

If you hear the "Yes" response, see if you can reliably tell the difference between your own thoughts and the subconscious. Explore asking your subconscious for the other responses—namely, "No", "I don't know" and "I don't want to tell you"—to see if auditory responses will work for you to communicate with the subconscious.

5. Other means of communication

When working with a patient who has difficult parts that block communication with the subconscious, it is possible to obtain communication with the subconscious with other unusual responses for "Yes" and "No". For example, with one patient who had some sort of programming—the deliberate creation of parts—my colleague and I were able to not alert the parts by teaching the subconscious to give a "Yes" response by making a sneer with her left, upper lip. This worked well for communicating, and we had some success working with her complex structures.

Summary

Most people can obtain communication and rapport with their subconscious. However, if you are having trouble and are not able to set up rapport with your subconscious, reread the Sections 3-3 through 3-5 and try this section again. If repeated tries at communicating with your subconscious are unsuccessful, you can assume that some aspect or part is blocking the communication. With continuing problems, do this.

T: **Can I talk with the part that is blocking communication with the subconscious?**

S: **No.**

Continue with the problem-solving in the way described in Section 3-5.

When there is no response for 30 seconds:

T: **Does the part that is blocking communication want more satisfaction and less pain?**

Continue to systematically try to resolve the barriers to treatment, and you will eventually resolve the barrier and set up contact with your subconscious.

If all else fails and you still want to treat your issues, consider finding a competent therapist. Get the names of competent therapists from your local Mental Health Department or the local women's sanctuary. These resources can give you a number of therapists to interview to see which will be suitable for you.

You can always check out my earlier book, *Emotional Freedom* (Flint, 2001), and see if Emotional Freedom Techniques are something you would like to try. It is based on the same theory, but you do the tapping on the outside to cause the treatment of issues. In that book, there is a chapter on inner-self healing that works with many people.

If all went well and you have communication with your subconscious, continue to the following section.

3-7 Assessing readiness for learning the treatment process

Practice communicating with your subconscious and get comfortable with your form of communication. It is important to know that any form of communication with your subconscious is subject to many influences that can result in an untrue answer. Always be aware that other parts can interfere with responses. Remember, just try to be curious, and deliberately avoid having any interest in the outcome of your questions to the subconscious. Remind all of your aspects, though you might not have any amnesic parts, that you want them all to join the Treatment Team.

Before you continue, think of the practice issue and ask:

T: **Think of the practice issue. Subconscious, is it safe to use the practice issue that we identified to test the treatment process?**

S: **Yes.** [Continue] or

S: **No.**

Look for some other issue that is less painful and check again with your subconscious. When your subconscious says the issue is safe to use, continue.

When you think that all your aspects are on the Treatment Team, you can find out if this is true with the following three questions:

1. Question one

T: **Subconscious, are all the aspects and parts members of the Treatment Team?**

S: **Yes.** [Continue]

When you get a "No," problem-solve.

2. Question two

T: **Do all the Treatment Team members want the subconscious to learn the treatment process?**

S: **Yes.** [Continue] *or*

S: **No.**

This calls for problem-solving. I start by asking:

T: **Is there a wee little baby part that is afraid?**

If you get a "No" or no response, ask the following:

T: **Is this part afraid of "big pain" or worried that your trauma memory will retraumatize the Main Personality?**

Continue problem-solving and clearing barriers.

Then, when it appears that all parts are on the Treatment Team, start with question 1 again. When you get "Yes" to questions 1 and 2, continue with question 3 by asking the confusing, double-negative sentence in a demanding voice:

3. Question three

T: **You mean there are no parts that don't want the treatment process to be taught?**

S: **Yes.**

You immediately go to the next section and teach the treatment process. If you wait, then another uneducated part might wake up.

S: **No.**

T: **Can I talk to that part that has some considerations about joining the Treatment Team?**

P: **Yes.**

You may have to reassure the part that the subconscious will not treat any part until it gives permission. Continue problem-solving the barriers and repeat questions 1 and 2 until you get a "Yes" to question 3; then continue to teach the treatment process. When I keep getting "No," I start worrying that the patient is responding with what he or she thinks is the correct answer. If you experience this, don't prompt the correct answer. I have often been wrong in my suspicion and found that a part was saying "No."

3-8 Learning the treatment process

Read this section after you get total agreement from all of your aspects. This is the section where your subconscious learns the treatment process.

T: **The subconscious will learn how to treat using an internal treatment process. No hypnosis, trance, or any other indirect means is necessary. I want you to be alert and aware of what you are reading. Read it with curiosity. This treatment process is taught by using a simple 20-second metaphor. The metaphor teaches a treatment process based on Thought Field Therapy, a tapping therapy developed by Dr. Roger Callahan** (Callahan, 1985, 1991, 2001). **Later, you will learn how to improve the treatment process, to get the subconscious to treat issues throughout the day, and how to treat specific issues. Now, I want to teach the subconscious the treatment process.**

Double-check so you will be sure that all aspects of your personality approve teaching the subconscious how to treat pain. Look for a "Yes" with the next three questions before you continue.

T: **Can I talk to the subconscious?**

S: **Yes.** [Yes #1]

T: **Do all aspects of your personality want you to learn the treatment process now?**

S: **Yes.** [Yes #2]

The following double-negative sentence tricks the parts with objections to respond "No." The subconscious, on the other hand, will respond "Yes."

T: **You mean there are no parts that don't have any objections to teaching the subconscious the treatment process?**

S: **Yes.** [Yes #3]

With "Yes" to these questions, you can continue. Otherwise, with any other response, it would be best to return to the last section or, if necessary, to reread the sections starting at Section 3-3. If you continue and teach the treatment process without getting "Yes" responses to the three questions above, it may be disrespectful to some aspects of your personality and these aspects may become barriers to treatment. Now you will read the metaphor that teaches the treatment process.

The treatment metaphor for Process Healing

T: [Draw the Figure 3-22 as you describe the treatment metaphor.] **Subconscious, imagine the brain is a soccer field, a smooth**

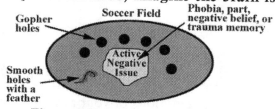
playing field with no
bumps. When the pho-
bia, negative belief,
painful memory, or part
becomes active and
moves onto the playing
field, gopher holes pop

Figure 3-22 The Healing Metaphor

up in a particular sequence. [Gophers are animals that burrow underground and push to the surface, leaving mounds of dirt.] **You can treat the emotion by remembering the sequence of gopher holes and gradually smoothing the dirt over each hole a little at a time with a feather in the remembered sequence, repeatedly, until the gopher holes disappear.** [Wait a few seconds.]

T: **Subconscious, do you understand how to diagnose and treat a painful memory?**

Usually, I get a "Yes."

When I get a "No," I initially assume that a prebirth part awakened and is responding to me. Prebirth parts can learn to respond for the subconscious and respond with a "No" because they aren't able to work like the subconscious and don't fully understand how to do the treatment process. If the "subconscious" continues to fail to understand, then:

T: **Is a prebirth part responding for the subconscious?**
P: **Yes.**

T: **Can I talk directly to the subconscious?**

At this point, you may have to problem-solve to get cooperation from the part causing the communication problem (see Sections 3-3 through 3-5).

When you are convinced that you have direct communication with the subconscious, ask:

T: **Subconscious, can you diagnose and treat the practice issue?**
S: **Yes.**

Explain to the patient what you want.

T: **I want you simply to focus on the practice issue and experience your emotions. See if you can experience the hurt gradually decrease after asking, "Subconscious, please treat this issue."**

On the other hand,

S: **No.**
T: **Subconscious, should we look for a different practice issue?**
S: **No.**
T: **Is there a barrier to treatment?**
S: **Yes.**

Go to Section 3-5 and problem-solve to find out if parts are blocking the treatment process. Though I believe the subconscious hears the metaphor, regardless of whether there is a barrier, sometimes I have reread the paragraph teaching the treatment process to the patient.

If you experienced the painful emotions of your practice issue going to zero, congratulations. It's a remarkable experience. Sometimes, there are parts that prevent the emotion from going to zero. If you felt the issue reduced from 8 to 5, for example, and stopped changing, you may have parts with pain to problem-solve and treat. Start off with:

T: **Subconscious, are there parts active or blocking the treatment process who are giving that remaining pain?**
S: **Yes.**
T: **Do those parts want treatment?**
S: **Yes.**
T: **Please treat those parts one after the other.**

When the answer is "No" and the parts don't want treatment, then continue to resolve any barriers until all the parts are treated. When the subconscious finishes treatment, you will feel the painful emotions for your practice issue become less intense or gone.

Your subconscious can now treat trauma issues. Next, you and your subconscious will learn how to problem-solve and resolve all the barriers that can arise while treating some traumatic issue.

3-9 Resolving barriers to treatment

When there are barriers to treatment, the brain is disorganized and the treatment process does not work. The information given below will help the subconscious or therapist problem-solve to resolve the barrier that is causing the disorganization. When problem-solving, if the part has problems about joining the Treatment Team, you may have to try all the reasons for treatment described previously in Sections 3-3 and 3-5. I listed additional barriers below in order, from most often used interventions to least used interventions. Of course, having this list is not going to remove the fun of problem-solving because human personalities can learn surprising and complicated patterns that block treatment. Later chapters describe complex memory structures.

Suppose that all aspects have joined the Treatment Team and your subconscious is actively treating aspects and painful memories. You can check in with your subconscious to find out if the treatment process is progressing well. You can find this out by asking:

T: **Subconscious, is the treatment going well?**
S: **Yes.** [Great] or
S: **No.**

You will have to problem-solve to resolve a barrier. The following barriers can block the treatment process. I describe each barrier with the general approach I use to resolve it. They are listed in descending order from the most frequently to the least frequently observed barrier.

Table of contents for this section

1. A part is talking for the subconscious

T: **Is there a part talking for the subconscious?**
S: **Yes.**
T: **Is this a prebirth part?**
S: **No.**

Continue problem-solving, following the problem-solving strategy described in Section 3-5 and using the information from this section.

S: **Yes.**

You have an active prebirth part. Prebirth parts learn to relay information from the subconscious to the Main Personality. They are often the parts that talk for the subconscious.

T: **Prebirth part, I know that your role in the personality has been useful, but your trauma and emotional pain will cause you to give distorted information to the Main Personality. You have much knowledge, wisdom, and understanding. If your pain is treated, your good coping skills are strengthened with positive emotions, and you join with the Main Personality, you will be more effective in protecting the Main Personality from pain and in finding more satisfaction. Are you willing to accept treatment?**

P: **No.**

T: **After treatment, you can join with the Main Personality and, when this happens, you can run the body with the Main Personality and have no conflicts. Would you like treatment now?**

P: **Yes.**

If the response is "No," review the advantages of treatment (see Section 3-3) with the part causing the barrier.

2. Parts are active

T: **Subconscious, are there parts active in the Active Experience?**
S: **Yes.**
T: **Do they want to join the Treatment Team?**
S: **Yes.**
T: **Please join the Treatment Team. It would help if you left the Active Experience and put your eyes and ears in to watch what's happening.**

I always intend to ask Treatment Team members to leave the Active Experience and put their eyes and ears in. This I assume reduces activity in the Active Experience. However, there are, usually, other aspects to deal with before you get all aspects on the Treatment Team.

S: **No.**

T: [To save time] **Are you willing to talk to a representative of the Treatment Team or the subconscious to learn all you need to know about the healing process? In this way, you can make an *informed* decision about whether to be treated?**

I usually shorten this to "talk to the subconscious," which usually works. With parts that are not communicating or with no response, I try to trigger any kind of response. It appears that any response helps the part to be willing to talk to the subconscious.

P: [After several attempts to establish communication] **Yes.**

T: **Subconscious, does this part want treatment?**

P: **Yes.** *or*

P: **No.**

T: **Does this part have pain so big that he or she is afraid to have it treated?**

P: **Yes.**

Go to the next barrier.

3. Pain is too great

T: **Does this part have big, big pain?**

P: **Yes.**

T: **Does this part know that the rate of treatment and the rest period between treatments can be adjusted to make the treatment process very safe?**

P: **No.**

T: **Are you willing to talk to a representative of the Treatment Team or the subconscious to get an explanation?**

P: **Yes.**

Otherwise, explain again about the treatment process and how safe it is. Refer to the treatment figure (Figure 3-20 on page 78), and draw the figure to explain the treatment process. With a "No," ask:

T: **Is this a fragile part that has so much pain that you fear flooding the conscious experience?**

S: **Yes.**

If it is a fragile part, explain the treatment interventions for fragile parts while drawing Figure 3-21 on page 79.

4. I want treatment now

T: **Do you want treatment now?**

P: **Yes.**

T: **Are you a member of the Treatment Team?**

P: **No.**

T: **Will you join the Treatment Team and be willing to be treated when the team decides it's best for you?**

P: **No.**

T: **Subconscious, would it be safe to treat this part right now and then continue treating the other part later?**

S: **Yes.**

With a "No," problem-solve.

You might have to use all your negotiating skills to resolve this issue. When there are two or more parts active and they both want treatment first, you can try the following:

T: **Subconscious, is there a conflict between parts that want treatment right now?**

P: **Yes.**

T: **Can you all decide among yourselves the order of treatment? Treatment takes only a few minutes** . . . *or*

T: **Subconscious, can you help them decide by telling them that treatment will only take each of them a few minutes?**

This may be a time to be creative to find some intervention to resolve the conflict. I have resolved conflicts by having the parts draw straws.

5. Part doesn't want treatment

T: **Is this a part that doesn't want treatment?**

P: **Yes.**

T: **Would you be willing to talk to the subconscious to find out all the information you need to make an *informed* decision about whether you want treatment?**

P: **Yes.**

T: **Great. Please do that.**

Sometimes, it's not this easy.

P: **No.**

T: **Did you just wake up?**

P: **Yes.**

Parts can awaken during the treatment process or when you are communicating with the subconscious. In this case, you can use the strategies provided in this section to problem-solve any barrier. Encourage the part to join the Treatment Team. Usually, the part will want more satisfaction and less pain and be willing to join the Treatment Team.

6. Treat the physiology first

Healing the physiology refers to a remembered neural connection between the trauma memory and the midbrain. This neural connection causes the midbrain to become sensitive to active emotions of a trauma. When the midbrain is sensitive, all the trauma emotions of the part can be easily triggered into the Active Experience. When the neural connection to the midbrain is treated first, then you can treat the emotions of the issue more safely. At this point, I seldom do this, but in the early years, I was always using this intervention to ensure the treatment process was safe.

T: **Subconscious, do I have to separate the content of the memory from the physiology connected to the midbrain to treat this issue safely?**

S: **Yes.**

T: **Should I treat the physiology first, before treating the content of the issue?**

S: **Yes.**

T: **Is it safe to do that now?**

S: **Yes.**

T: **Please treat the physiology.**

Sometimes, for some reason, the content has to be treated first. After treating the physiology, ask:

T: **Subconscious, please treat the content of the issue.**

7. Stored reversal

Stored reversal is a barrier that occasionally reveals itself. I seldom treat stored reversal. However, even though I don't do this intervention much anymore, I believe that my subconscious does it when necessary. The disuse of some interventions is caused by the subconscious communicating in another way (Flint, n.d.).

T: **Is there a barrier stopping the treatment?**

You would do the usual problem-solving and when you run out of ideas:

T: **Subconscious, is this barrier caused by stored reversal?**

S: **Yes.**

I usually explain what I am talking about to the patient and have him or her do the intervention.

T: **The corpus callosum is a structure that connects the right and left hemispheres of your brain. Usually, the front has a positive charge and the back has a negative charge. When the polarity of the corpus callosum is reversed, learning fails to occur. It appears as though this polarity reversal can be stored with aspects of memory. Then, when you trigger the memory into the Active Experience, it causes the reversed condition, and the treatment process will not work. The way to treat this condition** (see Figure 3-23) **is to have**

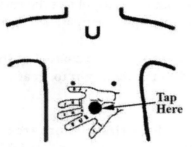

the patient place the back of his or her hand on the sternum, with the thumb down, and tap on the palm five times. This corrects this reversal, and the treatment process can resume. The subconscious can learn to perform this correction after a demonstration.

Figure 3-23 Correcting Stored Reversal

This technique is an intervention that simply works and may have no known connection to scientific fact. Now, can you put the back of your hand on your sternum and tap on your palm five times?

After the patient finishes, ask:

T: **Subconscious, is the barrier removed?**

S: **Yes.**

If you have done this correction before, you can simply ask your subconscious to do it:

T: **Subconscious, please correct the stored reversal.**

8. Wants more pain and less satisfaction

T: **Do you want more pain and less satisfaction?**

P: **Yes.**

T: **Do you mean that you find that choosing to have pain makes the pain you have feel less painful?**

P: **Yes.**

T: **Well, the pain you continue to avoid is pain that you learned many years ago. If you treat that pain in a way that doesn't hurt you, the Main Personality or any other aspects of the personality, you won't have to choose it anymore. Would you be willing to have your pain**

treated, have your positive qualities strengthened, and to join with the
Main Personality?

P: **Yes.**

Continue your treatment interventions.

P: **No.**

T: **Would you be willing to talk to the subconscious and get all
the information that you need to make an *informed* decision about being treated?**

Usually you get a "Yes." Otherwise, do the usual problem-solving.

9. A belief is blocking the choice to be treated

T: **Subconscious, is there a belief in this part that is blocking the
choice to be treated?**

S: **Yes.**

T: **Can I ask the subconscious to treat beliefs that are barriers
to treatment?**

S: **Yes.**

T: **Great.**

On the other hand:

S: **No.**

T: **Part, if I ask the subconscious to treat that belief without
asking you, would you be upset?**

P: **No.**

T: **Subconscious, please treat the belief.**

S: **Yes.**

Then continue to problem-solve to find and resolve the barrier.

10. Part without eyes or ears

Sometimes, parts formed *in utero* or at birth, as strange as it seems,
don't have eyes and ears.

T: **Subconscious, is there a part without eyes and ears?**

S: **Yes.**

T: **Can you communicate with that part?**

S: **Yes.**

Problem-solve to see if you can treat the part easily . . . *or*

S: **No.**

In this case, I imagine a part without eyes and ears moving in the
Active Experience, which stops the subconscious from communicating

or treating the part. I assumed that the subconscious could create neural activity that could slow or stop the part from moving.

T: **Can you create the neural activity to slow that part to a standstill and either communicate with or treat that part?**

S: **Yes.**

T: **Can you treat the part now?**

S: **Yes.**

Then continue to resolve other barriers and have the subconscious treat the part.

11. A part's emotions are active, but its other senses are dormant

T: **Is there a part active, but the eyes and ears are not active?**

S: **Yes.**

T: **I would like to ask the part that use emotions are active to come into the Active Experience. Can I now talk to that part?**

P: **Yes.**

T: **Do you want to join the Treatment Team?**

P: **Yes.**

Otherwise, problem-solve.

12. Toxic substances are disorganizing the brain

I seldom see this, but when I did see toxic effects, the subconscious was able to treat them so they didn't interfere with the treatment process.

T: **Subconscious, is there some toxic effect that is blocking treatment?**

S: **Yes.**

T: **Can you isolate the toxic effect from the memory, treat it separately, and then treat the content of the part?**

S: **Yes.**

13. Drug trauma is blocking the treatment process

T: **Subconscious, is there a drug effect that is blocking your ability to treat the part?**

S: **Yes.**

T: **Can you separate the drug effect from the content and emotions, treat it, and then treat the content and emotions of the part?**
S: **Yes.**

14. Part continues to refuse treatment or to respond, even after asking all the above questions

I am using this intervention more often because it saves time. It doesn't seem to cause any problems. However, I make sure that I continue to respect those parts that are not willing to be treated without giving permission.

T: **I want this part to know that I am only going to accept a "Yes" response as a "Yes" and all other responses as a "No." If I ask the subconscious to treat you without getting your permission to treat you, would you be angry with me?**

I usually get a "No" or no response.

S: **Yes.**

T: **Well, I am not going to ask the subconscious to treat you, but would this part mind if I asked the subconscious to treat the belief that is getting in the way of communication?**

S: **No.** [or no response]

T: **Subconscious, please treat that belief that gets in the way of communication.**

Sometimes, this works and I continue to treat the part. When it doesn't work, I continue with the usual problem-solving approach or try the following:

T: **Subconscious, if I asked you to treat the part without asking the part, and the part got angry with me, would it be in the patient's best interest to treat the part anyway?**

S: **Yes.**

I try to avoid using this approach, but when nothing works, I have used it effectively.

Summary

This section gave you many examples and resolutions of possible barriers that get in the way of the treatment process. The first few examples in the list are the interventions that you can test first. You are less likely to find the barrier to treatment as you try examples farther down the list. Again, I give these techniques mainly for therapists to use with patients with personalities that are more complex. When a therapist uses Process Healing enough, he or she gradually develops an intuition that helps find the barrier more easily.

Therapists and patients will find that, after using this technique for several months, resolving barriers becomes less of an issue as your treatment skills become entrenched. As trust is set up, your patient's subconscious appears to learn and use your current treatment skills. This is discussed in Flint (n.d.).

Now, if treatment of your practice issue did not work, here is what to do.

T: **Subconscious, can you diagnose and treat the practice issue now?**

S: **Yes.**

T: **Subconscious, please do that.**

T: [Addressing the person] **Simply focus on the issue and see if you can experience the emotions gradually decrease. Can you feel any change in the emotions?**

S: **No.**

T: **Subconscious, do you understand how to diagnose and treat pain?**

S: **No.**

This is unusual. Start problem-solving.

S: **Yes.**

T: **Is there is a barrier preventing the treatment?**

S: **Yes.**

Do one of the following: Look for prebirth parts or go back to the previous section and review the metaphor teaching the treatment process. You can review or reread this section to resolve any barriers to treating the issue. You can also ask the subconscious what to do by asking leading questions about possible solutions to get "Yes" or "No" answers.

Continue to the next section only after you have treated your practice issue. Remember, if your practice issue still has painful emotions associated with it, parts could be causing the emotions. The emotions should feel comfortable and normal after treating the issue.

3-10 The first interventions

This section will help you create treatment plans for each part on the Treatment Team. It will tell your subconscious of other support that is available to help the treatment process. Finally, the subconscious will learn how to be able to automatically treat negative beliefs, memories, and experiences, without involving the Main Personality.

Table of contents for this section

1. Develop treatment plans

T: **Subconscious, is it a good time to create treatment plans for all the members on the Treatment Team?**

S: **No.**

T: **Is there some aspect that wants treatment immediately?**

S: **Yes.**

T: **Subconscious, is it safe and politically OK to treat this aspect now?**

S: **Yes.**

T: **Please treat this part.**

S: **Yes.**

Sometimes there is more problem-solving to do, but generally, you can continue to give the subconscious and the Treatment Team instructions about making treatment plans.

T: **Subconscious and team members, remember the treatment plan has the rate of treatment and the rest time between each treatment. Adjust the rate and rest time for each part until all team members feel safe with the plan. If a fragile part is involved, select the treatment plan for fragile parts. All team members vote to approve the treatment plan. The decisions are made in consensus, which means all parts, 100 percent, vote "Yes" to accept each treatment plan for each part. However, each part is free to vote "Yes" or "No," depending on how safe he or she feels about the treatment plan. You all will have to negotiate to get consensus. When all members of the Treatment Team have a treatment plan, treating and integrating team members progresses in a safe, systematic, and orderly way. Subconscious, is it a good time to develop treatment plans for every member of the Treatment Team?**

S: **Yes.**

Of course, during the treatment process, uneducated parts can wake up, demanding parts awaken, or other issues can complicate the orderly progress of treatment. The approach to any barriers is described in the previous section. When there are many new parts that joined the Treatment Team, it is good to develop treatment plans for all the new members before continuing. In practice, when I convince a new part to accept treatment, I often ask the subconscious if it is safe to treat the part now, and then have the subconscious treat the part.

2. Resolve barriers to independent, automatic treatment

Three conditions prevent the subconscious from automatically treating negative activity in the Active Experience. Chapters 4 and 6 discuss other less common barriers to automatic treatment. The first is similar to the difficulty found in treating alcoholics. When an alcoholic says, "I want to quit drinking," "I want to drink" is embedded in the statement. This triggers all the positive and negative drinking memories into the Active Experience. This disorganizes the brain and blocks the treatment of the drinking urge.

This same process happens when the subconscious tries to treat an issue. When the subconscious thinks, "I want to treat that negative memory," all the memories having to do with getting treatment are elicited into the Active Experience by the embedded phrase, "I want to treat." The memories of going to mother, father, the doctor, dentist (for treatment), and so forth become active, and the Active Experience becomes disorganized. With all these active memories, treatment by the subconscious cannot take place.

These intrusive memories from other treatment experiences can be treated because negative emotions are the motivation for these intrusions. After treating the negative emotions associated with past experiences, the memories will not intrude or come into the Active Experience when the subconscious wants to treat something.

T: **Subconscious, please start this treatment at birth, before birth or as far back as necessary. Treat from then to now all beliefs, memories, experiences, and parts that get in the way of the belief that "I have a process within me and access to insight and knowledge to independently treat all memory structures on all levels that cause my mental and physical issues." Subconscious, can you do that?**

S: [I usually get a "Yes."] **Yes.**

If you don't get a "Yes," problem-solve. Check periodically to see if the subconscious is finished.

T: **Subconscious, have you finished doing the Change History?**
S: **Yes** or **No.**

The second barrier to automatic treatment is habits called Predispositions. When a negative aspect becomes active, there is a memory that causes a habitual response, a Predisposition, to deal with any negative aspect that comes into the Active Experience. The Predisposition conflicts with the subconscious when the subconscious tries to do treatment in the Active Experience. This conflict becomes a barrier to automatic treatment. The subconscious cannot treat the negative experience. You can treat this barrier in the following way.

T: **Subconscious, I want you to identify all Predispositions responding to negative memories that cause the conflict with the subconscious. Please treat the Predispositions so they will no longer occur when a negative memory becomes active.**
S: **Yes.**

Finally, sometimes, there are massive beliefs that prevent the subconscious from doing treatment. Ask the following to clear these beliefs.

T: **Subconscious, please clear all massive beliefs that interfere with treating negative issues in the Active Experience.**
S: **Yes.**

With these changes done, your subconscious should be able to treat most negative beliefs, experiences, and memories that come into your Active Experience.

T: **Subconscious, do you have the ability to treat issues independently and as needed?**
S: **Yes.**

I usually get a "Yes," and when I don't, I suspect a part is talking for the subconscious.

If all goes well, you will find your daily attitude becoming increasingly positive as the subconscious spontaneously treats negative beliefs, memories, and thoughts. Ask your subconscious, now and then, to see if he or she is still able to treat automatically. If not, problem-solve.

3. Put the subconscious into overdrive

Now that the subconscious has learned the treatment process and the Treatment Team members all have treatment plans, the following may facilitate the effectiveness of the subconscious. You won't understand this intervention (see Flint, n.d.), but it's my impression that this is good to do at this time. Jesus was known as a powerful healer, and his subconscious can serve as a consultant to your subconscious. Because you have not been led to think that this might be possible, if you think what I am suggesting is too weird to believe, just skip it. Otherwise, read or say the requests and notice whether you feel some activity in your brain.

T: **Subconscious, please treat any beliefs that will get in the way of communicating with and getting help from the subconscious of Jesus and compose and strengthen self-empowering beliefs in their place.**

S: **Yes.**

T: **Subconscious, please look around and contact the subconscious of Jesus.**

S: **Yes.**

T: [Wait] **Subconscious, have you made contact?**

S: **Yes.**

If "No," do further problem-solving.

4. Connect with other treatment support

Four different field or "energy" sources allegedly help with the treatment process. I will describe them to your subconscious and then ask the subconscious if he or she can use this energy source to help with treatment. I have no idea if any of this connects to reality. It is my impression that since I have been pointing out these supportive fields, the treatment is going faster. If you get a "No," a part is usually intruding and you have to stop and treat the part.

a. Heart field

T: **Subconscious, I am going to connect you with four field sources that may help the treatment process. The first is the use of the heart field in the treatment process. The field of the heart is 5,000 times stronger than the field of any other organ in the body** (Pearson, 1998). **When the heartbeat is in the Active Experience, then the heart field is easily used in the treatment process. When your subconscious is treating an issue, you may feel your heart involved in the treatment process. Subconscious, will you include the heartbeat in the Active Experience and use the heart field in the treatment process?**

S: **Yes.**

T: **Does the heart energy help the treatment process?**

S: [I always get a "Yes."] **Yes.**

When I get a "No" with any of these sources when I expect a "Yes," I usually find that a prebirth part or some other part has awakened and is interfering with the response.

b. Field receptors in the skin

T: **The second process is based on the notions involved with Therapeutic Touch. Have you ever experienced Therapeutic Touch?**

P: **No.**

T: **Well, to experience it, here is what to do. Have someone move the palm of their hand just over your shoulder and then slowly move their hand, two inches off your arm, down your arm to your fingertips. Do this in four to five seconds. Have them do this repeatedly. Usually, you will feel a sensation as the hand moves down your arm. The electric field from their hand is presumably stimulating field receptors in your skin. It is said that these field receptors are sensitive to the fields of all those who love and care for you and all who love and care for humanity (Krieger, 1993). In fact, some believe that this treatment process uses all positive fields from past generations. Subconscious, can you take this positive information from the field receptors from the entire surface of your body and use this field to help the treatment process?**

S: **Yes.**

T: **Subconscious, is this field a positive contribution to the treatment process?**

S: **Yes.** [I always get a "Yes."]

c. Brain stem

T: **The third source is a field that enters through the brainstem. Subconscious, can you use the field that enters through the brainstem in the treatment process?**

S: [I usually get a "Yes."] **Yes.**

T: **Subconscious, is this a positive field to use in the treatment process?**

S: **Yes.** [I always get a "Yes."]

d. Pineal gland

T: **The fourth field source that is seemingly helpful with the treatment process is a field produced by the pineal gland. Subconscious, can you use the field from the pineal gland in the treatment process?**

S: **Yes.**

T: **Subconscious, is this field a positive field for use with the treatment process?**

S: **Yes.** [I always get a "Yes."]

Summary

There you have it. You have just finished a series of sections where you have had the opportunity to learn the Process Healing Method. After you obtained total agreement from yourself and all of your aspects, you taught your subconscious how to treat using an internal treatment process. No hypnosis, trance, or any other indirect means was necessary. A simple 20-second metaphor for treatment taught your subconscious the treatment process. The metaphor describes the internal processes based on the tapping treatment I learned from studying Thought Field Therapy (Callahan, 1993). A patient's subconscious taught me that the subconscious could do the tapping without my involvement.

If your personality was receptive to learning the Process Healing Method, then you have a powerful self-healing tool that can last you a lifetime. It is easy to get upset and forget that, by simply asking your subconscious to do the treatment, you can treat those upsets. You can use Process Healing with parenting, marital, and job stress—even the stress of life. You can treat upsets with drivers, dogs, bugs or people in your life with Process Healing. By consulting with your subconscious, you can change your emotions and thoughts about behavior that you don't like, such as attending school, work, and so forth. You can treat the self-limiting or negative beliefs and experiences and strengthen positive, self-empowering beliefs.

To further clarify how to use the content of this chapter when working with yourself or someone else, reread the example in Chapter 2, starting on page 28, to relate the structure and contents of this chapter to the example. In Chapter 4, your will learn many interventions that you will need to help you address some issues more directly and completely.

Chapter 4

General Information and Basic Treatment

Introduction

Now that your subconscious has been introduced to the Process Healing metaphor, over the course of the rest of this book I am going to teach you how to use Process Healing. Starting with this chapter, the person receiving treatment will be referred to as the patient. That patient could be you, your friend, or the patient of a mental health worker.

The advantage of using the word "patient," even when you are working on your own issues, is that it makes it clear to you that your Main Personality is serving as a therapist to your inner dynamics—the patient. This shift in your thinking may help you to foster a detached view of the treatment and thus enable you to feel freer to address your own issues. The increased objectivity will also help in the problem-solving process. I am sure that your parts and your subconscious will easily adjust to this notion and will join in with you to work as a team in order to clear away any issues.

Therapists, on the other hand, are probably already comfortable with the patient terminology. However, I must emphasis the use of it because, by the end of the book, detaching from your issues in this way will increase your feelings of confidence in experimenting with and using the procedures suggested. The use of the word "patient" will bring the "treatment setting" to the treatment method. Getting comfortable with this clear definition of your function with respect to your patients will increase the chance that, as a therapist, you will start using Process Healing regularly in your practice.

This chapter provides the basic interventions for treating many trauma-based issues. In each case, it is the subconscious that performs an intervention to treat the painful emotions of trauma. With every intervention presented here, the basic premise is that the Process Healing treatment replaces the emotional pain of the trauma memories with neutral or positive emotions available from the treatment setting. After treatment, the trauma memories become memories without pain.

As you become more familiar with Process Healing, you can change the language used in the interventions, making adjustments to fit your style. And as a bonus, after working with yourself or someone else and developing a working familiarity, you can shorten the interventions by taking shortcuts, because the subconscious will know your intent and fill in the blanks (Flint, n.d.). It's always important to check to see that you have completed treating an issue.

The strategies and interventions presented in this section are grouped into arbitrary categories. Again, as you go through the steps, it is expected that you will refer to this portion of the book many times. Eventually, you will become familiar with the interventions, and they will become skills that you will automatically access when you need them. As a starter, while you read this chapter, try a few interventions on yourself. If the interventions don't work, look for barriers. Working this way through Chapter 4 will expand your skills in treating many mental health problems.

Here is a description of the following sections.

General information—The quality of patient participation is reviewed, including: assessment, tactics for working with difficult patients, the use of the Process Healing Method by laypeople, and the difficulties encountered in the treatment of parts.

Relating to patients and treating issues—Different tactics are given for identifying and treating issues, and for expanding the effectiveness of the subconscious. In this section, another Healing Process metaphor is given.

Routine interventions—Routine interventions such as memory tagging are explained. The concepts of Change History and Shadow Memories are introduced.

Treatment procedures—This section describes five procedures used in the Process Healing Method.

Strengthening and installing behavior—When unwanted behaviors are neutralized, positive behaviors are taught or strengthened to meet the patient's goals. Several choices are suggested.

Optimizing treatment—Optimizing involves creating shortcuts and accessing intangible and unusual options that help treatment.

Examples—Examples are given of unresolved problems, treating distractibility, deeper treatment options, and working with dreams.

Table of contents for this chapter

Strengthening and installing behavior

Optimizing the treatment

Examples

Summary

General Information

4-1 Patient participation during treatment

Perhaps one of first steps in establishing a working relationship with a patient is to instill a curiosity about the process. This curiosity can be established when you first teach, and then address any concerns about finger responses. Emphasize to the patient that it is important to leave his or her fingers relaxed and to be simply curious about which finger will rise or move. Point out that if a tingle is felt, the finger should be moved. This is to prevent you from hallucinating finger movements. After they are reminded several times to simply be curious, patients usually accept this new way of thinking and either work in the conscious state or go into a light trance to keep their conscious mind out of the treatment process. However, it is not always that easy to get co-operation from the patient. It can be difficult to experience a true finger response if the patient is unwilling to let go and just be curious. In these situations, it is useful to watch for other indices of response, such as jerks in the tendons of the fingers or body sensations. From the beginning, encourage the patient not to consciously take part in the treatment process, but simply to have curiosity about the treatment method with no expectations.

Let the patient know that if he or she actively joins in the treatment process by thinking or verbalizing a personal metaphor of some kind, the memory activity in the Active Experience caused by this thinking becomes a mild barrier. I treated one patient who consciously did EMDR by doing eye movements while the subconscious was treating. This sort of mental activity disturbs or distorts the Active Experience. The treatment process, therefore, slows down when the patient actively tries to understand what is going on or causes internal metaphors to become active. For the best results, the patient simply has to have an honest intention of accepting treatment and then be willing to watch the process occurring while supporting the subconscious and the therapist by taking part in solving problems as they arise. If the person or a part, for that matter, is repeating a thought to him or herself (for example: "This is weird," "I can do this," or "I won't do this"), then the treatment process will not work. The treatment process appears to work faster when the patient simply focuses on the brain and body sensations.

After treating an issue, the patient and therapist can then discuss the process and the constructs used. The therapist should be attentive to what the patient says because one can discover cues leading to other issues or suggesting solutions to problems. It is during these discussions that I often ask the subconscious "leading questions" to confirm my hypothesis or to further my understanding of a construct or process.

4-2 Mental activity during processing

The mental activity of a patient who continually processes information and keeps his or her mind active during the treatment process will always show a barrier to treatment. I had one patient who reflected on the barrier caused by thinking and was creating extraneous memory activity into his Active Experience. What he noticed was that the treatment was taking place only when he was in a state of total hopelessness and his thoughts were finally quiet. Usually when I encounter a barrier of this nature, there is some content or activity that is maintaining the active thought process. Here is an example of how I treated one of these barriers with the Structure Procedure (see Chapter 8-28).

T: **Subconscious, is there a structure of Layered Memories that has to do with the analysis of mental issues and metaphors?**

S: **Yes.**

T: **Please treat this structure and then do a Massive Change History.**

S: **Yes.**

In this example, this first query wasn't enough to quiet the patient's mental activity. The ongoing internal activity interfered with the subconscious' plans. Some problem-solving revealed that the negative emotions associated with the recurrent thoughts were very intense.

     T: **Subconscious, is there a memory structure in the Emotion System that serves the intruding thoughts?**

     S: **Yes.**

     T: **Subconscious, please treat the structure of Emotion Memories in the Emotion System that motivates the intruding thoughts.**

     T: **Yes.**

     This intervention got the treatment process going again.

     When you give consideration to these last two interventions, remember that they are not cookie-cutter interventions that will work with everyone. These are interventions fitting to this patient at this time. We encountered a problem; I suggested a resolution to the patient's subconscious and got a "Yes"; then I carried out the intervention to apparently resolve the problem. Many interventions offered in this book follow this paradigm. Let yourself be a flexible and creative problem solver.

4-3 Assessing the effectiveness of your interventions

     At the beginning of the next session, always assess the effectiveness of the interventions that you did in the previous session. This is the way to find out if you have to give more treatment to some of the previous issues. This practice can also give you valuable information to help you evaluate your effectiveness and give you ideas about strategy. However, there are some pitfalls that can distort your feedback.

     In most cases, the Process Healing Method will work painlessly and quickly. This is what we want, but when a therapist works in partnership with the patient to solve difficult problems, the patient may form an overrated value of the therapist because the interventions seem like magic. (They don't realize that it is straight behaviorism.) By being overrated, the patient will sometimes unconsciously find a positive outcome when there is none. It is important to keep this possibility in mind.

     Another possible pitfall that might distort patient feedback occurs when the patient gets preoccupied with current issues and forgets that other changes have happened, so the feedback is less positive than the actual changes reflect. In addition, the patient's system may have presented increased intrusions or pain, so it might seem as though the treatment has failed. This increased patient discomfort could be motivated by some part of the system either needing to gain the attention of the patient and therapist in order to obtain immediate treatment or even to hide a really big issue that some part doesn't want treated.

When assessing the effectiveness of the previous sessions, ask how the patient felt when he or she left the office, and how long the good feelings lasted. Then carefully explore the return of the problematic issues.

4-4 Working with difficult patients

One multiple personality patient (DID) resisted all my suggestions about just moving her fingers when she felt sensations in them. She wouldn't move her fingers. She became irate and threatened to leave when I tried to reason with her. I managed to keep her in the office and carefully treated the part that "hated" to take directions. I problem-solved and used the usual reframes to encourage this part to give permission for treatment. This turned out to be a significant intervention for her.

When I work with oppositional children, using creativity and humor are important. My rule is to follow the lead of the patient. For example, I've done sessions talking in metaphor to child patients while they were lying on the couch with their head under a pillow—with or without their fingers showing. Another time, a young boy lay face down on the floor with his arm on his back—fingers visible. I have done interventions using a raccoon puppet to ask the questions and made interventions with my best raccoon puppet voice. In another case involving a noncommunicative child with her head under a pillow, I talked to the child's mother in an obtuse way with embedded suggestions and interventions for the child's subconscious. Because the subconscious is always listening, I am always confident that I can communicate indirectly or directly with it.

A child whom I treated was a typical uncooperative patient. She was squirmy, agitated, and unpleasant. Fortunately, I was able to perform Emotional Freedom Techniques (EFT) with her. This involved having her tap on acupressure points while she or I said a reminder phrase relating to the issue (see Appendix V). This approach appeared to be working, but it was evident that she was going to become bored quickly, so I doubled up on what I was doing. While I was doing EFT, I continued talking to the subconscious, mentioning along the way that the subconscious could acquire my treatment knowledge with a nonverbal means of communication I was trying that was practiced by ancient First Nations elders (P. Adrian, personal communication, March 28, 2003). When the timing was right, I presented some of the Education Process. I observed that treatment was working when she admitted that she felt some sensations in her head. Her mother, who was present, looked unhappy with her difficult child. However, the girl gave me a warm, coy glance as she left. I was worried that the mother would end treatment because it didn't appear to be working. However, I was pleasantly surprised when they arrived for the second session. I think this girl was aware that she was making changes and wanted to continue treatment.

In the second session, the patient reported seeing changes at home and in school. For the first 45 minutes, she appeared relaxed and then she crumbled into tears of frustration. Her mother declared, "She can't be calm for over 45 minutes." Again, I worked intuitively and indirectly, asking the subconscious to tag and treat parts and the different behaviors that I noticed. She came in for a third session as a willing patient. My accepting, nonjudgmental stance with respect to any and all of her issues established the safety of the treatment setting required to help this patient.

4-5 Why treating dissociative people takes time

There is a reason that treating dissociative patients is more difficult than treating others. When the dissociative or amnesic parts are dormant, they can't be treated. Sometimes in patients with dissociative issues, it can take weeks or months of regular sessions to treat the same issue. Although the frequency of the symptoms relating to the issue decreases for some dissociative patients, it is hard to understand why the issue can't be treated in one session. The following metaphor may help the person understand the situation.

Our memory is like an empty room. As memories are created, little balloons of many different colors are inflated with emotions. With severe trauma, amnesic parts are formed into blue balloons, which are inflated with painful emotions. With many severe traumas, there are many blue balloons in the room (memory). Treatment involves deflating balloons. During treatment, only the blue balloons are active in the room. As we touch a balloon and treat it, the balloon is deflated because the touch lets the pain out of the balloon. Treatment is like working in a darkened room, where you can't always see what you are doing. As treatment proceeds successfully in the dark, there are fewer balloons and the blue balloons are harder to find. Initially, we can treat a lot of blue balloons and they are easy to find because they bump into us. But later, it is a hit-and-miss process, and we never know if there are more blue balloons to treat. As we treat more balloons, we find and treat them less frequently. We can never know when they are all treated. So, every once in a while, we expect to bump into one of those painful balloons from the past.

Relating to Patients and Treating Issues

4-6 Handling barriers when teaching the treatment process — First session

Some patients complete the Education Process of Process Healing more easily than others. Here is an example of a patient who took 80 minutes to get all parts on the Treatment Team and to have the Treatment Team and subconscious create treatment plans. This patient had an obsessive-compulsive and dissociative disorder, but initially I was not aware of any obvious parts activity.

From the beginning, I had difficulty getting the parts onto the Treatment Team. Some just didn't want to join and others awakened during the Orientation Process. I tried to identify the barriers by asking about issues such as wanting more pain and less happiness, fears of dying, loss of wisdom, overwhelming pain, or fears that the memory would retraumatize the Main Personality. I also used the inquiry, "Will you talk to the subconscious?" Some parts were willing to talk to the subconscious and, after the talk, joined the Treatment Team. Having the part talk to the subconscious is the fastest approach to resolving barriers. I had to problem-solve with many prebirth parts.

In another instance with this patient, a resistant part was willing to sleep until after I installed the treatment process. It turned out that the part wanted to watch the process and to decide later about joining the Treatment Team, which is logical given the changes that can occur with the use of Process Healing. At another time, after 10 minutes of trying all the tricks I knew, I asked and discovered that there was a part that could not hear. I asked the subconscious to communicate with the part and ask it to join the Treatment Team. This worked. I used this strategy again with two other parts.

In my effort to get all the parts on the Treatment Team, I again gave the reasons for treatment, then addressed the barriers to treatment, and finally presented the strategies for the treatment of intense pain. I also discussed what I think the parts experience after they join with the Main Personality. Finally, I installed the treatment process by having the patient's subconscious "read" my personal field and the wisdom of my teachers (Flint, n.d.).

Around the time that I was seeing this patient, I was still teaching that the treatment took place in the brain neural activity, though I was experimenting with treating in the personal field. Nowadays, I always assume that treatment is taking place in the personal field. Treating in the personal field seems to work faster and more thoroughly. After installing the treatment process in this patient, I continued to run into parts that awakened and didn't want to join the Treatment Team or receive treatment, so the process continued.

When I run into a barrier blocking communication with the subconscious and get no response from the aspect of the patient causing the barrier, I try the usual list of interventions described in Chapter 3. However, with continued noncompliance or noncommunication, I try the "treatment without permission" procedure described in Chapter 6-5. When I use that procedure and I get "no response" or "No" in response to the request, ask the subconscious to treat the "part." I assume the subconscious is doing the treatment anyway. I wait for a few minutes and then ask if the treatment is finished. With no answer, I assume the subconscious treated the part and I start problem-solving the next barrier. Sometimes I do the "treatment without asking" procedure several times without knowing if the procedure is working. After a period of time, in most cases, the subconscious starts responding.

While working with this patient, there was one part with whom I had no success, regardless of what I tried. The part simply didn't want treatment. In this case, when I used the "treatment without permission" approach, I got a "Yes" response that she would be angry. Out of desperation, I asked:

T: **Does this part want respect?**
P: **Yes.**

This worked and I went on to treat the part. With the next part, I ran into an impasse after she said, "Yes" to wanting respect. I tried to continue but got a "No" to treatment. Here's what I did.

T: **Do you want to talk to the subconscious?**
P: **Yes.**

After a few minutes, the part was willing to accept treatment. Notice that you have to be flexible and use your intuition or creativity to resolve barriers.

After 80 minutes of problem-solving, the subconscious was able to work with the Treatment Team to create a treatment plan for each part on the Treatment Team. We started treating issues.

4-7 The beginning of a session

When the patient comes in for another session, I ask if there is anything he or she wants to address. Then I ask if he or she experienced any intrusions or nightmares since the last session. I ask what changes were noticed. Next, I review the interventions that I did with the patient in the previous session to see if they were successful. If an intervention was not completely successful, I make a note of the continuing issue and add it to the list of issues to treat during the session.

At some point in this session, I ask directly to see if there is more than one Active Experience occurring simultaneously. If I find more than one, it will mean that it is possible for more than one treatment process to occur at the same time. Multiple Active Experiences will allow me to talk with the subconscious while treatment on some issues is processing. When there is only one Active Experience, then communication with the subconscious is more difficult during treatment. The communication causes extra activity in the Active Experience, which introduces a barrier to treatment. I ask the following:

T: **Subconscious, is there more than one Active Experience?**
S: **Yes.**
T: **Can we do a number of interventions at the same time?**

I usually get a "Yes." When I get a "No," it helps me to know that there is only one Active Experience, and my expectations about what can be accomplished are lowered.

Before I treat any of the issues that I have jotted down on my list during the first part of the session, my first intervention is almost always to get the subconscious working on treating issues that were tagged between sessions. Since I give homework to the subconscious to tag any negative memories or beliefs, I want to get the treatment of these tagged memories started at the beginning of the session.

T: **Subconscious, are there any tagged parts that want treatment?**
S: **Yes.**
T: **Subconscious, please treat the tagged parts, one after the other.**

I problem-solve any problems that might arise. Immediately after this intervention, here's what I do.

T: **Subconscious, are there any tagged parts that don't want treatment?**
S: **Yes.**
T: **I want to welcome all parts that don't want treatment.**

Then I problem-solve and get all these parts treated and joined with the Main Personality. I search for more parts that don't want treatment.

T: [Done. I repeat the question.] **Subconscious, are there any more parts that don't want treatment?**

S: **Yes.**

When there are more parts that don't want treatment, again I problem-solve and treat these parts. I continue asking this question until I get a "No." Just to be sure, I often ask the following question again:

T: [Done] **Subconscious, are there any parts that want treatment?**

S: **Yes.**

T: **Please treat them safely and with complete respect, one after the other.**

At this point, once satisfied that I have been thorough, I return to my notes and the list of old issues that need more work, and new issues that the patient or I identified. My patients often come to the session with lists of beliefs, behaviors or upsets that they want to address. Before I start treating anything, I check with the subconscious to see if what I want to treat is fitting. From this point on, I systematically treat all the issues available for treatment by addressing them one after the other. I remain alert to identify any other issues that might arise.

I always try to keep the session as comfortable as possible. However, in my enthusiasm, sometimes I have started treating issues too quickly without getting all of the feedback from the patient. I have to curb this tendency because some patients believe that therapy involves talking through issues and experiencing emotions. The Process Healing Method does not require this. When I treat patients who expect to talk, I explain that with "talk therapy," change sometimes doesn't progress as rapidly as with Process Healing. Even though I know such "talking it out" is not required for Process Healing to be effective, I do all I can to be sensitive to the patient who wants to talk at some length about something. However, after treating some issues, some conversation opens the space for the patient to have insights and the therapist to suggest positive beliefs. When I do talk about issues, before talking, I ask the subconscious to tag memories and parts triggered while we talk or to start treatment on parts that want treatment. In this way, we both get what we want.

T: [To the patient] **Before we start, can I put your subconscious to work?**

P: **Yes.**

T: **Subconscious, while we are talking, can you tag parts and start treatment with parts willing to be treated?**

S: **Yes.**

When I get a "No," I problem-solve.

4-8 Listen to the patient

There are many rather subtle signs in therapy that can lead you to issues needing treatment. I have made a list of some signs suggesting parts, dissociative processes, or memory structures. When I notice something that the patient said or did, I try to take the time to ask a few questions. I explore the content to see if there is an active part or aspect wanting or evading treatment. Here are examples of statements made by patients that encouraged me to explore.

Remarks that suggest parts:
- Suicidal feelings or attempts, and self-destructive actions, usually involve parts.
- High blink rate or the widening of the eyes
- Patient notices a loss of control with a behavior or feeling.
- "I feel like hurting (cutting) myself."
- "I cut myself, look."
- "It's like a cloud around my head." (The cloud left when a part was treated.)
- "I have this feeling in my ear." (I treated a part and the feeling went away.)
- "It started happening almost without my intent."
- "I could feel the depression move in."
- "I have no control, I just eat."
- [Embedded in a statement] "It's as if something comes over me."
- "I felt the fatigue (emotion, depression, pain) move in."
- "Confusion moves in or starts, with or without a trigger."
- "My mouth started talking and I wondered what I was going to say." This nine-year-old child had been suspended from school after "sassing out" his teacher.

Remarks that suggest Predispositions:
- "I just do it without thinking."
- "I hear, 'Oh, oh, here it comes.' "

When I identify and treat parts, I seldom know what caused the part or whether it was a dissociative or amnesic part or a memory structure. Often, the subconscious treats the symptom and the symptom stops or occurs less often. When the symptom continues, sometimes there are two or more aspects or parts that are related to the symptom that have to be treated.

4-9 Parts found through observation

Whenever the patient reports any unusual dreams, feelings, intrusions, or experiences that took place within one or two days of seeing me, I always address these experiences as aspects or parts. These reports usually identify an aspect or part that wants treatment and then it is a simple matter of treating the source of the intrusion.

During a session, many signs help me identify a part: A patient reports having a feeling or strong thought; a tic, an unusual movement, a thought, an out-of-context statement; a dissociative shift in the eyes, voice or word use. When I observe a sign, I look for the part that is causing it. My motto is, "When in doubt, look for a part." Of course, what I call a part can be an amnesic or dissociative part, a strong memory, or any other memory construct. I have discovered several significant issues for treatment using this approach.

Examples:

1. Flash in her eyes

While talking to the patient, I saw a flash in the patient's eyes.

T: [I saw a flash in the patient's eyes.] **Can I talk to the part that is flashing the eyes?**

S: **Yes.**

It was a part. After I treated and integrated the part, the patient volunteered that she always felt the eye experience and felt that it was out of her control.

2. Knees bouncing

A patient's knees were bouncing up and down. I labeled it a part by asking the following:

T: **Can I talk to the part that was bouncing her knees up and down?**

S: **Yes.**

After the subconscious treated and integrated the part, the knee-bouncing stopped.

3. A blurted thought

Another patient blurted out a thought that was incongruent with the context of the session. I inquired:

T: **Subconscious, did a part just make that blurt — and would that part like treatment?**

S: **Yes.**

The subconscious was asked to treat and integrate the part. Several more "blurt" parts were treated in the following sessions.

4. Physical sensation

Whenever a patient has any sensation in the body (stomach, heart or elsewhere), I label the presenting issue by saying:

T: **Subconscious, is there a part causing this stomachache?**
S: **Yes.**

Then I problem-solve and have the subconscious treat the issue.

5. A sigh out of context

Here is an example of noticing a response that led to the treatment of a part. We had just finished treating an issue and I asked if we were done. The patient gave a big sigh. Here is what I did.

T: **Subconscious, is that big sigh another issue?**
S: **Yes.**

T: **Is there a part related to the sigh who wants to be treated?**
S: **Yes.**

T: **Is there more than one part?**
S: **Yes.**

T: **Please treat these parts, one after the other, and then do a Massive Change History and everything.** [See Chapter 4-18 for the definition of "everything."]
S: **Yes.**

4-10 The patient's experiences lead to significant interventions

Whenever this patient visited his mother, he noticed that anything she said provoked a rush of anger and fear within him. This excessive emotional reaction prevented him from being able to express anything to his mother because he was tensed up and so filled with fear that he felt like a "weak little boy." I treated the anger by using the "weak little boy" metaphor.

T: **Subconscious, is there a "weak little boy" part?**
S: **Yes.**

T: **Does this part want to be treated?**
S: **Yes.**

T: **Please treat the "weak little boy" part.**
S: **Yes.**

Although there was more to do, this intervention cleared most of the anger that this young man felt when interacting with his mother.

4-11 Treating without knowing what you are treating

The patient said that his subconscious told him there was something to treat. Neither the patient nor I had any idea what the issue was. Here is how I handled the intervention.

T: **Subconscious, can I talk with you?**

S: **Yes.**

T: **Do you know what needs to be treated?**

S: **Yes.**

T: **Is it safe to treat it now?**

S: **Yes.**

T: **Please treat what needs to be treated and then do a Massive Change History and everything.**

S: **Yes.**

When I encounter a situation where the description of an issue is ill defined or vague, I resort to a strategy where I treat without knowing what I am treating. I do this by asking the subconscious if he or she knows what the issue is that we are trying to figure out. With a "Yes," I then determine whether it is safe to treat the issue and, if so, I ask the subconscious to treat it. When it is not safe, I problem-solve. Sometimes, though, it is best to determine the kind of memory structure requiring the treatment, for that will determine which treatment steps are necessary (see Chapter 8).

4-12 Construct interventions with a broad range of associations

The interventions used should be constructed to have the broadest range of associations. This is accomplished by wording the intervention so it will trigger the greatest number of dormant memories. For example: When doing the Sentence Procedure, use body movement or vocal emphasis to stress the intent of the sentence. It is probably true that the more emotion you create in the patient, the more memory elements are triggered into the Active Experience for the subconscious to tag.

Testing to see if your intervention worked is another instance where exaggerating responses is important. When you are testing an issue to see if the intervention worked, you are trying to see if the problem is still present. Carry out the test with a lot of emotion in the test scenario to increase the value of the test. For example, patients will find a difference between showing a person a can of beer and popping the lid and letting him or her smell the beer to see if it creates an urge. When you test fear of criticism, speak loudly with a scowl and a stern voice when you are giving sample criticism. The closer to reality the test, the more memory elements you will trigger. The more memories that you treat related to the issue, the more likely the treatment effects will carry over into the community.

When working with traumatic experiences, like robbery, sexual assault, auto accident, physical beating, and so forth, after the first step of treating the majority of the Emotion Memory, there is one more intervention to do. Have the patient slowly go through the experience like a movie, frame by frame, and treat any untreated emotions that arise (Shapiro, 1995). In this way, you can be fairly sure that the entire trauma was treated. Always do a Massive Change History and everything, including treating any Shadow Memories.

4-13 Loss of progress when the situation changes

I treated a patient for several months. He moved to get away from a drinking lifestyle, his controlling ex-mother-in-law, and an old girlfriend. Therapy focused on treating old traumas and addictions, as well as Predispositions to engage with his dysfunctional family and relationships in the community. We ended treatment after several months and he continued to do well while working locally. He was not drinking and was able to remain focused on who he was and where he wanted to go in his life. Then he decided to move back to his hometown, a small town where he was close to friends and relatives. It was here where he had been a "party boy."

After moving to his hometown, stresses relating to his health, fear of seeing old drinking friends, and added pressures at work resulted in his drinking a couple of times. Bouts of drinking urges and anxiety started. My interpretation, when he called, was that the old environment had triggered memories and parts not triggered initially in our therapy sessions. We scheduled a one-hour telephone session during which we were able to treat parts and memories.

It is always important to remind the patient that some parts and memories of any or all issues may remain intact and untreated. Some memories will undoubtedly remain dormant in memory and will become active later. If the patient has learned to use the subconscious between sessions, there is some chance the patient can treat these issues himself. Otherwise, the therapist can schedule an additional office or telephone session.

4-14 Teaching the subconscious the treatment method

Though it is possible the subconscious can learn the treatment process by chance or from someone who has learned it, I believe the subconscious does not usually learn "internal tapping" by chance. Normally, a person's subconscious is both ignorant of memory structures and the tapping treatment used to treat negative emotions. This section describes various ways to teach the treatment method to the subconscious.

When you point out the treatment method to the subconscious, he or she usually learns the process. The following case gives evidence to support this belief.

With a female patient, I did straight EFT in the first session. That night, after the session, she telephoned me because she was upset. While talking to her on the telephone, I quickly set up rapport with her subconscious.

T: **June, will you listen for a "Yes" or "No" in your conscious experience?**

P: **Yes.**

T: **Subconscious, can you recall the treatment method that we used today in my office?**

S: **Yes.**

T: **Can you use that process to treat the current upset?**

S: **Yes.**

While I chatted with her on the telephone about other matters, she felt her upset gradually subside. It was evident that her subconscious had learned to use EFT and did so with little direction on my part.

When teaching the EFT procedure, the subconscious can learn the process of tapping internally. At the beginning of the book, *Emotional Freedom* (Flint, 2001), I suggest that the subconscious can learn the treatment process presented. Later in this book, in the chapter on "Innerself Treatment," I give suggestions to the subconscious to enable automatic treatment. I have received reports from some readers that the internal treatment process taught in *Emotional Freedom* worked well for them.

4-15 Another metaphor for teaching the treatment method

T: **Imagine the brain as a large store that sells only radios. The store manager likes to keep it quiet. All the radios in the store are quietly playing. Then, some negative customer** [an emotion, a painful memory, or a trauma part] **comes into the store. The customer walks around and turns up the volume on several radios. The store manager** follows the customer around and notices what has changed. Then he or she turns the volume down on each radio a little at a time. He or she does this repeatedly, so the customer won't notice the noise level becoming quieter. When the customer leaves, the store is quiet once more. If that customer ever returns, the store remains quiet.

Routine Interventions

4-16 Routine interventions

Several interventions are good to do routinely. The basis for some of these interventions will be discussed in later chapters. Here is a list of the usual interventions I do regularly with all my patients:

Treatment plans — Direct the subconscious to work with the Treatment Team to create a treatment plan for each member.

Automatic treatment — Clear all the potential barriers to enable independent and automatic treatment by the subconscious (see Chapters 3-10-3 and 6-9 through 6-11).

The Healing fields — Tell the subconscious about the four fields that help the treatment process (see Chapter 3-10-2).

Treat the Predispositions — Treat the Protector-Controller and the negative Predispositions that are located in Memory II (see Chapter 4-24).

Collages in the Emotion System — Treat all collages in the Emotion System and associated memories (see Chapter 4-23).

4-17 Tagging memories

Tagging memories is a useful intervention. Once when I was working with a patient, I persistently asked the subconscious if there were any more parts in the personality. I kept getting a "No" answer. A year later, after treating many parts, an interesting insight occurred to me. When the subconscious does not have the awareness of the name of a part, or have some content or emotion of the part, the subconscious cannot trigger that part into the Active Experience. The subconscious needs a way to identify parts of interest. One way to identify parts is to know some content or emotions of the part that can be used to trigger it. Here is what I did.

The subconscious, it turns out, can do the simple intervention of tagging negative parts or memories when they become active. When the subconscious has a memory tagged, it can later easily activate or trigger the memory into the Active Experience by using the tag. The tag becomes part of the content of the memory of the part. The tag can then be used by the subconscious to activate the memory into the Active Experience. The Sentence Procedure uses the tagging method. As a rule, I try to get the subconscious to tag negative parts and memories between sessions. To do this, I say the following:

> T: **Subconscious, between now and the next session, please tag and treat any memory or part that gives negative sensory or emotional intrusions or detracts from getting satisfaction in life.**

Early in the next session, I do a follow-up with an intervention to treat memories and parts that have been tagged.

> T: **Subconscious, please treat all the aspects and memory structures you tagged between sessions.**

Sometimes, tagged aspects do not want treatment. Then you will have to problem-solve.

4-18 Change History explained

The Change History intervention is important. This is an adaptation of a powerful intervention used in NLP (Rice and Caldwell, 1986). There are two types of Change Histories. The first is the Change History of Memory III (see Figure 4-1). In this case, after the initial trauma is

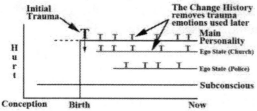

Figure 4-1 The Change History Procedure

treated, the subconscious treats the negative emotions or content of the trauma memory that is associated with other memories in our experience occurring after the trauma. For example, if you think of our experiences as being stored in books starting from birth to now, then a trauma found in book 10 has content or emotions that can be used in later books sprinkled throughout our life history. The Change History replaces the trauma emotions in all the books after the trauma with neutral to positive emotions.

Massive Change History

The second Change History is the one I call the Massive Change History. This Change History is similar to a simple Change History, but its scope is broader. The Massive Change History treatment involves reducing the intensity of emotions of all memories in the brain and body affected by the last intervention. All our organs and brain functions are to some extent associated with any belief, trauma, or part. When you treat a trauma, the treatment affects many memories because of associations with the trauma. Brain functions, organs, and parts are all run by memories. This includes Memories I, II, III, and any other memory in any system. I always use the Massive Change History Intervention after doing any intervention, and especially after treating a part, a negative belief, or any other issue that could have distorted memories following a trauma. I use the Massive Change History and everything regularly now rather than doing a Change History of Memory III.

Curiously, I just recently learned that the Massive Change History does not include the Change History of Ego States and Tandem Memories. Apparently, I have to be more specific when I give directions because Ego States are conscious state-dependent behaviors—namely, you can tell when they are happening. One can identify Ego States by noticing changes in your emotions and behavior that occur with changes in situations, like how you respond in church as opposed to in a police station, and so forth. Tandem Memories are caused by easy creation of Active Experiences that cause the creation of additional Memory IIIs (or Tandem Memories). It turns out that traumas can have effects on Tandem Memories similar to those they have on memories in Memory III. For this reason, I now also include Tandem Memories when I request a Massive Change History.

I include the treatment of Ego States and Tandem Memories with the Massive Change History by asking explicitly for the Change History of Ego States and Tandem Memories. It appears that just mentioning Memory III or Massive Change History does not trigger these other memories into the treatment process. By asking for a Massive Change History including Ego States and Tandem Memories early in treatment, the Subconscious will learn to do the Change History and the other memories automatically.

When the Massive Change History Intervention is taught to the patient's subconscious, I get specific about what is involved. Here is an example of what I often say when I ask for the subconscious to "please do a Massive Change History":

T: **Subconscious, when I ask you to do a Massive Change History, here is what is included in the intervention. Please do a Change History of Memories I, II, III, any other memory in any system including the Ego States and Tandem Memories, and treat the Shadow Memories** (see Chapter 4-19).

To be comfortable that everything is being treated in the Change History, I add on the word "everything." The subconscious learns that this means treating Memories II, III, the Ego States, the Tandem Memories and the memory of any system associated with the recent treatment. In addition, the subconscious treats any Shadow Memories relevant to the issue treated.

T: **Subconscious, please do a Massive Change History and everything with everything, referring to treating Memories I, II and III and any other memory in any system including treating the Ego States and Tandem Memories. Also, treat the Shadow Memories.**

I won't discuss Shadow Memories here because they are discussed in detail in the next section (see Chapter 4-19).

Examples:

1. Childhood neglect

When you want to treat the effects of early childhood neglect, here is what you say to the patient's subconscious. In this intervention, the subconscious triggers all associations with neglect from birth to now and treats the negative emotions that are present in the associated memories. At the same time as the subconscious is treating the negative emotions, he or she can be instructed to associate a feeling of well-being and confidence (or a self-empowering belief) with the memories.

T: **Subconscious, please do a Massive Change History and everything from birth to now including Ego States and Tandem Memories** [added for emphasis] **removing the effects of neglect, and then associate a feeling of well-being to the memories.**

2. Treating barriers

The Massive Change History and everything can also be used to treat memories that are in conflict with a desired belief or behavior.

T: **Subconscious, please do a Massive Change History and everything of all beliefs, memories, and experiences that serve as a barrier to the belief: "I am a capable person."**

3. The effect of traumatic memories

The Massive Change History Intervention is also useful to treat the effects of a variety of traumas or any other significant negative event that has intruded occasionally during a person's life. For example, suppose the patient was severely abused at age seven and as a result formed a disruptive amnesic part. After the successful treatment of the part, it is good to do a Change History to treat all memories affected by the activity of this amnesic part. I believe that doing Massive Change History in this way removes the effects of the trauma from our life experiences. I routinely use this intervention to treat the effects of traumatic experiences on a patient's life.

T: [I ask] **Subconscious, please treat the part, integrate it, and then do a Massive Change History and everything. Treat any negative impact caused by this part from the creation of the part until now.**

4. Self-limiting beliefs caused by trauma

When the subconscious treats all negative associations with the part (or any issue being treated) by using a Process Healing intervention, then any negative or self-limiting beliefs may have been treated at the same time. I believe it is good to replace these negative beliefs with a positive, self-empowering belief. To do this, I use the following intervention.

T: **Please do a Massive Change History and everything and change self-limiting beliefs to not true. Then, compose and strengthen self-empowering beliefs in place of the treated beliefs.**

In all my cases, I have the intention of doing a Massive Change History and everything after every intervention. Sometimes the subconscious learns to do this automatically and beats me to it.

4-19 Shadow Memories caused by trauma memory and parts activity

There were several interventions revealed by Kansky's subconscious (personal communication, October 6, 2003) that dealt with the effects of the activity of repeated trauma on memory in general. I have called these memories Shadow Memories. These are memories that carry some representation of the negative activity of parts or other recurring negative behaviors. The Shadow Memories are behavior and emotion activity induced into the neural activity surrounding the primary neural pathways carrying the negative behavior and emotions. These lingering Shadow Memories cause negative emotions or support negative behavior in our experience. By treating these Shadow Memories, I believe that the treatment of issues will be more complete and that there will be fewer underlying negative emotional experiences caused by lingering memories. These treatments have a calming effect.

T: **Subconscious, will you treat the Shadow Memories in Memories I, II, and III and do a Massive Change History and everything after completing each memory.**

I have found that Shadow Memories can be present in the Emotion System, and this can be problematic. When I work with the subconscious, it is possible to identify the emotions that need to be treated. In this intervention, you or the subconscious can repeat the intervention for each of the following emotions: anxiety, fear, sadness, anger, and discontent.

T: **Subconscious, there are five emotions that I want you to treat: anxiety, fear, sadness, anger, and discontent. Please treat the association structure in the Emotion System for anxiety. When the structure falls apart, tag each memory structure and treat the structures in the correct order. After treating each structure, please do a Massive Change History and everything including the Shadow Memories. Treat each emotion one after the other.**

While these interventions for the Shadow Memories seemed to work, I eventually incorporated the treatment of Shadow Memories into the Massive Change History Intervention.

Treatment Procedures

4-20 The year-by-year strategy

Sometimes it is fitting to treat systematically many traumatic memories formed from birth to now. This does not treat dissociated or amnesic memories but addresses negative emotions associated with simple memories in Memory III or Ego States. I do this by starting with any prebirth or birthing trauma, and then continue year by year with treating traumatic memories from year one to now.

T: **Subconscious, were there any traumatic memories created before birth?**

S: **Yes.**

T: **Are these traumas safe to treat?**

S: **Yes.**

T: **Please treat those traumatic memories and any negative beliefs in any order that you choose.**

T: [Wait] **Are you done?**

At this point I engage in just casual talk or I do some other therapy. I finish off this intervention with:

T: **Subconscious, please do a Massive Change History and everything, treating the effects of the traumatic memories from the creation of the memories to the here and now.**

The subconscious learns to do this automatically so you don't have to ask for a Massive Change History after treating each year.

Continuing:

T: **Subconscious, were there any traumatic memories created in year one?**

S: **Yes.**

T: **Are these traumas safe to treat?**

S: **Yes.**

T: **Please treat these traumatic memories and any negative beliefs, memories and experiences, in any order that you choose.**

T: [Wait] **Are you done?**

T: [Done] **Please do a Massive Change History and everything treating the effects of the traumas from the creation of the traumas to the here and now.**

Continue year by year.

T: **Subconscious, are there any traumatic memories in year two?**

S: **Yes.**

T: **Please treat them.**

T: [Wait] **Are you done?**

S: **Yes.**

T: **Subconscious, are there any traumas in year three?**

I continue this process year by year by following the same pattern. You can shorten what you say after the first few years. Sometimes, I write the years from year one to current age and simply cross them off as I progress. Some years do not have traumatic memories. Patients usually feel the processing and then experience a change in their experience of the past after this intervention.

4-21 The Sentence Procedure

The Sentence Procedure is a useful procedure to treat memories and parts that get in the way of treatment goals. I originally based the Sentence Procedure on my interpretation of Callahan's Psychological Reversal Correction Procedure (Callahan, 1985). For example, when a person says, "I want to treat my drinking urge," the statement also includes "I want to drink." The statement "I want to drink" triggers all the positive and negative beliefs and memories associated with drinking into the

Active Experience. These associated beliefs and memories, triggered by the statement, help to motivate the addictive behavior and block treatment by being active in the Active Experience.

Callahan handled barriers in the following way: The patient causes physical sensation by rubbing his or her chest or tapping on his or her hand. The physical sensation joins the memories. The added physical sensation blocks the memories from being triggered again when the statement is repeated. The physical sensation added to the problem memories is absent in the trigger required to treat the drinking urge, and so the problem memories are not triggered. This intervention blocks the memories from becoming a barrier to treatment.

All statements trigger positive and negative associated memories in the same way. The activity of these positive and negative memories also serves as a barrier to changing beliefs and behaviors because the active memories disorganize the Active Experience. The Sentence Procedure involves saying the sentence that triggers all the barriers to treatment of the issue. At the same time, I ask the subconscious to tag the memories triggered by the sentence. Then I ask the subconscious to treat tagged memories in the correct order by triggering the memories using the assigned tags.

The Sentence Procedure is an efficient way to treat associated unwanted memories activated when trying to treat maladaptive beliefs, behaviors, or addictions. I also use the Sentence Procedure to clear barriers to new beliefs and behaviors.

Here is how I ask the subconscious to do the Sentence Procedure on an issue. I usually give a detailed description of the Sentence Procedure the first few times I use it, as a way to teach the subconscious how to use it. Later in therapy, I shorten the request.

T: **I am going to do the Sentence Procedure. I want you to tag all the beliefs, memories, experiences and parts that become active in the Active Experience when I say, "I am never going to criticize people anymore." Then I want you to treat the tagged memories in the correct order. Then compose the best sentences to do the Sentence Procedure repeatedly until there are no further memories to tag.**

This intervention triggers all the memories that support being "critical of people." After giving the Sentence Procedure, you can continue with other interventions or sit around, chat and wait until the subconscious finishes doing the Sentence Procedure. I also use the Sentence Procedure when creating new self-empowering beliefs—by triggering and treating beliefs, memories, and parts that are in opposition to the new belief. You do this by stating the self-empowering belief in the Sentence Procedure.

T: **Subconscious, please do the Sentence Procedure on "I am worthy of life and worthy of love." When you finish treating the tagged memories, please strengthen this belief until it is true.**

In this case, the Sentence Procedure triggers all memories that get in the way of the self-empowering belief. After the subconscious finishes the intervention, I ask the patient to assess the degree of truth of the belief on a scale ranging from 0, not true, to 10, true. When the belief is not true—say, less than 10—I problem-solve, remove barriers and continue strengthening the belief until it is entirely true, a scale value of 10.

When you use the Sentence Procedure with a negative belief, you either compose a self-empowering belief by working with the patient or ask the subconscious to compose a self-empowering belief. After treating the negative belief, ask the subconscious to strengthen the self-empowering belief so the belief is true for the patient. Suppose the patient has the belief, "I'll always screw up." Use the opposite of the negative belief—a positive self-empowering belief—in the Sentence Procedure. This will trigger all the memories supporting the belief "I'll always screw up." Here's an example.

T: **Subconscious, please do the Sentence Procedure on the belief "I will do all I can to never make mistakes again." Then I want you to strengthen the belief "When I get clear information and attend to what I am doing, I can succeed."**

You can also add to the statement,

T: **Please compose good sentences for triggering barriers to the self-empowering belief and repeat the Sentence Procedure until the procedure no longer triggers memory barriers.**

Wait until the subconscious completes the task. Again, you can test the effectiveness of this procedure by having the patient think of the belief and assess its truth. If the belief is not 100 percent true, then problem-solve. The patient will usually experience the new, positive belief to be true. Here are four examples showing the use of the Sentence procedure.

Examples:

1. Strengthening self-love

T: **Subconscious, can we treat the self-love issue with the Sentence Procedure?**

S: **Yes.**

T: **Subconscious, please do the Sentence Procedure on "I love myself." Tag all the parts that activate and treat them in the correct order. If** there are any problematic beliefs, treat them until they are false, then compose self-empowering beliefs to replace them, and strengthen them until they are 100 percent true.

S: **Yes.**

T: **Please compose other sentences and repeat the Sentence Procedure until no more memories are triggered.**

S: **Yes.**

T: **Please do a Massive Change History and everything.**

S: **Yes.**

2. Reading barrier

T: **Subconscious, can we treat this with a Sentence Procedure?**

S: **Yes.**

T: **Subconscious, please do the Sentence Procedure on "I love to read." Tag all the parts that activate and treat them in the correct order. If there are any beliefs, treat them until they are false, and then compose and strengthen a self-empowering belief until it is 100 percent true to replace each treated belief.**

In some cases, I would list the beliefs that are problematic and work with them specifically.

3. Fear from a motor vehicle accident

You can stuff everything into one request.

T: **Subconscious, please do the Sentence Procedure on "I feel safe when I drive." Tag all the parts that activate and treat them in the correct order. If there are any beliefs, treat each belief until it is false, and then compose and strengthen a self-empowering belief until it is 100 percent true to replace it. Please compose additional sentences to use in the Sentence Procedure and continue until no more memories are triggered. Then please do a Massive Change History and everything.**

S: **Yes.**

4. Performance Anxiety

After working with a patient, the procedure requests can be shortened.

T: **Subconscious, please do a Sentence Procedure on "I feel relaxed and comfortable when I am driving a golf ball." Please do the Sentence Procedure and repeat it until you are done.**

T: **[Done] Subconscious, please do a Massive Change History and everything.**

S: **Yes.**

4-22 Treatment using structures of associations

All brain structures are massively interconnected (Freeman, 1991). This interconnectedness suggests that structures are associated when they have common content or emotions. In general, if the Content and Emotions Memories learned in one situation are similar to the Content and Emotion Memories learned in other situations experienced at any point in our lifetime, the content and emotions would all be associated in some way. For example, the structure of criticism would include memories from criticism at any time in our life, including criticism at home, from friends, teachers, and the criticism received at church, even though each occurred in a different place for different reasons. An association structure exists that joins all of the different experiences of criticism.

I assume that the association structure of any issue includes associations to all forms of memory structures, including amnesic parts and complex memory structures, which have common content or emotions created in the emotional situations. There can be a structure of structures — namely, structures associated because of some common property — consisting of beliefs, depression, fear, negative self-thoughts, suicidal ideation or any issue or emotion you can think of. For many interventions, you can use this structure construct to carry out an effective treatment intervention (see Chapter 7-5).

I call all the aspects, parts, and memories associated with a structure "memory elements of the structure." It turns out that by gradually treating the structure, all the emotions binding the structure together weaken and cause the structure of associations to fall apart. The memory elements appear to disengage from the structure. I instruct the subconscious to tag the memory elements of the structure when it falls apart. Then the subconscious can treat the memory elements in the correct order. This intervention is a powerful tool.

This interesting procedure has a surprising benefit. When the subconscious treats the emotions that associate to bind the structure together, the treatment also reduces the intensity of the emotions associated with the memory elements of the structure — in other words, memory structures of any aspects or parts are less motivated. This decrease in emotional intensity usually weakens barriers that might otherwise cause problems when the subconscious treats the tagged elements. This makes treating the memory elements less problematic. You can label any issue a structure and treat it as a structure. Note that occasionally there are parts that were elements of a structure, which require additional special attention and need to be addressed as they arise.

Example:

Black rage

A person came to me for help. He had served many jail terms because he went into black rages and beat people up. In the second session he revealed that he thought the anger was the result of his experiences in jail. This was the intervention:

T: **Subconscious, can you see the structure for all the negative jail experiences?**

S: **Yes.**

T: **Is it safe to treat the structure and tag all the memory elements of the structure when it falls apart?**

S: **Yes.**

T: **Please treat the structure, tag the elements as the structure falls apart, and treat the elements in the most correct and safest order. Please do a Massive Change History and everything as needed.**

S: **Yes.**

The processing was continuing as he left the office. Here are some other applications for which I have used this procedure: rapes, indecisiveness, procrastination, sexual issues, complex phobias, obsessions, compulsions, addictions, and depression. Usually, the patient notices the processing and a change in experience. With most issues, I have to do more than the structure process to treat the issue. The Change History intervention is another metaphor for treating a structure.

4-23 Treating emotion collages in the Emotion System

The most thorough intervention is to treat the collages of emotions in the Emotion System. The subconscious can apparently identify collages in the Emotion System that are associated with a particular emotion experienced by the patient. It turns out that the subconscious can follow associations from the collage of emotions and locate and treat the memory elements in Memories II and III, which are motivated by the emotions. This intervention adds another option for treating intense emotions.

This intervention can be used for treating aspects motivated by anxiety, depression, anger, and other emotions.

T: **Subconscious, should we treat the depression by using the Structure Procedure or by treating the emotions in the Emotion System? The Emotion System?**

S: **Yes.**

T: **Subconscious, will you please identify all the collages of depression in the Emotion System and treat the collages in the correct order? Treat the first collage, then follow the associations to the memory elements in Memory II and III, and treat each memory element in the correct order. When finished, do a Massive Change History and everything. Repeat this procedure for each depression collage in the Emotion System.**

S: **Yes.**

Occasionally there are parts that require special attention.

4-24 Treating Predispositions

The Predisposition construct is based upon Hal and Sidra Stone's (1989) work. Predispositions are parts or memory structures in Memory II that develop from before birth through about age four. When the first four years of a person's life have been filled with trauma or a dysfunctional family experience, many negative Predispositions can be learned during that period of development of Memory II. These negative Predispositions often disturb the life of the patient because they are habit-like reactions that respond to well-defined conditions in the Active Experience.

For example, when a negative thought enters the Active Experience, a Predisposition could respond to the negative thought with a typical response such as causing the thought to be dissociated—in other words, hiding the thought in the unconscious. However, the dissociated thought is still influencing the experience. Likewise, when "someone needing help" is present in the Active Experience, the response may be to behave in ways that will help the person. Other Predispositions are: to act on a specific impulse, to be defensive, to apologize unnecessarily, to reach for a beer or a cigarette, and so forth. Predispositions can affect our behavior in many positive and negative ways.

Sometimes Predispositions appear in pairs that represent opposite extremes, such as irresponsible-responsible, hate-love, or sad-happy. The point of treating the negative Predispositions is to stop their effects on behavior. There can be many parts in Memory II offering the same negative Predisposition. Predispositions are usually easy to treat and present no problems. So, when one treats Predispositions, you have to problem-solve to treat as many of the negative Predispositions as possible. Once a negative Predisposition is treated, it is joined with its opposite. Here is the way I have treated Predispositions:

T: **Subconscious, are there Predispositions that help to create this issue?**

S: **Yes.**

T: **Please treat all those negative Predispositions who want to be treated, one after the other, and join them with their opposite pair.**

T: **[Wait] Subconscious, are there Predispositions that don't want to be treated?**

S: **Yes.**

T: **Can I talk to the Predispositions that don't want to be treated?**

S: **Yes.**

T: **You all were created and learned your job in the first four years of your life. You are disrupting the patient with your behavior. The patient is now 27 and your behavior is upsetting her because she gets less satisfaction. Would you be willing to talk to the subconscious to find out how treatment will allow you to find more satisfaction in life?**

P: **Yes.**

With a "No," the barrier to treatment is handled by the usual solutions to barriers given in Chapter 3 but tailored to fit parts in Memory II.

One of the Predispositions in Memory II is the part that responds to the name Protector-Controller. This part is more intense than the Predispositions previously described. This part is like a protective part that serves to put protecting and controlling tendencies into the Active Experience. Protector-Controllers are sometimes difficult to treat if the early years of the patient were exceptionally traumatic.

The treatment of the Protector-Controller is carried out in the same way.

T: **Subconscious, can I talk to the Protector-Controller?**

S: **Yes.**

T: **Protector-Controller, are you willing to be treated so that you can offer constructive input to the Active Experience?**

P: **Yes.**

With a "No," I problem-solve to get the Protector-Controller to want treatment. Sometimes I say the following to either a "Yes" or "No" response.

T: **Protector-Controller, you have been serving well, but you were created in the first five years of life and the trauma you experienced at that time has resulted in your activity being a problem at this age. If the subconscious treated your trauma, you would base your activities on current emotions and you would work to get more satisfaction and**

less pain. Would you be willing to let the subconscious treat all of your traumatic memories?

P: **Yes.**

When I get a "No," I elaborate several times on positive qualities of treatment and integration. When this doesn't work, I look for other barriers that stop treatment.

With several patients, I had mistakenly believed that the subconscious had treated the Protector-Controller. I found out months later that it had not been treated. In another case, the Protector was independent of the Controller. Treating the subpersonality can have a noticeable effect on a patient.

4-25 Protocol for treating problematic beliefs

Here is the protocol for treating problematic beliefs. It incorporates the most powerful strategies for using the Sentence Procedure, the Structure Procedure, and for treating complex structures. Normally, beliefs can be changed easily. Sometimes, there are barriers that need to be problem-solved. Identify and list the beliefs that the patient wants to change, and ask the subconscious for the best order of treatment. Use this protocol on the first belief, and agree with the subconscious to call it the "belief treatment." Then you can systematically use it on the other beliefs. This procedure can be adapted for problematic behavior.

1. Do the Sentence Procedure.

T: **Subconscious, please do a Sentence Procedure on . . .** (state the positive belief) **. . . and tag the memory structures that became active. Take the emotions of the memory structures and treat the collages of emotions in the Emotion System; follow the associations of the collages back to memories in Memory I, II, and III, and treat them. Do this with each collage of emotions, and continue with the Sentence Procedure until complete.**

2. Treat the structure of Layered Memories that blocked this belief.

T: **Subconscious, please treat the structure of Layered Memories in the same way by treating the collages of emotions in the Emotion System, follow associations, and treat the memories. Repeat for each collage.**

3. Identify and treat the Predispositions that trigger the negative beliefs.

T: **Subconscious, identify the Predispositions that lead to this belief; identify the collages of emotions in the Predispositions and** complex structures; and treat them in the Emotion System. Follow the associations, and treat the memories in Memories I, II, and III. Treat any layering associated *to* the Predispositions, the Predispositions, and the complex memories in Memory III, one after the other.

4. Do a Change History in the Emotion System.

T: **Subconscious, when the treatment in the Emotion System is complete, please do a Change History in the Emotion System.**

5. Create beliefs to replace the treated beliefs.

T: **Subconscious, please create and strengthen beliefs that are positive and self-empowering to replace the beliefs that were treated.**

6. Do a Massive Change History.

T: **Subconscious, please do a Massive Change History and everything.**

7. Role-play situations to trigger any additional memories associated with the belief.

T: **Subconscious, if appropriate, imagine or role-play the situations where the belief is triggered and have the subconscious tag and treat any memory elements that are triggered. Repeat role-playing until memories are no longer triggered.**

8. Have the patient assess the negative belief to see if it is true and role-play the various situations where the belief may arise to see if he or she is completely comfortable with the new beliefs.

4-26 Treating massive beliefs

In several patients, I have encountered the situation where massive beliefs have stopped therapy or automatic treatment. I define massive beliefs as highly motivated beliefs, or beliefs with intense emotions associated with them. When a massive belief is related to the treatment issue it appears to interfere with the association process because the massive belief prevents the issue from being fully triggered into the Active Experience. This interference makes the treatment of the issue difficult or impossible. I routinely seek and treat massive beliefs because they can be so problematic. Fortunately, massive beliefs are usually easy to treat.

T: **Subconscious, are there any massive beliefs present in the unconscious?**

S: **Yes.**

T: **Can you treat all massive beliefs that get in the way of the treatment process?**

S: **Yes.**

T: [Done] **Please do a Massive Change History and everything.**
S: **Yes.**

Strengthening and Installing Behavior

4-27 Strengthening desired behavior

Sometimes there are behaviors that you want the patient to carry out that will help in establishing a better repertoire of behaviors. For example, you might want the patient to do something that would prevent an addictive behavior, to recover after a relapse, or to make a positive assertion. The difficulty with this is that the patient has no experience doing the desired behavior, so the behavior doesn't happen. To deal with the beliefs or behaviors that get in the way of the desired behavior, you can use the Sentence Procedure to trigger all the barriers blocking the desired behavior. Using the alcoholic urge as an example, you use the sentence, "No, thank you, I don't drink," in the Sentence Procedure to trigger in all the barriers to saying this assertive response. Then the subconscious can treat each of the tagged barriers.

When you strengthen behavior like "No thank you, I don't drink," you can test this statement in different situations familiar to the patient. This is similar to NLP future-pacing, in which you practice the desired behavior in your imagination. Have the patient imagine doing the wanted behavior in a familiar situation and assess how comfortable he or she feels saying the statement. When the imagined experience of saying the statement in the situation does not feel completely natural or comfortable, repeat this intervention, or problem-solve.

T: **Subconscious, please identify the source of the uncomfortable feelings and treat the uncomfortable feelings so the statement will feel completely natural and comfortable.**

This usually works. But remember to reassess this intervention at a later date because other parts often awaken to restore some of the anxiety or fear of making the desired statement.

4-28 Learning desired behaviors from books

The patient had experienced many years of abuse as a child and as an adult. This patient had major problems with interpersonal behavior. She was unable to relate intimately and in a connected way. Her relationship with her husband was strained because she didn't extend herself to him warmly. She was a passive partner who never wanted to snuggle and held hands limply. She had had many sessions with me and was comfortable with Process Healing. Here is how we treated this problem with interpersonal behavior.

T: **Subconscious, have you read about people who have had healthy and loving interpersonal relations?**

S: **Yes.**

T: **Can you take all the positive and loving behaviors and beliefs you learned from books and introject them into the patient, weaken incompatible behavior, and change all the negative beliefs to false, and then strengthen appropriate self-empowering beliefs?**

S: **Yes.**

This intervention took place after 25 sessions of the treatment of intruding parts and other issues. Usually, it is not an appropriate intervention early in treatment. Follow the lead of the subconscious.

Optimizing the Treatment

4-29 Creating shortcuts

Sometimes I am able to devise an intervention that can be used repeatedly to treat several similar issues without having to go through all of the steps each time. One example of this is the treatment intervention for addiction. The addiction procedure (see Chapter 10-3) can become a shortcut. When a patient has many addictions, I usually treat the first addiction by going through the treatment steps in detail. Then, assuming the subconscious remembers the addiction procedure, I simply ask the subconscious to do the addiction process on the next addiction that I want to treat. I have used the same sort of approach with beliefs.

T: **Subconscious, please treat the structure associated with the belief "I am worthless."**

T: **Subconscious, are you done?**

S: **Yes.**

T: **Can we use the structure treatment as a procedure and use it for the other negative beliefs that are present?**

S: **Yes.**

Patients often feel a processing sensation in some area of the brain immediately after asking such a question.

4-30 Increase the rate of treatment — Treat the Protector

Many barriers can exist that slow the treatment process. In one patient, I found that the Protector in Memory II was getting in the way of rapid treatment. It turned out that the Protector and Controller could either exist as independent processes (or parts), or they could be functioning as one integrated part. In this case, the Protector was independent and was creating the barrier.

T: **Subconscious, please treat the pain of the Protector and then do a Massive Change History and everything.**

S: **Yes.**

Remember that it is good in any case to treat the Protector and Controller and to integrate them.

4-31 Grounding at the end of the session

Some aspect or part of a person with whom I worked suggested that I should say the following closing statement at the end of the session.

T: **Subconscious, please ground the memories that we have touched today and reconnect them to the matrix of the universe.**

I initially didn't know if this closing statement had any connection to reality. Now I believe there is some basis for this intervention (Flint, n.d.). Most of the patients' subconsciouses to whom I say this at the end of a session confirm that making this statement is good. In this case, should I trust a patient's subconscious or should I trust western science?

Sometimes after I give the closing statement, the patient asks:

P: **What does that mean?**

My response is something like the following:

T: **It has to do with clearing from the brain impurities caused by our work and reconnecting broken connective pathways.**

P: **Do you believe this?**

T: **I don't know. Many patients' subconsciouses say that ending sessions like this is good to do. Subconscious, is this a good intervention to do at the end of the session?**

S: **Yes.**

I usually get a "Yes." In practice, I do not always close sessions with this statement.

4-32 Examples of unsolved problems in patients

I have not always had complete success in using Process Healing with my patients. Though I haven't always been successful, that doesn't mean the problem can't be solved. I will describe a few of the cases that I had trouble treating. The first three remain unresolved and the fourth was resolved using a different treatment method. (It is always good to have more than one card up your sleeve.) I operate with the belief that it's my problem when I cannot resolve the barriers for change. When this happens, I sometime start working for free because I can learn so much.

1. Secondary gain

The first case was a person on disability insurance. He had been on disability for several years and was experiencing depression, though he had a hobby that excited him and involved his going to social events. I tried every intervention I knew of or could imagine but had no success treating his depression. Still he came for therapy monthly. He was, I believe, making positive changes, but the facts of the case were such that if he treated his depression, he would have to go back to work. The secondary gain of being on disability insurance and doing his hobby was the barrier to becoming healthy again.

2. Lack of motivation

The second case was an 84-year-old male who had a severe smoking habit. He had trouble breathing and a terrible smoker's cough. I worked with him weekly for several months and did not succeed in making a dent in his 20-cigarettes-a-day habit. He reliably kept records of the number of cigarettes he smoked each day. It is interesting that he had carried a stop-smoking sucker in his pocket for weeks and never tried it. He had a heart condition and the subconscious said that quitting abruptly would be too stressful on his heart. We addressed the possibility of any secondary gain from my home visits and ruled this out as a barrier to treatment. Recently, I put him on a schedule and he cut the number of cigarettes smoked each day to 15. I continued to struggle with this unresolved treatment until I finally asked if he would flush all his cigarettes down the toilet, and he said "No." I concluded that he was not motivated enough to quit. As I have had similar difficulties with several other patients with addictions, I now ask all prospective addiction patients questions of this type.

Several months later, this old smoker was prescribed continuous oxygen support for his lung condition. His rate of smoking decreased, but one day he lit a cigarette butt in his bathroom. He forgot to take the oxygen hose out of his nose. The cigarette exploded, singed his eyebrows, and melted the hose in his nose. Now motivated, he stopped smoking immediately. Motivation, you see, is key to stopping addictions.

3. Unsolved barrier for communication

The third case is a woman who had spent 13 years trying to figure out why she was not feeling well. Initially, she was having aches and pains after she did physical work that others could do easily with no problem. However, from then on it got worse, with problems like canker sores, bladder infections, headaches, stomach problems, menstrual problems, and a list that goes on and on. She had one major illness every two weeks. She tried to get help from physicians, natural practitioners, acupressure therapists, hypnotherapists, naturopaths, physiotherapists, electroacupressurists, body workers, psychics, and most alternative practitioners. Many symptoms have not returned but muscle tension and weakness remain. She is diagnosed as having fibromyalgia. She came to see if I could treat her muscle tension and weakness.

I thought that there might be parts giving her tension—the weakness after physical exertion. I worked steadily for five sessions attempting to contact the subconscious or establish rapport with the part that was blocking communication. I tried everything including EMDR and EFT, and I had no success. She did find some success with EFT when she used it at home. Other than occasional finger responses, I made no headway. Now I believe that some very strong part or memory structure of some kind was blocking communication. I was unable to find the key to get communication started. She terminated treatment and said she might return when she has more time. This is an example of a patient I would welcome back, and perhaps for free. There is much I could learn from her case

4. Conscious intense trauma

The fourth case was a woman who experienced a number of robberies. She handled the first robberies without problems. A later robbery gave her intrusions of fear when she saw a robber look-alike or whenever someone put a newspaper on the counter. I easily installed the treatment method and successfully showed how the Process Healing Method worked by addressing a height phobia. Some parts were treated in order to bring the height fear to an acceptable level. I used two issues: standing on a ladder to screw in a light bulb and climbing a ladder to get on the roof of her house. The subconscious was effective in treating the phobia, at least in the office. However, when I addressed the robbery trauma, the subconscious was ineffective in reducing the pain of the memories. She showed immediate tearfulness and emotional distress. Obviously, I was not succeeding with the Process Healing Method.

I intervened with what almost always works, by doing the complete Emotional Freedom Techniques treatment on the fear caused by the robbery (see Appendix V). With the physical application of tapping on the EFT points, the pain decreased slowly, requiring about six EFT treatment cycles. At that point I thought that we had finished treatment of the issue. I checked her memory of the robbery and accidentally mentioned helplessness, and she burst into tears. The robbery related to a previous trauma, of which she was fully aware, and which also included feelings of helplessness. Again, I used Emotional Freedom Techniques to deal with the earlier trauma.

She canceled her next appointment because she felt good. A follow-up four months later revealed that the intervention was effective. She reported that she hadn't experienced any of the symptoms resulting from the trauma and has felt that her life was getting better.

My interpretation of this barrier to Process Healing was that the traumas were consciously available to the Main Personality. The intensity of the trauma flooded the Active Experience with active emotions and caused a treatment barrier. I believe that this activity of the trauma memory prevented the subconscious from being able do the treatment process in the usual safe sequence—treat-rest-treat-rest, and so forth. With this experience, I suggest that therapists learn the Emotional Freedom Techniques as taught in the book *Emotional Freedom* (Flint, 2001) or any other source as a backup intervention. Emotional Freedom Techniques are reviewed briefly in Appendix V.

4-33 Example of treatment distractibility

The patient said that she was, in general, easily distracted when trying to focus on something. After she drank a lot of coffee, she could hyperfocus for a period of time.

Here is how I approached this problem. I joined the association and dissociation parts, which were functioning independently, and then used the Sentence Procedure. I also checked for other structures that may have contributed to this problem.

T: **Subconscious, are the association and dissociation parts independent?**

S: **Yes.**

T: **Is this part of the cause of distractibility?**

S: **Yes.**

T: **Do the dissociation and association parts want treatment and to join with each other so they can work together?**
S: **Yes.**
T: **Please treat and join them.**
S: **Yes.**
T: [A part awakened.] **Subconscious, is this part willing to be treated and to join with the Main Personality?**
S: **Yes.**
T: **Please treat this part.**
S: **Yes.**
T: **Did this part contribute to distractibility?**
S: **Yes.**
T: [Wait] **Done?**
S: **Yes.**
T: **Subconscious, please do a Sentence Procedure with "I can concentrate without distraction" in both of the memories of the association-dissociation part and the Memories I, II, and III. Create other sentences and continue until you are done.**
S: **Yes.**
T: [Wait] **Are you done?**
S: **Yes.**
T: **Please do a Massive Change History and everything.**
S: **Yes.**
T: **Are there any other memory structures that contribute to these problems?**
S: **No.**

If "Yes," check for Layered Memories, fragments of the system, Predispositions in Memory II, trauma in Basic Neurostructure, Memory I or Memory II, and so forth.

4-34 Treating a dream

The patient had a scary dream bothering her occasionally for years. She outlined the major themes in the dream to me in some detail. I believe that dreams are related to daily experiences or past trauma or experiences and are for some reason triggered into the Active Experience when sleeping. The creative skill in the brain takes the active memories and organizes them into a story with a storyline. I explained this to her, and told her that I routinely have the subconscious treat the content and emotions of dreams. Treating a dream in this way usually stops the person from having the dream.

    T: **Subconscious, is it safe to treat this dream?**

    S: **Yes.**

    T: **Should I treat the content or emotions of the dream first? Contents?**

    S: **No.**

    T: **Subconscious, please treat the emotions of the dream in the Emotion System, follow the associations back and treat the memory structures, and do a Massive Change History and everything.**

    S: **Yes.**

    T: **[Done] Subconscious, please treat the content of the dream and then do a Massive Change History and everything.**

    S: **Yes.**

    T: **Subconscious, have we finished treating the dream?**

    S: **Yes.**

Summary

    You have read about a number of general interventions that you can use to treat yourself or others. Some of these treatment interventions were used early in the development of Process Healing and I no longer use them. I believe that these unused interventions are communicated to my patients by means of my subconscious, and if I didn't teach them here, you wouldn't know of them to communicate them to your patients. As I gain more experience, I regularly strike on interventions that appear to work faster and more thoroughly.

    As a review, here are the important interventions that I routinely use: I find that having the subconscious tag parts (Chapter 4-17) is an important metaphor to use in many interventions and between sessions. The Massive Change History and everything (Chapter 4-18) treats the effects of a trauma throughout the patient's life in any relevant system. I always use his intervention after any other intervention. Although I make the request for the subconscious to do this, I have found that subconsciouses usually learns to do the Massive Change History automatically after a treatment. Still, I frequently check to see that the subconscious has done it. I often use the Sentence Procedure (see Chapter 4-21), but treating structures of memories (see Chapter 4-22) or emotions (see Chapter 4-23) related to an issue may be a more efficient treatment. I continue to treat the Predispositions (see Chapter 2-24) and massive beliefs (see Chapter 4-25). I find myself increasingly using the treatment without getting permission (see Chapter 6-12). When treatment without asking is done with respect, it is useful to resolve barriers caused by parts that, for some reason, are not willing to say that they want treatment.

Chapter 5

How the Memory and Brain Work

In this chapter, you will learn in more detail about the different aspects in the brain and how the memory works. This is information you will need to resolve complex problems. I discovered the constructs of Process Healing while problem-solving complex issues and creating solutions or structures that worked to resolve issues. The more you understand what I discovered, the more creative you will be if you encounter complex structures. This chapter may take some studying, but I think it will be well worth your time.

I made up constructs of memory presented here to explain and treat different, and often difficult, clinical issues. Interestingly, the barriers themselves usually suggested the construct and how the construct caused a barrier to treatment. The constructs are imaginary memory structures. I created these memory structures to describe what I saw in my patients when I solved complex emotional problems. I have confirmed the validity of most of these constructs in therapeutic interventions with many patients. The constructs described in this book are not necessarily real; they just work as metaphors to help treat painful emotional issues.

The Structure of a Memory

The basic assumption of the theory is that memories run the mind and body just like programs run a computer. For instance, when you click on your e-mail icon, you activate a computer program, stored in memory, that runs your email program. In humans, such programs, known as memory, are stored in our brain. When a certain memory is activated, it causes our eyes to blink, lips to say what we are thinking, or our throat to swallow. The code in our memory causes neural activities that run specific physical or mental activity. Each memory is defined by a unique structure and is a program to cause some activity. Our memories are triggered like computer programs, although the triggers are sensory activity or active memory stimulation involving content or emotion. A memory structure associates *with* the other memories to do specific tasks. The associated memories are the code to run the body. So, to recap, each memory has a unique memory structure and associates *with* memories to run the body. I assume that memories run all activities in our body and brain.

Every memory that we have has a unique memory structure (see Figure 5-1) and it is the structure is the basic building block of all memories. Each memory structure has a collage of other, previously learned memory structures associated *with* it. The collage of memory structures, associated *with* a unique structure, all work together to activate neural activity to cause a

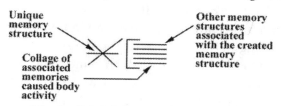

Figure 5-1 A Memory Structure

specific response. Notice that I italicized *with*. This is to create a distinction between *with* and *to*. Later you will learn that when memories associate *to* a structure, it affects the structure in a different way—namely, the memories associated *with* the structure cannot be modified.

A memory structure is like a tree with many branches that are also like trees. With the creation of a response, a new memory tree is formed. Other previously learned memory trees hang on the new tree, like branches, and cause the response. Memory trees hanging on the new memory tree work together and cause a unique mental or body activity like a visual memory, heart activity or an arm movement. The old memory trees or structures hanging on the new memory tree are called associated memories and form a collage of memories. In our behavior, collages of memories, each associated *with* unique memory structures, run our physiology to cause mental and body activity. Remember, there is a difference between associated *with* and associated *to* a memory structure.

Memory structures that are not active are dormant in our memory (see Figure 5-2). However, dormant memory structures are always potentially active in the sense that they are ready to be triggered into activity in the Active Experience. Most memory structures in our memory are dormant. Dormant memories are never experi-

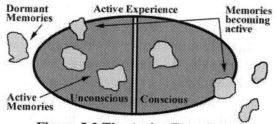

Figure 5-2 The Active Experience

enced in the conscious and unconscious Active Experience. Memories have to be active to be in the Active Experience. But even then active memories in the Active Experience are not always experienced. You experience an active memory only when it is selected to be in a collage of memory structures running your neural activity. Memory structures with a collage of memories are constantly created from the active memories in the Active Experience to cause all our behavior. There is a new memory structure with its collage of memory structures created for everything we do.

Here is another way to think about it. It is as if some memories are waiting at a bus stop for a bus. They are inactive and in the dormant state. Other memories are riding in the bus — active in the Active Experience. The memories waiting for the bus are called dormant. When these memories get on the bus, they become active. In other words, they enter the Active Experience and are called active memories. Many memories are on the bus in the Active Experience but only those memories that are suitable are used in a collage (memory structure) to manage the bus driver. Those memories used in the collage are the ones that are selected to work together to drive the bus. When the driver has to respond to an internal need (shift gears), or an external need (to respond to a stoplight), memories get on and off the bus. A new collage (memory structure) is formed to drive the bus using available active memories. Some of the un-used memories get off the bus but stay close by and are available to get back on the bus again and be used again in another collage. Memories are continually becoming active and going dormant as the internal conditions (the mechanics of driving) and the external conditions (the neighborhood) change. A selection process on the bus causes the most suitable memories to be used in collages to drive the bus. The fitting memories are assembled into a collage to give just the right response to the driver.

All activity in the bus (Active Experience) is organized to form a collage of active memories to get more satisfaction and less pain. As the neighborhood changes, active memories that are no longer relevant will sneak out the front door and become dormant again, while other, different memories will get on the bus and become active. Active memories, even the collage itself, which drives the bus, can be used in the next collage created to drive the bus. Sharing memories from collage to collage causes continuity in driving the bus. All active memory collages that we, our Main Personality, experience as thoughts and behavior are created from the memories in the Active Experience. Remember, the Active Experience is a theoretical or imagined construct that helps explain the complexities of our behavior.

Active memories in the Active Experience are the memories that can cause physiological activity that we experience at some level (see Figure 5-3, next page). Some of the active memories will be assembled into a collage in the Active Experience to cause activity in our body or in our conscious and unconscious experience. Collages of memories cause

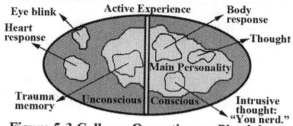

Figure 5-3 Collages Operating on Physiology

all our behavior as well as all brain and body experience. However, the Active Experience in our brain is even more complex than you might imagine. As you will read later, there can be many buses creating independent or parallel behaviors at the same time. For example, dissociative and amnesic parts can also be "buses." This is the reason changing behavior can be so complex. In most therapeutic approaches, we don't learn about communicating with the buses (parts), yet directly communicating with the buses is necessary to treat some problematic behavior. Process Healing gives us a way to communicate with all the active buses in our brain.

The Active Experience

Let us put the Active Experience in perspective. It will help you to have a clearer idea about what the Active Experience is. The Active Experience consists of all brain and body neural activity and active memories. Let's look at the Behavior System, the system that meets our survival needs (see Figure 5-4).

The Basic Neurostructure of the Behavior System causes the Behavior System. This Basic Neurostructure assembles information active

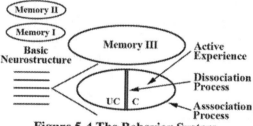

Figure 5-4 The Behavior System

in the Active Experience to create behavior and memory. The Basic Neurostructure works on neural activity — the sensations and memories that have to do with positive and negative emotions, basic needs, and the five senses. The Basic Neurostructure of the Behavior System processes all the memory and neural activity in the Active Experience. The result of the process is that a memory structure is created, which then associates *with* a collage of memories that will both become a memory and run the body to help us get more satisfaction and less pain. The memory structure is saved as a memory so it can be used again. In general, I assume there is Basic Neurostructure for thousands of systems that process the Active Experience to run some unique aspect of the brain and body.

However, the Behavior System is more complex. In the next section I will describe how the Behavior System develops in more detail. It is important to know this information because some of the applications of Process Healing involve treating the different structures of the Behavior System.

The Behavior System

The Behavior System develops from the activity in the Active Experience (see Figure 5-4, preceding page). The Active Experience is a construct that represents all neural activity in our brain and body. You will learn that Memory I, Memory II, and Memory III cause the activity in the Active Experience. Unique Basic Neurostructure for the Behavior System works on the activity in the Active Experience. The Active Experience construct simply represents all neural activity in the brain and body. The egg representing the Active Experience is helpful in describing active processes like trauma symptoms, parts activity, association and dissociation, conscious and unconscious, memory and creating behavior.

The Basic Neurostructure uses some of the active memories in the Active Experience to create a collage to cause the next response. For example, if I am moving my hand to scratch my ear and my nose starts itching, a change happens in the Active Experience. The next response incorporates the previous response with this new event in the Active Experience and creates a response moving my arm toward my nose. My hand changes direction to scratch my nose. The Basic Neurostructure responds to changes in the Active Experience. The process where the previous condition or response is used to create the next response is called a recurrent process.

State-dependent Memory

The behavior created by the Basic Neurostructure is more than just behavior. When each response is created, a new memory is also created so the response will be remembered. Here's the reason. The response involves the entire brain. The new memory created involves a new structure that is well defined in the brain. The memories associated *with* the new structure run some aspect of our body or behavior. After its activity, the structure in the brain is not lost or smeared away but remains as a memory that can be used repeatedly. In this way, body activity and behavior simply result in creating memories that can be used again. This property of the brain allows the Basic Neurostructure to create the response and memory at the same time. This is a highly adaptive skill given the ever-changing environment.

The Behavior System starts developing shortly after conception. Different conditions, as we develop from conception to adulthood, result in three distinct memory groups to be created in the Behavior System. Each memory group with unique common properties is called a memory structure in our Behavior System. The common properties are called state dependencies. State dependency is widespread in the brain and is a property that is used in many of the Process Healing interventions. It is interesting how state dependency causes the three memory structures to develop in the Behavior System. These memory structures are used in many treatment interventions.

In the beginning

Shortly after conception, neural development occurs, leading to spontaneous neural activity in the brain and body. Figure 5-5 illustrates this activity. This spontaneous neural activity (the little circles) is not organized — it is truly spontaneous. In a short time, when the neural activity becomes repetitive, a group of nerve cells associate and start working together to create memories and responses. I call this group of cells working together the Basic Neurostructure (see Figure 5-6). The Basic Neurostructure selects activities from the spontaneous neural activity to create a collage of neural activities (in brackets) — a memory, which at the same

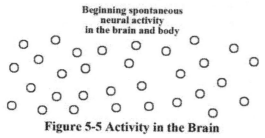

Figure 5-5 Activity in the Brain

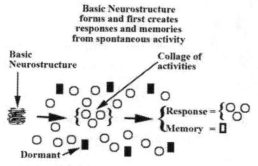

Figure 5-6 The Formation of Behavior and Memory Structures

time causes neural activity, otherwise known as a response. The response occurs when the collage of the memory is created. Initially, the memories created become dormant after making a response (dark boxes). A response is a newly created memory. Thus it begins: collage, memory, and responses leading to more collages, memories, and responses.

Any brain activity triggers the Basic Neurostructure to create memories and responses. Each memory has a unique memory structure. The common quality of the initial unique memory structures is simply neural activity. These memories accumulate between conception and birth to form Memory I. Memory I is defined as a state-dependent memory that only has memories that are related to simple neural activity.

Later, when the dormant memories and Active Experience have content in common, the dormant memories are triggered into activity (see open boxes in Figure 5-7). Instead of the spontaneous repetitive neural activity, the Basic Neurostructure starts selecting both active memories and spontaneous activity to create memories and responses. This continues until the active memories triggered outnumber the spontaneous activity. From then on, the collages for responses (in brackets, center, Figure 5-7) are primarily created from active memories. Memory I and the Active Experience (indicated by the shaded enclosures in Figure 5-8) are constructs to make it easier to talk about dormant and active memories and the Active Experience.

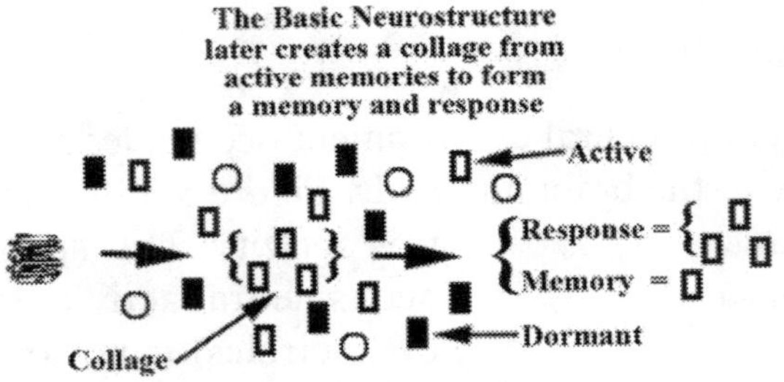

Figure 5-7 The Creation of Behavior from Active Memories

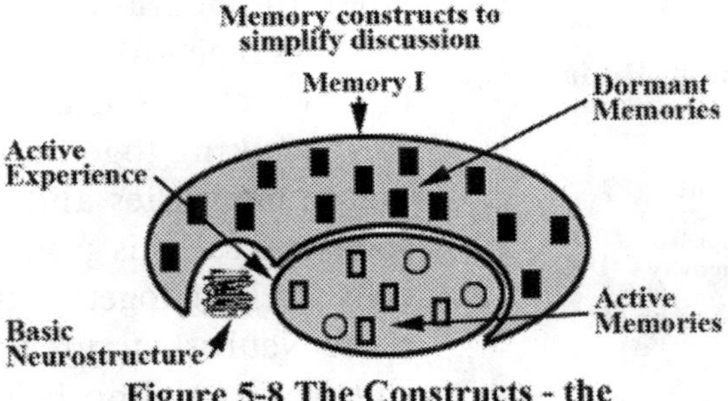

Figure 5-8 The Constructs - the Active Experience and Memory I

After Memory I is created, the Behavior System continues to develop. When sensory neural activity begins, a new state-dependent memory is formed that is called Memory II. Near birth, and when sensory experience, basic needs, and reinforcement and punishment begin, a third state-dependent memory is formed called Memory III.

Memory	State-Dependent Properties	Period of Development
Memory I	Activity	Conception to birth
Memory II	Activity, primitive sensory experience	Third trimester to age four
Memory III	Activity, operational sensory system, basic needs, positive and negative emotions	Third trimester to now

Table 5-1 The Properties of the State-Dependent Memories

Table 5-1 shows the properties of the three kinds of state-dependent memories that contribute to the creation of behavior and memories. The table also shows the period of development for each of the memories. It all starts with the fetus. As the fetus grows and different neural activity starts operating, three developmental stages cause the amassing of three independent memories. The development of each of these three memories overlap. Here is a detailed description of the conditions that cause the three memories to be unique and independent.

Memory I

The Behavior System forms in this way. At some point shortly after conception, some Basic Neurostructure begins working on primitive brain and body neural activity called the Active Experience. The Basic Neurostructure responds to the activity in the Active Experience to create a response and memory of the response assembled from this primitive activity (see Figure 5-9). The responses created in this process while *in utero* are in Memory I. These memories can be reused. The content of the activity in the Active Experience triggers some memories from Memory I into the Active Experience. The Basic Neurostructure

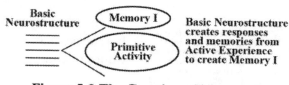

Figure 5-9 The Creation of Memory I

continues to take portions of the active memories in the Active Experience to create a collage that causes a response and memory of the collage. This process of creating responses and memories gradually adds more memories to Memory I. This is a learning process.

Creating a unique response and a memory of the response, which can recreate the response, is a pervasive property of our brain. Any activity in the Active Experience results in a response and memory. Therefore, any form of activity in the Active Experience causes a new memory or a change in memory. Memory I is a State-Dependent Memory based on neural activity in the Active Experience. The memory process caused by activity in the Active Experience is the property of the brain that Freeman saw when he decided that experience changes memory (Freeman, 1991).

After a memory is created, it can be elicited again into the Active Experience. When active, the memory can be used in a new collage for some neural activity. The memory structures created, building on previous memories, gradually become more complex as the neural activity gets more complex. The memories or memory structures preserved in Memory I reflect the increased complexity as the fetus develops. This memory process is efficient because these memories can be reused without creation or change. Changes in the environment either create new responses and memories or change old memories and emotions to get new responses. Memory I starts developing shortly after conception and continues to develop until birth. When active in a collage, the memories in Memory I can cause a response in our body. This same structural organization is repeated throughout the brain in various systems—namely a Basic Neurostructure with a unique memory operates on the Active Experience.

Memory II

As our brain and body continue to develop, Memory II starts to develop when primitive sensory stimulation (without sensations) begins to become active (see Figure 5-10). Memory II is also state-dependent. The state dependency is based on both neural activity *and* sensory activity. Memory I becomes less important but, nevertheless, continues to contribute to the Active Experience. The memories of Memory II are created

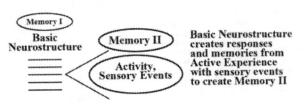

Figure 5-10 The Creation of Memory II

and take part in creating the new brain-body neural activity in the Active Experience. Now, both Memory I and Memory II provide memories that can be used in collages to create responses in our brain-body activity. From some time before birth to about 4 years old, Memory II continues to develop.

As we have seen before, the Basic Neurostructure processes the Active Experience to create a collage causing a response and a memory of the collage. The memory structures in Memory II learn to contribute to the Active Experience with strong responses that are like habits. These habit-responses are called Predispositions. All the Predispositions, taken as a whole, are called the subpersonality, an idea obtained from the work of Stone and Stone (1989). These strong Memory II responses provide the next immediate response in many situations. While many of these Predisposition responses are usually worthwhile, others cause problems and have to be treated. With continuing development, new survival demands and behavioral options activate.

Memory III

Similar to Memory II, as the complexity of our behavior increases, a new state-dependent memory is formed—Memory III. The creation process gradually shifts its role to work on all the neural activity related to

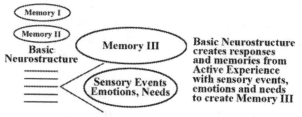

survival. With emerging positive and negative emotional experience combined with sensory experience and basic needs, a new state-dependent memory starts

Figure 5-11 The Creation of Memory III

developing (see Figure 5-11). Now the Basic Neurostructure uses elicited memories from Memory I, Memory II, and Memory III to create even more complex neural activity.

Memory III includes all memories of neural activity that have connection to simple stimulation, the five senses, positive and negative emotions (namely reward and punishment) and basic needs like water, food, and air. Memory III becomes the main memory, though Memories II and I continue to have impact on created behaviors. Memory III is always expanding by creating new memories. Imagine: All behaviors are the product of a constant creative process that is making collages from the Active Experience. The memories formed are heavily influenced, if not determined, by the memories we have learned in the past. These memories cause behaviors ranging in duration from seconds to minutes. Our dominant memory resource, Memory III, continues to develop gradually because of the activity of the Behavior System, which creates behavior and memories from our Active Experience to deal with the increasingly complex world.

Emotion Memories associated *with* Content Memories are also triggered into the Active Experience. They also organize into collages in what is called the Emotion System. Emotions associated *with* memories provide the motivation for the likelihood of the response and the intensity of the response. A dormant memory with intense positive or negative emotions is more likely to be elicited into the Active Experience than a memory with no emotions. Once active, the more intense the positive or negative emotion associated *with* a memory or behavior, the more likely the behavior is going to activate and happen. The Emotion System develops in a structure similar to the Basic Neurostructure and Memory I, but the development extends over our entire life.

Neural Activity and the Treatment Process

It has been observed that experience causes memories to change (Freeman, 1991). I call the creation of a response and memory a memory event. Any stimulation causes a memory event. This is the reason some treatments work fast. The safe, quiet treatment setting reduces the activity in the Active Experience. The absence of activity in the Active Experience keeps the memory structure of the issue being treated from being changed by the activity of other memories in the Active Experience. In the treatment setting, a memory event can change the content or emotions of an active memory.

The number of memory events is increased by novel, sensory stimulation, such as with eye movement (EMDR) or physical tapping on meridians (EFT or TFT). With repeating stimulation, the current relaxed or neutral emotion gradually replaces the painful emotions associated *with* a memory. This increase of memory events in the treatment setting causes the target issue to be created repeatedly in the Active Experience without changing its structure. This results in changing the content or trauma emotions associated *with* the structure of the issue. The current neutral to positive emotions of the treatment setting gradually replace the trauma emotions learned in the past. This combination of a quiet setting and artificially increased stimulation speeds up the treatment of trauma, beliefs, painful memories, and all other emotional issues.

Of course, there is no such location in the brain as the Active Experience. The term Active Experience is an imagined construct to describe all active neural experience related to brain and body. What about all these other imagined constructs, such as Memory I, Memory II, Memory III, dissociation and association parts, amnesia, and all the other memory structures that are discussed later? These constructs are useful to understand complex memory activity. The clinical effectiveness of these constructs used in treating mental issues gives legitimacy to using these constructs. Clinical problem-solving with complex behavior confirms the seeming fact that imagined structures used as metaphors influence the behavior created in the Active Experience.

When a treatment intervention with an imagined structure is found to work to solve a problem, it is tried with other patients. For whatever reason, the treatment structures in this book have worked with almost all patients with whom they have been used to solve a problem. The subconscious is the necessary feature of the brain that allows the constructs of this theory to work when used in treatment.

The Subconscious

The Subconscious (SC) is a system with a language that starts developing *in utero* (see Figure 5-12). The fetus learns words, phrases,

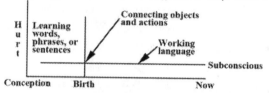 and sentences at a primitive neurological level. Learning a word in the primitive brain means the brain learns neural activity that directly represents a word. However, it

Figure 5-12 The Development of the Subconscious

does not yet have the auditory experience such as hearing the word or a meaning associated with that word. Following birth, when sensory experience starts, these words, phrases and sentences, learned without remembered sensory experience or meaning, associate *with* neural activity representing objects and actions. This addition of meaning causes a verbal system or language to develop. This language starts functioning, but the language is not experienced in the conscious experience. However, it becomes the language of a system that I now call the subconscious. In addition, it appears that all complex neural systems in the brain and body are structures that are associated with this verbal system. This means that you or the subconscious can conveniently talk with all complex neural systems. On the other hand, our personality works in a different way.

The Personality

Remember that all memories in Memory III are related in some way to stimulation, sensory experience, positive and negative emotions, and the basic needs of air, water, and food. The Behavior System starts forming Memory III at birth or maybe before birth (see Figure 5-13). Memory III continues to amass just by having our whole range of behaviors and experiences.

The Main Personality is a memory structure in Memory III. This personality is the personality that has run the body from before birth, from birth, or for the longest time. There can be many parts or other structures within Memory III. Sometimes, parts are formed through trauma or dissociation that will be described in

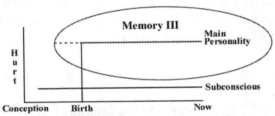

Figure 5-13 The Main Personality

detail later. These parts can either be hidden from the conscious awareness or be coconscious with the Main Personality. While the Main Personality is usually the naturally dominant personality, trauma parts can run the body while the Main Personality is dormant (see Figure 5-14). If the Main Personality has a severe trauma, a trauma part may become the dominant personal-

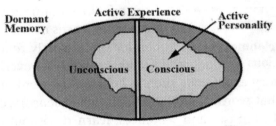

Figure 5-14 The Active Personality

ity. In general, an active personality is defined as being the part or parts that are currently active in the conscious Active Experience.

The active personality can be an amnesic part, a dissociative part, or the Main Personality. There can also be active parts that are in either the unconscious or coconscious in the conscious experience. The unconscious parts can give intrusions of emotions, body experiences, or thoughts into the conscious experience. These can occur either in the conscious experience or as a body experience viewed by the conscious experience—for example, a muscle movement, widening of the eyes, or even an unknown voice. See Appendix II for a visual description of the complexity of the Active Experience and parts activity.

The Difference Between the Personality and the Subconscious

Let me explain the difference between a personality and the subconscious. All experienced neural activity — emotions, senses, and behavior, for example — are active in the Active Experience. Behaviors created from the Active Experience are mostly responses of an active personality. The goal of the behavior is to get more satisfaction or pleasure and less pain. However, when a traumatic experience is active, it distorts the Active Experience with emotions or behaviors from the past. In turn, the distorted Active Experience distorts the response that is created. These distorted responses caused by a distorted Active Experience prevent gaining the goal of having more satisfaction and less pain.

The subconscious, on the other hand, experiences the neural activity that leads to the Active Experience but does not experience body sensations. For example, when I pinch myself on the leg, I feel the pain. The subconscious, on the other hand, only experiences the neural activity that leads to the pain, but does not feel the pain. The subconscious feels only a representation of all the activity in the Active Experience that was caused by the pinch without having a pain experience. Similarly, the language the subconscious uses is a representation of the language that we use. This allows us to communicate with the subconscious in our language. Further, since the subconscious does not physically experience pain or any sensation, it can communicate an accurate memory of our experience. It can do this without the distortion that trauma memories and reactions cause in the conscious experience.

Any severe traumatic experience always associates painful emotions *with* the trauma memory. Though not always a problem, when this trauma memory and the associated emotions are active in the Active Experience, they will distort the behavior of the personality. Interestingly, a severe traumatic experience can never damage the subconscious. However, the personality has filters, amnesic parts, and other aspects that can distort and hide a person's view of experience or memory. The subconscious, on the other hand, has no filters to cause distortion. It has the ability to see accurately the entire memory representation causing the activity in the Active Experience. Also, the subconscious is able to change the trauma in memories causing the most basic brain functions. This includes the Basic Neurostructure, the memories of the Behavior System, the Emotional System and the memories that serve brain and organ functions.

Association and Dissociation

The association and dissociation processes are normal, adaptive and, support the active personality. These processes are heavily involved in creating thoughts, experience, and behavior. The association and dissociation processes are important in our daily function. They are learned memories or parts in Memory III. They are like skills that are hidden and working in the unconscious.

With the initiation of conscious experience and reinforcement and punishment (pain and need reduction), apparent self-direction becomes a normal outcome of getting more satisfaction and less pain. Self-direction or executive function, in concert with the Basic Neurostructure, operates on the conscious experience to create responses. At the same time, self-direction leads to the association process, which prevents irrelevant memories from becoming active and the dissociation process, which conceals irrelevant active memories. The concealed active memories become active memories in the unconscious. The association and dissociation processes are used so frequently that they become skills in the unconscious.

Association process

The association process, formed early in life (see Figure 5-15), develops after our volitional behavior and the executive function starts. Be-

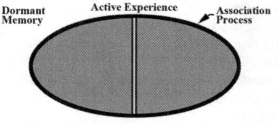

cause the Basic Neurostructure creates our behavior from the content of the Active Experience, the association process is learned to keep the Active Experience from becoming overloaded with the

Figure 5-15 The Association Process

content of irrelevant dormant memories. The association process manages the triggers that elicit dormant memories into the Active Experience. These triggers are the content and emotions of our active memories. The association process also has a verbal system and can engage in communication. When necessary, I interact with the association process as a part in the same way as I would interact with amnesic or personality parts.

Trauma to the association process can cause the mental problems referred to as loose associations and concrete (literal) thinking. Loose association, caused by trauma, occurs when many irrelevant memories flood our conscious experience. When a person has loose associations, he or she might speak in what is called "word salad," saying a stream of unconnected words. Concrete thinking is another trauma-related condition caused by the impact of trauma on the association process. This trauma to the association process leads to the inability to understand metaphors. For example, when a person says, "I'm going to run to the store," a person with concrete thinking might ask "Are you going to run in sweatpants or shorts?" Trauma to the association process can be treated to produce noticeable changes in behavior.

Dissociation process

The dissociation process is also a memory structure or part that works in the Active Experience (see Figure 5-16). This process is also cre-

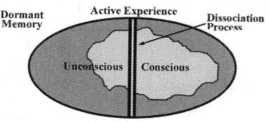

ated after volitional behavior and the executive function start. This dissociation part is in Memory III and is involved in creating behavior. The purpose of

Figure 5-16 The Dissociation Process

the dissociative process is to conceal irrelevant memories to reduce further the information to which we respond in our conscious experience. The dissociation process causes the conscious and the unconscious experience in the Active Experience.

The dissociation process, similar to the association process, was learned when our language and behavior began to respond to what we experienced in our Active Experience. There was so much unneeded stimulation in the Active Experience that this memory process was created to conceal the unnecessary activity. It does this by associating a memory or other neural activity *with* memories in the collage associated *with* the memory structure. A memory can then have sensory experiences, emotions, kinesthetic responses, or even memories experienced in the unconscious and out of the conscious experience. All memories have some dissociated content and emotions.

Because of the dissociative process, a memory can be active in either the conscious or unconscious experience or both. Remember, when memory is not in the Active Experience, it is dormant—that is, actively waiting to be triggered. For example, the memory for the answer to the question that I am about to ask you is not in your Active Experience and you don't know the answer. You don't know the answer because the answer is still dormant in your Memory III. Now I ask, "Can you remember an experience when you rode a bicycle?" If you had a memory of riding a bicycle, the memory is no longer dormant because it was triggered and you experienced the memory in your conscious Active Experience. It is now an active memory giving you an experience in the conscious Active Experience.

Dissociation and association and the Main Personality

The Main Personality (MP) is active on both sides of the dissociation process in both the conscious and unconscious experience (see Figure 5-17). The dissociation and association processes have similar functions—

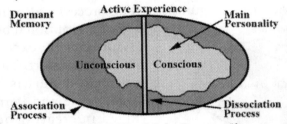

Figure 5-17 The Main Personality

the dissociative process to simplify the conscious experience and the associative process to simplify the Active Experience. They both screen out less relevant or painful memories.

One natural, adaptive function of the dissociation process is to hide (dissociate) painful experience from the conscious experience, spontaneously.

Usually, the two processes of association and dissociation cooperate with each other. They normally function as one process working on the Active Experience. However, trauma can damage both the association and dissociation processes. When damaged, they can function as independent processes. When this happens, the person has trouble focusing attention or concentrating without having intrusive thoughts or ideas in his or her conscious experience. Both processes can be treated by the subconscious. The treatment involves getting rapport with both parts by using everyday language and helping them understand the problem and the treatment solution. Then the subconscious can treat the trauma of the parts and join the association and dissociation processes into one integrated part. This treatment effectively reduces the number of intrusions when trying to concentrate.

The dissociation and association processes can be under voluntary control. With voluntary control of the dissociation and association processes, people can deliberately dissociate or hide painful experience from their conscious experience. When a person never wants to think about something again, these processes can be used to keep it in the unconscious — out of the conscious experience. The voluntary use of the dissociative and associative processes to hide a painful experience is called repression.

Creating Parts in the Personality

Dissociative parts and memory

Dissociative parts and memories form in a different way from amnesic parts and memories (described below). Dissociation is a normal property of Memory III that is useful in everyday behavior. The dissociation process is a memory structure. When this memory structure associates *with* other memories in a collage, it prevents the memories from being experienced in the conscious experience. It "moves" the memory into the unconscious experience. This memory activity is referred to as dissociation and the memories in the unconscious are called dissociated.

We can use the dissociative process to move trauma or negative experiences into the unconscious experience, thus making it a dissociated memory. The ease of dissociating many painful experiences can become a habit or a Predisposition. This often results in creating many dissociated memories. The use of dissociation in this way allows the Main Personality to have more satisfaction and less pain in the short run. Later, the dissociated memories associated *with* a traumatic experience can give us the intrusive emotional or sensory intrusions commonly noted in post-traumatic stress disorder. Dissociated memories usually show no ability to take over and run the body as a "personality" but only give intrusions. Dissociative memories are more like skills and don't have the executive function to manage and create all of our worldly activities. Although I call dissociative memories that run some aspect of the behavior "parts", they are really dissociative aspects of the Main Personality, such as intrusive thoughts, images and so forth. All dissociative intrusions occur while a personality part is active.

Many skills that we learn consciously like composing, editing our speech, writing, driving a car, and keyboarding, for example, gradually become dissociated skills as conscious control becomes unnecessary.

Then they start working automatically in the unconscious and provide useful skills in fitting situations. We learn these skills in our conscious experience and then dissociate them to our unconscious experience. These dissociated skills are the parts of our personality that, more or less, run hidden in the unconscious to simplify and still take part in creating our conscious experience. These unconscious parts that support our conscious behavior are active dissociative parts.

Dissociated trauma parts form in the same way that dissociated skills form. When a painful experience is repeated, including painful emotions and a pattern of behavior that is experienced over and over, the entire experience can become dissociated. The practice of dissociation in this repeating situation is similar to learning a skill that is later dissociated. These dissociated memories, which include behavior, can form dissociative parts. These dissociated parts can give intrusions that run the body like a skill, coconsciously, with the Main Personality. The dissociative parts do not have the executive function observed in the Main Personality or in amnesic parts. When a dissociative part runs the body, an observer can sometimes see a shift in a person's personality. Dissociative disorders can have both dissociated memories and dissociative parts.

There is another way that dissociation can hurt us. Dissociation is used when a negative experience is preventing the person from having a positive experience. In this case, the negative features of the experience can be dissociated. The Main Personality without awareness can dissociate information that prevents the person from getting satisfaction in some area of life. Dissociating the negative features can increase the possibility that the person can get satisfaction in the short run but can eventually lead to getting hurt by making a bad decision. A common example of a dissociated experience can be seen in the courtship of some couples. Some partners dissociate the significance of expressions of anger, like playful pinching, disrespectful language, punching holes in the wall, or taking pleasure in drinking a six-pack of beer every Saturday and Sunday. These are significant danger signals in the early stages of courtship. If marriage is the outcome of the courtship, then painful conflicts will often emerge later when the dissociation breaks down and the new partner is found to be an alcoholic or becomes violent. In this case, the Main Personality used the dissociation process to dissociate triggers for unwanted reactions that would prevent getting immediate satisfaction. Since your personality can have all of these different kinds of dissociative intrusions, they are included in what are called aspects of the personality.

Dissociation can also fall under voluntary control. Many people learn to put painful experiences out of their mind deliberately. They think, "I don't want to think about that" or purposely "push" the emotions down. When people learn to do this, it is called repression.

Amnesic parts and memory

The entire personality consists of all experiences or memories formed on the timeline from just after conception to the here and now. When amnesic parts are formed, the new personality parts take space on the timeline as amnesic memories (see Figure 5-18). Amnesic parts continue as parts of the Memory III, but because of the amnesia, the

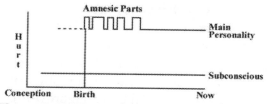

Main Personality does not easily access amnesic parts. They form during a unique, extreme, life-threatening trauma or when trust is broken. A unique experience is significant because the person has no memory to manage the new traumatic situation. With the absence of previous experience, and when the emotional intensity in a new trauma situation reaches a certain intensity or threshold, the intense emotions trigger relevant memories and emotions into the Active Experience independent of the Main Personality.

Figure 5-18 Trauma Causing Amnesic Parts

Basic Neurostructure and many other systems rapidly mobilize in a survival response (see Figure 3-9 on page 62). This rapid mobilization of memories and emotions "pushes" the Main Personality to dormancy, and the Basic Neurostructure and executive function work together to organize survival behavior. With mobilization, a new, unique neural structure forms that associates with the executive function and all the memories active during the trauma. This new structure is associated with all the experience during the trauma, but not to the Main Personality because there are few or no neural associations between the trauma part and the Main Personality while the Main Personality is dormant. The trauma part becomes an amnesic part.

Amnesic parts and memories are, more or less, independent of the Main Personality when active in the conscious or unconscious Active Experience. But amnesic parts distort the Active Experience and contribute to forming dysfunctional behavior (see Appendix II). This is in contrast to dissociative parts that are formed by the dissociative process, which prevents the dissociative memories from becoming active in the conscious Active Experience. Dissociations are also present in the memories of amnesic parts. Let me further explain how amnesic parts work in the personality.

Because of the rapid departure and re-entry of the Main Personality, few neural connections are associated between the trauma part and the Main Personality. The amnesia caused by the lack of neural associations effectively forms a barrier between the trauma memory and the Main Personality. It's simple — no neural associations, no communication. Yet, clearly all the behavioral resources available to the Main Personality, including the executive function, can also occur when a part is forming in a trauma. This means the amnesic part can be dealt with just like a personality. It remains a memory in Memory III, but the Main Personality cannot access or remember it.

Memory III can include amnesic parts created *in utero*, parts created during the birthing process, and parts created at any other time in

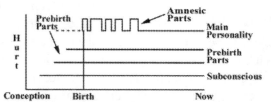

Figure 5-19 All Aspects of the Personality

life (see Figure 5-19). Amnesic trauma parts can be formed *in utero* when the mother experiences traumas such as the effects of drug abuse, an auto accident, a medical emergency or an intense trauma at birth. The parts that are formed before birth are called prebirth parts.

When an amnesic part is created early in life by a perceived, life-threatening trauma, the neural activity in many areas of the brain will be distorted with the trauma. This distortion of neural activity causes less intense trauma to easily mobilize the brain. This ease of mobilization creates more amnesic parts throughout life. Memory I, II, and other brain processes are changed in early trauma so rapid mobilization becomes a coping process under some forms of stress. When using Process Healing, readers will find dissociative or amnesic parts in their own or someone else's personality, although there is otherwise no obvious traumatic history to explain them.

Amnesic parts are completely normal and usually affect our behavior without our awareness of the active part. Normally, a person doesn't recognize the activity of such a part because he or she is used to the experiences and simply accepts them. These parts can be expressed as an intense phobic reaction, the presence of an emotion, a strange thought or voice, a muscle pain, or a tic. These are common, everyday experiences that a person accepts as normal, just a quirk, or who they are. The reason you will find amnesic parts when you use Process Healing is that by using the process, you intentionally set up rapport with all aspects of the personality and parts usually respond. Most of the time, these parts can be treated without even knowing how or when they were formed. Sometimes, without any prior reason, an amnesic or dissociative part that was never bothersome, or even noticed, wakes up and responds. It turns out that most parts, amnesic or not, in healthy people want to be treated. In fact, all parts want to be treated when they receive the information that answers all their questions.

Scope of Treatment

All personality activity, conscious or unconscious—namely, what we think and do, such as intrusive auditory, visual, or body feelings; dissociative and amnesic parts; and everything else, including brain and organ functions—are active memories. In this theory, I assume that each function in our brain and body has its own memory. All cells, organs, brain functions and other processes are run by their own memory. In addition, they are all interconnected. If everything is run by memory, there is no limit to what you can ask the subconscious to change. It either works or doesn't. One can try to change anything provided the subconscious says it is safe to try.

Summary

This chapter described the formation and function of the behavioral system. The constructs, the processes described—namely, the Active Experience, Memory I, Memory II, Memory III, the Behavior System, dissociation, and amnesia—all participate with increasing complexity in the Behavior System and other systems. These complexities will be described after the following chapter on problem-solving. In the problem-solving chapter, you will be exposed to some interventions described in detail in Chapters 7, 8, and 9. The skills learned in problem-solving will be useful to both those with less complex issues as well as those with more complex issues. In any case, the reader will have strategies to resolve most more difficult issues.

Chapter 6

Problem-solving

Problem-solving can be fun. Use your own curiosity as motivation to see what works and what doesn't. That is what makes problem-solving so interesting. Problem-solving is the way we remove barriers to treatment—barriers that distort or stop communication with the subconscious—and it also allows us to explore complex brain activity. Problem-solving is the primary activity that will lead you to discover new and interesting information about the human mind—what makes you tick. With luck, the basic course in Chapter 3 gives enough information to problem-solve and resolve most barriers. However, when the basic course is not enough, you can draw on the different strategies for problem-solving presented here. Don't worry about the strange constructs in this chapter because they will be described in detail in the following chapters.

This chapter gives you many routine problem-solving strategies. Furthermore, it gives you transcripts of problem-solving sessions that may help to free you to create metaphors to solve a barrier that haven't been discovered yet. I enjoy treating patients with difficult problems because they give me an opportunity to acquire interesting information while I am working with their specific issues. When I learn new interventions and constructs, I use them with other patients to confirm their usefulness as a metaphor.

Table of contents for this chapter

Possible barriers with parts and the subconscious

Trying something else

Expanding the method

Summary

Problem-solving Barriers

6-1 When to problem-solve

Problem-solving is frequently needed when communication with the subconscious or a part is distorted or stopped and you are at a loss for what to do to remove the barrier to treat the issue. As well, at times you may notice that responses by the "subconscious" are not always true and problem-solving can help rectify the situation. Because of this possibility, you have to be alert to identify when a part is responding as if it were the subconscious. Problem-solving involves identifying that a barrier exists and then treating it or offering a reframe of the barrier to remove it. Barriers can be detected by watching out for inconsistent responses—responses that don't feel quite right to you or even to the patient, who can often be a great help in picking up these inconsistencies. Here are some patterns of patient responses that would move me to problem-solving.

1. No finger response.
2. No progress in treatment—processing for a long time.
3. Too many "Yes" (or "No") responses in a row.
4. Treatment was completed too quickly.

5. Many "Yes" responses to "Are you still processing?" while the patient is not having an experience of treatment processing.

6. You expect a "Yes" or "No" and get "I don't know." Usually the subconscious gives a "Yes" or "No." When I get an "I don't know" or "no response" from the subconscious, I always ask if there is a part responding.

7. When the responses you are getting from the subconscious do not ring true and you feel uncomfortable about the answers.

8. You get "Yes" to leading questions that confirm information that is not possible or is theoretically or intuitively wrong. This is confirmed by problem-solving and finding that the source of the "Yes" was not credible.

6-2 How to problem-solve

Problem-solving is a creative task. Removing the barriers blocking treatment of memories or parts is the primary goal of problem-solving. In many cases, reframing the barrier, like the reframing described in Chapter 3-5, and 3-9, removes the barrier. Reframing means stating the problem in another way or adding information so the problem is no longer relevant or becomes self-empowering in some way. However, when reframing does not work, problem-solving involves investigating other ways to bypass barriers caused by unusual personality features (see Chapter 9). Problem-solving can result in creating new constructs or memory structures that work to treat the issues.

Here is how I problem-solve when I notice a barrier. Problem-solving involves asking a series of questions until I get a "Yes" response showing that the question identified the problem. With experience, you will know intuitively which questions to ask. A prompt sheet in Appendix I-1 will help you until you develop your own sense of the process. With successful problem-solving, you will be able to identify the type of barrier, which will then allow you to go to the next step of resolving the problem by doing an intervention or by reframing the issue.

I problem-solve by asking questions in an order similar to the following sequence of questions. First, I ask:

T: **Is there a part blocking communication or treatment?**

With a "Yes," I continue with questions in the order given here:

T: **Would this part talk to the subconscious to find out about treatment so he or she can make an *informed* decision about treatment?**

T: **Is this part worried about big, big pain?**

T: **Is this part worried that its trauma memory will retrauma-tize the Main Personality?**

T: **Does this part, who is blocking communication, want more satisfaction and less pain?**

T: **Does this part want more pain and less satisfaction?**

T: **Is there a conflict between parts?**

T: **Did this part just wake up?**

T: **Is this part worried that the social relations will change?**

T: **Is this a part without eyes and ears?**

T: **Would this part be angry if I asked the subconscious to treat it without asking?**

The more you use Process Healing, the more you will follow your intuition. I usually resolve barriers within three or four questions. Chapter 3 lists all the explanations and reframes that usually work to remove barriers. This chapter gives you examples of more complex barriers resolved by using strategies or constructs I have found useful.

6-3 A different class of barriers

There are barriers that cannot be treated or cleared with the information presented in this book. These barriers arise with intense trauma or torture and associate with parts or complex structures. Complex structures are usually not present in anyone without intense trauma. As trauma increases from minor trauma to intense trauma or torture, the memory structures become more complex. Not only does the complexity of structures increase, but so do the barriers that do not respond to my usual interventions. I have tried to figure out how to treat these barriers caused by intense trauma or torture. I could not do it with the simple association or learning-theory interventions that I had used up to this point. Before I understood the process underlying these barriers, I discovered I could use unorthodox procedures to clear them successfully. When I cleared these barriers, the patients almost always reported that they felt tingling from head to toe or a swoosh feeling coming off their torso, heart area, or some other part of their body. After the patient had this experience, the barrier was gone and treatment continued well. With this clinical data, I decided to use the metaphor *field* to describe this barrier that leaves the body with a swoosh feeling.

In this chapter, I occasionally refer to identifying and treating field barriers, and hope that you can bear with me with the field metaphor. It is just a metaphor, but when you learn the theory behind it, the metaphor leads to interventions that treat field barriers easily. I will not discuss the theory and interventions now because they are more complex than can be handled in this book. Normally, field barriers are not present in relatively normal people. If you ever exhaust all your resources trying to problem-solve a barrier, you can always ask the following:

T: **Is there a field barrier blocking treatment?**

A "No" will let you know that you are missing something. A "Yes" may generate some curiosity about what you are dealing with. A book is in progress that will provide the theory and treatment of field barriers within the context of the Process Healing Method (Flint, n.d.). For now, you can email me if you need support.

6-4 Using cues to solve problems

Whenever I am stuck and haven't any ideas left to try, I resort to asking the subconscious to give me a cue. The patient usually hears some words or sees an image that is the cue. Cues are not always easy to decipher. The subconscious uses metaphors, and not knowing what the subconscious is trying to communicate is not unusual. When the patient and I cannot figure it out, I ask for another cue. After I get the cue, the patient and I continue guessing what the subconscious meant by the cue until we discover its meaning. These cues help me identify and resolve barriers or show me how to treat a new issue. This strategy has often been useful. Here is an example.

Examples:

1. Using cues to expand understanding

The patient initially reported feeling good after a series of successful treatments. However, as time went on, the good feelings diminished and he became a little depressed. Some of his old issues returned. He added that he thought it was not a part causing the shift because he felt he had less dissociation and believed he was more grounded and down to earth. He did not give me much to work with other than the loss of the good feelings. I asked the subconscious about depression.

T: **Subconscious, do you know what is causing these experiences?**
S: **Yes.**

T: **Subconscious, is this experience caused by depression in the Main Personality?**
S: **No.**

It didn't take long to confirm that parts were indeed the problem by asking the next quick question.

T: **Are parts giving the depression?**
S: **Yes.**

With less dissociation, old issues were becoming more obvious.

T: **Subconscious, is there a reason you were not able to treat them?**

S: **Yes.**

We fumbled around suggesting possible barriers and finally I had to resort to asking:

T: **Subconscious, can you give us a cue?**
P: **I see "a green page."**

The patient and I couldn't guess what it meant. We fumbled around with this until I again returned to consult with the subconscious.

T: **Subconscious, can you give us another cue?**
P: **"A bright yellow light going up and down."**

I recalled the light bulbs going up and down suggestively at motels in the 1950s. The image was a cue for persons to stop at the motel and engage in sex. This was enough for the patient to come up with the answer.

P: **Concept of life.**

Here is what we finally decided after suggestive questioning of the subconscious: "With less dissociation, the system is more alive. Issues become more activated, become more problematic and, therefore, become more relevant to treat." In this case, understanding the cause of the apparent regression helped us both to feel more relaxed because the results of our inquiry supported our confidence in the treatment process and, in this case, eliminated the possibility of failure. We continued to problem-solve to treat the depression and other emerging symptoms.

2. Use of cues to find an intervention

The patient had had a difficult childhood and had been bullied by siblings and classmates. She developed a good working connection with her subconscious. Then we ran into a roadblock. For several weeks, we both encountered parts that responded with a "No" to any question. She knew it was not the subconscious because the part would answer "No" if she asked, "Is my name (her real name)?" To keep it simple, I called these parts, "No, no" parts.

T: **Is there a reason we have so many "No, no" answers?**
S: **Yes.**
T: **Can you give the reason to her?**
S: **Yes.**

She heard bullying in her head.

T: **Were parts created every time she was bullied?**

S: **No.**

T: **Are these Layered Memories that were created when she was saying "No" in her thoughts while she was being bullied?**

The Layered Memory intervention used here will be discussed further in Chapter 8-28.

S: **Yes.**

T: **Can you see a structure of Layered Memories that can give the "No, no" response?**

S: **Yes.**

T: **Please treat the structure of Layered Memories and any negative beliefs having to do with bullying, and so forth.**

S: **Yes.**

From working with other patients, I knew that parts could cause similar barriers that result in responses like the "No, no" responses. In this case, I simply used a Structure Procedure to treat the Layered Memories.

T: **Subconscious, please treat the structure of "No, no" parts.**

S: **Yes.**

I have also run into "Yes, yes," "No, yes" and "Yes, no" parts. These parts can be treated in the same way. Structures and Layered Memories are fully described in chapter 8. The same interventions may have to be repeated in later sessions.

This approach of getting cues from the subconscious is useful when you have tried everything and the subconscious signals that he or she knows a solution or an explanation. This method often leads to unusual metaphors to resolve a barrier or to get an explanation.

It sometimes happens that the patient reports to the therapist that he is getting information in writing that is visualized on an internal screen or hears a voice giving information and is at loss about where this information is coming from. I reassure the patient that this is quite common in Process Healing. This phenomenon also occurs within the therapist as well. Oftentimes, I have experienced intuitive information coming into my awareness that I cannot explain. If the information is helpful, I will use it and call it a gift. One has to know, however, that your own or the patient's parts can deceive you and mislead you with bogus information. The non-question intervention (Chapter 6-13) can usually reveal these deceptive parts.

Different names can be applied to the source of this internally generated information. I use the name with which the patient is most comfortable. Some of the names include Buddha, one-two, higher intelligence, and so forth. Any name given to the source of this unexplainable resource is simply a useful metaphor. It is important to be alert, to hear, and honestly evaluate the usefulness of the information or suggestions that you or your patient receive by this means. I have found these sources of information to be useful in therapy and theory building. The bottom line: If the information increases the power of the theory or treatment, it is safe information. If it works with several patients, then it is important and valuable information.

Sometimes I will inquire further of the subconscious about the source of this information and the answers can be quite startling. The discoveries I have made from these queries are the subject of the next Process Healing book dealing with field barriers (Flint, n.d.).

6-5 Resolve barriers with messages from the unknown

A forum member, Kathy Izzo, reminded me of a way to get clues or solutions for barriers. I had used this intervention years ago when I was treating with Neurolinguistic Programming. Basically, you forget about the issue or barrier and, before you go to sleep, ask your subconscious for a metaphor to give you the answer to the problem when you wake up. Though this can happen normally, from time to time, in some people's experience, a direct request works better. With patients, I would make the suggestion that they would have a dream or insight that would help solve the problem. Sometimes the patient would have a dream or intrusion one or two days before the session and that would be enough to help resolve an issue. This approach is very similar to asking the subconscious for a cue.

Here is what Izzo suggests: In a situation where you have run into a barrier, remain relaxed and positive and set a clear intention that you can and will resolve the issue. If you get frustrated, take a break. While you are on the break, ask your subconscious to send you a message that will lead to the understanding you need. When you run into obstacles that you can't figure out, ask a higher source to send an answer while you sleep. More often than not, you will dream what you need to know or awaken with the answer in your thoughts.

Exploring for Barriers

6-6 Finding other barriers to treat

Chapters 7 and 8 offer constructs discovered by problem-solving. These constructs are found in many of my patients. This section gives the series of questions I ask in order to identify a barrier caused by a construct or by one of the barriers described in later chapters. When I am at an impasse because I cannot find the barrier, I ask the subconscious the following lead-in question:

T: **Subconscious, are there any more barriers?**

After treating barriers already identified and still having a barrier for treatment, I ask the following questions. Frequently there are two or more barriers.

T: **Subconscious, is there a barrier in the Behavioral System?**

When the answer is "Yes," I ask the following questions:

T: **Subconscious, is it a Predisposition?**

T: **Subconscious, is it a problem in Memory I, Memory II or in the Basic Neurostructure?**

T: **Subconscious, is it easily created System Fragments?**

T: **Subconscious, is it an unusually strong belief that is blocking treatment?**

T: **Subconscious, are there floating structures in the Active Experience?**

When I find no barriers, I ask if there is a problem in Memory III.

T: **Subconscious, is the problem in Memory III?**

With a "Yes," I continue with the following questions:

T: **Subconscious, is the problem a Layered Memory or a part with a Layered Memory?**

T: **Subconscious, is the problem a memory layered with a fragment of the dissociation part?**

T: **Subconscious, is the problem a belief structure, a Layered Memory, a picture structure, or a fragment of the Behavior System?**

T: **Subconscious, is the problem a Tandem Memory within the primary Memory III?**

If I am still having problems, I explore for the more unusual forms of barriers (see Chapter 7).

T: **Subconscious, is the problem in the Emotion or Heart Systems?**

T: **Subconscious, is there a field barrier?**

The interventions to resolve these problems are easy to execute. Finding out what to treat to clear the problem or barrier can be more difficult. I routinely ask some of these questions early in treatment. Typically, I look for parts in the Emotion System, easily created systems, Predispositions in Memory II and the Tandem Memory. These are subtle, but important, because I find disrupting memory structures fairly frequently in my practice. The treatments of these structures are all described below or in later chapters.

By the time I finish these explorations, I usually have found the barrier requiring treatment.

6-7 Barriers involving the entire brain

This type of barrier, involving the entire brain, is believed to have major impact on the patient. Because the subconscious is a process involving the entire brain, a barrier of this nature can prevent treating a personality disorder, prevent the patient's access to his or her subconscious, and prevent independent treatment activity by the subconscious. You will notice three symptoms affecting the patients who have this barrier. First, the barrier prevents the person from communicating with his or her subconscious, except when he or she is in a treatment session or talking directly to the therapist on the telephone. Second, the subconscious cannot respond to a request by the patient to treat a belief, emotion or an issue. Finally, the subconscious cannot execute independent treatment of problematic parts and memories.

There is another problem caused by this barrier. It contributes to the severity of some personality disorders. In a normal personality, covert and overt conversation interacts with the subconscious to resolve conflicts and create normal, appropriate responses. When the brain barrier is present, the resolution of conflicts lacks input from the subconscious, which results in distorted perceptions, thoughts, conversations, and reactions in relatively normal situations in everyday life. The subconscious cannot access the activity in the Behavior and Emotion Systems and therefore fails to give beneficial input.

I ask the following question first in order to determine if the patient has a problem with an entire brain barrier.

T: **Subconscious, is there a barrier in the entire brain process that prevents the Behavior System from accessing the subconscious?**

S: **Yes.**

Then I continue to do the following intervention. So far, this treatment protocol has been routine.

T: **Subconscious, please treat this barrier.**

S: **Yes.**

T: [Wait] **Please do a Massive Change History of all the memories in the brain and body affected by this intervention.**

S: **Yes.**

T: [Wait] **Subconscious, please do a Massive Change History of the memories running the entire brain process.**

S: **Yes.**

This nearly always works to achieve communication with the subconscious and patients have noticed changes in the other symptoms of the entire brain barrier.

Possible Barriers with Parts and the Subconscious

6-8 More reasons for joining with the Main Personality

Here are more reasons offered by Jo Willems (personal communication, July 27, 2004) for getting treatment and joining with the Main Personality. Some of these reasons are different from the reasons provided in Chapter 3. Whenever you run into an aspect that persists in not wanting to join the Main Personality because he or she rejects the reasons to join, then you can try these reasons.

1. After integrating all aspects, you may experience an increase in knowledge and mental skills.

2. Physical body problems such as headaches and stress-related symptoms may be healed and this leads to general well-being.

3. Becoming a monopersonality leads to spiritual, mental and emotional growth and healing.

4. Memories become complete rather than broken up. After integration, the Main Personality uses memories without pain more efficiently because treatment removed barriers.

5. You will have more skills that are complete. Skills are related, so if all aspects are working together, you become more effective in getting more satisfaction and having less pain.

6. Painful memories give power to others. The more trauma memories you are able to treat and render powerless, the safer you will be. You will then be less accessible to those who might wish to harm you.

7. After treatment and integration, you stop experiencing internal intrusions and parts activity caused by external triggers.

6-9 Other barriers in the subconscious

Here is an interesting barrier that is also instructive. It showed up in the subconscious itself. The issue that caused this inquiry started when the patient said that he "had anxiety or fear about selling his art." He said that he also had similar fear about risk-taking behavior in many areas.

By working with the subconscious, I discovered a barrier in the whole brain process of the subconscious as well as 32 trauma barriers in the subconscious. His subconscious revealed, with leading questions, that this fear, which occurred in any risk-taking situation, was learned as a child in his home when he was seven years old. His father punished him at times when he felt good about being creative. This poorly timed punishment resulted in the Main Personality rejecting the possibility of making novel, risk-taking responses.

The subconscious participates in creating novel responses in children and at other times when a person is creative, confused, problem-solving, or is involved in the creative part of risk-taking. Punishing risk-taking traumatizes the creative activity of the subconscious process. Contrary to my assumption that the subconscious is not affected by painful experience, apparently the subconscious has to be active in the Active Experience to be creative. When a creative process is punished, the negative emotions become associated *with* that aspect of the subconscious that is creative. Therefore, with this patient, the response of the subconscious process in risk-taking situations was accompanied by the experience of fear associated *with* the creative aspect of the subconscious. The fear later experienced with creative activity in the Active Experience—the generation of novel responses—became a barrier to taking risks. This caused an illusion that there was a Predisposition not to take risks. This Predisposition appeared to influence all systems in all brain activity and was probably a significant cause for some pervasive personality problems.

The fear associated *with* the subconscious functioned as a Predisposition for giving fear to novel, risk-taking responses. A similar process involving behavior from Memory II caused the creation of Predispositions in Memory II not to help with tasks, not to do tasks, to shirk chores, and to set up others to do tasks, and so forth. Other examples of Predispositions formed in this way were procrastination, a feeling that he would die, shame, nervousness, and the belief that "nothing will work for me."

Here is how I treated this problem of a barrier in the subconscious.

T: **Subconscious, is there an emotion barrier in the subconscious that is distorting behavior?**

S: **Yes.**

T: **Subconscious, please treat all barriers or introjects in your memory safely, one after the other.**

S: **Yes.**

T: **Subconscious, please do a Massive Change History and everything of all memories touched by this intervention including the memory of the subconscious.**

S: **Yes.**

T: **Subconscious, please treat all Predispositions in Memory II that protected against anxiety in novel situations.**

S: **Yes.**

This resulted in a noticeable change in the patient's behavior.

6-10 Other barriers to automatic treatment

While developing the concepts of Process Healing, I observed that automatic treatment was happening in some of my patients—namely they felt treatment activity between sessions. Automatic treatment was an intriguing idea, for it meant treatment could continue between sessions. But it wasn't until after I had a dream that I deliberately tried teaching this automatic treatment to patients. The dream led me to clear the beliefs and memories that were incompatible with automatic treatment and a Predisposition in Memory II that responds to negative events in the Active Experience. (These interventions are given in Chapter 3-10.)

This intervention has worked well. I have had patients who have had the treatment process work constantly for months. Most often, the patient feels the treatment process active for brief periods during the day. I forewarn the patient that the treatment process can become intense and cause a headache or create intense emotions or fatigue. If this happens, I tell the patient to ask the subconscious to work at a slower pace.

P: **Subconscious, please do the treatment process slower so I do not feel these symptoms.**

Once, a patient complained of experiencing depression during a period of two months when I didn't see her. I had previously taught the subconscious how to treat by clearing the barriers stopping independent and automatic treatment by the subconscious. When she telephoned me, she had an appointment scheduled with her psychiatrist for antidepressants. I asked her subconscious to treat issues more slowly. I scheduled an appointment for her a week later. She came in for the appointment and said that after our telephone conversation her fatigue was reduced and she was feeling much better. Her fatigue was apparently caused by the intense treatment activity by her subconscious.

Automatic treatment can have an effect on the patient's day-to-day life and the patient should be made aware of this. As well, though I do not believe this to be necessary, I usually caution the subconscious to not be active when the patient is driving or using unsafe equipment.

My first interventions in teaching automatic treatment were short of what was possible because I did not teach the subconscious to work independently of the Main Personality. Eventually, I changed the request to include asking the subconscious to work independently of the Main Personality. The word "independent" in my request to the subconscious turned out to be significant. Including the word "independent" in the suggestion appears to cause the subconscious to treat more complex issues between sessions—issues formerly treated in the office.

Here are the six interventions that are sometimes needed to free the subconscious to treat independently and automatically:

1. Treat similar old memories

Patients usually expect to go to see someone to treat mental and physical problems. When the subconscious forms the intent to treat something, memories of treatment from the past become active in the Active Experience and disrupt the treatment process. These activated memories of going to doctors and dentists, and so forth, cause the disorganization in the Active Experience and thus create the barrier. Here is how to correct this barrier.

T: **Subconscious, can you do a Change History in Memory III, including the Ego States and Tandem Memories, and treat all beliefs, memories and experiences that will get in the way of the belief "I have internal treatment processes that can treat all my learned mental and physical problems and can work independently of my Main Personality?"**

S: **Yes.**

T: [When done] **Subconscious, please strengthen the belief, "I have the internal treatment processes that can treat all my learned mental and physical problems and can work independently of my Main Personality."**

S: **Yes.**

2. Treat Predispositions responding to negative emotions

Early trauma creates various Predispositions in Memory II. For example, one Predisposition could cause a "habitual" response triggered by an active memory with negative emotions. When a memory with negative emotions activates in the Active Experience, the active negative emotions trigger the Predisposition. An example is a Predisposition that dissociates active memories with negative emotions to the unconscious. This Predisposition that becomes active in the Active Experience responding to a negative event in the Active Experience causes a conflict with the subconscious. The conflict forms when both the subconscious and Predisposition try to operate in the Active Experience. The Predisposition's activity causes disorganization in the Active Experience and blocks the treatment process. To help the subconscious treat automatically, the subconscious can treat the Predisposition so it is no longer triggered by negative events. This eliminates the disorganization formed by the conflict. Here is how to ask the subconscious to treat the Predisposition that presents a barrier to automatic treatment.

T: **Subconscious, please treat the Predisposition in Memory II that prevents the subconscious treating actively and independently. Do a Change History on the Memory II and Memory III so the subconscious can give treatment leading to more satisfaction and less pain.**

S: **Yes.**

3. Treat massive belief barriers

Sometimes, there is a very negative and powerful belief that blocks treatment—for example, "Nothing will work" or "I can't heal." A belief like this can be so pervasive in the unconscious that the belief can block all treatment interventions. I treat belief barriers in the following way:

T: **Subconscious, are pervasive beliefs blocking automatic and independent treatment?**

S: **Yes.**

T: **Please do a Sentence Procedure with these beliefs, and tag and treat the beliefs, memories, and experiences in the correct order. Then, compose and strengthen positive, self-empowering beliefs to take their place.**

S: **Yes.**

Sometimes, a pervasive belief is orchestrated by a part that blocks automatic treatment. This part needs problem-solving and treatment.

4. Treat floating Behavior System Fragments

Sometimes treating Behavior System Fragments results in the need to do more treatment (see Chapter 8-25). Just like amnesic parts, the Behavior System itself can fragment. With treatment, the structures of behavior System Fragments will integrate into a more basic memory, namely Memory I.

In several cases, after treating these System Fragments, the fragments were not able to integrate into the Behavior System. A barrier in Memory I caused the inability of the System Fragments to integrate. When this happens, a remaining representation of the System Fragment (a structure) "floats" in the Active Experience and causes disorganization. This barrier blocks the possible automatic treatment process by the subconscious. The procedure for removing this barrier is given in Chapter 8-24.

5. Treat subconscious fragments

There can be subconscious fragments formed during the creation of System Fragments or with trauma in other systems. Fragments of the subconscious can become a barrier for independent, automatic treatment.

T: **Subconscious, are there any subconscious fragments blocking independent, automatic treatment?**

S: **Yes.**

T: **Please treat these fragments and integrate them with you.**

6. Treat field barriers

Sometimes, though unlikely, there are field barriers that attach to the subconscious to block the independent, automatic treatment. The field barriers are relatively easy to clear (see Flint, n.d.).

6-11 The intent not to heal is blocking treatment

After months of treatment, the patient said he experienced a buzz in his brain when the subconscious worked, and no buzz when it didn't work. When he asked his subconscious questions in my office, he would get no answers. However, when he was at his home and asked his subconscious questions without my being present, he got the wrong answers. The subconscious said this problem had been occurring from the first day of treatment. Using leading questions, we found that to solve this problem we had to treat a part. We discovered that we had to treat this part directly, but the part had a strong intent not to want treatment and not to make contact with the therapist. Furthermore, the subconscious told us that many other parts had a strong intent not to want treatment.

We did further problem-solving with the subconscious and found that a memory of not wanting treatment was associated *with* the part. This memory was giving the part intense negative emotions about treatment. This memory of not wanting treatment became associated *with* many parts during the creation of those parts. When one of these parts, with this memory, became active, the memory of not wanting treatment also became active and the part would not want treatment. The mention of treatment or healing would trigger all of these parts into activity and present a significant barrier. Here is how we finally resolved this problem:

T: **Subconscious, please slowly and safely treat the memory that gives this experience of not wanting treatment.**

S: **Yes.**

T: [Wait] **Subconscious, will you treat all parts that are associated *with* this memory, one after the other?**

S: **Yes.**

T: [Done] **Please do a Massive Change History and everything and treat the Shadow Memories.**

This intervention resolved the problem and the patient was again able to communicate with his subconscious. Another approach would be to treat the structure of memories associated with not wanting to heal.

Trying Something Else

6-12 Treating parts without asking permission

In the past when parts did not respond and nothing I did would elicit a response, I used to continue to struggle with the problem-solving strategies listed in Chapter 3-5. Out of frustration and desperation, I explored the concept of treating the parts blocking progress. I try hard to do it in a respectful way *without getting their permission* that still gives the reluctant parts the opportunity to assert their preference. I always remember that parts want more satisfaction and less pain. There can be a good reason for not wanting treatment and not wanting to join with the Main Personality. When I don't get a response and cannot find the reason, here are the five strategies that I try.

1. **Talk to the subconscious**

   T: **Will the part that is blocking communication talk with me?**

   P: **Yes.**

   T: **Would you be willing to talk to the subconscious and find out the answers to all your questions and considerations so you can make an *informed* decision about treatment and joining the Main Personality?** [Stress the word informed.]

   P: **Yes.**

   T: **Please talk to the subconscious.**

   After talking to the subconscious, the part will usually accept treatment.

   T: [Wait] **Subconscious, is this part willing to accept treatment?**

   S: **Yes.**

   T: **Please treat the part.**

   If the answer to the first question is "No," then I do the following:

   T: **Subconscious, does this part want more satisfaction and less pain in life?**

S: **Yes.**

T: [Wait] **Subconscious, is this part willing to accept treatment?**
S: **Yes.**

If "Yes," great. With a "No," it suggests the part does not want treatment, I continue to problem-solve by trying other barriers that might be relevant. After testing a number of barriers without success, or sometimes immediately, I go to strategy 2.

2. Treat without permission

I try to treat the part without permission by doing this intervention. I say the following:

T: **I am going to ask a question, and a "Yes" response is a "Yes" and all other responses and "no finger response" is "No." Now, if I ask the subconscious to treat this part without asking this part, will this part be angry with me?"**

When I wait a long time and don't get a "Yes," I say:

T: **Subconscious, will you treat this part slowly, safely and respectfully?**

I often don't get responses from the subconscious. I ask the patient if he or she feels the treatment process.

T: [Wait] **Do you feel the treatment going?**
P: **Yes.**

When nothing happens or I get a "No," I assume that the part continues not to want to heal, won't talk to the subconscious, and so forth. I try strategy 3.

3. Treat belief barriers without permission

Initially, I thank the part for responding to me. Next, I assume that there may be a belief that is blocking the part from exploring the possibility of treatment, so I try to treat the belief.

T: **Can I talk to the part blocking treatment (or communication)?**
S: **Yes.**

T: **Thank you for talking to me. I am going to accept all other responses as a "No" and only a "Yes" response as a "Yes." Subconscious, if I asked you to treat any beliefs in this part that are barriers for just considering treatment without asking this part, would this part be angry with me?**
S: **No.**

Usually I get a "No" response of some kind. Then I ask:

T: **Subconscious, please slowly and safely treat the beliefs that are stopping this part from considering treatment.**
S: **Yes.**

After the subconscious treats the belief—namely, changing the belief from feeling true to feeling false—the part is usually willing to communicate and eventually to accept treatment.

T: [Done] **Now, the subconscious can give you all the information about treatment so you can make an** *informed* **decision about joining the Treatment Team and receiving treatment. Are you willing to talk to the subconscious?**

This usually works, but if it does not, a little education about treatment usually helps to get the part to agree to receive treatment.

When I get a "Yes" to the question that indicates that the part would be angry if a belief were treated, I thank the part for communicating. I try Strategy 1 again or continue to problem-solve by explaining the reasons for treatment, or reframing the barriers for treatment, and so forth. Sometimes, I have found that after Strategy 2 and Strategy 3 do not work, I can go back to Strategy 1 and it works.

When further questions do not work, there are two additional approaches I can take.

4. Treat when in the best interest of the patient

The first approach that I take when I am desperate is the following.

T: **Subconscious, would it be in the best interest of the patient to treat this part even when this part will be angry with me if I ask you to treat him or her?**

S: **Yes.**

T: **Please treat this part.**

S: **Yes.**

I usually get a "Yes" response. With one patient I got a "No," but luckily Strategy 5 worked.

5. Acknowledge need for respect

I tried all of the strategies that came to mind and nothing worked. I was surprised by what came to mind. This approach, which was developed out of desperation, worked.

T: **Subconscious, does this part want respect?**

S: **Yes.**

T: **Will this part talk to the subconscious so he or she can give you all the information about treatment in order to make an** *informed* **decision about treating and joining the Treatment Team?**

S: **Yes.**

T: [Wait] **Is this part willing to be treated?**

S: **Yes.**

T: **Subconscious, please treat this part and give this part complete respect.**
S: **Yes.**

6-13 The non-question — Resolving blocks to communication

Sometimes there are parts that get in the way of direct access to the subconscious. When a patient gives no finger responses, there may be a problem. I find that one of the reasons for this can simply be my impatience. Some subconsciouses are quick responders and others take 20 or 30 seconds to respond. It's an individual style. However, generally when I get no responses I look for a part that is blocking communication. It is also a good idea to remain alert to inconsistencies in the responses from the subconscious. Every now and then there are distinct responses that are obviously not from the subconscious. Some examples are: "I don't know," following a long pause before the response; both "Yes" and "No" in succession; or a "Yes" or "No" that doesn't fit with your intuition. With any of these responses, I usually suspect that a part is speaking for the subconscious and the subconscious is not making the response. Here is how I confuse a part or parts that are blocking communication and get a response from the subconscious.

T: **Subconscious, is there a part blocking communication?**
S: **Yes.**

I set up rapport, problem-solve and treat the part.

With a "No" response or further inconsistent answers, I start problem-solving, trying to get in touch with the part that is confusing communication. I do the usual: more satisfaction and less pain; too much pain; trauma memory will traumatize the Main Personality; and so forth. Sometimes I use items from the whole list of potential problems until I get a "Yes" or "No." When I get any response, I thank the part for communicating with me. This breaks down the intent not to communicate, and communication goes easier after that.

If communicating with the subconscious is not working, or if you continue to get inconsistent responses, or you just want to get right to the point, there is a way to do it. You can ask the following non-question (Oglevie and Oglevie, 1997, 1999). This question is used to confirm that a "Yes" or "No" response was made by the subconscious.

T: **Subconscious, I am not going to ask if I am talking to the subconscious; I won't ask just now because it would be rude or unnecessary. No, I won't do it right now. I wouldn't even think of asking that** question. It is not right, but if I did ask that question—I am not going to do it—but if I did ask that question, would the answer be "Yes?"

When you get a "No," then work with the part that answered "No."

T: **Can I talk with the part blocking communication?**
Continue problem-solving.

This indirect form of questioning avoids all kinds of barriers. When you ask this non-question, create some space in time with irrelevant talk about something else. Make comments about not asking the question and about other irrelevant information. After some time, ask if the answer to the question was true. By extending the communication on and on, parts and the Main Personality become confused or forget the question and the subconscious is usually able to answer. This usually works to get the answer to your question when you suspect a part is giving inconsistent responses. With a "No," you shift into setting up rapport with the part blocking communication.

I often use this technique to find out if a part or field barrier is causing the block, or if there is some other barrier caused by an unusual structure. The use of a non-question is useful following other applications in which you have tried several interventions. It is also useful when the patient's responses lead you in an unusual direction and you find yourself wondering, "Can this be true?" In these situations, I ask the non-question.

T: **Subconscious, I'm not going to ask the question about whether the responses in the last 10 minutes have been yours, no I'm not going to ask that question** . . . (Make up a number of irrelevant comments) **. . . but if I did ask it, would it be true?**

With the response, I either continue the line of questions or start problem-solving.

When the information I am getting is in the form of metaphors with which I am uncomfortable, namely groundless or idealistic, I accept what the patient is saying and continue to hold some skepticism about the information as I continue exploring or treating.

When the line of questioning leads me to think the patient is responding consciously, I review the instructions about being a passive observer. I encourage the patient to simply relax his or her hands and be curious about what response the fingers will make. If the patient continues to make responses, I try the non-question. I have had only a few patients whom I had to confront about interfering with the process (see Chapter 4-1). In these cases, I easily resolved the problem and soon got valid responses.

6-14 Use a private line with the subconscious

Sometimes parts actively interfere with communication with the subconscious. When this happens, I try to form a private line with the subconscious. Most of the time this works well.

T: **Subconscious, can we form a private line for our communication by dissociating my voice from all aspects in the Active Experience and dissociating your responses from all aspects in the Active Experience?**

S: **Yes.**

You will notice when it doesn't work, because the communication problem still exists. After I have done this once successfully, all I have to say is the following:

T: **Subconscious, can we speak on a private line?**

S: **Yes.**

This is useful with torture survivors.

6-15 Moving memory for problem-solving

When a difficult problem arises and has all kinds of pitfalls, the subconscious can move the memory of the part or structure to its own memory. With the memory separated from Memory III, the subconscious can analyze the memory and find safe ways to get around the pitfalls without disturbing Memory III. Then, when the solution to the problem is obtained and will work safely, the subconscious can treat the problem in Memory III and any other memory in the brain that was included in the safe solution.

T: **Subconscious, please copy the memory of the memory structure into your memory so you can problem-solve and find the best and safest way to treat the memory. Look for any surprise triggers for self-protective responses and a simple solution for treating the entire structure.**

S: **Yes.**

T: [Wait] **Have you finished problem-solving?**

S: **Yes.**

T: **Is it safe to treat the structure in Memory III now?**

S: **Yes.**

T: **Please treat the structure.**

This is another intervention useful with torture survivors.

Expanding the Method

6-16 The spontaneous creation of a procedure

You can create procedures for use with a patient after one example. Occasionally, the treatment method used for one issue will work for other issues bothering the same patient or other patients. One example of creating a procedure was the development of the Sentence Procedure.

I developed the use of the Sentence Procedure while working with addicts. Beliefs and memories are triggered into the Active Experience when the addict says, "I want to quit drinking," so I thought, "Why can't I use this with other issues and beliefs?" Therefore, I asked the subconscious the following:

T: **Subconscious, can you tag all beliefs, memories, experiences and parts that become active when I say, "I am worthy of life"?**

S: **Yes.** [Of course.]

Then I started wondering if the subconscious could compose better sentences than I could to elicit beliefs, memories, experiences, and parts with the Sentence Procedure. It turned out that the subconscious could compose such sentences better and also repeat the procedure until no memories or aspects were triggered.

T: **Subconscious, can you repeat this treatment with the best sentences of your choice to trigger even more memory structures?**

S: **Yes.**

T: **Can you do this repeatedly until you trigger no more memories?**

S: **Yes.**

T: **Please do that.**

Next, I establish the name of this intervention for future reference.

T: **Subconscious, will it work if I call this procedure the Sentence Procedure?**

S: **Yes.**

Now I can use the Sentence Procedure with this patient by just saying that I want the subconscious to use the Sentence Procedure and suggest the desired, positive belief for the procedure. I have used this intervention for several other issues involving negative beliefs, including the treatment of addictions. When I want to strengthen a weak positive belief, I first use the Sentence Procedure to trigger and treat all beliefs or memories that will undermine the positive belief. Then I ask the subconscious to strengthen the positive belief.

6-17 Redoing previous interventions that were distorted by some barrier

Here is another intervention that is useful when a major barrier has possibly blocked the effectiveness of hours of treatment. This treatment depends on the subconscious remembering all previous interventions, which I trust is true. It is good for repeating weeks or months of treatment again for some reason. For example, when I discovered that Ego States were important to add on to the Massive Change History procedure, I asked for the following intervention.

T: **Subconscious, can you repeat the Massive Change History and include the Change History of the Ego States for all the interventions we have done since the start of treatment?**
S: **Yes.**

6-18 Exploring for answers—Discovering the Predispositions

This section describes how I initially developed the structures to describe what Stone and Stone (1989) call the subpersonality. The subpersonality, as you will read, is described as a number of parts that serve as Predispositions, like habits. I found these habits or Predispositions in Memory II. They consistently add a flavor to our behavior. The Predispositions often come in pairs—one that is helpful and the other hurtful to our behavior, (for example, accepting-critical). The negative Predisposition can be a pervasive problem in our behavior. In addition, there is also the Protector-Controller. This can be a single part or separate parts—the Protector and the Controller. The part or parts respond to protect us by modifying our behavior or by controlling our environment. Unfortunately, the Protector-Controller is responding based on what they learned in the first four years and are overreacting or reacting inappropriately to the current situation. These are significant constructs that are often relevant when treating difficult issues.

This section is a verbatim description of what I did when I first explored these constructs. Some of the constructs that I initially developed and which are described here were later changed as my working knowledge increased. This section is intended just to give an example of how I worked with the subconscious to develop these constructs. It is important to remember that this is only an example and not accurate. Read Chapter 4-24 to obtain the current approach for treating Predispositions.

Problem-solving as it is illustrated here is a questionable science. Read this to observe the problem-solving style, but don't believe any of the content of the exercise, because I found later that some of the metaphors and ideas I had at the time when I was developing the Process Healing theory were not entirely accurate. This is an actual example of my problem-solving process. I have added comments to bring the content a little closer to my current theory. Working with the subconscious and imagining causes and explanations for problems often results in unusual ideas being developed that are later discarded. However, even the content discarded from exploratory work often results in positive changes in the patient and provides significant contributions to the model.

My colleague Liz Medearis (personal communication, March 2, 2001) coaxed me into the following exploration of Hal and Sidra Stone's subpersonalities. She started by teaching me about the Stone's ideas and work with subpersonalities (Stone and Stone, 1989). She did this by working on my personal issues.

The subpersonality, in this context, consists of parts that give Predispositions learned in Memory II. The subpersonality consists of the Protector-Controller as one or separate parts, and pairs of parts that have opposite functions, such as love and hate. Certain experiences will trigger these Predispositions to warp behavior in a positive or negative way. Other Predispositions can manage brain activity, like the Predisposition to dissociate negative experiences in the Active Experience. The following is a rough description of Stone's treatment process that Medearis carried out with me. I'll describe how I related it to Process Healing by exploring the concepts and asking the subconscious leading questions.

This exploration occurred while Liz Medearis and I were talking on the telephone. Liz and I discussed subpersonalities and identified three of my subpersonalities (Controller, beach bum, and inner critic) that were relevant to some of my issues. Liz then explained that the intervention required me to assume different directions in my swivel chair and associate or anchor each direction with a subpersonality part when she communicated with it. I swiveled on my chair to one of the three different locations on my desk—right, left, or center, to associate each position with one subpersonality part. I had the fourth position, facing away from my desk, to talk with Liz.

Liz worked with the different parts and negotiated change by having me shift to the different directions associated or anchored to the part with whom she was working. After she completed negotiations, she did a treatment process. First she directed me to feel and assess the somatosensory experience of the two parts that were communicating in each chair position. Then she asked the parts to move next to each other in respective halves of the body. Again, I assessed the feeling. Then she asked to have half of the feeling of each part to overlap my body. Again, I assessed the feeling. Supposedly this breaks down the dissociative barrier and allows both parts to experience each other and to integrate partially. Homework was given to consciously attend to the intrusions of both parts and make a free choice about what to do with respect to the intrusions. To me this was confusing but interesting, because of the idea of subpersonalities. I didn't do my homework.

Here are some of the processes or parts in my subpersonality that were discovered by questioning my subconscious:

> Protector–Controller [A significant aspect in all people]
> Controller–enforcer
> Pusher–beach bum
> Pleaser–soul reality
> Joy–rational mind
> Creative being–inner critic
> Perfectionist–sloth
> Responsible–irresponsible

Now, I didn't know what to make of this model, so after we got off the telephone I did the following internal inquiry to find out more about the subpersonality, what it affected, and how to treat the negative subpersonality parts, namely the negative side of the subpersonality pairs. The inquiry I did below played some role in my work with the subpersonality. However, after I figured out how to treat the Protector-Controller and the negative Predispositions (subpersonality parts), the details about Predispositions became irrelevant.

Below is the relatively unedited transcript of the notes that I made of what occurred as I explored these possibilities with my subconscious. It is an example of how I asked leading questions of the subconscious as well as a record of my development of this segment of Process Healing. It is also an example of how I used my own processes to clarify questions about details of the model used with Process Healing.

T: **Can the subconscious help with what Liz was prescribing—namely, to become aware of subpersonality introjects, to recognize and ask the opposite's response, then to use free choice of how to behave?**

S: **Yes.**

I was not sure what I was asking here. I did not know the nature of the subpersonality. I fished around to see if the subconscious was familiar with any neural activity called the subpersonality that had positive and negative Predisposition pairs.

T: **Shall I develop a protocol to use in Process Healing?**

S: **Yes.**

T: **Is an aspect of the subpersonality one of the difficulties in deprogramming torture survivors caused by the "committee" obstructing change?**

S: **Yes.**

Oops, a deprogramming intrusion. I originally imagined the Protector-Controller was a committee consisting of the Protector and Controller. When the torture begins at an early age during the development of Memory II, the Protector-Controller and Predispositions would serve as barriers objecting to change. With ongoing pain, these parts would choose to have pain so that changing the pain is a barrier to treatment. Since they have significant influence on behavior, deprogramming becomes difficult.

T: **Does Jane's Ghetto model (see Frankel and O'Hearn, 1996) address the committee?**

S: **Yes.**

T: **Is there a quicker way to treat the interconnections and remove barriers caused by the committee?**

S: **Yes.**

T: **Can we do it in a simple protocol?**

S: **Yes.**

T: **Is the subpersonality in the memory running the Active Experience?**

S: **Yes.**

We were talking about Memory II. At this point, I did not have constructs such as the Basic Neurostructure or Memory I and II in my theory.

T: **Are these aspects of the subpersonality developed in the first five years of life?**

S: **Yes.**

T: **Is there much added after that?**

S: **No.**

T: **Is the goal: "Treat all the members (negative parts) of the subpersonality so they have the flexibility to work together to create overt and covert behavior and meet the basic needs of the individu-**

al and give the person power to run the body either consciously or unconsciously"?

S: **Yes.**

I forgot I did this until I reread my notes.

T: **Is there more to the goal than this?**

S: **No.**

T: **Will this bring self-awareness and consciousness of our Predispositions?**

S: **Yes.**

T: **Would one way of doing this be by treating and integrating all the opposing parts?**

S: **Yes.**

T: **Do all protection parts want treatment?**

S: **Yes.**

I find the Protector-Controller initially shows some resistance to treatment. Also, I later discovered that the Protector and Controller could be separate parts.

T: **After treating and integrating all the opposing parts, should the subconscious integrate them with the protection part?**

S: **Yes.**

I forgot that I did this too.

T: **Would it be more difficult with programmed people?**

S: **Yes.**

Oh, the intrusion again.

T: **With programmed people, would you just treat all the opposites and not integrate them?**

S: **Yes.**

T: **Can it be this simple?**

S: **Yes.**

T: **Should I refer to this as the primary subpersonality?**

S: **Yes.**

T: **If I do this on myself, will I notice differences immediately?**

S: **Yes.**

I didn't notice any difference, although my subconscious did.

T: **Are there more interventions I have to do to promote change?**

S: **No.**

T: **Was my speculation correct that the parts work that I did with Process Healing in the past dealt mainly with the memory of the**

Main Personality (Memory III) **and the parts work had little to do with the memory that runs the Active Experience?**

S: **Yes.**

I later learned that Basic Neurostructure, not memory, works on the Active Experience and the Active Experience consists of all neural activity in the brain and body. Earlier, I thought that Memory II ran the Active Experience. However, the response to this question was partially true. My previous parts work did not affect Memory II.

T: **So, is it true the memory that runs the Active Experience forms in the first five years of life? Then is it true that the Main Personality continues to form with the "memory that runs the Active Experience"** (Memory II) **remaining almost unchanged from then on?**

S: **Yes.**

This response is consistent with my patients' responses to this question. With my lack of clarity in understanding what is truly happening, it is remarkable that any of the metaphors I made up were as effective as they are. Remember, Basic Neurostructure runs the Active Experience. Memory II does not run the Active Experience, but it does, to some extent, distort all memories and behavior created from the Active Experience.

T: **Is this true for psychotic behaviors?**

S: **Yes.**

T: **Are psychotic behaviors learned in the first five years of life caused by the subpersonality?**

S: **Yes.**

This is worth exploring.

T: **Is this always true?**

S: **Yes.**

Although I got a "Yes" from my subconscious, I know that treating psychosis is not this simple.

T: **Will there have to be much negotiating with the subpersonality to get agreement to treat and integrate?**

S: **No.**

This seemed true. The Predisposition parts of the "subpersonality" are easy to treat, but the Protector-Controller can be difficult to treat.

T: **Is working with psychotics more complicated than working with normal adults?**

S: **No.**

Wrong—or I haven't discovered the structure or key to clearing psychotic behavior. If it is a dissociative-based psychosis, then there is generally no problem understanding the course of treatment. However, treating psychosis in any form is not easy.

T: **Do I have to negotiate with the subpersonality before I ask for the treatment and integration?**

S: **No.**

T: **Should treating the subpersonality be the first task I do in therapy?**

S: **Yes.**

I hadn't been doing this.

T: **Should I do it after I get the autotreatment set up?**

S: **Yes.**

T: **Will this make a significant impact on people?**

S: **Yes.**

T: **Would this be OK to do with a DID patient?**

S: **Yes.**

T: **Could a field barrier get in the way?**

S: **Yes.**

T: **Can I simply ask, "Subconscious, can you negotiate and treat all members of the subpersonality in the memory (Memory II) that affect the Active Experience in a safe, respectful, and self-empowering way?"**

S: **Yes.**

Remember, this is not an accurate statement of the question (see Chapter 4-24).

T: **Could there be any barriers to reaching this goal?**

S: **No.**

This is not true. I have found that Layered Memories in Memory II and fields can cause barriers for treating Predispositions.

T: **Shall I ask for integration in the same question?**

S: **No.**

T: **Shall I ask, "Protector, will you now integrate with all these treated members of the subpersonality?"**

S: **Yes.**

T: **Will I notice a difference?**

S: **Yes.**

T: **Will the differences be subtle in my experience?**

S: **Yes.**

T: **Will I respond differently to different situations because of this work?**

S: **Yes.**

T: **When Liz works with me again, will she notice a difference in how the parts work?**

S: **Yes.**

Oops! I noticed something that suggested that I was not talking to the subconscious. I used the indirect question method to make direct contact with the subconscious to try to figure out what was happening. Without writing out the detail, I asked the following as a non-question.

T: **Am I being deceived?**

S: **Yes.**

Again, I asked the following in the non-question format.

T: **Is it the Protector who is deceiving me?**

S: **Yes.**

Why did I ask this question? It just popped into my thoughts.

T: **Can I talk to the Protector?**

S: **Yes.**

T: **Can you treat the other parts of the subpersonality?**

P: [Protector] **Yes.**

What? This response didn't ring true to me. I asked with another non-question.

T: **Subconscious, can the Protector treat the other parts of the subpersonality?**

S: **No.**

T: **Is there a part in the memory running the Active Experience that can treat the parts in the subpersonality?**

S: **Yes.**

Again, I resort to asking a non-question.

T: **Is there a part in the memory running the Active Experience that can treat the parts in the subpersonality?**

S: **Yes.**

At that time, I labeled it "healer."

T: **Healer, did you learn how to do this when I taught the subconscious how to heal?**

S: **Yes.**

This seemed reasonable, but it turned out that this "healer" was the subconscious. The use of healer is a carryover from the past. I was mistaken at the time. It was another metaphor for subconscious.

T: **Healer, will I have to negotiate with the parts to heal them?**

S: **No.**

T: **Can we heal them just straight on?**

S: **Yes.**

T: **If you heal them without asking, will they be angry?**

S: **No.**

Later it occurred to me that, without reinforcement and punishment, there was no executive function in Predispositions so they are simply habit-like memories that can be easily treated. I asked the following with a non-question to be sure I was getting the correct answer.

T: **Asking any part, is it all right to ask the healer part in the memory of the Active Experience to heal the parts of the subpersonality?**

S: **Yes.**

T: **Is it true there is a part in the memory running the Active Experience that learned the treatment procedure when the subconscious learned it, and therefore knows how to heal by using it?**

S: **Yes.**

T: **Can I just ask the healing part, "Healing part in the memory that runs the Active Experience, please negotiate and treat all members of the subpersonality in the memory of the Active Experience, in a safe, respectful, and self-empowering way?"**

S: **Yes.**

I asked the following as a non-question.

T: **Healer part in the memory that runs the Active Experience, can you negotiate and treat all members of the subpersonality in the memory that runs the Active Experience in a safe, respectful, and self-empowering way?**

S: **Yes.**

T: **Can the part that heals integrate the parts after they are all treated?**

S: **Yes.**

I asked with a non-question.

T: **Can the part that heals integrate the parts after they are all treated?**

S: **Yes.**

T: **Could this intervention be a way to deal with functions or learnings in the memory that runs the Active Experience by using prompted or self-generated metaphors representing different functions?**

S: **Yes.**

It turns out the healer part was the subconscious. When I was creating constructs, I believed there was a healer part associated with each construct. Since then, I have found that there is only one subconscious, and I now work on that assumption. Whenever I find other subconscious fragments, as in System Fragments, in the Emotion System, or Layered Memories, I have the subconscious treat and join them with the primary subconscious. After months of experience, my general strategy to treat the Predisposition is given in Chapter 4-24.

I have learned much since I first explored with my subconscious how to identify and treat Predispositions. Though many interventions in this section are not correct, the incorrect concepts or metaphors were caused by my ignorance at this point in the development of my theory. My subconsciouses answers were based on my experience and honestly reflected my lack of knowledge up to that point. This example clearly shows that the subconscious is responsive to metaphors, even when they are later discovered to be inaccurate. I try to remind myself often that my theory and all other theories are simply metaphors, and they all have some element of truth. However, taken alone, they are all misleading. One way to evaluate interventions is to see how effective they are in treatment. Even when the interventions work, I always believe there are metaphors that will cause broader, more complete, and quicker changes.

Summary

This chapter gave the general interventions for your use in problem-solving when treating yourself or others. Included also is some of my own processing while developing some of the theory behind the Process Healing Method. Many of the treatment interventions I used early in developing Process Healing are now no longer used. As I gain more experience, I find more inclusive interventions that work faster.

I routinely use information in Chapters 6-1 through 6-7 when working with complex problems in people. I find myself increasingly treating without asking permission (Chapter 6-12). It seems respectful and tempers my impatience. Asking the non-question is useful because it saves a lot of time (Chapter 6-13). In the next chapter, you will learn about structures and trauma-causing structures.

Chapter 7

Interventions with Parts

Dissociative and amnesic parts are nothing more than memories. I try to treat these parts with respect; however, I pointedly avoid entering discussions in therapy about their role in the personality or about the trauma that created such parts. Sometimes the part wants to talk and I talk just enough to be respectful, but not too much. I find mapping a dissociative personality is unnecessary because I do not particularly need the information to treat the personality successfully. I avoid unnecessary dialogue by talking about parts as being normal and about the development of the personality. I go on to describe the advantages of healing and the safe treatment methods for intense emotions. I also attribute dysfunctional behavior to the survival demands that were present in the traumatic situation where it was learned. I normalize all the behavior the patient demonstrates, both the good and the bad, and let the patient know that the behavior, no matter how odd or unacceptable, was normal for the trauma situation. However, I also acknowledge that the problem behaviors displayed or reported are disruptive at this time in life for the Main Personality.

The memories for dissociative or amnesic parts are in Memory III. Remember from Chapters 3 and 5 that each part has a unique memory structure. The structure of the part has associations with memories that as a whole cause some form of internal or external behavior or neural activity. Recall that all dormant memories are always available to be triggered. This state of availability is the reason that, when I mentioned a bicycle, you had an intrusion of the memory of riding a bicycle. The memory activates and becomes active in the Active Experience. The dormant memory was responsive to an event, cue or stimulus that was similar to the content or Emotion Memory associated *with* its structure. This is also true for both dissociative and amnesic parts.

When there is a stimulus that matches the content or emotions of the part, the part triggers or floods into the Active Experience. It becomes active in the conscious or unconscious experience, or both, and causes some conscious or unconscious response. The subconscious can only treat and change memories that are active in our Active Experience. We do not experience dormant memories. Parts that are dormant and are not active in the Active Experience do not affect us. The content and emotions of parts are protected from change when they are dormant.

It is easy to change the content of memory. If I ask you to feel the love of your first cat, you may get an internal picture of the cat and have warm feelings. A tweak on your big toe adds the tweak to the memory of your cat. The content of the memory changed. Later, if I tweak the toe while talking about surfboarding, then the memory of your cat and associated feelings will flood into your experience (Dilts, Grinder, Bandler, and DeLozier, 1980). It is interesting to consider that everything we think and do causes flooding of collages of memories triggered by some cue in the Active Experience. Some of these flooding memories are assembled in collages that cause what we think and do.

Parts created by trauma or painful situations are just memories with unique structures. The structures have associations with many behaviors that are also used by our Main Personality. Language, muscle movements, speech and the emotions of an amnesic part can all be similar to the behavior shown by the Main Personality.

There are some important properties of parts that you should know about. Any content in the memory of the part can trigger or activate the part. When I say to an alcoholic patient, "I want to stop drinking," the phrase triggers parts and memories related to drinking into the patient's Active Experience. It does not matter to the patient's brain if I make the statement or the patient makes it. Therefore, when I use specific words to activate the Memory that I want to treat, I am using this property of the brain.

Example:
Deliberate torture

Some torture survivors have been deliberately taught to have some very angry parts that are difficult to control. These parts can have male or female names or be animals. Often, these are homicidal or suicidal parts. In one patient, I discovered that the person who created these angry parts also created other parts that could deactivate these angry parts. These deactivation parts had a deactivation code and were created by using relatively little pain. Working with this hypothesis, I eventually discovered that if I learned the name of the angry part—say, "George"—I could access the part with the deactivation code in the following way.

In this example, I had trouble getting George out of the Active Experience because he was running the body. Fortunately, I had previously used eye movements (EMDR) to associate a wall knock with the relatively strong, healthy part that usually ran the body. I put George to sleep by knocking on the wall to trigger in or activate the healthy part to push George to the dormant state—out of the Active Experience. I said then, "I would like to talk to the part that has 'George' and 'deactivate' in its program." The deactivation part became active and, after I obtained rapport, I would get the deactivation code and the fake deactivation code and then use the code to deactivate George. The patient felt waves passing through his brain whenever we deactivated these parts. From this case, you can see that it is relatively easy to use the content of memories as triggers to speed up treatment by using words to activate the memories you want to treat. When the memories are active, the subconscious can tag the memories and parts and treat them later.

Table of contents for this chapter

Summary

Identifying Parts

7-1 Looking for parts and noticing behavior

I have learned to listen carefully to my patients for what they say about body sensations, fleeting emotions, or any other strange verbal or physical responses that may occur. If a strange response looks distracting or problematic, I always ask to talk to the part that is causing the response. Usually, I get a reply to the effect that it was caused by a part, and then I continue to treat that part and all other similar parts. Invariably, the observed behavior that caught my attention goes away after treatment. Some of the observations that can lead to identifying parts to treat include: the sudden experience of an emotion, twirling hair, widening of the eyes, a look of dissociation, a chronic feeling, body sensation, chronic emotion, and muscle tension. Here is another example:

T: **Subconscious, can I talk to the parts that are bouncing your knees?**

S: **Yes.**

T: **Are these parts willing to accept treatment?**

S: **Yes.**

T: **Please treat these parts.**

S: **Yes.**

Notice that I spoke as though there were many active parts. I try to speak using plurals, like saying parts, to be more efficient. I believe that it speeds up treatment.

When a patient describes getting upset, having a blind rage, feeling numb, feeling depressed, or any other disturbing experience or activity, I always explore the experience with him or her. I want to know exactly how the patient experienced the change from feeling OK to feeling different. This could be a dissociative or amnesic part or memory triggered into the conscious experience. By carefully exploring the shift in consciousness, I can get some insight into the memory process that caused the shift. Unless I think it's a field barrier, I always refer to whatever caused the change as a part or parts as a way to keep the therapy simple. This line of questioning helps me to identify a dissociative experience. After I identify what I think is an experience caused by parts, I always ask the following question.

T: **Subconscious, can I talk to the part that gave the experience of depression?**

S: **Yes.**

I usually get a "Yes" and continue to treat and join the part with the Main Personality. If I get a "No," I problem-solve (see Chapter 6).

Thought intrusions revealed by the patient can also suggest dissociative or amnesic parts. Some examples include: "I have to stop therapy," "I can't do this now," "This doesn't work," "Nothing is going to change," or "That guy is a nerd." Here is an example of treating a thought intrusion.

T: **Subconscious, can I talk to the part that said, "I have to stop therapy"?**

S: **Yes.**

T: **Would this part like to be treated?**

S: **Yes.**

Take care of the part by either treating the part or problem-solving until it is treated. A word of caution: These kinds of barrier statements ("I can't do this," "I can't change, I have to have pain," etc.) can often be easily treated, however they also can be the entry into structured systems caused deliberately by some group or organization, so be prepared!

Sometimes you may encounter a protective part that may challenge you, literally. The best approach is to reassure the part that, after the painful emotions are removed, the positive protective behaviors will be strengthened with positive emotions. These behaviors will be available to the Active Experience after joining with the Main Personality because they are motivated by the positive emotions. They will be triggered appropriately by a relevant situation and may be used to create behavior. For this reason, I remind the subconscious to strengthen the motivation of those protective behaviors with positive emotions to make them available in a threatening environment.

With depression, obsessions or other personality features that are hard to treat, I look for barriers caused by trauma-based structures described in Chapter 8.

7-2 Working with parts causing issues

This is important to remember. When working with depression, obsessions, compulsions, addictions, and other intrusions, the subconscious can treat all the parts that are active that cause the problem. However, you must remain alert because, invariably, there are more dormant parts that will awaken later and cause the same symptoms. Expect to see the problem in the next session or many sessions later. When issue-related parts awaken, the patient will experience the issue again.

I always try to forewarn the patient that parts, similar to those that we have treated, may wake up days or weeks later. Usually, the parts or memories that cause later intrusions are easy to treat. On the other hand, in special cases you may find parts that cause later intrusions to be even harder to treat. These situations call for creative problem-solving.

One can activate memories related to an issue by using some quality or aspect of the issue to trigger and activate more parts associated with the issue you want to treat.

T: **Subconscious, please treat all parts associated with hair-pulling** (or any other content of the issue) **safely and respectfully and join them with the Main Personality.**

S: **Yes.**

Always do a Massive Change History and everything after an intervention with parts until you are confident the patient's subconscious will do it automatically.

Another intervention to increase efficiency in the treatment process is to ask the subconscious to use the content and emotions of the parts already treated to trigger and activate more memories and parts related to the issue.

T: **Subconscious, please use the content and emotions of the parts you have treated to trigger in more parts and memories. Please tag the active parts and memories and treat them in the correct order.**

S: **Yes.**

There is no real way to know if this works, although the patient's subconscious always confirms this procedure. Most patients feel the treatment process start after this intervention. After you ask for this intervention several times, it will usually become automatic for the patient's subconscious.

Here are other interventions that I routinely ask the subconscious to do when treating parts:

T: **Subconscious, please tag all beliefs, memories, and parts that become active and have negative motivation between now and the next session. When possible, treat these tagged memories one after the other in the correct order.**

S: **Yes.**

T: **Subconscious, please strengthen all positive coping behaviors and beliefs before joining a part with the Main Personality.**

S: **Yes.**

T: [Done] **Subconscious, after treating the parts, please do a Massive Change History and everything and treat any Shadow Memories related to this issue.**

S: **Yes.**

When the subconscious treats parts, the patient can sometimes feel some of the symptoms of the trauma. In addition, the treatment process can be so intense that it results in an uncomfortable headache for the patient. It is important to let the patient know that, when a physical symptom or headache is too intense, it is possible to ask the subconscious to slow the rate of treatment or to move the symptom into the unconscious during the treatment process.

T: **Subconscious, please move the pain of the symptom into the unconscious.**

or

T: **Subconscious, please slow the rate of treatment so I don't have these symptoms.**

S: **Yes.**

Treatment can result in fatigue due to all the brain activity, so the patient may become drowsy or fall asleep during the session. This fatigue can continue between sessions when the subconscious continues to treat the patient intensely. I routinely forewarn patients that the treatment experience can last several days, including feelings of fatigue in the brain, or even occasional trauma symptoms. I remind them to ask the subconscious to slow the rate of treatment or give me a telephone call if they ever feel too upset.

7-3 Use of body language to trigger parts

I attended a seminar in which Pat Ogden showed how she worked with trauma (Ogden, Nijenhuis, and Steele, 2002). She had the patient engage in postures that triggered emotional responses, with which she then worked.

I tried this with a patient who had been living with a man who was hurting her physically. The patient said, "I lived with a batterer. After the last trauma, I left and, since then, I have never drunk so much in my life." She clearly identified the trauma-based changes stemming from her experience. We catalogued all the changes that she noticed after leaving the batterer. These included a decreased tolerance for alcohol, increased urge for drinking, less sensitivity to insults, more distorted thinking, and more effort to be rid of any trauma-based experience. She also noticed that she was pushing people away and was not asking for help.

I treated the issue of pushing people away in the following way. I used Process Healing in combination with Ogden's approach by having the patient engage in a series of postures that triggered the emotional responses related to the issues of pushing people away and not asking for help. First I asked:

T: **Subconscious, please treat all parts and memories that are not ready to accept treatment in all areas of your life.**

S: **Yes.**

Sometimes you will do interventions that you don't understand. This intervention statement was an example of one of those times. Intuitively, I asked the subconscious to treat the parts and memories not ready for treatment, the patient immediately felt processing. The immediate processing confirmed that the statement was having some "positive" effect.

Next, I asked the patient to role-play (physically) the act of pushing someone away. The patient took a position that was similar to pushing someone away.

T: **Subconscious, please tag and treat beliefs, memories and parts that arise while pushing someone away.**

S: **Yes.**

I asked the patient to role-play (physically) reaching out for help. She had difficulty doing this, but made a symbolic reaching-out gesture with her arms.

T: **Subconscious, please tag and treat beliefs, memories and parts that arise while reaching out for help.**

S: **Yes.**

The use of body-oriented methods and Process Healing appear compatible. The body poses were symbolic of the barriers that she was feeling in her life. By assuming trauma-related poses, the patient elicited traumatic memories seemingly associated with that body metaphor. One can ask the subconscious to tag and treat the elicited traumatic memories. This was an experimental intervention for me but may be useful for those who engage in body work. Under the right circumstances, I will use a body-oriented method to facilitate treatment.

7-4 Similar parts always activate later

When we use an intervention to try to elicit and treat all the active parts, we usually don't elicit all the parts for that specific issue.

Other parts with the same issue activate later and the issue resurfaces. Treating the memories that cause an issue may be like peeling an onion. After we treat the primary memories that have intense emotions, then, later, memories with less intense emotions can become active in the Active Experience. Again, I forewarn my patients about the emergence of additional parts; treating intrusions today does not mean we have treated all intrusions. This discovery of more parts often occurs later when treating depression and obsessive or compulsive behaviors. Here is an example of this.

I worked with a patient for two years, treating a number of serious issues. One of his presenting problems was that he compulsively pulled out patches of his hair. He had to wear a hat to hide his bald spots. This compulsion was a difficult problem because it did not seem motivated by negative emotions. Through the following sessions we were able to learn that, when he was 15 years old, a spontaneous ejaculation occurred that allegedly caused the compulsion to pull out his hair. Other trauma in his life had already established the tendency to create new amnesic parts easily. Many parts contributed to the hair-pulling issue and other problems. We treated a great number of hair-pulling parts before the hair-pulling stopped between sessions. He did not pull his hair for two weeks—and then pulled another patch. We treated more parts. Then, after about six weeks with no hair-pulling, he pulled another patch. Again, we treated the parts that were pulling hair. Nothing happened for about three months, but then the symptom returned. I treated more parts. This is how treatment progressed until I had treated most, if not all, of the hair-pulling parts. The intervals between treatments increased until there were no longer any episodes of hair-pulling.

I have seen the same problem occurring with other behaviors, as in auditory intrusions, addictive behavior, bulimic behavior, and compulsive behaviors like repeatedly checking to see if a door is locked. It is important to prepare the patient for the possibility of re-emerging symptoms.

Parts Procedures

7-5 Treating parts and memories with common properties — The Structure Procedure

Neural associations link parts and memories with common properties. I call this network of associations for some property a *structure* (see Figure 7-1, next page). An association structure is the basis for state

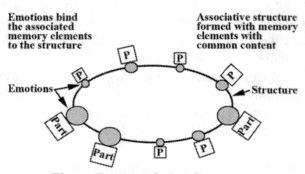

Emotions bind
the associated
memory elements
to the structure

Associative structure
formed with memory
elements with
common content

Emotions

Structure

Part

Part

Part

Figure 7-1 Association Structure

dependencies, which involve associations formed in situations with common content or emotions. An example of such a structure is what we see in Ego States. An Ego State is active when you notice yourself behaving differently in a church than you would in a beer parlor. On the other hand, severe trauma experiences like those inflicted in an abusive home, or in war or warlike experiences and so forth, cause dissociative and amnesic parts and other painful memories that are all associated in a structure. The common content or emotions of the memories from these experiences associate to form a structure.

The emotions associated *with* the memory structures bind the memories to the association structure. The aspects associated in a structure include parts, beliefs, Layered Memories, and memories of experience and so forth. These are called the memory elements of the structure. When the subconscious treats the emotions that bind the memory elements in the structure, the subconscious is also treating the emotions of the memory elements associated in the structure. Structures of torture survivors are more difficult to treat because some of the parts are highly motivated to protect the structure.

What was surprising to me was that when the subconscious treats the emotions holding the structure together, the emotions of the memory elements associated in the structure diminish in strength. The end result of treating the emotions of the structure is that the association of the memory elements in the structure breaks down and becomes disconnected. After the structure falls apart, the subconscious can tag all the loose memory elements from the structure—the memories and parts previously associated in the structure. Then, the subconscious can systematically treat all the tagged parts, one after the other, usually without difficulty. Because the emotions of the beliefs, parts, and memories in the structure are already partially treated, there are fewer barriers for treatment when treating these tagged memory elements.

Treating the memory elements of structures is not always easy. Sometimes, a few parts become active who continue to have strong emotions or have barriers to treatment that require problem-solving. Sometimes memories of the structure have field barriers.

Example:
Obsessive behavior

While working with a patient with an obsession, just for the heck of it, I asked the following question:

T: **Subconscious, are all the beliefs, memories, experiences and parts having to do with the obsession associated in a structure?**
S: **Yes.**

T: **Is it safe to treat the structure, and when it falls apart, to tag the memory elements and then treat them one after the other in the correct order?**
S: **Yes.**

T: **Please do it.**

The issue required more therapy, but the obsessive behaviors decreased dramatically.

In general, most other memory structures are suitable for treatment such as anger, short-fuse anger, frustration and agitation, depression, blocks to self-directed learning, residential school trauma, abusive relationships, abusive families, abuse in school, and so forth. There appears to be no danger in treating any structure that was normally formed by life experiences. However, if a structure was caused deliberately by systematic torture, then a therapist has to proceed carefully. Additional tips for treating structures based on torture are described in Flint (n.d.). The Structure Procedure can treat many memory elements (see Chapter 8-28 through 8-30). Memory elements include Belief Structures, Picture Structures, memory structures, parts with memory structures, Predispositions in Memory II, dysfunction in Memory I and Memory II. The Structure Procedure can help with dysfunction in other systems, such as memory elements in the Emotion System. Do a Massive Change History and everything after each intervention. If a negative belief is an element of the structure, ask the subconscious to compose a positive, self-empowering belief to replace the negative belief element of the structure.

T: **Subconscious, please compose a positive self-empowering belief to replace any negative belief that you treated and strengthen the positive, self-empowering belief with positive emotions until it is true.**
S: **Yes.**

7-6 Treating trauma memories through the Emotion System

Another way to treat many trauma-based parts and memories is first to treat the collage of emotions in the Emotion System caused by the trauma, then follow the associations from the collages back to the trauma memories and parts in Memory III, and then treat the associated memories and parts. Always do a Massive Change History and everything. Repeat this procedure with each collage of emotions memories associated *with* the trauma. Here is how to get started.

T: **Subconscious, is it safe to treat all the collages of emotions in the Emotion System associated *with* this trauma?**

S: **Yes.**

When you get a "No," problem-solve to figure out what has to be treated before you do this process.

T: **Subconscious, please treat a collage of emotions connected with this trauma, then follow the associations from the collage of emotions to the memory elements in Memory III, tag the memory elements associated *with* the collage, and then treat the memories one after the other. Then do a Massive Change History and everything.**

S: **Yes.**

You may have to treat active parts and a field here and there.

T: [Done] **Subconscious, please repeat this procedure with each collage of emotions associated *with* this trauma.**

S: **Yes.**

T: [Done] **Please do a Massive Change History and everything.**

S: **Yes.**

7-7 Treating the tendency to easily create new amnesic parts

Sometimes trauma damages various system structures and brain functions. This damage lowers the threshold of trauma required for the brain to mobilize and creates a new part. While working with a psychotic patient who had many parts, I discovered this problem of the brain routinely creating amnesic parts. I found that just treating parts without addressing the mechanism causing all the parts was a losing battle. The small traumas of day-to-day living were resulting in parts being created faster than I was able to treat them. Whenever someone yelled at this patient or he became angry, it appeared as if the brain mobilized to create a new part. Out of desperation to treat this tendency to easily create new parts, I resorted to the following:

T: **Subconscious, are parts created very easily?**
S: **Yes.**

I then went on to discover the procedure to stop the easy creation by asking leading questions. My patient had many parts. I wondered how it came to be that this patient created amnesic parts so easily. The patient told me that his mother told him that, when he was five years old, his father, while raising a garden hoe over the boy's head, yelled and threatened to kill him. He may have had a near-death experience that contributed to changes in the neural processes so that when his emotions got intense or someone yelled at him, this experience caused the easy creation of an amnesic part. Automatic creation of parts became a habitual response to any stressful situation because of the lowered threshold for brain mobilization. While simple flooding of intense emotions can cause a part, the easy creation of parts is caused by the flooding of emotions and the mobilization of other damaged brain structures. I estimated that he had more than 13,000 parts. I worked with the subconscious and learned how to treat the effects of the trauma so this easy creation of parts would no longer occur. I was eventually able to treat most of his parts (see Appendix VI).

I often find the easy creation of parts in psychotic patients, dissociative patients and patients with a personality disorder. When I work with patients who have parts, I normally use the following protocol to see if easy creation of parts is a problem. When the response is "No" to any of the following questions, I problem-solve to discover the cause for the "No." I often treat a barrier before I get the correct answer.

Below is a 16-step procedure that has been effective in stopping the easy creation of parts:

1. When I work with someone who has many parts or when I suspect easy creation, I assess the patient to see if parts are easily created by asking:

T: **Subconscious, does this patient have the tendency to create amnesic parts or other complex memory structures easily?**
S: **Yes.**

When the response is "Yes," I complete the following steps to stop easy creation of parts:

2. Early fixation caused by trauma before age three or four years can stop the gradual increase in the range of tolerance for negative emotional experience (Briere, 1991). The trigger threshold fixates at the age when the trauma occurred. This means that the Main Personality has not learned to manage emotions above the threshold. A lower and fixated trigger threshold (see Figure 7-2, next page) can contribute to the creation

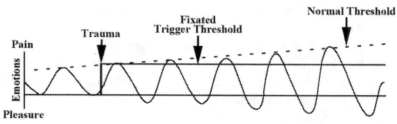

Figure 7-2 The Fixation of the Trigger Point

of parts with less than extreme fear. When the intensity of the emotions passes the trigger threshold, the more likely an amnesic part will be created by the flooding of emotions.

T: **Subconscious, was the range of emotional tolerance damaged to cause a low trigger threshold for mobilization?**

S: **Yes.**

T: **Subconscious, please do a Massive Change History from birth to now treating the trauma that caused the fixation of the threshold for mobilizing the brain. Then treat the effects of the fixation by doing a Massive Change History and everything and treat the Shadow Memories.**

3. The association process (or part) manages the activation of memories from the dormant state into the Active Experience. Trauma to the association process causes loose associations or concrete thinking. When trauma damages the associative part and allows the loose association of emotions, it contributes to easy creation of parts. When the patient experiences some strong emotions in the Active Experience, looseness in the association process allows the flooding of additional intense emotions into the Active Experience. The added emotions distort the Active Experience with the massive emotions contributing to the possibility that the brain will mobilize to survive. Here is how to treat this process.

T: **Subconscious, is the association process damaged, and does this contribute to the easy creation of parts?**

S: **Yes.**

T: **Subconscious, please treat the damaged memory in the association part and restore it to its normal function. Then do a Massive Change History and everything.**

I have found that I had to correct stored reversal (see Chapter 3-9-7) once when doing this procedure and, at other times, I had to clear some field barriers.

4. Diamond (1995) wrote about the thymus as a gland that responds to the quality of your environment. When a person is in a healthy

environment, the polarity of the thymus is positive; but when the environment is unhealthy, the polarity of the thymus is negative. It is not hard to speculate that the response of the thymus helps easy creation because the rapid change from positive to negative contributes to eliciting brain mobilization. Therefore, I have asked leading questions of the subconscious and determined that this hypothesis was correct and that treating the thymus is important.

T: **Subconscious, does the rapid change in polarity of the thymus contribute to rapid mobilization?**

S: **Yes.**

T: **Subconscious, please treat the trauma to the thymus that leads to a rapid change in the polarity of the thymus during emotional experiences.**

S: **Yes.**

5. What about Predispositions and the easy creation of parts in Memory III?

T: **Subconscious, are there Predispositions that contribute to easy creation?**

S: **Yes.**

T: **Subconscious, please treat the Predispositions in Memory II that respond to the presence of negative emotion in the Active Experience and support rapid mobilization.**

S: **Yes.**

6. Big traumas cause confusion in the Active Experience. Trauma to Memory II in the presence of confusion creates a Predisposition for confusion in the presence of trauma. With fairly intense emotions, the confusion caused by the Predisposition in Memory II contributes to mobilizing the brain. You can ask a question about this to see if the following intervention is needed.

T: **Subconscious, is there a Predisposition in Memory II that causes confusion that supports rapid mobilization?**

S: **Yes.**

T: **Subconscious, please treat the Predispositions in Memory II that cause confusion in the Active Experience when emotions get intense.**

S: **Yes.**

7. The amygdala and hippocampus structures are midbrain areas involved with mobilizing the brain in severe trauma (van de Kolk, Burbridge, and Suzuki, 1997). This damage sometimes causes hypersensitivity in the patient leading to exaggerated fear or anxiety responses.

T: **Subconscious, please treat the traumas to the memories running the midbrain and restore them to give normal emotional responses. Please do a Massive Change History and everything.**

S: **Yes.**

Sometimes, a field barrier associates to the memory running the amygdala.

T: **Subconscious, is there a field barrier distorting the function of the midbrain?**

S: **Yes.**

If the response is "Yes," the field barrier is treated.

8. Trauma can distort the neural activity in the forebrain right of center.

T: **Subconscious, please treat the trauma to the memory running the neural activity in the forebrain right of center. Please do a Massive Change History and everything.**

S: **Yes.**

9. I used my basic knowledge of neurostructure and trauma and guessed that the following neural area was important to treat.

T: **Subconscious, please treat the memory running the neural activity above the olfactory bulb. Then do a Massive Change History and everything.**

S: **Yes.**

Sometimes, I find field barriers with this intervention.

10. When the memory that runs the neurostructure near the right temple is distorted by trauma, the result can be an increase in the tendency to mobilize the brain.

T: **Subconscious, please treat the trauma to the memory that runs the neurostructure near the right temple. Then do a Massive Change History and everything.**

S: **Yes.**

11. The subconscious said that Basic Neurostructure working with the Active Experience promotes easy creation of parts.

T: **Subconscious, please treat the damage in the Basic Neurostructure of the Behavior System by adding and removing associations that promotes the easy creation of amnesic parts, then do a Massive Change History and everything.**

S: **Yes.**

12. It is unlikely, but there can be field barriers present that are associated with some memory that contributes to easy creation of parts.

When the trauma memory is activated, the field barrier activates and distorts the Active Experience by triggering intense emotions.

13. Trauma can distort the cellular memory in the entire brain.

I do not generally try to treat using the heart process. In this case, I was searching for whatever might work. My reasoning for using the heart field is that the heart emits a massive field and affects all cells in the body. I wanted to treat the cells, so I tried the following and it appeared to work. Since then I have used this intervention many times.

T: **Subconscious, please ask the heart process to treat the cellular memories damaged by trauma that support easy creation of parts, then do a Massive Change History and everything and treat the Shadow Memories.**

S: **Yes.**

14. Since all systems are interdependent, I reasoned that changes in one system would cause the need for changes in the other systems. To counter any negative effect, I do the following intervention to bring all systems up to date.

T: **Subconscious, please continue treating all the interconnections and responses of neural structures that we have addressed to provide a healthy neural condition. Please do a Massive Change History and everything.**

S: **Yes.**

15. Just to be sure, I ask the following question.

T: **Subconscious, please do a Massive Change History and everything with the new conditions and treat the Shadow Memories.**

S: **Yes.**

16. The changes made above may have caused changes relevant to all treatment interventions that were previously completed.

T: **Subconscious, please repeat all previous treatment interventions and then do a Massive Change History and everything.**

S: **Yes.**

Note: Though I don't usually do the following intervention, I have it here to show you that some accidents have unique effects on other brain structures. In order to complete treating the easy creation of parts, I had to treat one patient who had an auto accident that damaged or distorted the neurostructure of the Medulla. The following intervention completed the treatment for the easy creation of parts.

T: **Subconscious, please treat the trauma in the memory of the Medulla so it functions normally. Please do a Massive Change History and everything.**

S: **Yes.**

With this patient, this intervention stopped the easy creation of amnesic parts. In general, the 16 step procedure presented here has been effective in stopping easy creation of parts. However, I have been fooled and occasionally have to repeat the procedure. Another condition that causes easy creation of parts is given in Chapter 8-24.

7-8 Treating and integrating the dissociative and associative processes

Let us review dissociated memories. Memories can be active in either the conscious or unconscious Active Experience. In general, active memories are dissociated to become unconscious active memories. There is a dissociative process that causes dissociation. I believe that the dissociation process is a part that associates *with* all or some of the collage of memories of an active memory to cause all or part of the memory to be in active in the unconscious. The dissociative process operates like a part because it has our language and can be damaged by trauma.

With developing volitional behavior or executive function, before or after birth, a person learns dissociation as a skill to simplify the conscious experience. This dissociation process helps us focus our behavior and attention by dissociating irrelevant memories or skills and making them unconscious. Irrelevant memories in the conscious Active Experience would make the control of our thoughts and actions more difficult. The dissociation of an active memory makes the active memory unconscious—namely, the memory is still active in the Active Experience, but it is not in our conscious experience.

Focusing our thoughts, though, is a more complex process because the dissociation process usually works in tandem with the association process. Active memories and emotions in the Active Experience trigger dormant memories into the Active Experience. The association process filters or controls which dormant memories are triggered into the conscious or unconscious Active Experience. When patients have problems with intrusive thoughts while they are trying to read or focus their attention, I have found the associative and dissociative processes—both parts—are usually working independently. The dissociative process is being used to try to focus, but the associative part is letting intrusions into the conscious experience. These intrusions distract the person from focusing on the task. This problem can be helped by joining the parts. To explore, I often ask:

T: **Subconscious, are the association and dissociation processes independent?**

S: **Yes.**

I try to treat this problem by setting up rapport with both the dissociative and associative parts and then convincing them to accept treatment.

T: **Parts, when you are not working together, you are disturbing the Main Personality by making it difficult to focus and concentrate. This is frustrating and is a barrier to getting more satisfaction and less pain. Would you both be willing to have your trauma pain treated, have all your positive skills strengthened with positive emotions, and then join with each other so you can work together?**

S: **Yes.**

This usually works. Sometimes, however, there are other issues to address. When the association and dissociation parts are ready for treatment, continue with:

T: **Subconscious, can you treat and integrate the association and dissociation parts?**

S: **Yes.**

T: [Done] **Subconscious, please do a Massive Change History and everything.**

After integration, these parts work together to help the patient focus better on tasks. Patients usually say that they experience less distraction and are able to focus their attention better.

Example:

Distracting intrusions

Intrusions bothered this patient when she was trying to do a task at work. She had constantly intruding thoughts about what else she had to do. These intrusions distracted her from the task. The subconscious treated some parts related to this problem. When I talked further with the patient, she explained that she heard a voice just before the intrusions, "Oh, oh, here it comes." She could feel the start of the intrusion. The subconscious said that this verbal intrusion was not a part. I discovered that a Predisposition in Memory II gave this intrusion to the conscious experience. I had the subconscious treat the Predisposition. That was when I also discovered that there was a problem in the association and dissociation process. I treated and joined the independent processes. This ended the problem.

7-9 Treating trauma memories using the subconscious and the dissociative process

In adults, a person can voluntarily use the dissociation process to repress or hide painful memories. Remember the dissociative process responds like a part, but I am calling it a process to distinguish it from a normal part. It is more like a skill. Calling it a part would detract from the use of dissociation as the metaphor for the process that causes the conscious and unconscious activity in the Active Experience. The dissociation process can also dissociate painful memories involuntarily. When intense or recurring painful activities and memories happen and are subsequently dissociated, the dissociated memories can become a dissociative part. One day, while working with such a patient, I wondered if the dissociation process could remember all the dissociated negative memories and parts that had ever occurred. I was led to believe that it was possible and I asked the following of my patient:

T: **Subconscious, can you and the dissociation process work together and treat all the dissociated negative memories and parts from birth until now?**

S: **Yes.**

The response of the patient's subconscious suggested that the dissociation process and the subconscious could work together. Since then, I have used this intervention with patients for many years. Immediately after the intervention, most patients experience continuing treatment sensations. This intervention can be used to clear up negative memories that have a detrimental impact on our behavior.

More recently, I have been using the structure approach to do this intervention. The Structure Procedure seems more related to the way the brain works.

T: **Subconscious, can you see the structure of dissociated traumatic memories and parts?**

S: **Yes.**

T: **Please treat the emotions associated *with* the structure and, when the structure falls apart, tag and treat the elements of the structure in the correct order.**

S: **Yes.**

This intervention may be used to treat memories and tendencies implanted by hypnotic techniques. One example of this is the hypnotic implanting that can be observed in television advertising. Frequently, when patients learn to discriminate when they dissociate, they will often notice "buy me" reactions to some products in the grocery store—reactions learned via television. Memories and tendencies of this sort can be implanted by many other means.

7-10 Treating parts that help to run the body

Coconscious dissociated memories or amnesic parts, which have formed because of trauma, sometimes have positive behaviors or coping skills used to run the body. The motivation for the positive coping skills may come from the negative emotions learned in the trauma. By treating the negative emotions and integrating these parts, the patient runs the risk of losing some coping skills. After treatment, the emotions that motivated coping skills become neutral and leave the skills unmotivated. The end result is that the coping skills have little impact in the Active Experience. There are several ways to avoid this loss.

The following experience led me to recognize that some parts, motivated by pain, become active in order to contribute to positive coping skills useful to the Main Personality. In one case, I treated the parts and integrated them so fast that the patient ended up with no internal directions about how to cope with life in general. He did not produce behavior and became directionless. I suspect what happened was that the coping skills integrated with no associated emotions.

When coping skills join with the Main Personality without any associated emotions, no emotions remain to motivate the memory and the resulting coping response. Without some associated emotion, the coping responses will not carry much weight when behavior is created. Therefore, the positive coping responses are not available to participate in the creation of behavior. Now I take several steps to ensure the preservation of the positive coping responses formerly motivated by negative emotions.

First, treat the part and do not integrate it until the subconscious has associated positive emotions with the coping skills. The positive emotions will motivate the coping behaviors. This will support the coping response to be more relevant when active in the Main Personality and be more available during the creation of behavior.

Earlier in my learning, I asked the subconscious a few questions.

T: **Subconscious, does this part provide some positive coping skills?**

or

T: **Subconscious, does the part you are treating provide any positive coping skills?**

S: **Yes.**

Nowadays, I usually don't ask either of these questions but just give the intervention to strengthen positive coping skills in one statement.

T: **Subconscious, before joining this part with the Main Personality, please associate positive emotions with the positive coping skills to make them motivated when active in the Active Experience.**

S: **Yes.**

In cases where you are treating many parts, say the following:

T: **Subconscious, please treat these parts. Identify any coping skills that help the Main Personality function well in his or her world. Please associate enough positive emotions with these skills so they will work well when joined with the Main Personality. Then join the parts with the Main Personality. Please do a Massive Change History and everything.**

S: **Yes.**

Another approach is to assume there are positive coping responses in the part and ask the subconscious to associate positive emotions with the coping behaviors before integrating the part.

T: **Subconscious, please treat these parts, associate positive emotions with any positive coping behaviors, and then join these parts into the Main Personality.**

S: **Yes.**

Sometimes, treatment drastically weakens coping behaviors. The ignorance of others or oversight by a therapist may have produced integrated parts without strengthening the coping behaviors. This may leave the patient without coping behaviors. It is always important to strengthen the positive coping behaviors in a part prior to joining the part to the Main Personality. Fortunately, I learned from my own oversight that this can be done after the fact by making the following intervention.

T: **Subconscious, will you please do a Massive Change History and strengthen any weak coping skills with positive emotions so they will be more likely to be used in the creation of behavior?**

S: **Yes.**

Difficult Parts

7-11 A resistant young part wakes up

Young parts can wake up and feel that their function and presence in the person is important. They are not impressed with the benefits of treatment and refuse to deal with their pain. They may still feel very young, in spite of the physical age of the patient. They don't want to be treated. Sometimes, I do an intervention that creates confusion before I proceed to get the part to accept treatment and join with the Main Personality. The confusion is caused by taking a belief the young part has and then asking her to look at her current reality.

T: **Does this part want to heal?**

S: **No.**

T: [Resistant part—finally] **Part, do you know that you were created when you were little? That was many years ago. Look down at your legs and see that you have grown-up legs. After you are treated, you won't have pain and you can join with the Main Personality. Then you can run the body all day. Would you like treatment now?**

S: **Yes.**

It is not always this easy. There are many reasons for not wanting to heal. Sometimes I have to problem-solve for quite a while to find the key to getting the part to want to be treated.

7-12 Treating parts afraid to be active

With one patient, parts were popping in because the patient was getting healthy. But there were other parts that were afraid of getting healthier because they were afraid of waking up and becoming active in the Active Experience. They would put their eyes and ears into the Active Experience and then back out again because it felt unsafe for them. It was not possible to treat these parts directly. The subconscious said that there were 20 to 30 parts of this type. Some were punishing parts that often stopped the treatment from being effective. I did some problem-solving and the parts clearly did not want to be treated. I finally did the following:

T: **Subconscious, can we treat the structure of punishing parts? When the structure falls apart, please tag and treat the parts in the correct order.**

S: **Yes.**

By treating the structure, the treatment of the emotions weakened the resolve to not be treated. As the parts were treated, one after the other, I found that several parts were fragile and one feared that its trauma memory would traumatize the patient. These parts talked to the subconscious and eventually agreed to be treated.

7-13 Treating significant negative parts

It has been found that there can be significant negative parts that can give an assortment of negative emotions and behaviors to the patient. In one patient, we healed one significant negative part but another negative part remained untreated. She spent a week being stressed, moody, "snappy" and unhappy. The subconscious led me to the appropriate phrasing of a question in order to uncover significant negative parts.

T: **Subconscious, are there significant negative parts that need to be treated at this time?**

S: **Yes.**

T: **If I count up, can you tell me how many?**

S: **Yes.**

I counted up and the subconscious indicated how many parts there were. I continued to problem-solve and treat the parts. In this case, the patient's negative behavior was gone after the treatment.

7-14 Identifying parts with enormous pain—Fragile parts

Some patients have experienced frequent and severe trauma in childhood. When this happens, a part can learn to become active in the presence of all instances of severe pain and functions to take all trauma pain. The result is a part that has enormous pain and can have a distorted view of itself or life. Sometimes it is not easy to access these very fragile parts because they fear that they will flood the conscious experience and be damaging to themselves or others in the process. With patients who have a history of severe trauma, I always ask questions to see if there is a fragile part or a part that has taken all the extreme pain. There can be more than one part holding pain. It is important to look for them all and be aware that parts with intense emotions can take you by surprise when treating trauma. These parts can flood the conscious experience with powerful emotions or take over the body with suicidal, aggressive, or self-destructive acting-out.

The strategy for treating fragile parts involves being sensitive and identifying fragile parts and then being aware of different processes that can amplify the pain of the fragile parts. There are two ways fragile parts can be formed. The first is when a part experiences or takes all the pain during childhood; the second is when parts have had infantile rage.

The first problem is that by simply talking about a fragile part, one can cause the part to flood the conscious experience. Here is how I approach working with fragile parts to prevent getting in trouble with a flood of emotions.

T: **Subconscious, is there a part that has taken all the pain or feels extremely fragile?**

S: **Yes.**

T: **Is it safe to talk to that part without causing a flood of emotions?**

S: **Yes.**

With a "Yes," you continue carefully.

S: **No.**

T: **Subconscious, can you talk to that part without causing a flood of emotions?**

With a "Yes," continue carefully.

S: **No.**

T: **Subconscious, if we fill the Active Experience with safe parts, will it be safe for either you or me to talk to that part?**

With a "Yes," continue talking through the subconscious. Address any distorted images held by the part and any distortions in their current function. Normalize their fears by discussing the barriers for healing massive pain as described below.

The second way to have enormous pain is the presence of infantile rage. Infantile rage is often seen in patients with anorexia, control issues, or in personality disorders. Infantile rage may be potentially overwhelming to the whole system. Communication with parts with infantile rage has to be done carefully. The approach already outlined should be taken with parts with infantile rage. Take great care and caution when treating infantile rage because the flooding of emotions could cause damage to you, your office, or the patient.

T: **Subconscious, are there parts with infantile rage or parts that were present to take the pain?**

S: **Yes.**

When the therapist tries to work directly with massive emotions or infantile rage, the following three barriers can either block treatment or make treatment difficult. One or all of the barriers may be present.

1. Trauma in the association-dissociation part

The association-dissociation part may be pointedly keeping the fragile parts' rage out of the conscious experience and will continue to do so at all costs. Explaining the function of this barrier usually resolves the barrier.

T: **Subconscious, are the association and dissociation parts working hard to keep this rage or emotion out of the Active Experience?**

S: **Yes.**

T: **Well, the association and dissociation parts have always worked hard to keep this infantile rage out of the Active Experience and this strategy was important. This was important because the flood of emotions would retraumatize the Main Personality and create new parts. The association and dissociation parts did a good job.**

Explain the positive functions of the association-dissociation process and get rapport.

T: **Infantile rage can be treated safely with the help of the association and dissociation processes. They know how to control fragile parts carefully and prevent emotional flooding. They can use this skill to help the subconscious orchestrate a very slow and safe treatment rate of the infantile rage.**

Then make the following intervention.

T: **Subconscious, can you work with the association-dissociation part and safely treat this infantile rage? Please review the treatment plan before you begin treating.**

S: **Yes.**

This treatment is similar to the treatment in Chapter 3-5-2, which has added features.

2. A Predisposition barrier

Memory II has learned a Predisposition to keep this rage out of the Active Experience. Treat the memory that causes this Predisposition by asking the subconscious the following:

T: **Subconscious, are there Predispositions in Memory II that are keeping the infantile rage out of the Active Experience?**

S: **Yes.**

T: **Subconscious, please treat the Predispositions in Memory II that work to keep the infantile rage out of the Active Experience.**

S: **Yes.**

Example:

Uncovering and treating infantile rage:

T: **Subconscious, is some infantile rage underlying the problem behavior?**

S: **Yes.**

The part is contacted using the cautious approach described above. If the part wants to be treated and join the Main Personality, then the one can start working with the subconscious to determine the barriers and safeguards that may have to be taken.

T: **Subconscious, is there is a field barrier associated with the trauma underlying the rage?**

S: **No.**

If "Yes," assess and remove any field barriers.

T: **Subconscious, can you safely treat, in small increments, both the Predisposition that keeps this rage out of the Active Experience and the trauma memories causing the rage at the same time?**

S: **Yes.**

T: **Please do that.**

If "No," then do the following:

T: **Subconscious, is trauma in the association and dissociation parts blocking the treatment of the infantile rage?**

S: **Yes.**

Review Chapter 3-5-2 for the procedure for treating this barrier and intense emotions.

3. Field Influence

Field barriers can amplify the pain. The first step when treating fragile parts, then, is to determine if a field barrier is attached to the trauma memory. The field barrier activates when the trauma memory becomes active and triggers additional emotions that increase the rage. This results in disorganizing the Active Experience and blocking the treatment process. Since field barriers trigger relevant negative emotions independent of the emotions associated *with* the trauma itself, the active emotions in the Active Experience cause a barrier to treatment. Emotions caused by a field barrier can cause the part to flood the Active Experience. When a field barrier is present, treat the field barrier before treating the trauma.

T: **Is there a field barrier associated *with* this trauma?**

S: **Yes.**

When there is a field barrier associated with the trauma, use a treatment given in Flint (n.d.).

7-15 Parts causing psychotic behavior

One patient had a psychotic problem that involved the constant, intense intrusions of parts that simulated four significant people in her life. The intrusions reflected the interests of these people and had similar voices to four people she had known in the past: three previous boyfriends and the current girlfriend of one of the boyfriends. She was also bothered by parts simulating many other acquaintances, but their intrusions were much less intense.

Associated *with* these intrusions were kinesthetic sensations that created the experience that she was actually receiving speech from these people—in other words, thought intrusions. In addition, she felt that she was sending her thoughts to others, or thought broadcasting. She had been put on medication, but it had not stopped the psychotic intrusions. I dealt with her somatic experience of communicating and receiving thoughts by clearing parts in the Kinesthetic System (see Chapter 8-36). After the thought intrusion and broadcasting was treated, I then focused on treating the intrusive experiences. She thought these experiences were real, so I knew that beliefs would have to be treated to resolve this issue.

I started with the most annoying part.

T: **Subconscious, is Roscoe a part in Memory III?**

She said "No," but the subconscious knew otherwise.

S: **Yes.**

T: **Can you treat this part?**

S: **No.**

T: **Are there field barriers blocking the treatment of this part?**

I had some problem treating the field barriers, but by using the approaches in Flint (n.d.), I was able to clear the field barriers.

S: **Yes.**

T: **Are there a lot of Roscoe parts?**

S: **Yes.**

T: **Can you treat all the Roscoe parts, one after the other?**

S: **Yes.**

T: **Please do that.**

After some problem-solving, the three other major parts were treated. Additional parts simulating this group of people awakened in later sessions.

T: [Done] **Subconscious, are there beliefs that support her belief that her somatic experiences are real?**

S: **Yes.**

T: **Is there a structure of beliefs that can be treated?**

S: **Yes.**

T: **Please treat this structure of beliefs until they are false, and then compose and strengthen self-empowering beliefs to take their place. Then do a Massive Change History and everything.**

S: **Yes.**

I turned my attention to the minor players in her intrusions that she described as "all those other people." These were all people who she had known in the past. Before treating the "other people," I wondered if there was some unique type of easy creation that was causing these parts.

T: **Subconscious, are there ways that the simulated conversation with people with whom she comes in contact are learned as part-like or part structures?**

S: **Yes.**

T: **Is this caused by trauma to Basic Neurostructure, Memory I, and the creation of some Predispositions in Memory II?**

S: **No.**

I have had some experience so I make off-the-wall guesses. This time I was wrong, but when I am correct, it saves time. I would treat these structures in the usual way—Basic Neurostructure (see Chapter 8-37 through 8-41), Memory I (see Chapter 8-33), and Predispositions in Memory II (see Chapter 4-24). When I am wrong, I run through the possibilities of structures or process one at a time. In this case I was definitely wrong. I continued.

T: **Is there a constellation of System Fragments** (see Chapter 8-23) **that causes these parts?**

S: **Yes.**

T: **Please treat the constellation of System Fragments in the usual way.**

I guided the subconscious through the treatment procedure (see Chapter 8-23).

T: **Subconscious, have we finished treating and integrating the System Fragments causing these problems?**

S: **Yes.**

Now as I turned my attention to the minor parts, she experienced her inner world getting increasingly quiet.

T: **Subconscious, do you see a lot of "other people" parts that are intruding?**

S: **Yes.**

T: **Can you treat the "other people" parts that want to be treated one after the other?**

S: **Yes.**

I dealt with the people parts that did not want to be treated by the usual problems solving techniques (see Chapter 6).

With several more sessions, this woman was able to resume attending college at half time, concentrating on her studies. She started relating to others in a relatively normal way and experienced fewer psychotic symptoms. Four months after treatment ended, the intrusions were all but gone and she was tapering off the medication that hadn't stop the intrusions. However, this treatment was not a success. Later, the patient moved to another state, started having intrusions, consulted with a doctor and was put back on medication. My guess is that untreated parts that had been dormant at the time of seeing me became active. Further use of Process Healing may well have completely eliminated the issues over time.

Summary

This approach to working with parts takes the mystery out of doing this work. Usually, amnesic and dissociative parts are easy to treat because of the following incentives: getting more satisfaction or happiness and having less pain and having the opportunity to run the body from morning to night. This leverage makes it easy to convince parts that it is good to be treated and integrated. Though these approaches are not the last word on treating unusual or novel parts, this chapter gives the reader a good start to handle most parts issues that arise. As you will find in the next chapter, memory structures can complicate the treatment of parts. In addition, parts can be formed in other systems. The basic treatments for these unusual memory conditions are presented and will give ideas for treating structures yet to be discovered.

Chapter 8

Memory and Structures

Memories cause everything we think and do. Recall that each memory is a unique memory structure that is created with a collage of associations *with* previously learned memories—old memory structures. As we get older our memories are more complex just by virtue of having more of them to build on each other to behave in the increasingly complex environment. The structures are all normal but can present problems. The therapist can be challenged when he or she encounters a structure not previously encountered or covered specifically in this book. This chapter gives many examples of structures that will help in problem-solving. While you read the chapter, notice that the structures are frequently elaborations of previous structures. Mixing and matching old structures, so to speak, formed the new structures. You cannot make major errors while problem-solving. Whatever path you take to solve the problem is OK. So, feel free to mix and match structures when you are baffled by the problem and in search of a solution.

Memory and system barriers are all memories. This chapter describes the formation and treatment of memory barriers and system barriers. The distinction between memory barriers in Memory III and system barriers that involve the Basic Neurostructure, Memories I, II, and III, or other systems, will be examined in detail.

Basic to the understanding of Process Healing is the fact that trauma can cause memory barriers in Memory III. Unusual circumstances during trauma can cause the association of one or more memories *to* the memory structure created during the trauma. Remember, the association of a memory *to* a memory structure makes it hard to treat the memories associated *with* the memory structure. This causes some barriers for treatment, which I call Layered Memories. The memory layered *to* the memory structure must be treated first.

There are two kinds of Layered Memories. The first Layered Memory involves associating one amnesic part *to* another amnesic part. Because you can find two or more parts stacked in this way, I call this type of memory structure *Stacked Parts*. The second type of Layered Memory has a memory structure that's not a part associated *to* a base memory. I call this memory structure a Layered Memory. This distinguishes between two different structures. These structures are both easy to treat, but you have to be aware of the possibility of such a structure in order to ask the correct leading questions to find out whether they are present in the patient.

System barriers differ from memory barriers because they involve Basic Neurostructure, Memories I, II, and III. These barriers to treatment are also caused by trauma, but they occur in the formative stages of the personality and are actually a duplication of primitive structures. The early trauma causes a process similar to easy creating of amnesic parts. In one case, I discovered system barriers that involved the duplication of the Behavior System. In another case, the barrier involved duplicating Memory III.

This might sound very complex, but the reality is that both System Fragments and duplicate Memory IIIs are easy to treat; however, it is important that you also treat the effects of the trauma which caused the initial creation of these structures. Keep in mind that it is important to treat the cause of easy creation of structures to avoid the problem of more structures being created while the patient is in treatment. Also, one can treat parts and other structures in the Emotion System and the Heart System. Another potential system barrier is the formation of a second Behavior System. This system appears to operate independently from the primary Behavior System.

Other sources of problem behavior can come from distortions in the Basic Neurostructure. These interventions are rare, but when you find any unusual barrier, there is always a chance the Basic Neurostructure adds to the cause of the barrier. How things are associated can be unexpected and surprising, like the infinite combinations possible in the game of Lego. Chapter 8 gives you an introduction to common structures and, by the time you've finished reading it, you will know that problem-solving involves mixing and matching memory structures with which you are familiar.

Table of contents for this chapter

Structures in Systems

Subconscious

Summary

Structures in Systems

8-1 Systems participating in our behavior

The figure below explains most of the systems identified in this book that participate in running our brain and body (see Figure 8-1). These systems are all involved in generating our behavior. There may well be other systems that exist that I have not yet found. The systems listed are the ones that have emerged, as needed, to solve problems. I have learned of no complications stemming from creating a new system to solve a problem. My assumption that memory runs everything supports the approach of composing any metaphor or memory construct necessary that relates to and solves the problem.

In Figure 8-1 (next page), the fine bars on the left of the Active Experiences represent the Basic Neurostructure as it is related to the Active Experience. Each system has its own Basic Neurostructure operating on the neural activity in the Active Experience. Each system has memory that contributes to the Active Experience. The Basic Neurostructure

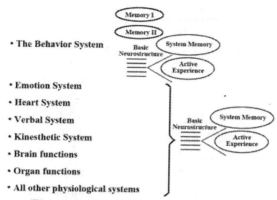

- The Behavior System

- Emotion System
- Heart System
- Verbal System
- Kinesthetic System
- Brain functions
- Organ functions
- All other physiological systems

Figure 8-1 Neural Systems in Our Body

creates a response from the activity in the Active Experience that operates on the physiology to run some brain function, muscle, or organ. A memory is changed or created when the response is created. This is true for all systems. The Basic Neurostructure for the Behavior System creates our behavior from the Active Experience, which receives contributions from the three memories, Memories I, II, and III, and internal and external stimulation.

Just as described earlier for the Behavior System, the active memories in the Active Experience are used by each system to create memories and responses to govern the activity of a system, whether it is a brain function, heart, or muscle activity. From our earliest activity, within each of our systems, responses amass efficiently to form a system memory. The bottom line of our reality is that the Basic Neurostructure of all systems operates on the Active Experience to create collages by selecting from the available, active memory structures from each system memory to control some aspect of our brain or body.

The Behavior System is different from most systems in the brain and body. The Basic Neurostructure of the Behavior System is first responsive to initial simple neural activity. Then we develop sensations and later more complex sensory experience, including basic needs and responses to positive and negative emotions, all of which occur during the development of the system. This causes the creation of three state-dependent memories— Memories I, II, and III.

The Basic Neurostructure operates on *in utero* neural activity in the Active Experience and creates Memory I. Neural activity then is the common property of memories in Memory I. The development of Memory I begins shortly after conception and stops developing at birth or a little later.

At some point before birth, the developing neural system makes it necessary for the Basic Neurostructure to perform behavior that is more complex, and this results a new state-dependent memory to handle the new complexity. Activity and sensory stimulation define this new state-dependent memory,

Memory II. Now Memory I and Memory II participate in creating responses in the developing Behavior System.

The complexity of the developing Neurostructure continues until some point before birth, where, along with the development of the five senses come the basic needs—air, food, and water, as well as the need for stimulation, and the responsiveness to reinforcement and punishment. All of this creates a new state-dependent memory called Memory III. Memory III starts accumulating memories as the child experiences and behaves in the physical world. All three Memories participate in the Active Experience to contribute to the formation of collages to perform specific behavioral activity. With internal and external stimulation, the system is in a constant state of change from the impact of content and emotions and the current responses of all relevant systems triggering into and moving out of the Active Experience.

Subconscious

8-2 Barriers to auto-treatment

As discussed earlier, automatic treatment by the subconscious is a most effective and efficient way to use Process Healing. However, sometimes it is not always possible to get auto-treatment to work as effectively as it should. With the aid of the subconscious, I have found several barriers to automatic treatment in various patients. If the patient has not been able to experience the results of automatic treatment, here are interventions based on memory and structure theory that may clear possible barriers.

Examples:
1. A belief restricts the Active Experience
I guessed that there was a massive unconscious belief that blocked the treatment activity of the subconscious by blocking or distorting the association process. I find this barrier fairly frequently. In one case, I found a field associated with the belief.

T: **Subconscious, is there a massive belief that is stopping you from automatically treating negative events in the Active Experience?**
S: **Yes.**
T: **Can you treat that belief?**
S: **No.**
T: **Is there a field associated with that belief?**
S: **Yes.**

Just as the subconscious can learn to treat trauma in our memories, he or she can learn to treat fields.

T: **Can you clear the field and then treat the belief?**

S: **Yes.**

2. A part in the Emotion System blocks automatic treatment

I initially called this a Predisposition, but later discovered that it was a part in the Emotion System. Almost any metaphor that approximates the neurostructure causing our behavior works to reach the treatment goal.

T: **Subconscious, is there a part in the Emotion System that stops automatic treatment?**

S: **Yes.**

T: **Subconscious, is it safe to treat the part that blocks automatic treatment?**

S: **Yes.**

T: **Please treat it.**

S: **Yes.**

3. Memory I structures causing barriers to auto-treatment

The Active Experience can have many Memory I structures that can block auto-treatment. An example of this subtle barrier was found when I was doing treatment over the telephone. In this case, when we were on the telephone talking together, this barrier did not come into play, but when I hung up, the activity of these structures began and apparently blocked the auto-treatment in the patient. These structures can cause activity in the Active Experience that blocks treatment. Chapter 8-25 describes the treatment for these floating structures.

4. When subconscious fragments form Layered Memories

In the presence of trauma, memories important for survival are layered by the subconscious to prevent them from changing. This fragmenting by the subconscious undermines its full function.

T: **Subconscious, are there Layered Memories that are layered with a fragment of the subconscious?**

S: **Yes.**

T: **Please treat the subconscious fragments and join them with you and then treat the Layered Memories.**

S: **Yes.**

5. Field barriers associated with the subconscious

When there is still a barrier to automatic treatment, you can look for a field associated with the subconscious.

T: **Subconscious, is there a field associated with the subconscious?**

S: **Yes**.
T: **Please clear the field.**
S: **Yes.**

8-3 Barrier caused by a surrogate subconscious

The patient tried all week to use the subconscious and it did not work. In session, while we were trying to treat the tendency to create parts, we discovered the reason. There was a surrogate subconscious.

T: **Subconscious, does this patient easily create parts?**
S: **Yes.**

I tried to use the treatment for easy creation and found a barrier to communicating with the subconscious. I inquired about fields and treated some fields and other field complications. Some patients can tell me when parts become active and this patient mentioned that a part had become active.

T: **Subconscious, please treat the part.**
S: **No.**

Using the non-question intervention, I asked, "Is there a part called the subconscious?"

S: **Yes.**

I treated the part called the subconscious. Then I started exploring a little.

T: **May I talk to the true subconscious?**
S: **Yes.**
T: **Has there been a fake subconscious active in the last five sessions?**

The patient had not been able to contact his subconscious for five sessions.

S: **Yes.**
T: **Does the fake subconscious want to be treated?**
S: **Yes.**
T: **Please treat the fake subconscious.**
S: **Yes.**

The following is an intervention worth remembering.

T: [Done] **Subconscious, do you remember all of the interventions we did in the last five sessions?**
S: **Yes.**

T: **Please repeat the interventions that we did in the last five sessions and do a Massive Change History and everything as appropriate.**

S: **Yes.**

I wondered how the patient learned a part called subconscious. Usually when I run into this, someone has deliberately created a part called subconscious to confuse a therapist.

T: **Subconscious, was the fake subconscious put in deliberately?**

S: **Yes.**

T: **Were memory structures put in deliberately?**

S: **Yes.**

Because of what I have encountered in other patients, I was thinking of various mind-control techniques used in some unpublished research experiments, but in order to be sure, I thought I would explore further. I asked the patient if he could remember any lost time, waking up upset, missing days, and so forth. The patient remembered that in grade five he was afraid of going to sleep. At that time he believed that sleep was a form of death, and he put off going to sleep because he wanted to live. The result was that he was getting only four hours of sleep every night. Still today, he has trouble going to sleep.

T: **Subconscious, was this experience the cause of structures?**

S: **Yes.**

T: **Are they relatively benign, giving only occasional problems such as intruding anxiety and sleep problems?**

S: **Yes.**

T: **Subconscious, please treat the structures one after the other.**

Here, I could have become misled by believing some bad guys deliberately created the structures. In this case, because he believed he would die if he allowed himself to go to sleep, the child inadvertently created the structures to protect himself. He was not the victim of an organization doing experiments. The fake subconscious may have been a protective part helping the child stay alive and maintaining the five-year-old strategy of not sleeping.

Behavior System

8-4 The Behavior System

The Basic Neurostructure creates our behavior in the Behavior System, which, in simple terms, is all the behavior that is generated from active memories in the Active Experience. In other words, the Active Experience is a construct representing the neural activity from which our behavior is assembled. In Figure 8-2 (next page), which

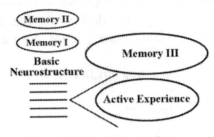

Figure 8-2 The Behavior System

summarizes the structural components of the basic Behavior System, the ellipse drawn around the Active Experience distinguishes dormant from active memories. The Basic Neurostructure creates our behavior from all activities in the brain and body and other active memories in the conscious and unconscious experience that are represented in the Active Experience.

The Active Experience is not a well-defined region in the brain. It represents neural activity from all areas of the entire brain and body. At any one moment, a collage forms from the activity in the Active Experience, causing a response that will lead to more satisfaction or to less pain. The next response is based in part on the present response. The visual image of the ellipse containing the Active Experience helps us to conceptualize the process of building memory collages that cause our behavior and memory. At the same time, it allows the use of the dissociation process to cause the conscious and unconscious experience in the Active Experience.

Memory I is a memory that starts with simple neural activity and primitive responses that occur between conception and birth. These memories are occasionally found to contribute to the cause of some problematic issues. Memory I memories are usually treated without difficulty, but you have to be specific when directing treatment to them.

Memory II contains memories developed from experiences prior to birth through the first four years of life that are related to activity and sensory sensations. This memory is based upon primitive sensations and neural activity. Many Predispositions, like habits, are formed in Memory II and can be problematic to our behavior. Also, the Protector-Controller, a collection of behaviors that automatically occur to protect us or control our environment, is formed as Memory II amasses. The Protector-Controller and Predispositions are usually easy to treat. Predispositions can also be associated *with* or *to* other structures in Memory III. Interestingly, parts in Memory II are usually easy to treat because they do not show executive function. They are essentially skills learned early in life.

Memory III is based upon neural activity, positive and negative emotions, and the basic needs. Memory III contains the Main Personality with Ego States, Tandem Memories, memories, amnesic parts, dissociative parts, and the memory of all neural activity related to each of the memories. The dissociative and associative processes are considered to be parts that are also in Memory III. Most of our behavior is created from memories in Memory III.

8-5 The Verbal System

The discovery of the Verbal System came about when I encountered situations where I had no idea how to explain the source of verbal intrusions. I asked if there was a Verbal System. According to the patient's subconscious, this system started independently from the Behavioral System when the baby was crying and vocalizing. It initially formed like a tandem system, but, because of its specialized form of behavior, became an independent, encapsulated system in Memory III. It might be similar to an Ego State—a state-dependent memory associated with speech. The Verbal System is different from other memories in the Behavioral System because it appears to generate self-organized novel or creative verbal utterances. The appearance of self-organization is caused by the memories being associated *with* Predispositions in Memory II.

I have found other memory structures in the Verbal System of several patients, including Layered Memories, Belief Structures, Picture Structures, beliefs, and parts. The patients who showed these aspects of the Verbal System were patients with severe negative self-talk, procrastination, and smoking addiction. In one psychotic patient, the Verbal System was the source of memories that gave verbal intrusions from which he assembled sentences in answer to questions. The resulting answers were out of context, rambling, and failed to answer questions I asked.

T: **Subconscious, are there memory structures in a Verbal System that contribute to negative self-talk?**

S: **Yes.**

T: **Shall I use the Structure Procedure to treat all the memory structures in the Verbal System related to negative self-talk?**

S: **Yes.**

T: **Please treat the structure of memory structures in the Verbal System that provides negative self-talk in the conscious experience.**

S: **Yes.**

After each intervention, I ask

T: [Done] **Please do a Massive Change History and everything, including the Verbal System, and treat any Shadow Memories.**

S: **Yes.**

T: [Done] **Please treat the structure of Belief Structures in the Verbal System that provides negative self-talk in the conscious experience.**

S: **Yes.**

T: [Done] **Please treat the structure of Picture Structures in the Verbal System that provides negative self-talk in the conscious experience.**

S: **Yes.**

T: [Done] **Please treat the structure of parts in the Verbal System that provides negative self-talk in the conscious experience.**

S: **Yes.**

T: **Subconscious, are you finished treating the Verbal System?**

S: **Yes.**

If "No," problem-solve.

This intervention has been routine. However, I have occasionally run into fields that block the treatment. I have used this intervention with difficult cases, and though I have not found any miraculous changes, I am sure that it contributes to reducing the source of some problematic verbal behavior.

Layered Memories

8-6 Layered Parts in Memory III — Stacked Parts

I first discovered a case that showed the formation of Stacked Parts when I worked with a patient who had accidentally experienced intense electric shock for some duration. With this survivor, I tried to treat the base part that had experienced the shock, but the treatment wouldn't work. Problem-solving revealed a stacked structure with seven layers formed during the trauma. I pictured this structure as a pyramid with seven layers. I called this structure *Stacked Parts* (see Figure 8-3).

Since then, I have seen many patients with Stacked Parts.

With the shock victim, the increasing intensity of the electric shock caused more Layered Memories or parts to form. The first or base part formed rapidly. When the intensity of the shock increased, the experience became intense and novel again and

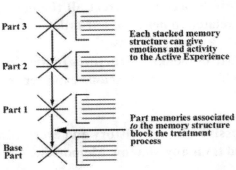

Part 3

Part 2

Part 1

Base Part

Each stacked memory structure can give emotions and activity to the Active Experience

Part memories associated *to* the memory structure block the treatment process

Figure 8-3 Stacked Amnesic Parts

was responded to as a new trauma. The brain mobilized a second time to survive and formed a second part. The second part associated *to* the first part. The pain continued to increase, became novel, and caused the third part to form, which associated *to* the second part. The pain increased, became novel, and caused another part to form. This layering process continued in this way to create seven Stacked Parts. I have seen parts stacked with three, seven, and 56 layers. Sometimes, more than one part associates *to* the same layer. It is rare for stacked trauma parts to occur without torture or intense, unavoidable, increasing pain.

Stacked parts offer an interesting challenge. When you try to treat the base part of Stacked Parts, you cannot treat the memories associated *with* the base part because of the treatment barrier formed when a layered or Stacked Part is associated *to* the base part. When a part associates *to* a base part, the association effectively anchors the emotions of the base part, preventing treatment. A structural attachment occurs when the memory structure of one part attaches *to* the memory structure of another part. Memories usually associate *with* a memory structure to become part of the content of the memory. Memories attached *with* a memory structure do not cause any problem in the treatment process. A memory—in this case, a part—associated *to* the base memory structure interferes with treating the base memory or part. However, the treatment of Stacked Parts is relatively straightforward.

The first step in treating Stacked Parts and Layered Memories involves identifying which of these structure types are blocking the treatment process. With Stacked Parts, the goal is to work toward getting all the Stacked Parts to want treatment; for example, Figure 8-3 shows three Stacked Parts. Convincing Stacked Parts to want treatment is usually quite easy to do by using the reframes provided in Chapter 3. When the Stacked Parts are ready for treatment, the subconscious can simply treat and integrate the parts, one by one, from the top layer down to the base layer. As you progress treating the parts from the top of the stack down, integrate or join the treated parts into the Main Personality. Even though the timelines of the parts sometimes overlap, they can all seemingly be treated and joined with the Main Personality.

T: **Subconscious, is the barrier or problem caused by Stacked Parts or Layered Memories in the personality?**
S: **Yes.**
T: **Are there Stacked Parts active?**
S: **Yes.**

Problem-solve until all the Stacked Parts want treatment and want to join with the Main Personality.

T: **Subconscious, please treat the parts from the top layer to the bottom and join the parts with the Main Personality as you finish treating them. Please do a Massive Change History and everything as needed.**

S: **Yes.**

Sometimes, some of the Stacked Parts have fields associated with them. In this case, you have to clear the fields before treating the part (see Flint, n.d.). It is possible to have more than one part attached *to* a part at different levels in the stack of parts.

Examples:

1. Picking angry women

The patient had a history of picking angry women for his live-in relationships. As it turned out, one of his parts, with parts stacked to it, acted upon the belief: "You deserve it." This resulted in doomed relationships because this Stacked Part structure arranged for him to choose angry women, thus contributing to his misery. When treating the Stacked Part, I found the upper layer of the stack had two fields associated with it. The second part had three layered fields associated with it. I asked the subconscious to clear the fields and treat the parts. Then I discovered a conflict between the parts in the stack. After resolving the conflict and treating the parts, a Massive Change History and everything was done. In addition, two more parts required treatment, and one of these was associated with a field. Once this was addressed, we learned that the base part was afraid to heal. I worked with the base part and treated the fear and the trauma. This shows the complexity of Stacked Parts.

2. An athlete with no feelings

In this example, the patient had no feelings. The patient was an athlete, a hockey player, and, as a child, prided himself at being able to handle pain. He was as tough as they can get, and he grew up without having either positive or painful feelings. He was out of touch with his feelings. I speculated there was a part that took all the negative feelings.

T: **Is there a part that handled all the pain in your youth?**

S: **Yes.**

Further problem-solving found two Stacked Parts: one with four Stacked Parts and the other with three Stacked Parts. These parts were treated and, following some other treatment, the patient started having both positive and negative feelings.

3.Stacked parts in a torture survivor

I had seen Stacked Parts before in torture survivors but did not fully understand the mechanism or the effects of Stacked Parts. When I tried to treat a trauma memory in a torture survivor, I couldn't do it. Now I understand what was done to create such barriers.

This barrier to treatment in torture survivors was the result of a part being deliberately associated *to* the base part (see Figure 8-4) to create a Layered Memory. The base part or memory is a personality part

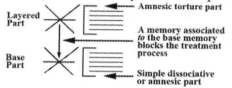

Figure 8-4 Part Caused by Torture

created as an amnesic part, more or less in the same normal way as discussed in Chapter 3. Another deliberately created trauma part was taught specific instructions during the torture and was deliberately associated *to* the base part. The instructions are usually something the part has to do—a task. This task, when triggered, has to be completed to avoid the trauma pain remembered from the torture. Following the instructions for the task is an avoidance response. The cue for triggering the task is also learned when the victim is learning the instructions. This cue can be as simple as two snaps of the fingers. Some layered parts are also taught how to block treatment and are themselves difficult to treat because they have to be triggered to find them; otherwise, they remain dormant. I found that I had to treat the layered torture parts before I could treat the trauma that initially caused the base part. Needless to say, by treating torture survivors I learned a lot about brain processes and memory.

8-7 Belief Structure

Belief Structures are common structures in Memory III (see Figure 8-5). A negative Belief Structure is a Layered Memory that maintains a belief that is disruptive to a person's behavior. Everyone has be-

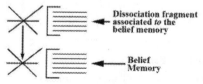

Figure 8-5 Belief Structure

liefs that limit what we can do in our lives. Some of these beliefs are Layered Memories. A memory associated *to* the structure of a negative Belief Structure stops the treatment process from changing the belief to false. The memory typically associated *to* the Belief Structure is a fragment of the dissociation process.

I discovered Belief Structures when I was working with a patient who believed that when something in his life was working well, it would end and he would never experience it again. Some of the positive experiences and behaviors lost to him included independent treatment by the subconscious, having a fully open heart, and having the opportunity to give "good vibes" to others. By treating various barriers, these positive experiences became briefly available to him again, but he could not retain the experiences for any extended period.

With leading questions, the patient and I discovered how Belief Structures are formed. A fragment of the dissociation process in Memory III was associated *to* the structure of the belief that "positive experience is not possible." This belief prevented the patient from experiencing positive experiences or behavior. The belief was in a Layered Memory, which was not easy to treat. Without changing this layered belief, the belief would remain as a pervasive trait of the personality. Here is how the Belief Structure formed. The patient learned the belief that "no positive experience is possible" when his mother punished positive experience at a crucial point in his childhood. The belief was a memory, preserved and reaffirmed by the mother's constant negative responses to the boy's positive experiences. In forming this belief, a fragmented dissociation part associated *to* the memory structure of the belief. This learning created a Layered Memory, which resulted in a belief that could not be treated easily. Here is the sequence of events that caused the belief.

There is a dissociative process that is available during the creation of behavior and memory. This dissociation process is in Memory III and works in the Active Experience. Normally, the Basic Neurostructure associates the dissociative process *with* some memories to make all or part of those active memories unconscious. In our example, when the patient's good experience or positive behavior was punished, he experienced confusion. This experience created the negative belief, namely — "positive experience is not possible." It happened in the presence of confusion and resulted in a fragment of the dissociation part associating *to* the memory structure of the belief. This layered belief was experienced repeatedly, and effectively disrupted the positive emotions associated *with* positive experiences. Here is how to treat Belief Structures.

First you have to find if Belief Structures are present.

T: **Subconscious, are there any Belief Structures or structures that have memories or layered dissociation fragments blocking their treatment?**

I included memories to be sure that all possibilities were covered.

S: **Yes.**

T: **Subconscious, please treat the fragments of the dissociation process and join them with the dissociation part.**

S: **Yes.**

T: **Subconscious, now treat the memory structures of the beliefs that serve as a barrier to positive experience.**

S: **No.**

In this case, before the intervention could work, we found a field was blocking positive experiences (see Flint, n.d.). I asked the subconscious to treat the field.

T: **Is there a field barrier?**

S: **Yes.**

T: **Subconscious, please treat the field associated with this belief.**

S: **Yes.**

T: **Subconscious, now treat the memory structure of the belief.**

S: **Yes.**

T: [Done] **Subconscious, please do a Massive Change History and everything.**

To replace the function of the treated belief, I always do the following.

T: [Done] **Please compose and strengthen self-empowering beliefs with positive emotions to replace the beliefs you have just treated.**

The patient had a conscious belief that none of this would work. After the treatment, he said the belief that "if something good happens, it will never happen again" no longer felt true. In the following week, the patient felt what he described as his heart opening.

8-8 Picture Structure

After discovering Belief Structures, it occurred to me that people have pictures about how the world should be. By studying NLP and taking EST training (Erhard, 1976), I learned about how "rigid pictures of how things should be" could lead people to become upset when reality did not meet with their picture. So, I explored whether there was something unique about these picture memories that made them hard to treat; in other words, were there "Picture Structures"? I found a likeness between Picture Structures and Belief Structures, but Picture Structures had multiple memories associated *to* the memory structure that gave the picture to the Main Personality (see Figure 8-6, next page). Here is how I discovered and developed this idea.

I had a patient who had a particular picture that led him to get upset whenever he asked his wife if he could pour her a cup of tea.

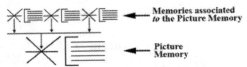

Memories associated *to* the Picture Memory

Picture Memory

Figure 8-6 Picture Structure

She always refused his request by saying that she would do it. This upset him. I noted that he had a picture that he would be caring if he showed his love by pouring her a cup of tea. The upset was a reaction to his failure to meet this picture of himself. He wanted to treat that reaction, so we started problem-solving and developed a procedure for treating Picture Structures. We had tried to treat some of these pictures prior to developing the procedure, but were not altogether successful. The first step was to discover if there were such Picture Structures. With further questioning, the treatment revealed itself. This is the same problem-solving strategy that I have used repeatedly.

T: **Subconscious, are there any picture memories that we have not successfully treated?**

S: **Yes.**

T: **Are these picture memories Layered Memories?**

S: **Yes.**

T: **Do they have dissociation fragments associated *to* them?**

S: **No.**

T: **Is there a regular memory structure associated *to* them?**

S: **Yes.**

I guessed with the next question.

T: **Is there more than one memory associated *to* the picture memory?**

S: **Yes.**

T: **Subconscious, can you easily treat picture memories?**

S: **Yes.**

T: **Subconscious, please treat all picture memories by first treating all the memories associated to the picture memory and then treat the picture memory itself.**

As always, I wanted to strengthen any positive, adaptive, self-empowering memories that can contribute to making life more satisfying.

T: **Please compose and strengthen a self-empowering memory with positive emotions to be more flexible and adaptive than the memory we just treated.**

S: **Yes.**

Now when I run into problematic pictures, I do the following:

T: **Subconscious, can you see the picture memory that causes this reaction?**

S: **Yes.**

T: [I explain.] **The memory that is providing the rigid picture is a memory structure that has several memories attached to it. This makes treating the picture memory difficult. Treating picture memories involves treating memories attached to the picture memory. Can you treat memories attached to the picture?**

S: **Yes.**

T: [Wait] **Now, can you treat the memory that causes the picture and change it so there is more flexibility to respond comfortably to what is real?**

S: **Yes.**

I have found fields associated *to* the Picture Structures. So far, they appear easy for the subconscious to treat.

I found this picture memory construct in other patients. This structure is formed seemingly by a dysfunction in the association process. Apparently, during the creation of the Picture Structure, the association process allows other memories to associate *to* the picture memory. It appears as though the association part has a memory of all the Picture Structures and it is possible for the subconscious to work with the association process to treat all the Picture Structures.

8-9 Personality traits as Layered Memory structures

The Layered Memory structures in Memory III can be disruptive (see Figure 8-7). These memories are difficult to treat when you don't

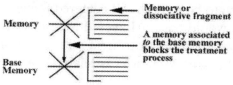 identify them for what they are. An example of Layered Memories can be seen in cases where negative personality traits or self-defeating tendencies become problem-

Figure 8-7 Layered Memory

atic for the patient. These negative behaviors, the cause of the emotional distress, are Layered Memories that provide rigid pictures or expectations of how life should be. Sometimes, these Layered Memories provide verbal intrusions. Layered Memories have to be treated differently because a memory layered or associated *to* the memory interferes with the treatment process.

Layered Memories become problems when they cause negative influence on the behavior created in the Active Experience. Sometimes these Layered Memories are not caused by trauma. These memories can form early in life and involve Predispositions. When an unusual or novel situation occurs, a Layered Memory can be created. This happens when the behavior of the person is conflicting with reality and causes confusion. The resulting confusion between a Predisposition and the conflicting behavior causes a fragment to split off from the dissociative process and associate *to* the memory structure of the conflicting behavior to form a Layered Memory. The maladaptive memory, a belief or picture of how it should be, becomes untreatable because of the dissociative fragment associated *to* its memory structure. The conflicting maladaptive behavior becomes permanent because it is a Layered Memory.

The base memory can still take part in creating behavior, but treatment requires the layer to be addressed specifically before treating the base memory. The behavior caused by the maladaptive Layered Memory adds a personality trait in Memory III, which can provide a maladaptive personality pattern. The maladaptive pattern can range from denial in addictive behavior to psychosis and thinking disorders.

Examples:
1. Treating dependency feelings and behaviors

The woman was dealing with a number of dependency issues. The dependent feelings and behaviors were in Layered Memories that responded in certain situations to cause the dependent pattern. The dependent patterns included: feelings of abandonment and of emptiness without men in her life, the willingness to walk on eggshells rather than to cause anger, complying without assessing her own needs and wants, the need to control, the use of denial, the need to be right, a self-centered focus, and feelings of confusion. Situations would trigger Layered Memories that would give these responses. They were difficult to treat with traditional therapy approaches, but treating Layered Memories is relatively easy using Process Healing.

T: **Subconscious, are there any Layered Memories or memory structures that are causing these dependency behaviors?**

S: **Yes.**

T: **Are fragments of the dissociative process associated *to* these Layered Memories?**

S: **Yes.**

T: **Subconscious, please treat any fragments of the dissociation process and join them with the primary dissociative part.**

S: **Yes.**

T: [Wait] **Subconscious, please treat the problem memories, and compose and strengthen self-empowering behaviors.**

S: **Yes.**

T: **Subconscious, please do a Massive Change History including the Ego States and Tandem Memories and treat any Shadow Memories.**

S: **Yes.**

2. Sensitivity to light

The patient said that sometimes she had an extreme sensitivity to light. The subconscious reported a damaged dissociation process. Fragments of the dissociative process associated *to* the damaged memory that was light sensitive. After trying to treat the part, I discovered it had seven layered dissociative fragments. This was a Stacked Memory consisting of seven stacked dissociative fragments. There was also an associated field. I started with:

T: **Subconscious, can you treat the field barrier?**

S: **Yes.**

I had previously taught the subconscious to be able to simple treat fields without my intervention.

T: [Done] **Subconscious, please treat the seven dissociative fragment layers by starting at the top and progressing down to the first layer. Treat each layered fragment and integrate the fragment with the main dissociation process.**

S: **Yes.**

T: **Subconscious, can you now treat the light-sensitive part?**

S: **Yes.**

T: **Please treat the part.**

S: **Yes.**

T: [Done] **Subconscious, please do the Massive Change History.**

S: **Yes.**

This Layered Memory structure was formed when the patient was about five years old. At that time, she was locked in a dark cellar with several other children for four days without food or water. Such an experience is consistent with light sensitivity. Adding to the horror, all the children were naked. The environment became smelly and messy. There was much crying and yelling. When the patient heard other children crying, she became confused because she did not know whether she herself or another child was crying. Apparently, this confusion resulted in a fragmentation of the dissociation part. The fragmented dissociation part associated *to* the memory of becoming accustomed to darkness. This created the Layered Memory structure causing her to experience sensitivity to light. The base memory was the memory that caused the light sensitivity. After treating the Layered Memory structure and the base memory, the light sensitivity was no longer a problem. I wondered if this problem involved a Tandem Memory III.

T: **Subconscious, is there a Tandem Memory III that becomes coconscious during these feeling states?**

S: **Yes.**

Treating Tandem Memory III conditions is described later in this chapter.

3. Treating the structure of Layered Memory structures

This intervention speeds up the treatment of various unique Layered Memory structures by treating the structure of Layered Memory structures such as beliefs, pictures, Predisposition memories, and parts with Layered Memories.

T: **Subconscious, please treat the structure of Layered Memory structures. When the structure falls apart, tag all the memory elements of the structure, and then treat the Layered Memories slowly and safely, in the correct order. After treating each structure, please do a Massive Change History and everything and strengthen suitable self-empowering beliefs or behaviors.**

S: **Yes.**

4. Treating intrusions caused by Layered Memories

The patient had problems with her memories intruding. The subconscious said that Layered Memories caused the intrusions. This is an example of treating the tendency to create Layered Memories easily.

T: **Subconscious, does minor trauma cause the spontaneous creation of new Layered Memories?**

S: **Yes.**

T: **Subconscious, please treat the tendency to form Layered Memories easily by doing a Change History in Memory I, Memory II and Memory III.**

S: **Yes.**

T: **[Wait] Subconscious, are you done?**

S: **I don't know.**

T: **Is this a part that awakened?**

S: **Yes.**

T: **Do you want treatment?**

P: **Yes.**

T: **Subconscious, please treat this part and complete the other task.**

S: **Yes.**

T: **Are you done?**

S: **Yes.**

T: **Subconscious, please treat all the Layered Memories in Memory III, strengthen the positive coping memories with positive emotions, and join them to the Main Personality.**

S: **Yes.**

As a reminder, we know that any treatment of Layered Memories will not treat all Layered Memories. Some of the Layered Memories may be dormant and not accessible to the subconscious at the time of treatment.

8-10 An emotion layered *to* a memory in Memory III

This is the case of a patient doing treatment on his own to address a history of fright and flight responses. While working on these issues, he apparently triggered an emotion in the Emotion System associated *to* a Layered Memory in Memory III. The Layered Memory became active and blocked the ability of the subconscious to communicate with the patient. Apparently, the Layered Memory, present from childhood, could not become active until the emotion in the Emotion System became active. The patient contacted me because the self-treatment had activated that emotion, and once the emotion became active, the memory was activated and remained active, blocking all communication with his subconscious.

T: **Please treat all Emotion Memories in the Emotion System that are the memories associated *to* the disruptive memories in Memory III.**

S: **Yes.**

T: **Subconscious, can you treat all Layered Memories that are blocking the patient's communication with the subconscious?**

S: **Yes.**

T: **Please do a Massive Change History and everything.**

S: **Yes.**

8-11 Spontaneous formation of Stacked Memories

This patient came to see me because she had intruding memories that were problematic. The subconscious reported Stacked Memories caused the intruding memories. With further questioning, I discovered the Stacked Memories were spontaneously forming. By using the constructs of Process Healing, it was a relatively simple matter to develop an intervention to treat this issue. Though I don't do this intervention much anymore, for some reason, I am including it so you are familiar with it in case you ever need it.

    T: **Subconscious, are Stacked Memories forming spontaneously?**
    S: **Yes.**
    T: **Subconscious, please treat the tendency to form Stacked Memories easily by doing a Change History in Memories I, II and III.**
    S: **Yes.**
    T: **[Wait] Subconscious, are you done?**
    S: **I don't know.**
    T: **Is this a part that awakened?**
    S: **Yes.**
    T: **Do you want treatment?**
    P: **Yes.**
    T: **Subconscious, please treat this part and complete the other task.**
    S: **Yes.**
    T: **Are you done?**
    S: **Yes.**
    T: **Please treat all the layers in the Stacked Memories in Memory III from the top down. Treat all the base memories and strengthen self-empowering coping memories with positive emotions before integration.**
    S: **Yes.**
    T: **Please do a Massive Change History and everything.**
    S: **Yes.**

This appeared almost too easy. I suspected that, because these structures are formed easily, the intensity of the emotions with the stacked and base memories were weak.

8-12 Easy creation of amnesic parts caused by a Layered Memory

Easy creation can be caused by a novel Layered Memory. A Layered Memory is formed when an Emotion Memory in the Emotion System is associated *to* the memory. The Layered Memory, in this case, is also associated *with* a Predisposition. The Predisposition is also layered. When the Layered Memory is triggered by the Predisposition, the memory of the Layered Memory brings in the conditions necessary to cause the creation of amnesic parts. It causes the Active Experience to mobilize to create a new amnesic part. The following is a good example of how various memory structures are pooled together to solve a problem.

T: **Subconscious is there an easy creation process that causes amnesic parts?**

S: **Yes.**

T: **Is this a Layered Memory with an emotion associated *to* it and that is associated *with* a layered Predisposition in Memory II?**

S: **Yes.**

T: **Please treat the layers on the Predisposition first, then the Predisposition, then the Emotion Memory in the Emotion System, and then the Layered Memory. Then do a Massive Change History and everything and treat Shadow Memories.**

S: **Yes.**

8-13 Easy creation of other structures

The easy creation process has been discussed in other chapters including amnesic parts (see Chapters 7-7 and 8-12) and easily created systems (see Chapter 8-24). Easy creation is an example of the flexibility of the brain. Included here are four other examples of easy creation that I have discovered in my patients. In all of these examples, when I discovered there was a great number of the structures, I simply asked if there was an easy creation structure creating these structures. With problem-solving, I figured out an intervention to treat the easy creation of structures. I cannot guarantee the same intervention will be effective in all patients who have easy creation of the structures described.

Examples—treating easily created structures:

1. Predispositions—The treatment involved treating the Basic Neurostructure, Memory I, and Memory II, in that order.

2. Layered Memories — The treatment for easy creation of Layered Memories was to treat the Basic Neurostructure and then the Predisposition that created the Layered Memories.

3. Stacked Memories—I had a patient who had a number of Stacked Memories. They were something like Stacked Parts but were memories. The treatment of easy creation of Stacked Memories was to treat the Basic Neurostructure and then treat Memory I. This stopped the easy creation of Stacked Memories. The Stacked Memories were treated from the top down.

4. Tandem Memories—The treatment of easy creation of Tandem Memories was to treat the Basic Neurostructure and then treat Memory I. The easy creation of Tandem Memories was learned in utero when stimulation overwhelmed the Active Experience.

Predispositions

8-14 Predisposition structures

Predisposition structures are simply Picture Structures in Memory III layered with memories that are associated *with* Predispositions in Memory II (see Figure 8-8). When the reality does not match the picture,

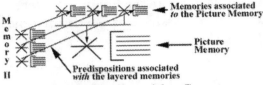

there is an upset caused by the activity of some Predispositions in Memory II. The predisposed responses intensify the patient's responses when-

Figure 8-8 Predisposition Structure

ever the reality does not match the picture. The activity of the Predispositions in the Active Experience stops treatment because of the disorganization.

Treating the Predisposition structures involves the subconscious treating the Predispositions in Memory II, the memories associated *to* the picture memory, and then treating the picture memory. This is relatively easy to do. It also appears as though the association part has a memory of all Picture Structures. The subconscious can work with the association part and treat all the picture and Predisposition (picture) structures in the system.

T: **Subconscious, are there any picture memories that are associated *with* Predispositions?**

S: **Yes.**

T: [Wait] **Subconscious, please treat the Predispositions associated *with* the Layered Memories of the picture memory.**

S: **Yes.**

T: [Wait] **Subconscious, please treat all the memory structures associated *to* the picture memory.**

S: **Yes.**

T: [Wait] **Please treat the memories in the picture structure so they are more self-empowering.**

S: **Yes.**

T: **Subconscious, please do a Massive Change History and everything.**

S: **Yes.**

I have found these Predisposition structures often enough to routinely look for them. In one case, the treatment process became so intense that I now forewarn my patients about this possibility.

8-15 A Predisposition associated *with* a Layered Memory

Problem-solving can reveal other variations of the structures we have seen. In this case it was a Layered Memory that had a Predisposition in Memory II associated *with* the Layered Memory. Here is how it was treated:

T: **Subconscious, is there a Layered Memory associated with a Predisposition?**

S: **Yes.**

T: **Subconscious, please treat the Predisposition first, then the Layered Memory, and then do a Massive Change History and everything.**

S: **Yes.**

8-16 Predisposition associated *to* a Memory III

The patient treated some memories between sessions that were significant. They were memories learned at age one. The symptoms he noticed included the feeling of being seized with fear in the heart area, being spaced out, and experiencing anticipatory anxiety. Neither he nor I could get a handle on how to treat the anticipatory anxiety until we tried the described intervention. Problem-solving revealed a Predisposition in Memory II that was associated *to* a memory in Memory III. When a response to a trauma was created in Memory III (at age one) and, simultaneously, a trauma response in Memory II created a Predisposition, the Predisposition associated *to* the trauma memory in Memory III.

T: **Subconscious, please treat the Predisposition in Memory II, the memory in Memory III and then do a Massive Change History and everything.**

S: **Yes.**

The patient immediately noticed that the lifelong anticipatory responses were greatly diminished.

8-17 Parts with a Predisposition structure

In one patient, I found a part that I was having difficulty treating. This put me into the problem-solving mode where I soon discovered a part with a Predisposition structure associated *to* it. Though I have not run into many of these structures, it is worthwhile to know that any memory structure can associate *to* parts (see Figure 8-9, next page). It turns out that when a memory structure associates *to* the structure of a part, the

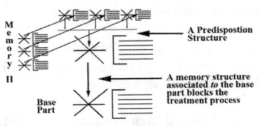

part cannot be treated until the memory structure is treated. Notice that the same pattern of structures keeps appearing in more complex structures and in different systems. Here is how I treated this layered part.

Figure 8-9 Part with Memory Structure

T: **Subconscious, can you treat this part?**

S: **No.**

I continued problem-solving and became frustrated because none of my inquiries resolved the problem. I determined there were no field barriers. What next?

T: **Subconscious, is there a structure associated *to* the part that is blocking treatment of the part?**

S: **Yes.**

I inquired about the various types of memory structures associated *to* the structure. I tried belief, memory, stacked, and Predisposition structures. It turned out there was a Predisposition structure associated *to* the part.

T: **Subconscious, is it a Predisposition structure associated *to* the part.**

S: **Yes.**

T: **After we treat the Predisposition structure, can we treat the part?**

S: **Yes.**

T: **Subconscious, please treat the Predispositions, the Layered Memories, the base memory, and then the part.**

S: **Yes.**

Now that I understood the situation, the part was easy to treat. Sometimes, there are fields blocking the treatment, and it is not always a part with a memory structure associated *to* it.

Predisposition parts are created during a trauma while the Predisposition structure is active in the Active Experience. During the creation of the memory structure for the trauma part, the Predisposition structure associates *to* the structure of the part. The layered structure associated *to* the part results in a barrier for treating the part.

8-18 Treating a part that was unsafe to treat — A five-structure part

This patient always felt dead inside. He had the same dead feeling when he made mistakes or when someone asked him to do things. We had been working intensively together for more than a year, and I felt it was strange that this condition continued so persistently. Eventually, the subconscious or a part told me that it was not safe to talk about the cause of this dead feeling. Aspects associated with the creation of that part did not want to talk about it because it was not good for the Main Personality to know, and he didn't have to know.

T: **Subconscious, do you know the feelings that we are talking about?**

S: **Yes.**

T: **Are these feeling safe to treat?**

S: **No.**

T: [After 20 questions] **Subconscious, so the feelings are dangerous to treat because treatment can damage the Heart System. The part doesn't want treatment because there is some danger.**

S: **Yes.**

I had to clear a field.

I continued problem-solving and discovered the part causing the dead feeling was in the Heart System as well as in the Emotion System, the Behavior System, Memory I and Memory II, and even the subconscious. I called it a 5-part. (I miscounted.) There were fields in all five systems associated with this 5-part. The subconscious was able to clear all the fields easily by using an unorthodox approach.

The subconscious was willing to treat the 5-part, but when trying to offer ways to treat the 5-part by treating the systems one by one in different combinations, the proposed intervention was always unsafe to use. I took the following strategy to solve this problem safely. I have used this same procedure with varying success with torture survivors.

T: **Subconscious, can you dissociate my speech and your responses from all aspects of the brain and body?**

S: **Yes.**

T: **Is it safe to talk openly now?**

S: **Yes.**

T: **Can we call this the "private line" in the future?**

S: **Yes.**

T: **Subconscious, can you map the memories that compose this 5-part into a memory that the 5-part, other parts, and Main Personality cannot access? Then can you safely problem-solve in that memory to discover the safe way to treat this complex 5-part?**

S: **Yes.**

T: [Wait] **Can you do it?**

S: **Yes.**

This form of problem-solving was important to find and plan a safe treatment strategy without tipping off the 5-part or other hostile parts in the Memory III.

T: **Is it safe for me to know how you treat the 5-part?**

S: **No.**

T: **Is it safe to treat that part now?**

S: **Yes.**

The patient felt the treatment process start, which suggested that something was happening. The whole process took about 35 minutes.

I questioned the 5-part about its role in the personality. The 5-part did not act as a subconscious. It created feeling states, barriers for doing projects, as well as blocking heart-felt responses, interfering with communication with the subconscious, and it also supported mood swings. The 5-part contributed to the patient's mild Asperger's syndrome. Primarily, the 5-part affected motivation and helped maintain dysfunction by putting the patient out of step with the here and now.

The 5-part formed at the age of five years. Though the situation was a trauma experience, the subject would not have seen the experience as a trauma. The experience activated and involved the Heart, Emotion, and Behavior Systems and Memory I and Memory II. It involved a sequence of events with his father punishing him at the end the sequence. The boy was trying to learn how to hammer a nail under his father's guidance. He missed the first nail. This upset his father. When he tried the second time, he missed again and his father dismissed him again with much verbal punishment.

As I see it, the sequence of events began with good feelings, involving the Heart and Emotion Systems. Because his father was helping him, Memory I and II were active because he was at that stage of development. The confusion caused by good feelings and receiving the verbal punishment at the same time brought the subconscious into the Active Experience. The verbal abuse triggered painful emotions that associated *to* all the components of the part that were active at the same time to resolve the conflict. So, the trauma emotions associated *to* a five-memory system—the 5-part.

The danger lay in the possibility of a misstep in the treatment approach, which could apparently both make the psychological condition worse and irreparably damage the ability to experience heart feelings. The possibility of damaging the patient with an intervention is the reason for always checking with the subconscious as to whether the treatment will be safe.

Curiously, this patient noticed in some situations that he could ask one question of the subconscious in his thoughts and get one answer and then ask the same question aloud and get another answer. The subconscious indicated that, with the weak activity of the covert question, the 5-part could control the response to the question. However, when the patient asked aloud, the greater intensity of the verbal response in the Active Experience would overwhelm the 5-part and allow the subconscious to make the response.

Tandem Memories

8-19 Duplication of Memory III—Tandem Memory

I had previously considered Memory III as a solitary memory system constantly expanding with new memories, which, in itself, was not subject to trauma. I had become accustomed to patients' subconsciouses talking to me while actively treating issues. However, the subconsciouses of a few of my patients were not able to treat and talk at the same time. These subconsciouses wanted me to be quiet while they were treating an issue. I finally started asking questions: Is there only one Active Experience? Are there more than one Active Experiences? I found that with some patients, there was only one Active Experience, but with other patients I discovered many Active Experiences operating in tandem (see Figure 8-10). When there is more than one Active Experience, it makes treatment easier and faster because treatment and communication can take place at the same time.

A patient led me to one possible explanation of how more than one Active Experience can form. When this patient was a child, he allegedly became so angry, because of jealousy, that it overwhelmed his Active Experience. Consequently, the Basic Neurostructure created another coconscious memory or Tandem Memory III with its own Active

Experience to handle the increased neural activity (see Figure 8-10). The Tandem Memory contained the memories providing executive function.

Another time, while I was problem-solving a difficult system, it occurred to me that it was possible for the increasing overload of the Active Experiences to result in the creation of additional Tandem Memories and Active Experiences. This would explain multiple Active Experiences. When this Tandem Memory was, on occasion, coconscious with the

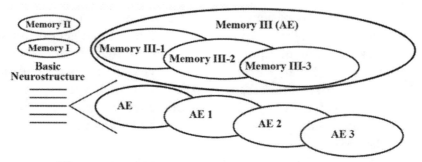

Figure 8-10 Memories Operating in Parallel

Main Personality, it might create a noticeable experience. These Tandem Memories are different from the creation of trauma parts. Memory III contains most of the trauma parts. The inclusion of these Tandem Memory IIIs in Memory III can give subtle intrusions of feelings, thoughts, and behavior. I have treated subconscious fragments apparently formed during the creation of Tandem Memories. The primary subconscious can treat the Tandem Memory IIIs and treat and integrate the subconscious fragments.

Having Tandem Memory IIIs is a relatively frequent condition. When a patient comments on different feeling states occurring in some situations, or an attempt to identify parts fails, then it is easy to look for Tandem Memory IIIs. In such a case, an explanation may be necessary to educate the subconscious:

T: **Subconscious, are there memories in the Tandem Memory IIIs that are causing problems in thoughts and behavior?**

S: **Yes.**

8-20 Treating Tandem Memory IIIs

Treatment of the pain and trauma in Tandem Memories is relatively easy. Initially, as I treated and integrated the Tandem Memories, I soon found that I no longer had several Active Experiences, but only one

Active Experience. I concluded that when you treat Tandem Memories it is best not to integrate them because you want to maintain the ability to have multiple Active Experiences in the patient. Supposedly, a record of Tandem Memory IIIs is found in Memory I.

T: **Subconscious, is there a record of Tandem Memory IIIs in Memory I and can you use the record to help identify and treat all Tandem Memory IIIs?**

S: **Yes.**

I think the subconscious can use the record of Tandem Memory IIIs to treat these structures faster. Here is the protocol to treat Tandem Memory IIIs.

T: **Subconscious, please treat all Tandem Memory IIIs, but do not join them with Memory III.**

S: **Yes.**

Sometimes, the trauma that causes the Tandem Memory IIIs can also cause easily created subconscious fragments. If there are any subconscious fragments, treat these fragments and join them with the main subconscious:

T: **Subconscious, please treat all subconscious fragments and join them with the main subconscious.**

S: **Yes.**

T: **Subconscious, please do a Massive Change History and everything.**

S: **Yes.**

Tandem personalities can have structures that are more complex. I usually envision treating the Tandem Memories from the most recent memory created to the first created. If this doesn't work, try another strategy.

T: **Subconscious, can you treat the Tandem Memory IIIs?**

S: **No.**

T: **Are these stacked Tandem Memory IIIs?**

S: **Yes.**

T: **Can you treat the stacked Tandem Memory IIIs in the most appropriate order?**

S: **Yes.**

In one case, this didn't work. I tried to treat the memories in the opposite direction from the bottom up.

T: **Please treat the stacked Tandem Memory IIIs from the bottom up.**

S: **Yes.**

T: [Done] **Subconscious, please do a Massive Change History for each Tandem Memory III.**

T: **Yes.**

This usually works, but there may be other unusual Tandem Memory structures yet to be discovered. You may have to get more specific in describing what you want to treat in the Tandem Memories.

8-21 Treating the tendency to form Tandem Memory IIIs

Similar to the tendency of the brain to mobilize easily and create parts in Memory III, I found that it was also true that early trauma can create conditions to allow the easy creation of Tandem Memory IIIs. Here is how to treat the trauma memories leading to the easy creation of multiple Memory IIIs:

T: **Subconscious, please treat the memories in Memories I, II, and III that make it easy to create Memory IIIs and subconscious fragments.**

S: **Yes.**

T: **Subconscious, please treat the Basic Neurostructure that operates on the Active Experience in the Behavior System to stop easy creation of subconscious fragments and Tandem Memory IIIs. Treat the Basic Neurostructure by adding and subtracting neural connections to remove the tendency to create Tandem Memory IIIs.**

S: **Yes.**

To solidify the treatment of the memories that caused this duplication of Memory IIIs, I introduced a barrier to help prevent the reactivation of easy creation of Memory IIIs. Ask the following to create this barrier:

T: **Please associate dissociation fragments *to* the memories just treated in Memories I, II, and III so a new trauma will not reactivate the treated memories.**

S: **Yes.**

Sometimes the problem of easy creation of Memory IIIs may be more complex. With problem-solving, a subconscious suggested the following interventions to complete this treatment.

T: **Subconscious, please treat all situational contexts that lead to easily created systems.**

S: **Yes.**

T: **Subconscious, please do a Massive Change History and everything of memories affected by these changes.**

S: **Yes.**

T: **Subconscious, please treat any trauma or parts in the Emotion System that help the creation of Tandem Memory IIIs.**
S: **Yes.**
T: **Please do a Massive Change History and everything.**
S: **Yes.**

Several other interventions that were suggested to complete this intervention are given in Flint (n.d.).

8-22 The Content-Emotion Memory—Depression

The Content-Emotion Memory is another unusual memory in Memory III. It is a state-dependent memory that consists of memories that have emotions associated *with* the Content Memories—namely, the sensory experiences. Usually, the emotions are associated *with* the other neural activity that was active at the time of the trauma (see Figure 2-1, page 26). This Content-Emotion Memory was discovered when addressing a continuous condition of depression. The patient had a pervasive feeling of "deadness" for years. It was through the usual problem-solving technique of "taking a guess" that I found this Content-Emotion Memory. The depression content was motivated by negative emotions. Treatment turned out to be easy.

T: **Subconscious, is there a state-dependent memory in Memory III that has depression content associated *with* emotions?**
S: **Yes.**
T: **Is this memory system contributing to the depression and the feeling of deadness?**

At this point, you would customize the above question to see if this Content-Emotion Memory is the cause of the issue.

S: **Yes.**
T: **Subconscious, please treat all the negative emotions associated *with* the content in the Content-Emotion Memory.**
S: **Yes.**
T: **[Done] Please do a Massive Change History, including the Content-Emotions memories, the Ego States, Tandem Memories, and treat any relevant Shadow Memories.**
S: **Yes.**

In this case, the patient felt a calm spread over him. I next asked all the questions I could think of to try to disprove the presence of the Content-Emotion Memories, and failed. Content-Emotion Memories may not be present in all patients.

System Fragments

8-23 System Fragments — How to find and treat them

System Fragments are fairly common, although I initially did not expect this would be so. I first discovered System Fragments after I'd worked with a patient for about 11 weeks using the Process Healing Method. The patient had a personality disorder. We treated many parts, beliefs, and experiences in the usual way in the Active Experience. We had made some progress but, although no longer flooded with emotions, he was still avoiding social situations. He reported feeling more centered and also said that when he was alone he was more able to maintain a sense of calmness because there were fewer triggers for his avoidance behavior. However, to the frustration of both of us, if he encountered a trigger, the avoidance behaviors would return in full force. He complained for several sessions that whenever he felt good, he would start feeling bad.

The patient was smart and it didn't take long for him to become adept at working with his subconscious and treating parts and field barriers. But at times, nothing would work. Finger responses or other muscle-test results were often inconsistent. The relapses into his old avoidance patterns occurred when "his brain fried," meaning he became disorganized. Curiously, when his Active Experience was disorganized, he felt good and centered; otherwise, he felt haggard and harassed. I suspected the disorganized condition was the cause of a barrier to treatment, and it would occur when many memories or parts were active in the Active Experience at the same time. He said that when he felt better he also felt divided and was very confused. Feeling divided was a cue that I did not understand immediately.

Usually I started a session by asking if there were any issues that the patient wanted to treat. I inquired about earlier interventions to see if they were lasting. In one of the later sessions, the subconscious said the problem was not a part, the Main Personality, the Basic Neurostructure that runs the Active Experience, or a field. I fooled around and finally asked:

T: **Subconscious, is there a second Active Experience?**
S: **Yes.**

Now we were getting somewhere. Here is where the "feeling divided" came from. I soon discovered that this second Active Experience was in a fragmented Behavior System. This was not the same as an Active Experience caused by a Tandem Memory III. The fragmented Behavior System was the source of the process causing his strange experiences when the Active Experience was disorganized. Over our many sessions I had apparently treated many related parts and memories in Memory III serving the regular Active Experience, but I had not managed to treat any of the other memories serving the fragmented systems.

I worked with the patient and the subconscious to figure out how the fragmented Behavior System was formed. The other System Fragment apparently came into existence when he was about one year old. The subconscious said there was no avoidance process then. The Basic Neurostructure was still in a formative stage. His brain operated fast and he was smart. At the time he experienced a mild trauma caused by the mother when she gave him verbal instructions to be a different person. She said, with much emotion, "Why can't you be more like your father?" This forceful comment apparently caused the Behavior System to fragment with an Active Experience and a memory. Up to the time I started therapy with him, the System Fragments and main Behavior System worked in parallel and both learned essentially the same thing. I had been treating one Behavior System but not the System Fragments. The System Fragments continued to maintain and show avoidance and other problematic behaviors.

I first believed there could only be two System Fragments. I later found there could be many (see Figure 8-11). Since System Fragments form in a unique context, I grouped them in the context in which they formed. I did not bother to find out what caused the context, but simply called them constellations of fragments. I had initially believed that there was a unique subconscious related to the easily created fragments, but this was also inaccurate. The unique subconscious was not needed to treat the trauma in the System Fragment. It was possible for the primary subconscious to carry out the all interventions of the entire treatment process.

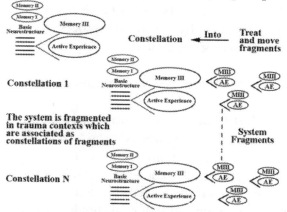

Figure 8-11 Behavior System Fragments

Before I lead you through the problem-solving, which led to the discovery of System Fragments, here is how I currently treat easily created systems:

T: **Subconscious, are there any System Fragments?**

S: **Yes.**

T: **Constellations of System Fragments form under similar conditions. Are there several constellations of System Fragments?**

S: **Yes.**

T: **Please treat the fragments in each constellation and then join the fragments into one fragment representing each constellation.**

S: **Yes.**

T: [Wait] **Please treat each constellation fragment and then join the constellation fragments into one fragment.**

S: **Yes.**

T: **Please treat the remaining fragment and join it with the Behavior System.**

S: **Yes.**

T: **Please do a Massive Change History and everything.**

S: **Yes.**

T: **Subconscious, are there any floating fragments to deal with?**

S: **No.** [If "Yes," then go to Section 8-25.]

The treatment of System Fragments works easily with patients and takes about 3 to 10 minutes. I usually explain the process to the patient while the subconscious is treating the patient.

8-24 Treating the tendency to create System Fragments

Generalizing from what I had learned about easy creation of parts, I soon determined that damage to the Basic Neurostructure contributes to the easy creation of new System Fragments. This discovery led to the development of the following protocol. Whenever I find System Fragments, I always ask the subconscious if the System Fragments tend to be easily created and if we should treat any cause for this tendency to create System Fragments. Here's the protocol:

T: **Subconscious, is it easy to create System Fragments?**

S: **Yes.**

T: **Subconscious, please treat the trauma in Memory I, Memory II, and Memory III so it will no longer be easy to create System Fragments.**

S: **Yes.**

T: **Subconscious, please treat the Basic Neurostructure that operates on Memories I, II, and III. Add or subtract neural connections in the Basic Neurostructure so the easy creation of System Fragments stops.**

S: **Yes.**

T: **Subconscious, please treat the context that caused easily created System Fragments.**

S: **Yes.**

T: **Subconscious, please do a Massive Change History and everything.**

S: **Yes.**

T: **Subconscious, please treat any trauma or parts in the Emotion System that helps the easy creation of System Fragments.**

S: **Yes.**

T: **Please do a Massive Change History and everything.**

Check in later sessions to see if this intervention was complete. Sometimes there is a problem when the System Fragments integrate into the primary Behavioral System. For some reason, the structures of the fragments will not join properly and remain "floating" in the Active Experience. The next section discusses the treatment of floating structures.

8-25 Floating Structures in the Active Experience

Floating structures in the Active Experience result in an unusual treatment barrier. These floating system structures disorganize the Active Experience, which often results in slowing down the treatment rate and causing a disorganized conscious experience. The activity also blocks the ability of the subconscious to treat issues spontaneously between sessions and the patient from communicating with the subconscious.

Following problem-solving, I found that floating structures were caused by the incomplete integration of constellations. The treated structures failed to integrate into the Behavior System. A barrier in the Basic Neurostructure and Memory I of the system was the cause of this incomplete integration. This barrier in the Basic Neurostructure leaves the basic structure of the trauma part unintegrated and free to "float around" in the Active Experience without emotions or memories.

We already know that the subconscious can treat System Fragments and join them to form a single fragment for each constellation of fragments. Just like parts, the floating System Fragments operate as one after they are all joined with the Behavior System. When these floating

System Fragments join with the Behavior System, they do not lose their uniqueness but associate *with* the structure of the Behavior System to operate in harmony.

This floating fragment phenomenon can also happen with amnesic parts. With some patients, I have found that by simply asking the subconscious to integrate the amnesic parts, the associations are exchanged; however, the Memory I component of a part can prevent it from integrating into Memory III. Often, the cause of this problem is that the Basic Neurostructure or Memory I of the main Behavioral System has a barrier, which prevents the Memory I of the part from integrating. When the Memory I of the treated part fails to integrate, I have found that it will often float in the Active Experience. These floating amnesic part fragments disturb the experience or behavior of the person, as well as the treatment process and communication with the subconscious. Whenever I am desperate, I look for floating fragments. Here is the way to clear these floating fragments of parts or Behavior Systems.

T: **Subconscious, are there any floating fragments in the Active Experience?**

S: **Yes.**

T: **Subconscious, please treat the barrier in the Basic Neurostructure and Memory I in the Behavior System.**

S: **Yes.**

T: [Done] **Please integrate the Memory of the fragments into Memory III.**

S: **Yes.**

T: **Please do a Massive Change History and everything and treat any relevant Shadow Memory.**

I found that some symptoms of mild Asperger's syndrome in a client were in part caused by floating structures. Treating the floating structures was one of the steps in treating the syndrome.

8-26 Treating subconscious fragments

Sometimes, patients create subconscious fragments when System Fragments are formed. This can also happen with other trauma. I initially included the treatment of subconscious fragments in the procedure to treat System Fragments and constellations of fragments. Later, I learned the subconscious could directly treat all subconscious fragments and join them with the primary subconscious. Sometimes field barriers need to be addressed.

T: **Subconscious, are there any subconscious fragments in the Behavior System?**

S: **Yes.**

T: **Is safe to treat these subconscious fragments?**

S: **No.**

T: **Is there a barrier?**

S: **Yes.**

T: **Are fields associated to the subconscious fragments?**

S: **Yes.**

Remember, it is possible to teach the subconscious how to treat fields.

T: **Can you clear the fields and then treat and join the subconscious fragments with the subconscious?**

S: **Yes.**

8-27 An Independent Behavior System

It is possible to have an Independent Behavior System operating, as I discovered in the following example. With this particular person, more than 15 sessions were held trying to treat a part that seemed impossible to treat. The part appeared to have knowledge beyond our expectation and consistently outwitted my patient and me in our problem-solving attempts. I tried all the interventions in my experience. All my attempts to find the solution were thwarted by disguises put up by the part. This part was not created on purpose by someone else to thwart a therapist, but was a genuine and very clever self-protective part of the personality. The part could verbalize through auditory intrusions and was quite candid about how inept I was.

In desperation, I guessed that this was a separate Behavior System with an independent Active Experience, memory, and subconscious, and therefore was completely independent from the primary Active Experience. Apparently, a severe head trauma resulting in a near-death experience, sometime between the ages of one and four, was the cause of this part's creation. The primary subconscious and Active Experience went into protection mode and closed down all functions. The separate Behavior System was created and took over with an independent Active Experience. The environment presented a condition of "total unwantedness" that became the pervasive theme of the part in the system. The part felt pain when the patient was feeling happy or moving forward in some way and, on the other hand, happiness when the patient was sad. This part wanted to stay in total control. This part had a "mind of its own" and was committed to the goal of the punishing mother by undermining the patient's efforts to intentionally advance in life. The part also produced many negative verbal intrusions, often identical to the punishing words of her mother. In other Independent Behavior Systems caused by total "un-wantedness" were abandonment and severe neglect.

In this case, the subconscious could not easily communicate when the part generated by the Independent Behavior System was active. Even after I had a model of the part, I continued to have trouble treating it. I tried all of the interventions described in this book and some less conventional interventions including fields. I was grasping at straws. The best I could do was to get the part to consider that she had a fear of being wanted. The part was willing to consider this as a "problem"—one that she might agree to have treated. The good outcome was that, three sessions later, the part allowed the subconscious to treat the fear of not being wanted and to move the part into Memory III.

Now we had a brilliant disruptive part in Memory III. Three sessions later, after many reframes and treatment of odds and ends, the part joined with Memory III. This intervention will be given in detail in Flint (n.d.). The patient still was not able to move forward voluntarily. This was resolved in later sessions by using esoteric interventions to treat and integrate a part that had a belief imposing "no to everything." This was the keystone we were looking for, on and off, for 26 sessions.

To summarize, a new Behavior System is created when some intensely severe trauma causes the Basic Neurostructure to fragment. The new Behavior System develops independently from the main Behavior System. The Emotion System serves both the new and the main Behavior System. Here is an intervention for treating a simple Independent Behavior System.

T: **Is this problem caused by an Independent Behavior System?**
S: **Yes.**

T; **Are all parts in the Independent Behavior System willing to be treated?"**
S: **Yes.** [If "No," problem-solve.]

T: **Subconscious, please treat the colleges of emotions in the Emotion System. Follow the associations and treat the memory elements in the Independent Behavior System and Memory III in the main Behavior System.**
S: **Yes.**

T: [Done] **Subconscious, please do a Massive Change History and everything and join the Independent Behavior System with the main Behavior System.**

S: **Yes.**

T: [Done] **Subconscious, please do a Massive Change History.**

S: **Yes.**

Structures

8-28 Treating the structure of Layered Memory structures

I believe that this intervention speeds up the treatment of various unique Layered Memory structures by treating the structure of layered structures. This intervention treats memories, Belief Structures, Picture Structures, Predispositions, and parts with Layered Memories. It could well be that this intervention will treat all forms of layered structures in Memory III.

T: **Subconscious, will you treat the structure of Layered Memory structures, and when the structure falls apart, tag all the elements of the structure and then treat the Layered Memories slowly, safely, and in the correct order? After each structure is treated, please do a Massive Change History and everything and strengthen the suitable self-empowering beliefs or behavior.**

S: **Yes.**

Of course, if any Layered Memory structures are dormant, the inactive memories will undoubtedly awaken later and will then have to be treated.

8-29 Treating structures related to significant issues

The Structure Procedure is a useful intervention to treat most any issue. Five significant structures have been defined, consisting of associations to problematic behaviors and emotions. When I treat these structures, I treat each one on the list, one after the other. I ask for a Massive Change History and everything after each treatment. There always exists the possibility that all structures are associated in some way, so I begin with the following:

T: **Subconscious, please treat the structure of all structures and then do a Massive Change History and everything.**

S: **Yes.**

T: [Done] **Subconscious, please treat each structure in the correct order and do the Massive Change History and everything after each structure.**

S: **Yes.**

In the case of the patient with mild Asperger's syndrome, questioning led us to believe that there was a structure that linked all the background structures and a garbage can structure, too—the structure of forgotten memories. As improbable as this sounds, the intervention led to the patient immediately feeling calmer. Then I asked the following:

T: **Subconscious, please treat the structure of all problematic structures.**

S: **Yes.**

T: **Subconscious, please treat the structure of all trauma structures.**

S: **Yes.**

T: **Subconscious, please treat the structure of all learning structures.**

S: **Yes.**

T: **Subconscious, please treat the structure of all negative dissociation structures.**

S: **Yes.**

T: **Subconscious, please treat the structure of all trauma emotions.**

S: **Yes.**

The patient was sleepy by the end of the session.

8-30 Treating the structure of trauma emotions

Trauma creates collages of trauma emotions in the Emotion System. These emotions are the motivation for problematic behaviors in individuals who suffered the trauma. This is different from a Structure Procedure because the Structure Procedure uses associations between content and emotions to identify the structure of common memory elements (see Chapter 7-5). The present intervention involves using the associations from all the different trauma responses to the collages of trauma emotions in the Emotion System. Once the collages of trauma emotions are identified, we know that the collages of emotions in the Emotion System have neural associations to the memory structures in Memory II and III that bind emotions to trauma memory structures. This intervention first treats the collages of trauma emotions in the Emotions System and then uses the associations between the treated trauma emotions and trauma memory structures to identify and treat them. It is believed that this treats many more trauma structures in Memory II and III because the associations are like tags used to activate memories that would otherwise remain dormant. This intervention, therefore, is efficient and effective in the treatment of many issues, including: personal issues, obsessions, compulsions, complex memories, trauma behaviors that are reinforced by the environment, and so forth.

T: **Subconscious, can you identify the behavioral effects of the trauma and find the association links to the collages of emotions in the Emotion System and tag them?**

S: **Yes.**

T: **Please treat the collages of trauma emotions in the Emotion System one after the other, and after treating each collage, follow the emotions to the memory structures and treat them in the correct order. Then do a Massive Change History and everything. Repeat this for every collage of trauma emotions in the Emotion System.**

S: **Yes.**

Below is an example of an intervention that was used to treat parts in a structure. It can also work for intrusions, memory structures, and beliefs.

T: **Subconscious, I am going to read the following intervention to see if it is safe to do. "Find the basic trauma that underlies the structure. Look for resets, suicidal memories, and so forth so you are not taken by surprise. Go to the basic trauma in the Emotion System, and treat the emotions in the Emotion System, and then treat the links to the peripheral parts. Disempower the parts by treating the remaining emotions in the parts. Strengthen the positive behavior of the parts with positive emotions and join the parts with the Main Personality." Is this intervention safe to do?**

S: **Yes.**

T: **Please do it.**

S: **Yes.**

If the subconscious says "No," then problem-solve, making sure that the intervention you suggest is safe and appropriate. This intervention apparently releases most of the parts with no pain and allows positive qualities to be strengthened, and then integrates the parts. Nevertheless, some parts may have to be treated individually. As always, if it does not work, problem-solve.

One patient said that this process was like "peeling an onion." He felt a constant processing sensation. My subconscious suggested that going to the core of the issue in this way was treating what needed to be treated, and that it was fast.

Emotion System

8-31 Parts in the Emotion System

Occasionally, I will find a part in the Emotion System that increases the emotional response of problematic behaviors like obsessive-compulsive disorders and depression. Specifically, what I call a part, in this case, is a collage of emotions that became associated *with* a memory structure forming a specific emotion. I still refer to these collages of emotions as parts because it is easier. Usually treating parts in the Emotion System is straightforward.

T: **Subconscious, are there parts in the Emotion System that contribute to this issue?**

S: **Yes.**

T: **Can you treat the parts and do the change histories?**

S: **Yes.**

Later, you will see, other memory structures can be found in the Emotion System.

8-32 Stacked parts and Layered Memories in the Emotion System

A patient felt mortified by a comment he made to someone. He confessed to me that he frequently felt this mortification and believed that this shame feeling blocked his ability to relate comfortably to people, and also limited his competence in coping with the communication mistakes he often made. Problem-solving and treating this issue resulted in an interesting insight, for I discovered Stacked Memories and layered parts within the Emotion System.

T: **Subconscious, is the behavior that gives the feeling of mortification a memory structure?**

S: **No.**

T: **Is the behavior a part, a field, or an Ego State?**

S: **No.** [To each guess]

I made other guesses and finally:

T: **Is it a Belief Memory?**

S: **Yes.**

T: **Please treat the Belief Memory.**

S: **No.**

After more problem-solving, I found I could not treat the mortification emotion because it was the base of what I thought was a stacked

Emotion Memory in the Emotion System. We found two memories stacked and associated *to* the Emotion Memory.

T: **Please treat the stacked Emotion Memory in the Emotion System starting at the top and working down.**

S: **No.**

More problem-solving, and we ruled out fields, Stacked Parts, and Predispositions in Memory II as the source of a barrier. The memory associated *to* the Emotion Memory was a Belief Memory in the Behavioral System—in Memory III.

T: **Subconscious, please treat the dissociation fragment associated *to* the Belief Memory in Memory III.**

S: **Yes.**

T: [Done] **Please treat the Belief Memory in Memory III and compose and strengthen a self-empowering belief to take its place.**

S: **Yes.**

T: [Done] **Please treat the Emotion Memory and follow the association to the memory structures in Memory III and treat them in the correct order.**

S: **Yes.**

T: [Done] **Please do a Massive Change History and everything.**

S: **Yes.**

The patient reported that this intervention resulted in an overall relaxed feeling that lasted the whole week.

In the following session I made another discovery. The subconscious reported that the treatment in the Emotion System was significant. We explored and found Layered Memories in the Emotional System that had formed during trauma. When the trauma emotion was actively associating with the trauma memory in Memory III, and when a new belief formed because of the trauma, the emotion created to associate *with* the belief would associate *to* the Emotion Memory associated *with* the trauma memory. The Emotion Memory therefore became a Layered Memory. Apparently different beliefs, like feeling helpless, hopeless, and worthless, can result in two or more emotions becoming stacked to the basic trauma emotion.

T: **Subconscious, are there any stacked Emotion Memories in the Emotion System?**

S: **Yes.**

T: **Please treat the stacked Emotion Memories from the top down.**

S: **Yes.**

Sometimes, I look for memories of the creation of trauma structures that may be used to speed up treatment. I am not confident that I ever have success at this. However, this is an example of looking for one of those memories.

T: **Subconscious, is there any aspect of memory who remembers all the stacked Emotion Memories in the Emotion System?**

S: **Yes.**

With problem-solving eliminating various possibilities, the subconscious revealed the association process could identify the stacked emotions.

T: **Subconscious, please work with the association process and treat the stacked Emotion Memories in the Emotion System.**

S: **Yes.**

This last intervention presumably treated all the stacked Emotion Memories in the Emotion System.

8-33 Heavy feeling from Memory I

The patient was being treated for ongoing painful feelings that he had had since early childhood and which had persisted throughout his life. This was the final ongoing feeling to be treated. It soon became apparent that a memory (or memories) in Memory I had emotion associated *with* it from the Emotion System. This memory, with the emotion to motivate it, associated with every behavior that occurred, thereby giving what the patient described as a heavy feeling.

T: **Subconscious, please treat all memories in the Emotion System that are associated *with* memories in Memory I.**

S: **Yes.**

T: **Please do a Massive Change History and everything and treat the Shadow Memories.**

S: **Yes.**

8-34 Comparison memories in the Emotion System

The subconscious was directing treatment. Questions revealed that a memory in the Emotion System required treatment. This memory was the motivator of negative moral comparisons that were used to make critical assessments of self and others in everyday life.

T: **Subconscious, please treat the memory collages in the Emotion System that motivate negative moral comparisons.**

S: **Yes.**

T: **[Done] Is there a structure of memories in Memory III that provides the comparisons?**

S: **Yes.**

T: **Subconscious, please treat the structure of comparison memories in Memory III, tag and treat the memory elements in the correct order, and then do a Massive Change History and everything.**

S: **Yes.**

T: **Please create comparison memories that would be more adaptive in appropriate situations and then do a Massive Change History and everything.**

S: **Yes.**

The patient said that this intervention led to the elimination of negative comparisons with mundane issues.

8-35 Treatment of a memory covered with a towel

The subconscious of a patient gave me permission to find and treat issues. This led to an interesting intervention after I found a problem with a memory in the Emotion System:

T: **Subconscious, is the issue a memory structure in the Emotion System?**

S: **Yes.**

I asked the following questions.

T: **Tried before? Part? Young trauma? Floor or rug? Trauma memory?**

S: [All] **No.**

I asked if I could treat the Emotion Memory structure and discovered a barrier. I asked if it was a part, Layered Memory or field, and so forth. We finally found a memory structure in Memory III associated *to* the Emotion Memory. The Emotion Memory was hidden with a towel (in Memory III), that couldn't be removed. (A towel? Well, that's what I got.)

T: **Subconscious, please change the color of the towel to green.**

Why? Green is a healthy color.

S: **Yes.**

T: **Please treat the trauma of the towel and integrate it with the Main Personality and then do a Massive Change History and everything.**

S: **Yes.**

T: **Subconscious, please treat the memory in the Emotion System and do a Massive Change History and everything.**

S: **Yes.**

This is an example of accepting what you get from the patient and using it in the treatment.

Kinesthetic System

8-36 Treating the Kinesthetic System

I discovered this system when I was working with a person's self-esteem. When I asked if there was any other system that had to do with increasing this person's self-esteem, the subconscious revealed the presence of another system, one I had not discovered yet. After some serious problem-solving, we found a Kinesthetic System that appeared to generate a low-level background feeling of well-being in normal people. In my patient's case, damage to the Kinesthetic System became a barrier for fully experiencing self-love, positive self-esteem, and the feeling of confidence. After its existence and qualities were discovered, here is how I had the subconscious treat the Kinesthetic System.

T: **Subconscious, can you treat the Kinesthetic System?**

S: **Yes.**

T: **Please treat the barriers to positive self-esteem and good feelings in the Kinesthetic System and strengthen the memories that will give positive self-esteem and good feelings to the patient.**

S: **Yes.**

Double-check and look for additional related issues to treat:

T: **[Done] Please tag and treat all parts triggered and activated by the last intervention.**

S: **Yes.**

I have had the subconscious treat the Kinesthetic System in several patients. They have all felt the treatment process begin and experienced varying degrees of positive change in their self-love and self-esteem after the treatment.

Basic Neurostructure

8-37 Basic Neurostructure leading to negative traits

A patient had some negative personality traits and wanted to treat these issues. The following intervention was recommended by the patient's subconscious. Frequently with neural interventions of this type, the patient feels some activity in his or her brain.

T: **Subconscious, do you see the cause of the negative personality traits?**

S: **Yes.**

T: [after further leading questions] **Is it caused by the Basic Neurostructure?**

S: **Yes.**

T: **Can you add and subtract neural connections to eliminate the negative personality traits?**

S: **Yes.**

T: [Wait] **Are you done?**

S: **Yes.**

T: **Is it all healed?**

S: **No.**

T: **Are there some conditions that you cannot treat?**

S: **Yes.**

This is an interesting intervention, suggested by the subconscious, where the subconscious changes memories to compensate for some problematic issue in the Basic Neurostructure.

T: **Can you modify some memories to compensate for the response of the Basic Neurostructure that you cannot treat so the result will be a healthy system?**

S: **Yes.**

T: **Please do it.**

S: **Yes.**

8-38 Speeding up treatment with Basic NeuroStructure Procedures

Dean Kansky (personal communication, September 2, 2003), in conversation with me, said his subconscious had some suggestions that would make a difference when clearing trauma or negative behavior. The interventions involved making adjustments in the Basic Neurostructure to get the Behavior, Emotions, and other systems active and responsive during treatment. This leads to faster changes.

1. Behavior System

T: **Subconscious, will you add and subtract neural associations in the Basic Neurostructure of the Behavior System to optimize its responsiveness during treatment?**

S: **Yes.**
T: [Wait] **Please do a Massive Change History and everything.**
S: **Yes.**

2. Emotion System

T: **Subconscious, will you add and subtract neural associations in the Basic Neurostructure of the Emotion System to optimize its responsiveness during treatment?**
S: **Yes.**
T: [Wait] **Please do a Massive Change History and everything.**
S: **Yes.**

3. Kinesthetic System

T: **Subconscious, will you add and subtract neural associations in the Basic Neurostructure of the Kinesthetic System to optimize its responsiveness during treatment?**
S: **Yes.**
T: [Wait] **Please do a Massive Change History and everything.**
S: **Yes.**

8-39 Treating maladaptive responses caused by the Basic Neurostructure

The patient felt upset because he easily followed what others suggested without giving thought to what he wanted in a situation. He came to me in order to learn to communicate with greater ease, negotiate his needs, and be able to compromise. He also displayed some odd verbal responses and a strange pattern to his speech. I discovered the cause of his undesirable behavior was in the Basic Neurostructure of the Behavior System. This action of the Basic Neurostructure was an adaptation to the punishing behavior of his mother and was caused by a trauma in his first year of life. Basic Neurostructure is especially susceptible to environmental influence between conception and one year of age.

T: **Subconscious, please treat the trauma in the Basic Neurostructure of the Behavior System by adding or subtracting associations to eliminate the problem behavior.**
S: **Yes.**
T: **Please do a Massive Change History and everything.**
S: **Yes.**

The patient never mentioned noticing a change, but he did not refer to himself as "a lackey" afterward.

8-40 Treating compensations in Basic Neurostructure caused by trauma

Another feature of the Basic Neurostructure is the ability to compensate for trauma. An example of this was found in a patient who noticed a miserable and unusual feeling whenever he thought he was feeling better. The subconscious said that this had to do with a trauma that we had previously treated. Before this trauma was treated, when the trauma memory occurred and chronic misery was being experienced, the Basic Neurostructure compensated for the negative effects. The Basic Neurostructure adapted to remove the negative effects of the trauma. This shift in the Basic Neurostructure eliminated the experience caused by the trauma—namely, the misery—by making some other response that changed the experience so the patient was no longer aware of the misery. According to the patient's subconscious, the shift or compensation on the part of the Basic Neurostructure is a more effective way of "dissociating" hurt caused by intense trauma. I haven't observed this phenomenon before or since. However, after treating the trauma, we discovered that the compensatory response of the Basic Neurostructure could become a problem by causing an unusual feeling in the patient. So, though unlikely, it is possible that after a trauma is treated, a compensatory adjustment in the Basic Neurostructure will require treatment. Other structures in Memory II, Memory III, Tandem Memory IIIs, and in the Emotion System were also involved in this compensation for trauma. The treatment for this compensation problem can be given to any one of these memories and structures as needed, but the Basic Neurostructure always has to be treated.

T: **Subconscious, please add or subtract associations in the Basic Neurostructure of the Behavior System and any memory system to stop any compensation activity that is no longer needed.**

S: **Yes.**

T: [Done] **Please do a Massive Change History and everything.**

S: **Yes.**

8-41 Treating quiet spaces in the brain

If you assume that, after conception, brain activity was very diffuse with no particular memory systems or well-defined pathways, then learning can be preserved in all areas of the brain. This suggests that any early trauma could also be stored throughout the entire brain. Here's a hypothesis about how this might happen when the fetus is initially restricted in activity early after conception. As the fetus develops, physical constraints increase that might possibly create a traumatic response. These traumatic responses are remembered in all areas of the brain. As the brain becomes more specialized and regions are devoted to specific functions of the brain and body, the early trauma is changed and is no longer a problem. But in the quiet places of the brain, which are not subjected to a lot of neural activity, these trauma experiences remain. These trauma experiences in the quiet places of the brain are the underlying motivation for a pervasive experience of shame and may well contribute to the experience of shame after birth. Here is the way to treat this problem:

T: **Please treat all the quiet spaces in the brain that were traumatized in utero and after birth.**

S: **Yes.**

T: [Done] **Please do a Massive Change History and everything.**

S: **Yes.**

Recall the vignette in Chapter 1 (see page 11) in which the quiet spaces were treated by repeated applications of the 9-Gamut Procedure (see Appendix V)? The tapping intervention can also be applied to this issue.

Summary

In this chapter we discussed barriers caused by structures in memories and systems. Problem-solving usually revealed the interventions to use to treat complex structures found in patients. These interventions have been used successfully with a number of patients. Using them with yourself or others will validate most of these interventions. When you find a barrier or issue that is not caused by a structure given in this book, you can creatively combine any of the known structures and check with the subconscious to determine if that new structure will resolve the barrier. In such a situation, it is important to remain relaxed, optimistic, flexible and, most of all, expect to resolve the barrier.

Part II

For the
Therapist

Chapter 9

Treating Personality Issues

Whenever you work with yourself or as a trained professional with a patient, you can encounter some real risks that must always be assessed. I assume that if you are treating serious issues you are either a trained mental health professional or are working with one. Although Process Healing can be used to handle most of the possible risks, treating people with an unknown history always requires some basic assessment.

An assessment is important to rule out serious issues. Briefly, you ask the patient about suicidal or homicidal thoughts or plans, assess your patients for any major traumas that could lead to the flooding of emotions, look for dissociative processes such as losing time, assess for addictions, and psychotic behavior, and so forth. It would not hurt to do a formal mental-status examination to rule out more severe issues. Information about mental-status examinations can be obtained by doing a web search. It is your responsibility to protect the patient from misdiagnosis or from missing some unusual physical issue. It is always good to have the patient have a physical examination to rule out other causes for apparent mental dysfunction.

When the patient has a severe depression or any incapacitating issue such as anxiety, fear, or an eating disorder, always discuss the possibility of medication and ask him or her to consult with his or her physician and request a consultation with a psychiatrist. If the patient is reluctant to try medication and is also incapacitated by the symptoms in some way, suggest having a few sessions of treatment to see if it is effective in reducing the symptoms. If no progress is made after several sessions, ask the patient to consider medication. Know your limits. When you see an illness or condition that you are not trained to treat, politely refuse to treat, and refer the patient to other therapists who have the necessary experience.

The most common issues encountered are related to fear or anxiety. This makes treatment of many issues straightforward. However, personality issues come in recognizable patterns or diagnostic categories for which training in the diagnosis and treatment of personality issues becomes useful. In my experience, patients do not usually come to therapy with a known personality diagnosis; they do not ask to have their narcissistic or schizoid personality treated. They come with a list of symptoms that are affecting their way of life—symptoms that they don't want any-more. These are the symptoms that you will treat. However, unless you are a mental health professional, you will not have the training or access to personality testing for a proper diagnosis of how the symptoms fit into some diagnostic category.

In this chapter, I describe common issues, intrusions, system is-sues, and neurological issues. In the section called Common Issues are suggestions for treating basic anxiety, personality patterns, sleep issues, dreams, grief, shame, guilt, Core Issues, and self-perpetuating behav-iors. Remember, what I give in these sections are suggestions and not a thorough, systematic analysis of the issue with the appropriate treat-ment strategies. Everyone is unique and will require problem-solving to resolve issues. In most cases, these are easily resolved. Later in this chapter you will find examples of ways to strengthen desired behaviors and beliefs. Other examples suggest treatments for improvement of self-esteem, positive beliefs, self-empowering behavior, the need to feel loved, and forgiveness of the perpetrator.

The next section deals with intrusions. The examples of intru-sions are rather varied—a feature of human uniqueness—but these ex-amples give a number of ideas about treating intrusions. The nice quality of intrusions is that by recording the frequency at which they occur, you can always get a measure from which to judge the effectiveness of your treatment intervention. I usually get an estimate of the number of intru-sions per day or week and then, in following sessions, ask if and how often the intrusion occurred that week. Many intrusions are caused by parts or Layered Memories and are easy to treat. Remember that some parts and Layered Memories are not active during the session and can become ac-tive later. Treating intrusions involves problem-solving to determine the structure of the intruding memory. Some of my most difficult issues have been intrusions, but in the course of problem-solving I usually learned something new that works with other patients.

The final two sections of this chapter give examples of system issues and issues having to do with neurostructures. The examples illus-trate several strategies that can be used to treat unusual issues.

The best strategy when treating a personality issue is to get the subconscious to help identify the structure that is causing it. When you problem-solve and find a barrier or a novel issue, assemble a combina-tion of structures related in some way that the subconscious will accept as the structure causing the issue. Once this metaphor is developed and accepted, then you can treat the barrier.

Treating personality issues is not always easy. As the intensity of the trauma increases and the intelligence of the patient increases, the more complex the memory structures become. The reason for this is that a quick brain can be very creative in forming the more unusual, problematic memory structures and System Fragments. The treatment of a severe personality disorder may require many sessions.

Paradoxically, the success of Process Healing can also slow the treatment process because most patients, when they experience positive results, want to treat all the little annoying issues that are not easily treated by regular therapy. It is as though once they see that subtle annoyances can be treated, they continue in therapy because they experience progress. On the other hand, even though you can see progress, invariably, for each issue you treat in a session, there are many aspects related to the issue that are still dormant and will not show up until a later session. This delayed expression of issues has ultimately resulted in the development of treatment strategies that have broader treatment effects because they trigger other related memory structures.

This chapter will give professionals some direction in the treatment of major personality issues and help in changing the self-limiting beliefs, habits, obsessions, and compulsions that reduce the quality of life.

Table of contents for this chapter

Strengthening Behaviors

Intrusions

System Issues

Neurology

Summary

The Basics

9-1 Treating personality issues

At the beginning of each session, I like to ask patients what they want to change or which issues they want to work on. Normally, the patient gives me a list of issues and I go to work on them. I start by asking the subconscious which one is best to treat first. Sometimes, treating the first issue resolves all of the others. I generally use the structure approach. Process Healing, I believe, is "evidenced-based therapy" in the truest sense because change in the issue is assessed immediately following treatment, and treatment is modified and continued until the desired outcome is obtained. Review of the issue in following sessions often requires additional treatment. This is a strategy used in Neurolinguistic Programming (Rice and Caldwell, 1986).

Though the content is vast and varied, treatment of personality issues follows a definite seven-step protocol:

1. Identify the issue. Usually, the patient identifies the issue in terms of an emotion or behavior, such as "I have this 'wingy' feeling every time I go out." Be sure to use the patient's wording ('wingy,' in this case) in the intervention. This serves to trigger in the memory aspects that are associated with the patient's feeling.

2. Obtain a baseline for the issue by having the patient imagine a situation where it arises. This is the basis for evidence-based therapy—namely, to treat and then test for your effectiveness. Get a score of the intensity of the issue on a scale from 0 to 10 and a measure of its frequency per day or week.

T: **When you imagine yourself walking out of your house, on a scale from 0 to 10, how intense is this wingy feeling?**

P: **An 8.**

You will ask this again at the end of the treatment to assess the effectiveness of your interventions and see how complete you were in treating the issue. You are making progress if the score decreases. Repeat the test for treated issues in the following sessions.

3. Suggest an initial intervention such as the Sentence Procedure or the Structure Procedure to start treating the issue. I believe that you save time by asking the subconscious if the intervention you want to use is the best intervention.

T: **Subconscious, is the Sentence Procedure the best intervention to use with this issue?**

S: **Yes.**

T: **Subconscious, please do the Sentence Procedure with the sentence, "I will not feel wingy when I leave my home," and tag all of the memory elements that activate, and treat them in the correct order. If there are any beliefs, treat the beliefs so they are no longer true. Then compose a self-empowering belief, and strengthen it until it is true.**

S: **Yes.**

Here is an example of using the Structure Procedure with this issue.

T: **Subconscious, should I use the Structure Procedure to treat this issue?**

S: **Yes.**

T: **Subconscious, please treat the structure of memory elements that give the wingy feeling. When the structure falls apart, tag the memory elements and treat them in the correct order. If there are any** beliefs, treat the beliefs so they are no longer true. Then, compose and strengthen self-empowering beliefs to take their place.

S: **Yes.**

4. Ask the subconscious if this issue has been completely treated.

T: **Subconscious, has this issue been completely treated?**

With a "No," you check for barriers and then start asking about simple structures in Memory III and then progress to more complex structures, and then to system structures or structures in other systems. Remember to do a Massive Change History and everything and treat the Shadow Memories after each intervention. Here are a few structures that I would try:

- Memories
- Layered Memories
- Parts
- Predispositions
- Belief or Picture Structures
- Part with a Layered Memory
- Layered Memory associated *with* a Predisposition
- Part with a Layered Memory associated *with* a Predisposition
- Structure in an Ego State or Tandem Memory
- System Fragments
- Memory or structure in another system
- Independent Behavior System

If the subconscious says no to everything on this list, ask:

T: **Subconscious, have I treated this structure before?**

S: **Yes.** [Problem-solve]

If you get a "No," you start creating new memory structures with unusual combinations of known structures. You can also ask the subconscious for cues to help you guess the strategy to treat the issue completely.

5. If appropriate, ask the subconscious to compose and strengthen the desired behavior to replace the behavior just treated. Issues sometimes involve ineffective behavior or behavior that creates the wrong response from other people. Though treatment usually weakens these behaviors, I like to strengthen positive behaviors to take their place. I frequently take time to work with the patient to compose some behavior that feels comfortable to the patient.

T: **Subconscious, can you strengthen positive, self-empowering behavior to replace the behaviors we have just treated?**

S: **Yes.**

6. When you have finished treating the issue and strengthening a replacement behavior, test the issue in the original situation to see if the experience of the issue has changed.

T: [To the patient] **Now, imagine yourself walking out of your house. How strong is the "wingy" feeling?**

P: **I feel completely relaxed walking out the door.**

If the experience is not at 0 or an appropriate level, repeat the steps above to bring the score down to the desired level. When it appears that you are done with this issue, continue to step seven.

7. Use the Futurepace Intervention (see Chapter 9-3) with the issue to practice the change in many different situations.

T: [To the patient] **Select four or five situations where you have felt this wingy feeling and then one at a time review these situations in slow motion and see if any uncomfortable emotions or wingy feelings are experienced. Subconscious, please tag and treat any emotions or memories that activate during this process.**

S: **Yes.**

When the patient discovers additional issues or emotional spots, problem-solve and treat those issues by repeating the above steps. It is often useful to discuss the situations that the patient reviewed to see if there was any point in the situations where they needed to do or say something (positive behavior) to make the situation more comfortable. If so, compose and strengthen the appropriate statements and do the Futurepace Intervention again.

9-2 Treating complex structures with Predispositions

It is important to know that Predispositions can be associated *with* complex structures. With an extreme trauma or traumas during a developmental stage, Predispositions can be associated *with* memories in Memory III or associated *to* structures in another system. I usually inquire about Predispositions when I am treating a personality issue. Predispositions are like habits because they are triggered by situational cues. Many traits of personality disorders can be caused by memory structures triggered by Predispositions. An awareness of these possible structures is useful when treating some personalities. I am reminding you with a list of possible combinations because these combinations are commonly found in personality disorders:

1. Layered Memories, Belief and Picture structures (Chapter 8-7 through 8-8)

2. Predisposition Structures (see Chapter 8-14)

3. Layered Memory with a Predisposition associated *with* the memory (see Chapter 8-15)

4. A part with a Layered Memory with a Predisposition associated *with* the Layered Memory (see Chapter 8-17)

5. In general, a review of Chapter 8 will remind you of many structures that are found in personality disorders. It's important to have this information available when you problem-solve.

In most cases, the Predisposition is treated first, before treating the remainder of the complex structure.

9-3 The Futurepacing Intervention

Futurepacing means that the patient imagines doing the desired behavior in various settings in the future. This is an NLP intervention. While imagining a future situation in which the issue may arise, the patient looks for an experience of negative emotions, memories, or beliefs that will get in the way of the desired behavior. After identifying these negative emotions, work with the subconscious to treat them. Use the Sentence Procedure to weaken all beliefs, experiences, and memories that get in the way of the desired behavior you want to strengthen. After you have treated all the barriers and strengthened the desired behavior, test the results by using the Futurepace Intervention with the desired behavior in that situation again.

Another way of using the Futurepace Intervention is similar to the Sentence Procedure. Have the patient imagine doing any desired behavior in some situation, and then immediately ask the subconscious to tag and treat any memory structures or emotions observed in the Active Experience that would get in the way of the desired behavior. Continue this, repeatedly, until the goal behavior can be imagined to happen naturally with comfort and confidence—for example, when the patient is offered a cigarette, the goal is to have the patient respond with, "No, thank you, I don't smoke" and feel completely natural. Then you use the Futurepace Intervention with the desired behavior in many different situations. This associates the desired behavior to those situations, so that when the situation arises the desired behavior is triggered. In most cases, the desired behavior simply occurs spontaneously and naturally and seems congruent with the patient. When you find additional issues while doing a Futurepace Intervention, problem-solve the issues and treat them.

Common Issues

9-4 Treating basic anxiety

Anxiety is a frequent issue that presents. Massive anxiety can be associated *with* a memory structure or parts; therefore, some awareness and precautions for emotional flooding are necessary. Panic attacks are an example of massive anxiety usually caused by fragile parts. Always check with the subconscious to see if it is safe to treat the issue. Usually, the treatment of anxiety is a routine, easy intervention. This is an example of how I treat basic anxiety.

T: **Are there parts or memory structures with anxiety that need treatment?**

S: **Yes.**

T: **Is it safe to treat these parts or memory structures, one after the other?**

S: **Yes.**

T: **Please treat them, one after the other.**

S: **Yes.**

T: **Are there any parts that do not want to be treated?**

S: **Yes**

Problem-solve until all other parts are treated and integrated. Be sure to ask about fragile parts and treat them appropriately.

On the other hand, anxiety can be treated in the Emotion System.

T: **Are there collages of anxiety for this issue in the Emotion System?**

S: **Yes.**

T: **Please treat a collage of anxiety for this issue in the Emotion System, and then follow the associations to memory structures. Treat them in the correct order. If there are beliefs, treat the beliefs until they are not true, and compose and strengthen positive, self-empowering beliefs to take their place. Do a Massive Change History and everything. Repeat these interventions for each collage for this issue.**

S: **Yes.**

In a case of chronic anxiety, I continue with the following:

T: **Subconscious, are you done?**

S: **Yes.**

T: **Subconscious, please do the Sentence Procedure, "I will not have this anxiety or these fears." Tag all memory elements that became** active and treat them in the correct order, one after the other. Then do a Massive Change History and everything.

S: **Yes.**

T: **Subconscious, are there layered parts that contribute to these issues?**

S: **Yes.**

T: **Please treat them.**

S: **Yes.**

Sometimes, parts become active during the treatment—for example, a baby part awakened at this time. I treated the baby part and then continued to treat the anxiety issue. I look for Tandem Memory IIIs that could contribute to chronic anxiety.

T: **Subconscious, are there any Tandem Memories that contribute to chronic anxiety?**

S: **Yes.**

T: **How many?**

P: **Eight.** [The patient heard the number in her thoughts.]

T: **Can you treat the anxiety in each of the Tandem Memory IIIs? Then, do a Massive Change History and everything.**

S: **Yes.**

When I was learning Process Healing, I made a minor error and treated and integrated multiple Tandem Memories into one Tandem Memory, and then integrated the remaining Tandem Memory into Memory III. I eliminated the multiple Active Experiences and, by doing so, hampered treatment, because there was only one Active Experience to work with. Therefore, I now treat Tandem Memories because they all may have the some pain and negative memories, but I do not integrate them into Memory III. Tandem Memories run the independent Active Experiences, which are a positive asset for the person.

9-5 Personality patterns treated as structures or beliefs

The following are examples of several personality patterns treated with a Structure or Belief Intervention. If this type of intervention does not work, problem-solve to treat the issue.

Examples:

1. **Defensiveness**

The patient said that whenever she had to explain anything to others, she felt driven to prove that she was "not wrong" in the explanation of what she was doing. Here's how I began the intervention;

then I continued to test and problem-solve until I felt confident that the issue was completely treated. The issue, as always, was reviewed in the following sessions.

T: **Subconscious, is there a structure of defensive behaviors that we can treat to handle all these defensiveness problems?**

S: **Yes.**

T: **Please do that.**

2. Mother-in-law reaction

This woman always felt moody, hypersensitive, and took a defensive stance when she was around her mother-in-law.

T: **Subconscious, is there a structure of memories associated with the mother-in-law, which we can treat to handle the moody behavior, hypersensitivity, and defensive stance around her mother-in-law?**

S: **Yes.**

T: **Please do that.**

3. Emotions related to conversing

This patient always felt a surge of emotions when she was trying to converse with people.

T: **Subconscious, is there a structure associated *to* emotions, which becomes active when she tries to converse with people?**

S: **No.**

T: **Is it a belief?**

S: **Yes.**

T: **Please treat the belief that causes this problem and strengthen the willingness to converse when you do the Massive Change History and everything.**

S: **Yes.**

In this case, I didn't have the subconscious compose a replacement belief but instead strengthened the experience of feeling comfortable when conversing with others.

4. Dwelling on negative things

This patient had the problem of always dwelling on negative thoughts. After some investigation with the subconscious, I asked:

T: **Is this a massive belief that looks for the negative in everything?**

S: **Yes.**

T: **Please treat the belief that finds something negative in everything, and create and strengthen a positive, self-empowering belief to replace the treated belief, and then do a Massive Change History and everything.**

I ask the subconscious to create a positive, self-empowering belief as the means to install a positive belief. Sometimes, the patient or I compose the positive, self-empowering belief, such as "I look for the good in everything," but at other times I just make a general statement: "Subconscious, please create and strengthen a positive, self-empowering belief and replace the treated belief." Either way works fine.

9-6 Treating sleep issues

When I have a patient who has not been sleeping well, I assess for depression or drinking a stimulant late in the day or at night. Then I ask questions to determine exactly what he or she sees as the problem. He or she may be sleeping lightly, waking up several times a night, having recurrent dreams, waking up with a start, having trouble falling asleep easily, or waking early. Sometimes, the details I get from my questioning will lead me to precisely what needs to be treated. Below are examples of interventions for treating sleep issues. I usually ask the subconscious whether the intervention is necessary to treat the sleep issue.

Examples:

1. Parts wake up and interact

T: **Are parts keeping this patient awake at night?**

S: **Yes.**

T: **Subconscious, please treat, one after the other, parts that wake up during the night.**

S: **Yes.**

T: **Subconscious, please tag and treat all the parts and memories that become active when I say, "I am going to sleep with a quiet mind." Then generate other sentences to trigger more disruptive memories until no more are triggered. Then treat them one after the other.**

S: **Yes.**

2. Unusual parts are active at night—parts without eyes and ears

This patient felt an active mind at night but could not really identify any kind of intrusions that were coming into his thoughts. I fumbled around and finally discovered what was keeping him awake.

T: **Subconscious, are there parts without eyes and ears waking up at night?**

S: **Yes.**

T: **Subconscious, please generate some activity to slow down the parts without eyes and ears and then treat them one after the other.**

S: **Yes.**

Sometimes, problem-solving is necessary to treat parts without eyes and ears. I also used the Sentence Procedure here to activate other parts that were involved in keeping him awake.

3. Activity in the Active Experience—Predispositions

A patient was having problems sleeping and the resolution came down to this intervention—after a lot of problem-solving.

T: **Subconscious, are there Predispositions interfering with sleep?**

S: **Yes.**

T: **Subconscious, please treat the Predispositions that interfere with sleep.**

S: **Yes.**

4. Active mind preventing sleep

When the patient has an active mind keeping him or her awake, I ask the patient to do the Tapas Acupressure Technique (TAT, see Appendix VI) while thinking the typical thoughts he or she has after going to bed. I then instruct him or her to say the following:

T: [While the patient is holding the TAT pose] **Please clear any barriers for having a good night's sleep.**

S: **Yes.**

I instruct the patient to hold the pose until any feeling in the brain or under the fingers stops or until the thoughts or pictures stop streaming through her consciousness.

5. Diet issues

I ask the subconscious if any of the following drinks or snacks interfere with sleep: coffee, chocolate, alcohol, and late meals. I work with the subconscious to determine a cut-off time for eating snacks and meals, and so forth.

T: **Subconscious, does the patient eat or drink anything that tends to keep her awake at night?**

S: **Yes.**

T: **Can you tell me at what time she has to stop eating or drinking?**

S: **Yes.**

Then I work with the subconscious to get a specific time by asking questions like the following:

T: **Subconscious, should fluids be taken after 9 p.m.?**

S: **Yes.**

T: **After 10 p.m.?**

S: **No.**

T: **After 9:30 p.m.?**

S: **No.**

By asking questions in this way, then the time to stop drinking fluids can be determined. In this example, I asked the patient to stop drinking fluids after 9:30 p.m. to see if he or she slept any better.

9-7 Working with dreams

I suppose I could do a brief dream analysis with my patients that would probably reveal or trigger some issues. Instead, I usually explore briefly by asking the patient if the dream conveys any message. Sometimes this reveals issues that should be treated, particularly when the dreams happen one or two nights before our scheduled session. My belief, though, is that dreams are artifacts of the Active Experience. I don't know if the occurrence of dreams has to do with processing the previous day's experience or past memories, but I do believe that some memories or past intense experiences spontaneously become active in the Active Experience. Our brain organizes what is active into some form of plausible experience, and a storyline, either literal or in metaphor, is formed.

Dreams have content and emotions. Rather than trying to interpret the dreams I assume that, by treating the content and emotions, the treatment process will lead to the treatment of the appropriate memories causing the dreams. In most cases, Process Healing will stop the dreams from occurring again.

T: **Subconscious, do either the emotions or the content of the dream have to be treated?**

S: **Yes.**

T: **Should I treat the content first?**

S: **Yes.**

T: **Please treat the content of the dream.**

S: **Yes.**

T: [Done] **Subconscious, do the emotions associated *with* the dream have to be treated?**

S: **Yes.**

T: **Please treat the emotions associated *with* the dream, follow the associations back to the memory structures, and treat the structures in the correct order.**

T: [Done] **Subconscious, does a Massive Change History and everything have to be done?**

S: **Yes.**

T: **Subconscious, please do that.**

S: **Yes.**

Sometimes dreams do not have to be treated, but more often, either emotions or content, or both, have to be treated.

Example:

Cartoon picture dreams

I had seen the patient for several sessions. Over Christmas, she had a large number of dreams. As usual, I tried to treat the content and emotions associated *with* the dreams. All but one of the dreams were successfully treated. I asked the patient to tell me about the dream. The patient was a torture survivor. She was reliving the content of past memories by means of dreams. In her dreams, all of the ugly, terrifying experiences were portrayed as cartoons. The cartoons lightened the intensity of the content of the real experience but were nonetheless problematic. I started to deal with the parts giving the cartoon dreams. This patient heard sentences said by the subconscious that she then relayed to me.

T: **Subconscious, are there cartoon parts that are *associated with* this dream?**

S: **Yes.**

T: **Do these parts want to be treated?**

S: **Yes.**

T: **Please treat these parts, one after the other.**

S: **Yes.**

T: **[Wait] Are all the parts treated?**

S: **No.**

T: **Does this part want to be treated?**

The following is an example of the subconscious communicating in words.

S: **The part can't understand you because it's humming and can't hear you.**

T: **Humming?**

S: **The humming protects the part from the trauma pain.**

T: **Subconscious, can you talk to the part?**

S: **Yes.**

T: **Subconscious, can you treat the humming and the big, big, pain together so this part and no other part or the personality feel the pain?**

S: **Yes.**

This seemed to work, and the patient felt more relaxed and no longer had cartoon dreams.

S: **Yes.**

T: [Done] **Subconscious, can you now treat the parts one after the other?**

S: **Yes.**

One week later — in session.

P: **I noticed that I touched my ear for some reason.**

T: **Subconscious, is this a part that is connected to the cartoon dream?**

S: **Yes.**

T: **Please treat that part, slowly and safely.**

S: **Yes.**

Working with such "agents" or "helper entities" used to stretch my credulity, but now I look favorably on any form of positive influence that works for the patient. Though I trust the subconscious to operate in the best interest of the patient, I frequently do safety checks to be sure that the patient does not get damaged in any way.

9-8 Treating grief

Grief can be a sensitive emotion to treat. Some people with extreme grief are comfortable experiencing it because they believe that experiencing emotions is part of the grieving process. Others find that grief interferes with their life and would rather reduce the grief symptoms by treating them directly. Exploring and treating a patient's grief must be done in a very sensitive way to show complete respect to all parts concerned.

The least intrusive way to treat grief is to use a Sentence Procedure. Use "I feel my grief at a comfortable level" as the initial sentence. This will trigger almost all grief-related beliefs, memories, and parts that would perpetuate the grief.

T: **Subconscious, please do the Sentence Procedure with "I feel my grief at a comfortable level" and tag and treat the memory structures giving grief, until the grief is at a comfortable and appropriate level of intensity.**

T: [Done] **Please do a Massive Change History and everything.**

There may be aspects or parts that have some belief about death of a loved one and grief. When you run into this, discuss with the patient, in detail, the pros and cons of treating grief. I have had patients decline treatment of their grief when I first approached the issue. In the next session, they ask to have their grief treated.

In some cases, I suggest that the patient write a letter to the lost loved one. This is also appropriate with estranged parents, family, or friends. I ask my patients to include in the letter all the things they dislike and all that they love and appreciate about the person, citing instances of both. I tell them to write the letter so that the recipient will know that it is a loving letter. While writing the letter, a full range of emotions will probably be felt. I ask the subconscious to tag and treat any beliefs, memories, or parts that carry negative emotions experienced while writing the letter. When the patient is satisfied with the letter, it can be disposed of in a symbolic way or mailed to the person.

9-9 Treating a basis for shame

The emotional basis for shame is learned *in utero*. Shame is a common emotion that occurs when an individual takes responsibility for a trauma. Children have a tendency to take responsibility for situations they can't control. I believe that the feeling of "shame" stems from the dissonance experienced when physical constraints are placed on the free response of the fetus—namely, as the fetus gets larger, the control of movement decreases. I call the negative stimulation of constraint and the subsequent response "experienced" by the fetus through this loss of control *fetal dissonance*. Later on in life, the experience of losing control can be interpreted as doing something wrong and thinking you caused it. This can lead to self-blame or shame. Fetal dissonance, an emotion experienced as shame, later associates *with* experience involving loss of control and magnifies the experience that is responded to with shame. Hence, the shame is experienced more intensely.

This shame stemming from *in utero* trauma dissonance can have a pervasive, life-long effect on a person's experience. As a child or adult, the lack of control of any kind can trigger fetal dissonance, which adds additional motivation to the shame associated *with* the current experience. Having the feeling that you or your body did not respond appropriately in a trauma situation will trigger shame. Shame can be a chronic underlying emotion that may be especially pervasive in a traumatized person. Even with a trauma-free childhood, many of our negative beliefs are shame-based. Here are some examples of treating shame.

Examples:

1. Treating with a Change History

Here is an intervention to treat fetal dissonance experienced as shame.

T: **Subconscious, please do a Change History in Memories I, II, and III, and treat all in utero traumatic dissonance underlying beliefs, and then strengthen appropriate, self-empowering beliefs.**

S: **Yes.**

T: [Done] **Subconscious, please do a Massive Change History and everything.**

S: **Yes.**

2. Treating through the Emotion System

T: **Subconscious, is there a collage of shame emotions in the Emotion System?**

S: **Yes.**

T: **Please treat the Shame emotions in the Emotion System, and follow the associations to other memory structures in Memory III, the Ego States, and Tandem Memories, and treat them in the correct order.**

S: **Yes.**

T: **Please do a Massive Change History and everything.**

S: **Yes.**

T: **Are we done?**

S: **Yes.**

9-10 Treating the fear of change

The patient had a boyfriend who was thinking of leaving her. I asked how upset she would be if he left. She said she was more afraid of change than of losing the relationship. As a further example of this fear of change, she described an incident where she purchased a cell phone. By the time she got home, she had a lot of anxiety about the purchase, simply because of the change in her life caused by buying the phone. She said this always happened to her when things changed in her life.

T: **Subconscious, can we treat this fear of change with a Sentence Procedure?**

S: **Yes**

T: **Subconscious, here is the sentence: "I feel totally comfortable with all changes." Please do the Sentence Procedure and repeat it in different ways until you are done.**

S: **Yes.**

T: [Talking to the patient] **When you think about the loss of your boyfriend, how does it feel?**

P: **Overwhelming.**

T: **Subconscious, are dependency needs feeding into this pain?**

S: **Yes.**

T: **Is there a Predisposition in the Basic Neurostructure, Memory I, II, or III that causes the dependency needs?**

I just guessed that the cause of dependency was in the Basic Neurostructure, Memories I, II, and III.

S: **Yes.**

T: **Can you change the Predispositions for dependency in the Basic Neurostructure, Memories I, II, and III? Then could you do a Massive Change History and everything?**

S: **Yes.**

T: **How does it feel now when you think of the loss of your boyfriend?**

P: **I feel sadness in my heart.**

T: **Subconscious, is this normal grief?**

S: **Yes.**

Now, I would approach this in another way. These last two interventions were close enough to the internal conditions to get the appropriate treatment done. Later interventions have shown that just treating the Predispositions in Memory II and the Layered Memories in Memory III would be as effective. Memory I and the Basic Neurostructure were probably not involved in this issue.

9-11 Shame and guilt

The patient suffered shame and guilt as a result of a number of angry outbursts he had exhibited with friends over the last four years. I asked him what he felt when he imagined himself socializing with friends. He reported feeling full of shame and guilt. It was apparent he had self-limiting beliefs involving shame and guilt that would continue to distract him when he socializing. I used the Fetal Shame construct and found it was consistent with this patient's issue.

T: **Subconscious, please do a Change History in Memory I, Memory II, and Memory III. Treat the Fetal Shame learned *in utero* through age four, and later, that motivates the self-limiting beliefs. Can you also strengthen self-empowering beliefs?**

S: **Yes.**

T: **[Done] Subconscious, can you do a Sentence Procedure with "I no longer feel this guilt and shame around my friends"?**

S: **No.**

This intervention was in the third session and I figured the subconscious knew how to do the Sentence Procedure. I was wrong. I explained it again and asked for the intervention again.

T: [Done] **Subconscious, please do a Sentence Procedure with "I no longer feel this guilt and shame around my friends."**

S: **Yes.**

T: **Please treat the beliefs, memories and parts in the correct order, and create and strengthen positive, self-empowering beliefs to replace the treated beliefs.**

S: **Yes.**

T: **Please do a Massive Change History and everything.**

T: **Yes.**

T: **Subconscious, have we finished treating this issue?**

S: **Yes.**

I asked him to again visualize socializing with his friends. He said that he felt relaxed and comfortable.

9-12 Treating the Core Issues

The patient wanted to work on Core Issues: issues that are pervasive in our behavior. Neither the patient nor I knew what his Core Issues were. We decided to have the subconscious give us cues to lead us to them. We identified the Core Issues in the following way.

T: **Subconscious, can you give him a word or symbol in the conscious experience that will lead us to discovering the Core Issues?**

S: **Yes.**

Usually the patient sees or hears some word, symbol, or image. I take this cue and work with the patient to guess what the cue means until the subconscious signals that the guess is correct. Some patients see or hear phrases or complete sentences in response to questions. Sometimes, the subconscious makes covert comments with hidden information or uses humor during problem-solving, which gives a clue to the solution. When the subconscious responds with a symbolic clue like a heart, rain cloud, smoke, a word, and so forth, you ask leading questions about the meaning of the symbol. Eventually, you will strike on a statement that identifies the solution. When nothing works, you will have to ask for another cue. The more you problem-solve, the more your intuition will help you find solutions.

In the above case, we started looking for the Core Issues in the following way:

T: **Subconscious, do you know what the Core Issues are?**
S: **Yes.**
T: **How many Core Issues are there?**
S: **Nine.** [I counted aloud until I reached nine and then got a "Yes" response.]

The patient knew the first Core Issue and, when she voiced it, the subconscious validated her suggestion. The first Core Issue was a sense of being incomplete.

We asked for cues for the remaining eight Core Issues. She got the response in her thoughts, and we worked together to clarify the meaning of the cues listed below. Each cue is given in bold, followed by the interpreted meaning.

Cue: **Mountain**–Overresponsible—makes a mountain out of a molehill
Cue: **Love**–Barrier for self-love and loving others
Cue: **Electricity**–She overextends herself
Cue: **Life**–Preoccupied with small things and missing life
Cue: **Sexuality**–Barriers to enjoyment of sexual activities
Cue: **Winter**–Mild depression
Cue: **Animals**–Allergy
Cue: **Selflessness**–Relates in a one-down position

The subconscious said treatment would be easy but we had to deal with processes in the basic systems. Apparently, in this case, all the Core Issues were related to the same trauma. We used three steps in the treatment.

1. Normalize processes in the basic systems

The first step, according to the subconscious, involved normalizing the processes in the basic systems. The basic systems involved some of the neural structures known to be involved in behavior and trauma. I guessed all of the basic systems except one. Again, I asked the subconscious to give a cue. The cue was "white." I guessed the Visual Perception System, which was correct. The intervention required treating the basic systems in the correct order—from simple to complex.

The order of the systems treated (from simple to complex) was: Visual Perception System, right forebrain area, above the olfactory bulb, the thymus, the midbrain, Kinesthetic System, Emotional System, Behavior System, Heart System and the Spirit System. (Spirit System is a construct that I used occasionally in the past.)

T: **Subconscious, please add and subtract associations to normalize the behavior of each of these systems, one after the other.**

S: **Yes.**

2. Do a Massive Change History

T: **Please do a Massive Change History and everything to extend the effects of the last intervention in the Emotion System, neutralize triggers in Memory III, and adjust the memories in all relevant brain and body systems. Then treat the Shadow Memories that were associated _to_ the issues.**

T: **Yes.**

While asking for the Massive Change History, I added the request to extend the effects of the previous intervention because an intuitive guess suggested a connection. I figured there were triggers in Memory III that were necessary to activate the Core Issues. All or none of it may have been necessary. If I had been off base or incomplete, I trust that the subconscious would have said "No."

3. Treat the Core Issues

T: **Subconscious, please do a Structure Procedure for the first Core Issue and, when the structure falls apart, tag and treat the memory elements in the correct order. Make all negative beliefs false, and then compose and strengthen positive, self-empowering beliefs to replace the treated beliefs for this Core Issue.**

S: **Yes.**

T: [Wait] **Please do a Change History and everything to extend the effects of the last intervention in the Emotion System and neutralize triggers in Memory III, and adjust the memories in all relevant brain and body systems. Then treat the Shadow Memories that were associated with this Core Issue.** (The wording of this Change History was approved by the subconscious. The intervention had to be worded precisely to get the correct outcome.)

S: **Yes.**

T: [Wait] **Do a Massive Change History and everything and treat the relevant Shadow Memories.**

Step 3 was repeated for each Core Issue, one after the other.

T: **Subconscious, please do step three on each Core Issue.**

S: **Yes.**

The patient and I waited while the subconscious treated each Core Issue in the list.

9-13 Treating self-perpetuating behaviors

Self-perpetuating behaviors are self-destructive behavior patterns that are rewarded simply by doing the behavior. The patterns involving reward make the self-destructive pattern more likely to happen and difficult to change. Listed on the following pages are the 25 self-perpetuating behavior patterns that the environment supports and maintains and, therefore, can develop into undesirable lifelong habits leading to pain and dissatisfaction. Theodore Millon (1981) uses these self-perpetuating behaviors in his description of severe personality disorders. I include the descriptions of self-perpetuating behavior as suggestions for the patient to review. They may or may not be present in the patient or may be insignificant. If these patterns exist in an adolescent, they may be at an early stage. The descriptions give the most negative outcome when the self-perpetuating patterns are taken to the limit. For the sake of brevity, I describe the patient as a male.

Though I now use the subconscious to determine whether it is necessary to treat the behavior in the patient, one can use the Millon Clinical Multiaxial Inventory–III (Millon, 1981) to determine with some accuracy which, if any, self-perpetuating behavior tendencies might be present in the patient. Here is how I assess for the presence of a self-perpetuating behavior in my patients:

First, I have the patient read the list of self-perpetuating behavior patterns provided below. I assume that even though the patient may not acknowledge the issue, the subconscious will have a more accurate perception and will identify the problematic behavior patterns. I asked the subconscious if the pattern is present in the patient and whether it should be treated. Here is an example of how I do this.

T: **Please read these descriptions of the self-perpetuating behaviors that lead to personality disorders.**

P. **Yes.**

T: **Subconscious, do I have to treat the self-perpetuating behavior leading to impassive and insensitive behavior?**

S: **Yes.**

T: **Please treat the memory structure and Predispositions that support this self-perpetuating behavior and, after any beliefs are treated, create new, self-empowering beliefs to replace the treated beliefs and strengthen them until they are true.**

S: **Yes.**

T: **Please do a Massive Change History and everything.**

S: **Yes.**

T: [Done] **Are we finished treating the memory structures that support this self-perpetuating behavior?**

S: **Yes.**

If you get a "No," problem-solve. Problem-solving may involve dissecting the description of the self-perpetuating behavior, and isolating the memory or system structure that causes it.

Repeat this intervention and progress through the remaining descriptions of self-perpetuating behaviors by asking the subconscious if the self-perpetuating behavior needs to be treated. When the subconscious says "Yes," repeat the above intervention.

The 25 self-perpetuating behavior patterns are:

1. Impassive and insensitive behavior

He cannot communicate very well and is almost unresponsive to others. For these reasons, he does not attract others and fades into the background in social situations. When relating, the contact is usually brief and is an empty, emotionless interaction. He is seen as boring. His contactless behavior and the tendency to be alone perpetuate and increase his detached style.

2. Reduced perceptual awareness

He does not see and respond to social stimuli fully because he levels or "smooths out" emotional situations, which results in taking emotions out of his experience. Therefore, he sees the world through a filter that reduces his experience of the emotional quality of social events. Reduction of the experience of positive and negative emotions removes the possibility of learning a more varied and socially involved life.

3. Social inactivity

Because of his style of having little social contact or emotional connection with others, he perpetuates this pattern of social inadequacy. Although he may actively preserve his responsibility in work or school, his isolated style prevents the possibility of having new experiences. Choosing to behave this way, he preserves this detached style, which prevents him from having experiences that could change this basic isolative pattern of behavior.

4. Active social detachment

He actively chooses to stay away from people and this choice limits his exposure to positive experiences that could revive his interest in reaching out and taking risks with other people. The dangerous quality of this form of behavior is that he is left to become preoccupied with his own thoughts and impulses. Left to his inner world, his thoughts will be obsessed and will tend to further separate him from others. As he continues to lose contact with people, he develops a loss of touch with reality and forms irrational thought patterns.

5. Suspicious and fearful behaviors

He may be suspicious and show fearful behaviors. These behaviors will not only distance him from others but they will often invoke reciprocal reactions of fear that further separate him from others. The reactions of others will further his suspiciousness and fearfulness so he will be caught in a response style that is difficult to break.

6. Emotional and unending hypersensitivity

He may show emotional and perceptual hypersensitivity by being painfully alert to signs of deception and humiliation. Although this may be protective, it may also become a pattern of identifying and intensifying problems that most people overlook. This behavior brings these problems to his awareness, which heightens the pain he wants to escape.

7. Intentional interference

He may deliberately interfere with the quality of his thought processes to alter and hide from himself what is present in his reality. Defensively, then, he deliberately destroys the clarity of his thoughts by intruding irrelevant distractions, tangential ideas, and conflicting emotions. By misperceiving his environment, he tends to disrupt his relationships, which further increases his original problem and, therefore, intensifies his alienation from both himself and others.

8. Self-depreciation

It would be typical of him to play down his own achievements and underestimate his abilities. His tendency is to perpetuate this dependent style by accentuating his real shortfalls in competence and downplaying his virtues, talents, or achievements. This leads other people to avoid placing confidence in him, which, in turn, perpetuates his self-depreciation.

9. Avoidance of adult activities

Because of his possible sense of inadequacy or fear of failure, he may avoid taking part in adult activities which may present risk to him. By doing this, he perpetuates the loss of opportunity to mature and grow independently. Therefore, he becomes even less confident and more dependent on others.

10. Clinging social behaviors

A person with this personality style tends not only to see real shortfalls in his competence, but he depreciates what virtues and talents he does have. This may be done to prevent others from expecting him to assume responsibilities he would rather avoid. This leads others to believe that he is, in fact, incapable of being responsible and, therefore, they will lose confidence in his abilities. This, in turn, allows him to deepen his self-image of incompetence, and thus, promote further use of self-depreciation to avoid responsibilities. The pattern becomes self-perpetuating.

11. External preoccupations

He tends to be highly sensitive to the external world and is directed by it in a way that leaves him with a false picture of reality. By responding to external cues in this way and not integrating and internalizing his experience, he makes responses that appear impulsive and not thought out. This style stops him from developing a fund of experience and coping skills. He needs external events to give him direction.

12. Massive repression

He tends to repress or "forget" experiences and emotions, which forces him to depend on others to direct his behavior. Because of the empty space in his memory, without emotions and reflections on experience, he lacks the skills to adapt and learn new behaviors for various situations. This leaves him without the opportunity to learn and grow and leads him to be completely dependent on the environment. Therefore, he may not have grown beyond childhood and shows the behavior and values of an adolescent.

13. Superficial social relationships

He may draw excessively on friends and acquaintances to give him the stimulation and attention that he needs to give him an identity. His friends tire of him and without that external stimulation, he feels lost, empty, and alone. Faced with this, he finds someone or creates some excitement in his environment to fill the void. He may show a pattern of behaviors where he is at times euphoric and at other times sad.

14. Illusion of competence

He may feel that he already knows what is necessary to do well in life. This belief leads him to brag and act proud but, underneath, he questions whether he can really pull it off. Thus, he safeguards his inflated self-image by never attempting new challenges. Owning an inflated opinion of himself and not venturing out to create and develop his skills, he may fall behind his peers in development. His shortfalls become obvious to him and to others. After a period of boastfulness, public awareness of his shortfalls leads him to feel false and empty. This can result in the defensive formation of paranoia and delusions.

15. Lack of self-control

His illusion of confidence and superiority may lead him to ignore social control in the form of social rules and expectations, in order to get what he "deserves." Eventually, he will have to tell lies to justify breaking rules and agreements. Bending rules, telling lies and distorting reality are now necessary to protect his illusion of superiority. Lacking the social controls, he moves further away from objective reality.

16. Social alienation

He may lack respect for others and think poorly of their actions, judgments, and opinions. Because of his felt superiority, he may often get into disagreements that result in further loss of respect for others. With his inability to respond socially and his disrespect for the rights and property of others, he may increasingly alienate others. This will further isolate him from any opportunities to heal a distorted view of the world or develop an understanding of others. Feeling rebuffed, after a period of sadness, he may further distort his view of the world in order to feel confident again. In time, he will create situations that drive away potential friends, thus confirming his opinion of himself. With few social controls and little self-control, his fantasies speed up, and the break from reality develops into a delusional system protecting him from reality.

17. Perceptual and cognitive distortions

For all of us, our view of the world requires us to fill in details to create a meaningful picture. When he has old anger and resentment, events in his experience may falsely appear to be negative, leading him to feel rejection where there is none. He reacts to the negativity he feels and gives an aggressive response. His response prevents him from recognizing and getting positive attention offered by others. This gives him another self-defeating outcome and prevents him from getting a positive reaction that could change his view of the world. Therefore, he further increases his resentment and anger and strengthens the distortion. He is creating punishment from which he cannot escape because he projects it into his experience.

18. Degrading affection and cooperative behavior

He may have learned to put down any expression of positive affection and cooperation and to show a lack of feelings for other less fortunate people. This is a defensive tactic against rejections and rebuffs that he has had in his past. His not showing positive affection, empathy, or cooperative behavior provokes others, who feel threatened, to move away from him and not to show tender feelings toward him. He is now creating the very environment that evokes and confirms his cold attitude.

19. Creating true antagonisms

He may have aggressive behavior or attitudes and enjoy intentionally bothering other people to prove his strength and competence. With success, he may become cocky and bristle with aggressiveness. These conflict-seeking behaviors provoke distance and rejection by others and eventually may lead to aggressive retaliation. Such conflict may nurture or develop a vigilant state that leads him to have to prove himself again.

20. Pervasive rigidity

He stays in situations that are familiar because he wants approval and does not want to be criticized. This keeps him restricted to existing self-expectations and to familiar situations. His thought focuses on single issues and he sticks to them without deviation. This results in repression of his emotions and creative imagination, while he leads a deliberate and mechanical life. It prevents him from having new experiences and from developing a more flexible behavioral style. This rigidity keeps him from changing past behavioral patterns.

21. Guilt and self-criticism

He probably has a set of unbending rules for himself—learned from his parents. An internal dialogue keeps him from deviating from those rules and even introduces considerations for every decision he makes. He intends to be proper and responsible. If he is not, he badgers himself with guilt and self-punishment. He has internalized external controls so well that internal sanctions and directions restrict his opportunities for behaviors different from the past. His past activities and behaviors are therefore continued without any hope for change.

22. Creation of rules

His behavior is so restricted by severe internal sanctions that a part of him wants to rebel. To deal with this, he creates new rules to help him guide himself and judge others. In addition, the more restrictive he finds the external rules, the less effort he has to spend controlling himself. By increasing the severity and number of rules that constrict his behavior, both internally and externally, fewer new opportunities will be experienced. This style will further narrow his range of behavior.

23. Negativistic and unpredictable behaviors

He may show negativistic and unpredictable behaviors. He may act erratically and waver from one course to another or try to achieve incompatible goals. These behaviors undermine his effectiveness so he cannot commit himself to one clear direction. This ambivalent behavior may paralyze his growth. In addition, people like him may behave in ways that undo positive contacts with people. This push-pull relationship with the environment creates the same environment that taught him these behaviors. He may eventually produce anger and withdraw from people altogether.

24. Re-creating disillusioning experiences

He may have experienced re-creating disillusioning experiences. The repeated experience of expecting disappointment causes a growing ambivalence that creates an unconscious process, which supports him to re-create disillusioning experiences that parallel those of the past. Even with ambivalence and a pessimistic outlook, he may enter relationships looking for the best. At some point in the relationship, he may test it to see if it is, in fact, a solid relationship. This eventually ends the relationship. This experience recurs in different ways and further reinforces his pessimism.

25. Anticipating disappointment

He may have the habit of anticipating disappointment. Having learned in the past that good experiences do not last, he unintentionally undermines the good experiences so that they do, in fact, change. This then reinforces his belief that good experiences do not last and perpetuates a self-defeating cycle where he feels further discontent and disappointment.

Strengthening Behaviors

9-14 Strengthening positive beliefs

Sometimes, you can easily strengthen positive habits. Three interventions are useful to do this: the Sentence Procedure, the Structure Procedure, and the Futurepace Intervention. These are similar because they all trigger behaviors (that are incompatible with the goal belief), which are then tagged and treated. As always, a Massive Change History and everything should be used in conjunction with these three interventions, making a total of four interventions, thus:

1. Sentence Procedure

Here is the direct approach using the Sentence Procedure.

T: **Subconscious, please do the Sentence Procedure with the belief "I am comfortable with success." Tag and treat all the elicited memory structures in the correct order.**

S: Yes.

T: **Subconscious, will you do a Massive Change History and at the same time strengthen the belief, "I am comfortable with success"?**

S: Yes.

T: **I want to test the effects of these interventions. When you think, "I am comfortable with success," on a scale of 0 to 10, how true do you experience that statement?**

Continue problem-solving until the statement is completely true.

2. Structure Procedure

First, you have to evoke some elements of the structure you want to treat and then do the Structure Procedure:

T: **Subconscious, I want to strengthen the statement, "No, thank you, I don't smoke." Can you identify the structure of all memories that will become barriers for this statement?**

S: **Yes.**

T: **Please treat the structure of memories that are barriers to the response, "No, thank you, I don't smoke." Tag the memory elements when the structure falls apart and treat them in the correct order, reduce beliefs to not true, and compose and strengthen self-empowering beliefs to take their place.**

S: **Yes.**

T: **Please strengthen the belief "No, thank you, I don't smoke," until it is completely true.**

S: **Yes.**

Go on to step 3 and use the Futurepacing Intervention and problem-solve until the new behavior feels completely natural to the patient.

3. Futurepace Intervention with tagging

Here is an example of another approach to strengthen a new belief or behavior. Ask the patient to visualize a situation where he would express his new belief or the desired behavior:

T: [Ask the patient] **Please visualize or imagine saying, "No, thank you, I don't smoke" in a typical situation that may occur in the future.**

Then ask the subconscious to go to work.

T: **Subconscious, please tag any beliefs, memories or parts that became active and are incompatible with this non-smoking belief. Treat the tagged memories in the correct order and strengthen the likelihood of this response in appropriate situations.**

S: **Yes.**

T: [Wait] **Subconscious, are you done?**

S: **Yes.**

T: [Done] **Will you visualize or imagine doing that again?**

P: **Yes.**

T: [Wait, then to the patient] **Does saying, "No, thank you, I don't smoke" feel completely natural to do or say in that situation?**

P: **No.**

T: **Subconscious, please treat any emotion that prevents that behavior from feeling completely natural.**

S: **Yes.**

There can be other problems that keep the desired behavior from feeling completely natural. In this case, you can do the Sentence Procedure or the Structure Procedure to elicit and treat all beliefs, memories, and parts that prevent the desired behavior from feeling completely natural.

4. Massive Change History

The Massive Change History is also useful to strengthen beliefs and behavior. It is not as powerful as the Sentence Procedure or Structure Procedure, but it is occasionally useful to strengthen some behavior when you are doing a Massive Change History after some other intervention.

T: **Subconscious, please do a Massive Change History and everything, and also strengthen all memory structures supporting the belief "I love myself."**

S: **Yes.**

Any behavior or belief can be strengthened or weakened in this way.

Examples:

1. Changing a belief

Here is how the belief change is done with the belief, "I can't do well in school."

T: **Subconscious, please do the Sentence Procedure with the self-empowering belief, "When I study hard, I can do my best." Tag and treat all memories that become active in the correct order.**

S: **Yes.**

T: [Done] **Subconscious, please treat the negative belief, "I can't do well in school," until the belief is not true.** Then strengthen the self-empowering belief until it is completely true.

S: **Yes.**

Wait until the subconscious finishes. Check with the patient and see if the patient experiences the self-empowering belief as completely true.

T: [Done, but the belief is not experienced as completely true] **Subconscious, please treat the structure of barriers that are preventing** this self-empowering belief from being experienced as completely true. Then, continue strengthening the self-empowering belief.

S: **Yes.**

You may still have to do some problem-solving to neutralize barriers that are more difficult. Some beliefs are based on extensive trauma histories and will not be a quick fix. In these cases, treat the trauma history before strengthening the desired belief.

2. An example of defining a procedure to treat many beliefs

When the patient is aware of many beliefs that have to be changed, I will approach this intervention by having the patient write down all the negative or self-limiting beliefs that get in the way of his doing well in life. Group the beliefs with the aid of the patient and treat them one group at a time. Work with the subconscious to determine the order in which the beliefs or groups of beliefs should be treated.

T: **Subconscious, does the order in which these beliefs are treated matter?**

With a "Yes," work with the subconscious to define the order of treatment. Start with the first belief or group to be treated. Make up a self-empowering belief that will replace the negative belief. Use the Sentence Procedure to elicit beliefs, memories and parts that support the negative belief by choosing a sentence that is directly opposite the negative belief. This will elicit all the memories that oppose changing the negative belief. The use of the Sentence Procedure will make it easier to strengthen the self-empowering belief.

T: **Subconscious, please do the Sentence Procedure using the belief, "I will never smoke again." Tag and treat the memories that activate in the correct order.**

S: **Yes.**

There may be barriers to completing the Sentence Procedure. At some point after initiating the Sentence Procedure, ask the following:

T: **Subconscious, have you been able to complete the Sentence Procedure?**

S: **No.**

With a "No," if the subconscious is not processing, you have to problem-solve. First, look for any parts and then check for other possible barriers.

T: **Subconscious, please repeat the Sentence Procedure.**

S: **Yes.**

T: [Done] **Subconscious, please treat the self-limiting or negative beliefs and, at the same time, compose and strengthen all relevant self-empowering beliefs to take their place.**

S: **Yes.**

T: [Done] **Subconscious, please do a Massive Change History and everything, treat the effects of the negative beliefs and strengthen memories supporting the self-empowering beliefs.**

S: **Yes.**

Have the patient state the belief and see if the patient experiences the belief to be true. If the belief is not experienced as completely true, problem-solve until the belief is completely true.

In the interest of saving time, I define the intervention used with the first belief to be a procedure.

T: **Subconscious, can the above strategy be used as the procedure to treat other self-limiting beliefs?**

S: **Yes.**

Work with the patient to create a self-empowering belief for each belief or group of beliefs to be treated.

T: **Subconscious, please use the procedure that we used for changing beliefs, the "Belief Procedure," to make the self-empowering belief completely true.**

S: **Yes.**

This appears to work. The unique "Belief Procedure" saved a lot of time with this patient. Now the disempowering beliefs can be treated one at a time. Notice that I referred to the previous series of interventions as a procedure. The name Belief Procedure can be used in the future with this patient to treat beliefs. Remember to test the truth of the old and new beliefs to be sure that the intervention worked.

9-15 Strengthening self-esteem

This intervention is based on an NLP technique. The patient had poor self-esteem. We'd had many sessions together and had cleared many issues related to self-esteem but had not addressed the treatment in this way before.

T: **Subconscious, please take the emotions from examples of positive self-esteem in Ann's history and replace the negative emotions of all experiences that led to a negative self-esteem with Ann's positive emotions. Do this from before birth until now.**

S: **Yes.**

T: **Please do a Massive Change History and everything and treat the Shadow Memories.**

S: **Yes.**

The patient reported feeling greater self-esteem and more self-love.

9-16 Forgiving the perpetrator

The perpetrator of an old trauma can still have some effect on our system and behavior whenever we hate or hold a grudge. Ideally, then, it is good to try to arrange for the patient to forgive the perpetrator. However, if you feel that approaching the notion of forgiveness is totally out of the question for a patient, be very sensitive and don't discuss the possibility of forgiveness. With patients who may be open to this idea, here is what I say.

T: **You may not want to forgive the perpetrator at this time but, until you do, the lingering negative feelings for the perpetrator are going to affect your life. When you are ready to get over the trauma completely, it would be good to consider forgiving the perpetrator. This does not mean that you have to like or associate with the perpetrator. Forgiveness just means that you have removed the last remaining effect of the trauma from your system. You will always know that what he did to you was wrong. He was and may still be an unsafe person and you will protect yourself and others from him or her when necessary. Is it appropriate for you to think about forgiveness at this time?**

If the patient is not ready to forgive the perpetrator, I turn my attention to other issues and, when appropriate, make a transition statement like the following:

T: **It is possible to learn and experience forgiveness whenever you want.**

To teach forgiveness, you can do a Sentence Procedure.

T: **Subconscious, please do the Sentence Procedure with "I forgive Mr. Bad Guy." Tag and treat all the triggered memories in the correct order. If there are any beliefs, treat the beliefs until they are no longer true and compose and strengthen self-empowering beliefs to replace them.**

S: **Yes.**

The subconscious will then treat all beliefs, memories, experiences, and parts that are related to not forgiving this person. Then I do a Massive Change History.

T: **Subconscious, please do a Massive Change History and every-thing and give the patient the feeling of forgiveness for the perpetrator.**

S: **Yes.**

On the other hand, I often combine asking forgiveness with a Massive Change History in this way.

T: **Subconscious, if it is appropriate, will you add the feeling of forgiveness to the effects of the trauma or memory of the perpetrator as you do the Massive Change History and everything?**

Usually, the patients report a neutral feeling or a feeling of forgive-ness after this intervention.

Intrusions

9-17 Treating a racing mind or obsessions

I have found that the Tapas Acupressure Technique (TAT) (Flem-ing, 2003) (see Appendix VI) is very effective to stop racing minds and obsessions. It is a safe intervention and the patient can do it at home as needed. Of course, TAT is another powerful intervention that can be used for treating allergies and many mental issues. It is worth taking training in TAT or buying the manual (Tapas, 2005).

Example:

The patient obsesses on her fear

This patient has the problem of experiencing fear around groups of people and losing her ability to communicate effectively. Here is how I used TAT to treat this issue. I started the intervention by explaining how to do the TAT pose and the Three Pose Procedure (Wakefield, 2002) (See Appendix VI). With this procedure, the patient does a pose with the one hand, then the other hand, and then with both hands. I explain that during the pose process, the obsessive thoughts may stream through her thoughts as if tied together. I explain that all the negative emotions con-nected to the thoughts are stripped off the thoughts so they will no longer occur spontaneously. The negative emotions serve as motivation for the thoughts to occur. Without the emotions, these thoughts will not occur without choice.

T: **I want you to imagine you are talking to four people.**

P: **OK.**

T: **Do you feel the fear?**

P: **Yes.**

This image triggers the structure of thoughts connected to talking to four people. If she obsesses, these thoughts may be linked together.

T: **Now do the TAT procedure and think, "I am treating the origin of my fearful thoughts." Continue doing the pose until you no longer have a feeling in your brain and the pictures or thoughts stop streaming through your thoughts.**

When she brought her hands down, I asked her to do the pose with the other hand in front and, when this treatment was complete, I asked her to do the pose with both hands. Then I tested again by having her imagine that she was conversing with four people and, if she experienced obsessing on fear, I had her treat the obsession with the three-pose TAT again. When no obsessive thoughts were obtained, I repeated this process with 10 people, again, treating the obsession. Then I had her imagine that she was on a bus full of teenagers and treated the obsession. After I repeated the test with a busload of teenagers for a second time, the patient felt calm in that imagined situation.

9-18 Treating panic caused by hyperventilating

Though this example does not directly use any Process Healing Method, it is important to be aware of the problem because it is a fairly common occurrence. The patient complained of anxiety and panic attacks. I usually try to notice how fast the patient is breathing. This contact was over the telephone so I listened to his breathing pattern in the telephone receiver. Optimal breathing rate is about 12 breaths per minute. This patient was breathing 22 breaths per minute. I explained to him that with a fast breathing rate, any anxiety results in deeper breathing at the same rate. When this happens, the brain is soon overloaded with oxygen. I explain how the brain responds to too much oxygen in the blood by stopping further breathing. The person would soon find it hard to breathe, which would lead to more anxiety and forced breathing. This eventually would result in the other symptoms of hyperventilation. I explained that the solutions to hyperventilation are relatively simple and involve breathing into a brown paper bag or holding one's breath. When the oxygen level drops to normal, the symptoms go away.

The intervention for patients who have a rapid breathing rate and problems with anxiety is to have them practice diaphragmatic breathing. Instruct them to stretch out with their back to the floor and put two big books on the stomach. Then practice breathing at 12 breaths per minute by pushing the books up to inhale and let them drop to exhale. I have them inhale for four seconds and then exhale for four seconds. When they do this homework and make breathing at 12 breaths per minute a habit, the anxiety and panic attacks will not occur as often, if at all. I ask them to do an Internet search for further details about hyperventilation.

9-19 Involuntary switching into others

In Neurolinguistic Programming (Rice and Caldwell, 1986), I learned how to teach people to switch into another person's experience to get a sense of their emotions. This was done by learning to go into a light trance to experience the other's emotions. However, this skill can be a symptom for some people. In a constantly punishing situation with a raging parent or partner, going into a light trance or switching into the aggressor is learned as a survival strategy. Victims who have to protect themselves from the aggressor's anger or rage learn to switch into the aggressor's emotions to assess their safety. This is a survival technique for them. If it feels unsafe, they move out of the situation.

I assess for this issue by asking women to close their eyes in my presence. With their eyes closed, the eyelids flutter. This is a dissociative response or light trance state that was learned by being raised in a family or living in a relationship where it was necessary to walk on eggshells, and the subject learned to go into trance to become extremely aware of the other's emotions as a means of self-protection. When she is in a light trance, she is more suggestible and is less likely to get hurt. Since most perpetrators are male, this light trance state is often triggered simply by the presence of a male. Here is the way I explore for this habit:

T: **Please close your eyes. Do you notice them fluttering?**

P: **Yes.**

T: **Have you ever been asked to go for coffee by some man and said "Yes" without thinking? Later, you wondered why you said, "Yes"?**

P: **Yes.**

I discuss the reason for asking this question in the following way:

T: **Well, it is possible that you learned to go into a light trance around an angry man when you were younger. Now you go into a light trance when you are around any man. Here is how you can treat this problem. Slap your cheeks lightly as though you are waking up, and after a few slaps, pinch your thumb and index finger briefly. Do this several times.**

I demonstrate what I want her to do as she learns it. Sometimes the patient has to be instructed to pinch only briefly because repeating or holding the pinch for more than a few seconds will undermine the intervention.

T: **Now I want you to switch into me, as I play depressed.**

P: **OK.**

I try to look sad and think of my sick cat or deceased parent to generate depressed emotions.

T: **Do you feel my depression?**

P: **Yes.**

T: **Now, pinch your fingers and see if you can feel yourself move back into your center.**

P: **OK.**

T: **Did you experience the feeling of becoming more centered or clearheaded?**

P: **Yes.**

If or when they get the feeling, you ask them to practice switching in and out of people, first with the pinch, and then by a conscious decision.

This intervention gives patients a little more control over their lives. Often, they notice the switching has had an effect in other areas, such as switching into product brand labels seen in stores, which is then accompanied by an urge to buy the product.

A vivid example of this was a patient growing up with a mother who had a dissociative identity disorder. She said that she was highly vigilant as she grew up. After the intervention, she said she was able to observe when she switched into other people. A week later, she said that she could switch out of people by choice and was not absorbing the negative experiences of other people when she spent time with them.

Professionals and laypeople who switch into their clients or patients all day acquire the sad emotions and often take them home with them. It is important for them to learn to switch in and out of their clients so they do not pick up their clients' negative emotions.

9-20 Treatment for fear of abandonment

The fear of abandonment often accompanies childhood trauma and other traumas. Though there is no single cure for all cases, I have found some interventions that will generate changes in patients who experience the fear of abandonment.

T: **Subconscious, does this patient have a fear of abandonment that is interfering in healthy relationships?**

S: **Yes.**

T: **Are there Layered Memories with links to Predispositions that cause much of this problem?**

S: **Yes.**

T: **Please treat the Layered Memory by treating the Predispositions first and then treat the Layered Memories.**

S: **Yes.**

Sometimes, fields block treatment.

T: **Subconscious, are there parts that want to be treated who are associated *with* the fear of abandonment?**

S: **No.**

T: **Are there parts that don't want to be treated who are associated *with* the fear of abandonment?**

S: **Yes.**

Here I have to determine the cause of the barrier and reframe the problem. Usually it is either because of too much pain or because the trauma memory would retraumatize the patient. I treat the barriers and then ask the following:

T: **Subconscious, please strengthen behaviors and memories that will allow the perception of the circumstances of people leaving Joe's life to soften or block the feeling of abandonment.**

S: **Yes.**

I do several Sentence Procedures with the following sentences. I remind the subconscious to create self-empowering beliefs to replace any negative beliefs.

"I am worthy of love and worthy of life."

"I am proud of myself and my accomplishments in life."

When there are particular people who have caused the feeling of abandonment, most often mother or father, I ask the patient to visualize the parent.

T: **Subconscious, please tag all memory elements that become active and treat them in the correct order and, after treating negative beliefs, compose and strengthen self-empowering beliefs to replace them.**

S: **Yes.**

In some cases, the patients have felt alone and empty after treatment. When this occurs, I try to find a situation in which they have felt nurtured and fulfilled. Sometimes it is with a pet or a special friend. I have the subconscious take these emotions associated *with* the memories of being nurtured and use the Massive Change History to replace all the "alone and empty" emotions associated *with* the painful memories. Usually this works to clear this issue.

9-21 When your patient hears a voice—"Who said that?"

I have many patients who hear voices in their thoughts. It might sound strange, but I view this as a healthy sign. Many of these voices are neutral or even helpful. Some voice intrusions with a trauma history can make destructive comments. Though these can be helpful, I am not talking about voices based on trauma. The voices I am referring to are not the same as the example in Chapter 1, of the paranoid patient with thousands of intrusive voices. A good example of the voices I am talking about is one patient with whom I worked for many sessions. He felt an epiphany when he first heard a voice directing his attention to issues that needed to be treated. These voices can sometimes be very helpful both in identifying issues to treat and in problem-solving treatment plans in difficult and unusual issues.

Some patients who have dissociative issues hear what they call *helpers* and believe that they are getting help from parts in their system. I have had patient helpers help me with solving or explaining the issues of torture survivors, spiritual issues, or the structure of the dissociative system. Occasionally, I get an e-mail post or a phone message from a helper or part that used the computer or telephoned without the Main Personality's awareness. These sources of information are very helpful and often serve to speed up or clarify treatment. I try to form a treatment relationship with these helpers and eventually treat and integrate them.

The most unusual form of help is when the helper voice takes the patient and me totally by surprise. I have had one such patient who was allegedly sent to me by two "enlightened beings in the ninth dimension" to teach me some new treatment interventions to aid in the treatment of her more difficult issues. This patient was a very successful person, with a good administrative job, and was healthy in most ways, but couldn't advance within her company. She would always block the advance in some way. She and I were both surprised by the voices she heard in her thoughts and relayed to me. They appeared instructive and knowledgeable about any question I asked. The patient suffered extreme trauma from the very beginning of her life, with four years of unique personalized cult abuse and years of extreme, vile verbal abuse and physical punishment, including a number of near-death experiences. The cult abuse and emotional damage provided complex structures and other phenomena that were exceptionally difficult to treat. These voices both tutored and provided me with unique Process Healing techniques. Were they really enlightened beings? I'll never know for sure, but what I do know is that this patient made tremendous progress using the interventions suggested by these voices. All of the interventions were consistent with the theoretical basis for Process Healing and will be presented in Flint (n.d.). Most of them have worked for other patients. Be alert and willing to engage with a helper from any source in your patient whenever you find one. It just makes good sense to evaluate and use the unique information offered.

9-22 Physical pain—Tense shoulders

When this patient was a child, he had a number of ugly warts on the back of his neck. He didn't want anyone to see them, so he kept his collar up and his shoulders hunched. Even though he eventually had the warts burned off, for more than 30 years he continued to turn up his collar and hunch his shoulders. His shoulders were chronically tense.

T: **Subconscious, can I talk to the part that keeps the shoulder muscles tense?**

S: **Yes.**

T: **Do these parts want to be treated?**

S: **Yes.**

T: **Please treat these parts.**

S: **Yes.**

His shoulders relaxed and continued to be relaxed when I checked the following week. He still kept his collar turned up.

System Issues

9-23 Mood changes—Treating trauma in the Heart System

When trust is broken in any early-life trauma, sometimes damage is done to the Heart System, which stops love responses in more normal situations. This results in a lack of heartfelt empathy and a loss of guidance from the level of the heart. Here is the way to treat this Heart System issue.

T: **Subconscious, please treat all the traumas that damaged the Heart System.**

S: **Yes.**

T: [Wait] **Subconscious, please do a Massive Change History and everything and include all other memories affected by the Heart System.**

S: **Yes.**

9-24 Treating behavior that does not feel good

The patient was isolated, grouchy and distant to her partner at home, and distant from people at work. She said she was depressed and had a great deal of pain. She thought that there might be a part that was the source of the depressed, angry moods. Trying a different way to identify the part, we came across something very interesting.

T: **Subconscious, does she have everyday behavior that does not feel good?**

S: **Yes.**

T: **Is it a part in the Emotion System?**

S: **Yes.**

T: **Are there many parts?**

I called the structure parts when I did this intervention, but I believe that these were collages of emotions with no history.

S: **Yes.**

T: **Are these emotion intrusions with no history?**

S: **Yes.**

T: **Subconscious, please treat all negative emotion parts in the Emotion System.**

S: **Yes.**

T: [Done] **Please do a Massive Change History and everything and treat the Shadow Memories.**

S: **Yes.**

The subconscious gave a very energetic "Yes" to the suggestion of treating the Shadow Memories.

9-25 Treating the absence of positive emotions

The patient had never been able to get out and do the things he wanted to do. We analyzed the problem and found that the usual positive emotions that people have when they are doing what they want to do were absent. In fact, the patient lacked positive emotions for anything he did.

He had no memories of positive experiences. We discovered that we could use the Heart System to trigger positive emotions. Here is how we did it.

T: **Subconscious, can we associate a response from the Heart System with a Predisposition to provide positive emotions?**

S: **Yes.**

T: **Can we use preexisting Predispositions?**

S: **Yes.**

T: **Please associate aspects of the Heart System to the Predispositions appropriate for experiencing emotions.**

S: **Yes.**

T: **Please associate the weak positive emotions in the Emotion System with the Predispositions.**

S: **Yes.**

We did not have to do a Massive Change History. After treatment, the expectation was that, in situations where positive emotions were appropriate, the situation itself would trigger the Predispositions that would, in turn, trigger the Heart System to cause some positive emotions. I tested the intervention by asking the patient to imagine that he had just finished cleaning up his bedroom. He claimed he felt some positive emotions. The subconscious said the positive feelings would increase over time.

Neurology

9-26 Distorted Basic Neurostructure

In early child development, before the Basic Neurostructures are available to run various systems (say, in the first three weeks after conception), a trauma can distort the pre-Basic Neurostructure, which consequently distorts the later development of the Basic Neurostructures that create behavior, heart activity, and emotions. I believe that, in some cases, this form of distortion may lead to difficult personality disorders. The most severe forms of personality disorder may be examples of this early life distortion.

An example where this may have happened was observed in a patient whose mother contemplated having an abortion because she had some blood problems.

T: **Subconscious, was there early trauma that distorted the development of the Basic Neurostructure?**

S: **Yes.**

T: **Is it safe to treat that trauma and the Basic Neurostructure?**

S: **Yes.**

T: **Please treat that early trauma and the effects of that trauma on the Basic Neurostructure. Then do a Massive Change History and everything.**

S: **Yes.**

9-27 Process erased by fever

The problem for this patient was that he had a tendency to shut down systematically and avoid anything that had to do with risk-taking. He said that it was not so much "a thing of anxiety" but more like an absence of motivation. After a few treatments he reported some feelings of being motivated to do things but this would fade after a brief period. He mentioned that it felt like he was being blackmailed or shut down. This is where the treatment started.

T: **Subconscious, should we go in on blackmailed or shut down? Blackmailed?**

S: **Yes.**

T: **Is it in the Main Personality?**

S: **No.**

T: **Can you give us a phrase?**

The subconscious started giving responses in the form of auditory intrusions.

S: **Something erased early in life.**

T: **What do you mean, something erased?**

S: **Something developed that was erased.**

T: **In what system did this happen?**

S: **Heart System.**

T: **Was it caused by trauma?**

S: **No, a form of sickness caused the erasure at age four.**

T: **Did the parents know?**

S: **No, neither the patient nor family members knew.**

T: **What was it?**

S: **A high temperature destroyed a specific area of the brain.**

The patient said that this made sense because he had many episodes of fever in his life. Here is the intervention that we believe worked:

T: **Subconscious, can you map the heart memory prior to the trauma into a new memory, and then develop this memory from then to now?**

S: **Yes.**

T: **Please attach the new memory to the Behavior System.**
S: **Yes.**

T: **Please do a Massive Change History and everything and treat any Shadow Memories.**
S: **Yes.**

The patient reported that his willingness to take risks improved.

9-28 Chronic punishment of experience

The patient had long complained of not getting things done, not enjoying anything, and wilting under criticism. His latest experience of this occurred while he was enjoying yoga exercises and his partner criticized him. He immediately stopped experiencing pleasure from the yoga. This was the first time he had noticed his lack of enjoyment, and because of that awareness, became upset believing an activity that he'd once enjoyed was no longer available.

Problem-solving revealed that the undermining process was not a part and that it was not in the Behavior System—well, not all of it. Apparently a Predisposition in Memory II, associated *with* a collage of negative emotions in the Emotion System, was triggered by criticism and enthusiasm. This Predisposition triggered negative emotions that associated *with* the positive experience. The negative emotions served to counteract the positive emotions, the activity would not be enjoyed, and he would stop doing the activity.

T: **Subconscious, please treat the collage of negative emotions in the Emotion System.**
S: **Yes.**

T: **Please treat the Predisposition that was associating the collage of negative emotions *with* activities experienced with enthusiasm.**
S: **Yes.**

T: **Please do a Massive Change History and everything and treat the Shadow Memories.**
S: **Please treat the Basic Neurostructure in the Behavior System by adding and subtracting associations in the Basic Neurostructure to get a self-empowering outcome with enthusiastic experiences.**
S: **Yes.**

T: **Please do a Massive Change History and everything and treat the Shadow Memories.**
S: **Yes.**

This undermining of his enthusiasm was also a problem in many other areas of his life. It was possible that this was the reason for the avoidance behaviors that upset him. Such Predispositions can serve to undermine positive experience or enthusiasm in anyone's life. Some of the areas where this can happen include:

- Enjoying male company
- Physical activities
- Food
- Visual experiences
- Tactile experiences
- Physical pain

- Enjoying female company
- Intellectual activities
- Sex
- Auditory experiences
- Reading
- Receiving gifts

Other problem situations identified by the patient's subconscious included: public places, comparison thoughts, smells, completion of projects, and thinking about things. Apparently, these activities, rather than being associated with punishing consequences, were associated *with* the Predisposition, which then associated negative emotions to the experience. Furthermore, in this case example, whenever the patient had a positive experience with a woman, he would immediately become fearful and this would trigger a flight-or-fight response. I treated the Predispositions that undermined his enjoyment of many of these areas in his life by doing the following:

T: **Subconscious, can you see a structure of Predispositions associated *with* negative emotions that can be treated and then, when the structure falls apart, tag each of the memory elements and treat them in the correct order?**

S: **Yes.**

I was curious about whether it would be useful to treat any beliefs formed by the experience of criticism.

T: **Subconscious, is there a structure of beliefs that has to do with criticism?**

S: **Yes.**

T: **Please treat the structure of beliefs that are related to criticism. When the structure falls apart, treat the memory elements of the structure in the correct order and treat the negative beliefs until they become false. Then compose and strengthen positive self-empowering beliefs until they are true.**

S: **Yes.**

T: **Subconscious, is there a structure of beliefs that causes barriers for success?**

S: **Yes.**

T: **Please treat the structure of beliefs that obstructs the experience of success. When the structure falls apart, treat the memory elements of the structure in the correct order, and treat the negative beliefs until they become false, and compose and strengthen positive self-empowering beliefs until they are true.**

S: Yes.

T: **Subconscious, please treat the collage of negative emotions in the Emotion System, and follow the associations to memory structures, and treat them in the correct order.**

S: Yes.

T: **Please treat the Predisposition associated *with* the collage of negative emotions, and associate it with positive emotions and enthusiasm.**

S: Yes.

T: **Please do a Massive Change History and everything and treat the Shadow Memories.**

S: Yes.

Additional barriers were found, which were treated by the techniques discussed in Flint (n.d.). The patient noticed positive changes.

Summary

This chapter presents a number of examples to give you ideas for creating your own interventions when treating personality issues. Today, I would treat many of the issues in this chapter differently from the earlier treatment methods described here. In general, I would follow the Structure Procedures that are offered in Chapters 8-28 through 8-30. These earlier approaches usually lead to the resolution of challenging and problematic issues. Some of the interventions given in this chapter illustrate that relatively vague interventions can work to create change. The wording of an intervention does not have to be perfect. It just has to work. I hope that this will help you feel more comfortable as you get creative to problem-solve complex issues.

Chapter 10

Treating the Symptoms of Complex Issues

The Process Healing Method is simply an Education Process that trains the brain, and thus the patient, to think in a specific way—and it is a natural way. I say this because everything I have observed confirms these methods as a natural healing process. Incredible as it may seem, changing the way we think can often change the way our bodies and minds respond to what life throws at us. Consider the impact that a patient's way of thinking has on the course of a cancer: The link between a positive frame of mind and a positive outcome has been well documented. I believe Process Healing is a thinking and problem-solving paradigm that offers a systematic way to access some of the powerful tools drawn from within our own minds, memories and perhaps the soul—in other words, from within our humanity.

This chapter addresses symptoms of complex mental disorders such as depression, addictions, psychosis, and obsessive-compulsive disorder. While reflecting on my current approach, I have concluded that I use the same tactics to treat the symptoms of all mental issues. I started out thinking that I would have protocols for different mental disorders but I use a protocol only for addictions. Because some symptom may be present in many mental disorders, I am giving my experience and speculations about treating the various symptoms.

I must emphasize again that three assessments should always be made.

First, assess for any suicidal thoughts. This is not only to discover early in treatment whether the problem is present but also to assess the intensity of the thoughts regarding suicide. You also want to know the extent of a patient's social support and whether to make a referral for assessment for medication. If you are not comfortable dealing with a suicidal person, then refer the person to a therapist with experience in this area.

The second assessment is to determine whether the patient should receive a referral to a family physician for a physical examination and perhaps a psychological or psychiatric evaluation. This is to rule out brain damage or disease, or any systemic basis for the patient's symptoms. Any rapid change in a person's personality can be caused by brain damage and merits having it checked out. The cause could be a motor-vehicle accident, a fall, a brain tumor, or some organic imbalance. It is important at least to ask when the patient last had a physical. The patient about to have a physical should be coached to write down all physical and emotional symptoms so the doctor can get a clear picture. Frequently, therapists and even doctors miss a physical illness or a condition that might be causing the mental problems presented by the patient.

As an aid to becoming more familiar with symptoms of brain damage or a systemic disease, Taylor (1981) has written an excellent programmed manual that teaches how to do a neuropsychiatric mental status examination. This is a book designed to teach professionals to recognize the verbal behaviors and physical conditions that suggest the possibility of neurological disorders. If you are not a trained therapist, do not attempt formal neuropsychiatric mental examinations of anyone. However, if you have some awareness of the symptoms of brain or systemic problems, it puts you in a better position to recognize and classify disturbed behavior caused by them. When you identify a disturbed behavior, you should refer the person to the appropriate therapist to receive further assessment or treatment.

The third assessment is for any addictive behavior, such as medication, street drugs, alcohol, or eating disorders like bulimia or anorexia. Addictions are common and are frequently missed by therapists. Addictive behaviors can undermine the treatment of many issues, and therefore it is important to assess for addictive behaviors in the first session.

In the first part of this chapter, I will describe my standard approach to treating patients. The remainder of the chapter will give my experience or conjectures about the way to treat various complex mental issues. I have categorized the symptoms into: depression, addictions, obsessions and compulsions, affect issues, manic behavior, thought process disorders, delusions, psychosis, war survivors, and barriers to peak performance. My descriptions are more suggestions than actual road maps of how to do it. The issues treated in this chapter are often the consequence of bizarre and traumatic early-life situations. For this reason, each patient is unique and usually the treatment should be made to fit the person rather than trying to fit the person to the treatment. Keep in mind that this is a creative process.

Some of the symptoms described in this chapter are not considered treatable by the mental health profession. However, I believe most symptoms are often treatable using Process Healing. Treatment success is achieved when you are creative and able to find memory structures causing the symptoms. Be sure the patient receives appropriate referrals to rule out other causes for the symptoms and is under medical or psychiatric care if appropriate. Explain clearly the rationale for your treatment to the patient, the patient's family, and the doctor. Have the patient complete a 'Consent for Treatment Form' that is clear about the experimental basis for treating his or her symptoms.

As a psychotherapist, my focus is on mental and emotional issues. Although I have treated some physical ailments with great success and have had varying degrees of success with others, I lack the follow-up documentation to make any definitive statement. Nonetheless, I am especially encouraged by the preliminary unpublished results of treating various physical issues, as reported by Joaquin Andrade (personal communication, February 11, 2004).

When exploring how Process Healing might help resolve a personal physical problem, the reader is encouraged to be creative, for the outcome is often determined by the unique personal fit of the approach. It is also important to take all of the precautions necessary to assure a successful outcome. Some brief examples of treating physical issues are given at the end of this chapter.

Table of contents for this chapter

Mental Issues

Physical issues

Summary

Mental Issues

10-1 Treating mental issues—the general protocol

When a new patient walks into my office, I usually start off by describing my education and work history. I also describe the different types of treatment that I can use such as EFT, EMDR, TAT, and Process Healing. I emphasize the Process Healing Method. This is a way of allowing the patient to adjust to the treatment setting and get a sense of who I am. Then I ask what brought him or her to my office and I make a list of all the symptoms he or she describes. I ask leading questions to rule out fragile dissociative processes and to determine whether he or she has a dissociative disorder. During this assessment, I look for suicidal ideation, addictions, or physical problems and then determine whether it is appropriate to refer him or her to their family doctor or a psychiatrist. After assessing the patient and collecting all the relevant information before treatment, I establish rapport with all aspects of the personality and get the aspects on the Treatment Team. When given permission by the Treatment Team, I teach the subconscious the treatment method. Then I do a sample treatment with a phobia or something of that nature and have the subconscious and Treatment Team create treatment plans. Finally, I have the subconscious treat the barriers that prevent it from being able automatically and independently to treat issues that arise between sessions. After all of this, I start addressing the issues.

I usually start by treating all the parts that want to be treated and problem-solve and treat all the parts that do not want to be treated. I repeat this until all parts are waiting for treatment. With that done, I treat any suicidal aspects or memories present. If the patient is self-mutilating, I treat the parts that want to mutilate. Then I start treating the patient's issues. I usually have a list of the issues so treatment can be systematic. When there are extreme emotions, I treat the emotions in the Emotion System and ask the subconscious to follow the associations back to memory structures and treat the memory structures in the correct order. Sometimes, there are collages of extreme emotions—for example, rage. In this case, I ask the subconscious to treat the collages in the best order and follow the associations of each collage back to treat the memory structures. Then I ask the subconscious to do a Massive Change History and everything. Next, I ask the subconscious to repeat the procedure with each of the other emotion collages. I do this with all the emotions that are relevant to the patient such as: rage and anger, sadness, fear, anxiety, panic, disgust, shame, guilt, and grief. I have not yet treated subjection, dejection, and aversion. I ask the subconscious which emotions should be treated and read the list. I treat the emotions in the order indicated by the subconscious.

When general treatment does not completely treat the issue, I start suggesting various memory structures to the subconscious until he or she indicates the structure that caused the problem. I usually find that when an issue is pervasive, one of the following structures is involved: Layered Memories, Predispositions, layered parts, or System Fragments. I treat the memory structures and, if there are many similar structures, I look for some process that is causing the easy creation of structures. I occasionally find an easy creation process present that has to be treated before I can proceed.

Some mental health issues are more complex in nature. This chapter summarizes treatments I have used with various complex disorders. The interventions described in these cases are not necessarily complete because all people are unique with their own assortment of memory structures. What I include here are interventions I collected from my notes. These interventions should be taken as suggestions, not protocols. I have summarized what I have done for many of my patients with each issue. Because the interventions can progress rather rapidly throughout a treatment session, I have undoubtedly missed some of the interventions that took place.

The interventions described are not one-session cures. The target issue may linger for weeks or months, although the patient will usually experience progress with each session. The big barriers to problem-solving will become more obvious as you continue to problem-solve for many sessions. In cases that require a lot of creative treatment and problem-solving time, I always assume that I have not found the key to treating the issue. When I have trouble progressing with an issue and my creativity is exhausted, I inquire about fields. I sometimes use the more advanced Process Healing techniques that involve fields (Flint, n.d.). The existence of fields in this context has not been firmly established by science. But whether fields are a real phenomenon or a metaphor for other memory structures, fields frequently appear to be the problem, and treating fields usually clears the way for further progress. Finally, always keep in mind that however intent you are on clearing the barriers, it is important to assess whether the patient wants to continue. If he or she is becoming discouraged, it may be best to refer him or her to another therapist before he or she wants to quit seeing you and loses interest in therapy.

10-2 Treating Depression

Depression can be caused by either great sadness in the Main Personality or by aspects giving thoughts and emotions to the conscious Main Personality. I always check to see if there is a part that is causing the depression. Then I look for parts related to the symptoms of depression, such as: fatigue, suicidal feelings or thoughts, confusion, negative beliefs, and so forth. When you treat depression, list the symptoms and systematically go through each of the symptoms by asking the subconscious if there is a part that is giving that symptom. Expect to find more than one part involved. Start with suicidal thoughts. When the subconscious confirms that several parts are causing some symptom, I get permission to determine the number of parts by counting up until the subconscious gives me a "Yes" to indicate the number. I ask questions that could trigger more parts requiring treatment. In the next session, I review the symptoms and treat additional parts as needed.

Treating depression is not easy. Usually, all the traumas that caused the depression have to be treated. Always use the Massive Change History and everything after every intervention. Usually depression leaves people without the resources needed to initiate positive experiences, or sometimes they struggle with lingering negative beliefs. Many self-damaging beliefs may have to be changed and positive beliefs installed in their place. Futurepacing is needed to set goals, to practice new behavior to generate more interests and activity, and to increase the possibility of getting more happiness and satisfaction in life.

Interventions for depression

If possible, treat the suicidal thoughts first. These may be parts formed early in life when suicide appeared to be the only way to escape the pain. These negative thoughts can be treated with the Sentence Procedure. Check to see if the patient thinks about suicide between sessions. Sometimes patients tell you later about suicidal close calls but will not let you know at the time. I make contracts with patients to call me before they attempt suicide. The contracts usually contain a clause giving me permission to alert their support network. If necessary, I talk them into going into the hospital when I have no other options.

Guilt and self-reproach based on a past or present situation are often the motivating causes of depression. I have found that when the guilt and self-reproach have been treated, the depression tends to be less intense. Assess and treat Fetal Shame (Chapter 9-9). Check to see if the depression is associated with an early trauma. Depression can be treated as a complex emotion in the Emotion System. When the motivation has been treated (by treating the emotions in the Emotion System and following the associations back to memory structures and treating them), the patient usually feels a change in the intensity of the depression. When the cause of the depression is an ongoing situation, treatment can be more difficult. Then you have to focus on changing the current situation by composing reframes and treatment.

Beliefs like helplessness, hopelessness, and worthlessness can be treated using the Sentence Procedure or the Structure Procedure. Look for other beliefs that may be associated with feeling depressed and treat them in a similar way. Replace treated beliefs with self-empowering beliefs. When a patient presents evidence of mood swings, like feeling worse in the morning and better in the afternoon, I would look for parts that are active in the morning and treat them all. Similarly, for symptoms of early-morning waking or insomnia, I would look for parts as the source of the problem. Eating disorders may often be resolved by treating the depression, but if this is not effective, treat the eating disorder separately (Chapter 10-3). Any irritability in a patient's behavior can be treated with the

Sentence Procedure to trigger the relevant memories. Use the Emotion System to treat the trauma emotions and motivation for irritability. Treat triggers for irritability such as Predispositions or Picture Structures. All of these symptoms could be present as a Predisposition, a problem in the Ego States or Tandem Memories. Complex memory structures or even easily created systems may well exist that contribute to the depression and the symptoms. Remember always to do the Massive Change History and everything after each intervention.

Example:

An introspective depressed person

This patient stated that he had depression on and off for years. He said that he had experienced it several times the week before the session. He described the feeling as gloom, thinking negatively, feeling hopeless and helpless: "What's the use? Life is not worthwhile." He said, "I'm not too great to be with. I say things and then I reflect on my thinking, 'What did I say that for?'" He feels the depression is in his face. He added, "When I am depressed, I don't want to talk about it." The marked symptoms and the irregular experience of depression led me to believe there were parts underlying the depression.

Depression parts were treated one after the other and I problem-solved with parts that did not want to be treated until they accepted treatment. Depression collages in the Emotion System were treated. There were layered parts that gave negative memory intrusions. Several constellations of easily created systems were treated. Other parts intruded during the treatment. A year later, contact with the patient revealed that these episodes of depression were no longer experienced.

10-3 Treating addictions

I usually weed out the unmotivated patients by asking if they could flush the addictive substance down the toilet to show both them and me that they are committed and motivated to quit using. When patients hedge on tossing out the addictive substance, I tell them that treatment would probably fail and they would be wasting their money. Some patients are not motivated enough to end their addiction or to be in therapy. However, when the patient's response to this question leads you to believe that he or she wants to quit the addiction, continue with the addiction protocol presented here. Screening for motivation in this manner often weeds out addicts who are encouraged to get into therapy by a spouse or some authority. I expect the addicts to make their own appointments. If your client were addicted to alcohol, I would strongly encourage him or her to join Alcoholics Anonymous. Have him or her attend each of the available AA groups to see which is best for them.

Educate the patient and teach the treatment method. Have the subconscious clear any barriers to automatic treatment. Treat parts that want to be treated and parts that do not want to be treated and problem-solve until they are all treated. If there are addiction withdrawal symptoms, list them all and ask the subconscious to treat them one at a time, from the worst to the least intense symptom. Remember to do a Massive Change History and everything after each intervention. Here is the protocol for addictions.

1. List the addictions, such as drugs, marijuana, alcohol, tobacco, food, sex, and so forth, and with the help of the subconscious, order them from the first to be treated to the last. Start treating the first addiction prescribed by the subconscious.

2. Ask the subconscious if there are any field barriers connected to the addiction. If there are, ask if they will get in the way of the treatment. If the patient says the following is true for him or her, "I can have one drink, but if I have two, it's as if something comes over me and I have to drink everything in sight," I interpret this as a field process that adds motivation and, possibly, problem behaviors to the drinking addiction.

3. Then do the Sentence Procedure with, "I want to quit drinking." Ask the subconscious to tag all elicited memories, beliefs, experiences, and parts, and treat them in the correct order. Then do a Massive Change History and everything. Have the subconscious generate statements for the procedure until all the beliefs, memories, experiences, and parts related to drinking are no longer triggered.

4. Ask the subconscious if the tagged memories or the parts should be treated first.

   a. If memories should be treated first, ask the subconscious to treat the memories safely, one after the other.

   b. Then treat the parts. Are there parts contributing to the addiction? Do they want treatment? If they do, ask the subconscious to treat all parts safely, one after the other. Check for more parts.

   c. When the parts do not want treatment, problem-solve, and treat the parts.

5. Ask the subconscious if there are collages of emotions in the Emotion System that support drinking. Treat the collages and then have the subconscious follow the associations to the memory structures and treat them in the best order. You may have to problem-solve here.

6. Explore with the subconscious about other structures that may be involved with the addiction. Ask the subconscious about Predispositions, System Fragments, Independent Behavior System, parts in the Emotion System, and so forth. Problem-solve and treat these structures.

7. Strengthen the patient's motivation to stop the addiction. Do the Sentence Procedure on "I want to quit drinking" or "I don't want to smoke," and so forth. After the procedure is done, strengthen these beliefs.

8. Talk about all the places where the addiction is likely to occur or be mostly enjoyed and ask the subconscious to tag and treat all of the memories triggered by this conversation. Make a list of the situations you talked about so you can test the patient's response later. Treat the positive memories of the addiction first and then treat the negative memories. Ask the subconscious to repeat this by generating statements to activate as many beliefs, memories, and behaviors as possible. Test the addictive urge when talking about the situations on the list and assess the patient's addictive response.

9. Teach a social response.

   a. Ask the subconscious to treat all beliefs, behaviors, and memories that get in the way of "Thank you, I don't drink," or whatever is appropriate for the addiction being treated. (For example, treat positive beliefs for doing the addictive behavior, avoiding old trauma pain, or barriers to taking responsibility.)

   b. Strengthen an appropriate response, such as: "Thank you, I don't drink," until it feels true to the patient.

   c. Visualize several situations where this response is appropriate. Have the patient imagine saying this response so the subconscious can treat triggered memories until the statement feels completely natural to say.

10. Check for more fields. Imagine your first drink. What do you feel? If your drinking tendency arises gradually, explore for a field; otherwise, look for parts.

11. Have the patient imagine him or herself in a situation where he or she had a relapse and started doing the addiction again. Treat addictive urges and compose with the patient a strategy to avoid the addiction in the situations leading to the relapse. Test the strategy repeatedly until it feels completely natural to the patient.

12. Remove beliefs that support the addiction. Here are some examples for drinking.
    a. "I can't feel high energy unless I drink." Treat the motivation for this belief and all memories related to the motivation. Then strengthen, "If I eat and sleep well, I won't be as sad and will feel more energy."
    b. "I have to drink to have fun." Treat the motivation for this belief, and all memories related to the motivation. Then strengthen the belief; "I can have fun without drinking." Do the Futurepace Intervention with this belief in many situations until it is completely true.
    c. "Celebrations are a time to party." Treat the motivation for this belief. Strengthen the belief, "I can party and have fun without drinking. If I am not having fun, I can leave."

13. Recovering from a relapse requires a belief that can lead the patient back into sobriety. I have the person imagine having a drink. Treat all beliefs that are triggered when sobriety is broken. Treat the negative self-talk so the statements are not true, and strengthen a positive statement that will protect the person from falling into the addiction again, such as, "Now I know I am still vulnerable. I'll stop drinking and do my program." Use the Futurepace Intervention until the patient can imagine a slip in sobriety without feeling like a failure or feeling addicted again.

14. Treat all the interconnections between the treatments that were done. Who's to say what this does? But someone's subconscious suggested this to complete treating the addiction.

15. The subconscious will remember this addiction protocol. Simply ask the subconscious to repeat this protocol for treating the next addiction on the list. Be sure to check to see if the protocol worked for the next addiction.

Examples:

1. Food addiction

The patient was a recovered drug addict but continued to have food-addiction problems. It looked more like an obsession. She had intrusions about eating food, when to eat, and what to eat. Many parts and Layered Memories were giving constant food intrusions. Some parts expressed a fear of her sexually acting out if she became attractive. Other parts blocked the eating compulsion by causing her to starve herself, and then she felt shame for feeling hungry.

Treating this addiction involved treating many parts and other memory structures. She was encouraged to start an exercise program. Beliefs such as "I hate my body" and "I can't lose weight" were treated. By successfully losing weight, the results would feed into her fear of success. The food obsession was treated in several sessions with TAT (see Appendix VI). The anticipation of losing weight increased her fear of getting raped or hurt in some way. In a later session, she found that she ate to sedate herself. If she ate fast, she would go to sleep; parts caused this tactic. Treatment involved treating many parts, memory structures, and beliefs.

In a later session, during the time when she was losing weight, a part that wanted to get bigger was treated. More than a year later, after she asserted the food issue was done, we made the following interventions:

T: **Subconscious, please work with the dissociation process to treat all dissociated food-related memories that are intruding into the conscious experience.**

S: **Yes.**

T: **Please treat all beliefs about getting treatment and compose self-empowering beliefs to take their place.**

S: **Yes.**

T: **Please treat the system of satiation and deprivation that was distorted by traumas.**

S: **Yes.**

T: **Please treat the parts that are avoiding dealing with hunger.**

S: **Yes.**

T: **Please treat the structure of malnourished experiences.**

S: **Yes.**

T: **Please treat the structure of forced-feeding memories.**

S: **Yes.**

T: **Subconscious, please treat the traumas at birth.**

S: **Yes.**

The net result was that, although she retained some of her excess weight, she was comfortable with her body and eating was no longer an issue for her. She continued to eat healthfully and to exercise.

2. Sexual addiction

Sexual addiction can include engaging in intercourse with many partners, spending long hours on the Internet viewing pornographic content, or renting pornographic movies. Often, these people have a sexual abuse history from an early age, which stimulated the motivation for casual sex with a high sex drive. Here is a general outline based on what I did to treat one patient with a sexual addiction:

a. Have the patient take steps to stop watching porn on the Internet or in rented movies. This may involve having his partner or a relative monitor his behavior.

b. Have the patient make an exhaustive list of all the sexual experiences that he can remember from the earliest age. These are important to treat because the motivation for the addiction is based mainly on this early experience.

c. If child abuse is involved, this is where boundaries are discussed. Strengthen appropriate boundaries. Discuss his masturbation fantasies. Encourage age-appropriate fantasies.

d. Treat these sexual abuse traumas and look for sexual addiction-related parts and Layered Memories that may have Predispositions associated *with* them.

e. Treat the rage and anger associated with the abuse. Identify the triggers that evoke the sexual addiction and systematically treat the emotions that support these triggers.

f. Treat the addictive or obsessive sexual emotions in the Emotion System and the Kinesthetic System.

g. Test the treatments by having the patient imagine examples of being around seductive women or children of various ages.

h. Treat any thoughts or urges that are triggered, such as "wanting to get to know the woman and having sex."

i. Treat the boundary issues regarding women. Boundaries are like beliefs, so the intervention involves identifying the poor boundaries, treating them and then composing a socially acceptable boundary to protect the patient, as well as women and children.

Check with the patient and subconscious and repeat the interventions suggested here as needed over a series of treatment sessions. Sexual addiction is based on a complex traumatic sexual abuse history. Continue testing and treating to see if further treatment of any memory structures, relevant to the issue, is necessary. Consult often with the subconscious to search for additional interventions—or interventions that should be repeated.

Three months after completing treatment of the sexual addictive behaviors, the patient in this example reported that he was not experiencing the intense drive to view pornographic material or to engage with good-looking women. He said that he was able to appreciate the beauty of women without experiencing a sexual interest in them. This assessment of the sexual addiction issue was ongoing over the duration of the treatment.

10-4 Treating Obsessive-Compulsive Disorder

Working with obsessions and compulsions usually involves treating many parts and memory structures. The first step is to look for and then treat the memory structures that automatically create parts or memory structures. When treating parts that intrude, you can be led to believe that all the parts were treated in one session. However, it always happens that before the next session, or even many sessions later, another part will become active and intrude again. For example, when working with the patient who had the hair-pulling compulsion, which I mentioned earlier, I worked many sessions to finally get a week with no hair-pulling. Three weeks later, the patient pulled a patch in his scalp. We treated more parts after this episode. Three months later, he pulled a small patch in his scalp. Again, we treated more parts, and since then he has had no problem for six months.

Obsessive-compulsive disorder is a complex issue that can sometimes be treated by simply treating parts. However, in other patients the intervention could well include everything you learned in this book and require problem-solving for many weeks. Different people can have different complex causes for this disorder.

Examples:
1. Obsessive patient
The patient called herself scatterbrained and obsessive. We had treated many structures that gave obsessive thoughts. However, she was still obsessed with thoughts at work, and they were interfering with her productivity. The line of questioning presented here resulted in the detection of a basic obsessive structure that I had missed earlier in treatment:

T: **Subconscious, is there a basic obsessive structure that we have missed?**

S: **Yes.**

After probing around a bit, I discovered the basic obsessive structure that caused this issue. It consisted of Predispositions in Memory II that were layered and associated *with* Layered Memories in Memory III.

The layering of Predispositions in Memory II protected them from being easily treated.

T: **Subconscious, please treat all the dissociative fragments associated *to* Predispositions in Memory II and then treat the Predispositions. Then, treat the Layered Memories in Memory III.**

S: **Yes.**

T: [Done] **Subconscious, were all those layered Predispositions easily created in some way?**

S: **Yes.**

Here is how the structure that causes the easy creation of Layered Memories was formed. A trauma occurred. A Predisposition memory in Memory II became layered when a dissociation fragment was associated *to* the Predisposition memory. This new, layered Predisposition memory was also associated *with* the dissociation part in Memory III. In a later trauma, when the dissociation part fragmented to associate *to* a new Layered Memory in Memory III, the fragmented dissociated part included the layered Predisposition associated *with* it and created a new, layered Predisposition in Memory II. This structure made the new Layered Memory difficult to treat under normal circumstances because a layered Predisposition was associated *with* it. The creation of Layered Memories of this kind seemingly happened repeatedly. Here is the treatment of the structure that caused the automatic creation of a Layered Memory with a protected Predisposition.

T: **Subconscious, please treat the dissociative fragment associated *to* the Predisposition and then the Predisposition associated *with* the dissociation process. Then treat the Layered Memory.**

S: **Yes.**

So, now I was interested in testing the outcome of these interventions. I asked the patient to produce the thoughts that bothered her at work. She said that they were a little less intense.

T: **Subconscious, can you tag and treat any Predispositions that may have become active?**

S: **Yes.**

I asked her to try to come up with more thoughts, and she said it became a little harder to think of them.

T: **Subconscious, can you tag and treat any Predispositions that may have become active?**

S: **Yes.**

I asked the subconscious if we should do the TAT pose (see Appendix VI). She carried out the TAT intervention on the thoughts with both the left and right hand. We followed with a Massive Change History and everything. The following week she found that she could hold her attention to the task she was doing.

2. Treating behaviors with repetitive qualities

A subtle chronic pain caused by a particular type of trauma occurring around the time of birth can be motivation for repetitive behaviors. This trauma is caused by the conflict between the fetus' behaviors and tendencies for behavior inherited from the parents (Flint, n.d.). The pain caused by this trauma is subsequently avoided by the activity of repetitive behaviors. The resulting repetitive behaviors can be the major cause of issues such as addictions, obsession-compulsion disorders, chronic disorders, rebellious behaviors, and depression.

The following intervention was used to treat a patient who had many of the behaviors caused by this particular type of trauma. In the following example or protocol, the order was not determined by questioning the subconscious but developed as I thought of them. You will notice that some of the interventions seem unusual. I was being creative and these unusual interventions were accepted by the subconscious. The interventions were carried out one after the other. Field barriers occurred with several of the structures. (The patient's "Yeses" are omitted.)

T: **Subconscious, is there a trauma at birth that causes the repetition of this person's issue?**

T: **Subconscious, please treat birth trauma.**

T: **Treat the structure of Layered Memories in the dissociative process.**

T: **Treat the structure of beliefs that support external reference.**

T: **Treat the structure of parts with Layered Memories, and memories that support repetitive behavior.**

T: **Add and subtract associations in the orbital cortex so it will produce normal behavior.**

T: **Subconscious, please treat the Protector-Controller and treat all the Predispositions in Memory II that lead to repetitive behavior.**

T: **Treat the Basic Neurostructure of the Emotional System to normalize any activity that would stimulate repetitive behavior.**

T: **Treat the Basic Neurostructure of the Heart System to normalize any activity that would stimulate repetitive behavior.**

3. Here are more interventions from patients who had OCD.

OCD can be difficult to treat. Often the solution for eliminating OCD involves interventions that are unusual. These are some of the interventions I use when I treat OCD patients.

T: **Treat the collages of OCD emotions in the Emotion System, follow associations back to memory structures, and treat the structures in the correct order.**

T: **Treat the memory structures in Ego States that cause OCD behaviors.**

T: **Subconscious, please add and subtract neural associations in the Basic Neurostructure of the Behavior System to eliminate OCD tendencies.**

T: **Please treat parts with Picture Structures associated *with* Predispositions.**

T: **Subconscious, are there any fields that support OCD behavior?**

The repetitive behaviors were no longer experienced by the patient.

10-5 Treating thought-process disorders

Serious thought-process disorders are not too common. It would be good to review Taylor's book (1981) to become familiar with the various kinds of thought-process disorders. It is unlikely that you will see a patient with a thought-process disorder unless you work in a mental health facility. However, if you meet or treat a person with a thought-process disorder, suggest a neuropsychological or a psychiatric evaluation to rule out brain damage. If the patient has been evaluated for brain damage or intends to be evaluated, and if the patient is willing, you might try to treat the thought-process disorder. It would be an interesting issue to try to treat.

I am giving some examples of thought-process disorders that I have treated with some, but not complete, success.

Examples:

1. Word salad and tangential speech

This patient was diagnosed as schizophrenic and used tangential speech. That is, when trying to answer a question, he assembled phrases that never really addressed the question. After years of treatment, he finally revealed that he created sentences in conversations from a selection of auditory intrusions. This resulted in his giving unusual, tangential answers to questions and making tangential statements in conversation. He often spoke in disconnected phrases. Medication did not reduce these symptoms, which, in my experience, suggests that the problem was a dissociative disorder. (Typically, drugs do not work with symptoms of dissociative disorders. They can help to reduce emotions, improve the ability to focus, and lower the rate of switching, which is important, but they do not treat the underlying disorder.)

The intrusions seemed like parts or Layered Memories. In the first session, after we treated many parts, he noticed a decrease in the rate of internal phrase intrusions. But by the next week the intrusions were back. We continued from week to week until the patient reported no intrusions. His mother reported that his relatedness and ability to communicate and organize his life steadily improved over this period.

The process of speech creation usually takes place in the unconscious, through the assembly of appropriate words or phrases to build a meaningful and coherent response. The following is an explanation of how this patient's problem came about:

T: **Subconscious, is there a structure that I have not worked with before that causes this problem in communication?**

S: **Yes.**

T: **Does this have to do with the formation of associations?**

S: **Yes.**

T: **Does this have to do with Memory I and Memory II?**

S: **Yes.**

T: **Is there a structure?**

S: **Yes.**

With leading questions, I discovered that a structure—a composition process—was formed in Memory I when the patient started to respond with mismatching phrases. The patient allegedly started talking this way because he thought it was amusing. This style of assembling mismatching phrases created a structure (involving both Memory I and Memory II) that formed tangential sentences. Normally, structures in Memory II learn to take part when forming meaningful utterances in the unconscious. However, in this case there was trauma to Memory II, which caused the patient to compose verbal utterances in his conscious experience. The trauma in Memory II was treated to normalize these psychotic verbal phenomena and resulted in the elimination of intruding phrases.

There was a period of adjustment as he learned to create responses specifically to what he heard and knew to be true. While this patient remains disabled in subtle ways, his ability to communicate, focus, plan, make decisions, and run his life improved. Curiously, I also managed to treat another interesting psychotic feature of this man. He only experienced the first phrase of received language—for example, from people, when reading sentences, or hearing dialogue in movies. Treating this psychotic symptom also contributed to his doing better in life.

2. Thought-process disorders

The following are examples of thought-process disorders that would be interesting challenges to treat. Most outpatient therapists never see patients with severe thought-process disorders. The patients or families of such patients often cannot afford the expense of years of treatment. Medication is the standard course of treatment. However, the educational value of treating a motivated patient with a severe mental disorder makes it worthwhile to consider reducing or even waiving the fee.

One advantage of treating these serious thought-process disorders, other than helping the patient, is to develop a model of the brain processes creating these symptoms. These individual models will expand our knowledge of how the brain works. Whoa . . . ! When I think of brain processes, I automatically fall into thinking of hardwired structures that create our speech. But with the development of speech, we must go through a learning process where the receptive speech process comes first. This is the process that receives auditory input and converts it into a personal experience providing meaning. Then comes the expressive process that converts memory activity in the Active Experience into sounds or spoken words. Then, with simple words, the composing process starts, which then grows in complexity as the number of words increases. This requires the learning of syntax so the words can be arranged into a well-formed sentence. As the environmental demands increase, editing is required to juggle words and syntax to achieve clear expression. We then end with five dissociated processes that can all be involved in thought-process disorders: receptive process, expressive process, composing process, syntax process, and editing process. If any of these processes get damaged early in childhood, then it is possible that a thought-process disorder will arise.

My suggestions for the treatment of the thought-process disorders are just hypotheses. They are presented to give you some idea about how to look at the problem and construct an intervention. These thought-process disorders are usually found in mania and schizophrenia but are also associated with brain damage or chronic brain disease. Therefore, it is important to assess for the possibility of brain damage and refer the patient to a neuropsychologist or a physician for evaluation. If the problem is a brain tumor or lesion in the brain, then treatment with Process Healing probably will not work. If the patient is diagnosed with schizophrenia or mania, then the behavior may be memory-driven and treatable.

When being treated for thought-process disorders, the patient may hide his or her internal process or may not discriminate the sequence of conscious events that leads to the disorder. The patient who had tangential speech revealed his process to me only after two years of therapy. If I had been more systematic in my interviewing or had tried earlier to uncover the process leading to his disordered speech, perhaps I could have treated this issue more readily.

The first goal is to establish rapport with the patient. Some patients may behave in ways that make it nearly impossible to communicate or they may be uncooperative. These problems are treated first. When communication is difficult, I assume that the subconscious uses normal language and I try to establish rapport with it.

I had a colleague who was skillful in working with schizophrenics. He found that if he tried to interpret the disordered speech, he could eventually learn the patient's language and communicate with the patient meaningfully (B. Post, personal communication, 1970). Treatment would involve leading the patient back to an acceptable language of communication. This suggested that the thought and speech processes were working properly but that some form of trauma possibly distorted the organization or meaning of words and phrases used in thought and speech.

Patients with each of the following thought-process disorders can be given careful interviews to try to get some idea of what to treat. I have broken the thought-process disorders into groups: speech characterized by intrusive patterns; rate-of-speech symptoms; speech lacking meaning; repetitive patterns of speech; and word distortions. By working closely with the subconscious, you will get help in your problem-solving. I am going to list the disorders under each category and then suggest how to approach the patient to analyze and treat the disorders.

1. Speech characterized by intrusive patterns

Flight of ideas—the person's communication jumps from topic to topic. Multiple lines of thought may be observed in the symptom. The shifts in topics can be caused by external stimuli.

Circumstantial speech—communication that is intact but out of context; phrases are interspersed so that the response to a question takes a roundabout route before reaching the goal.

Tangential speech—the patient talks around the point but never reaches the goal.

Thought blocking—the patient stops speaking in the middle of the sentence.

Derailment—the patient shifts from one line of thought to another in the middle of the sentence. It is sometimes triggered by a specific word.

Non-sequitur—a statement or reply that has no relevance to what preceded it, or an argument where the conclusion does not follow from the assumptions.

If rapport can be achieved, perhaps the following suggestions will be useful for problem-solving these thought-process disorders. In each of these intrusive patterns of speech, there does not seem to be a problem with syntax. I would therefore look for independent association and dissociation processes and treat any trauma in these processes before joining them. These processes, if independent, could have the effect of causing the patient to talk around an issue or to insert out-of-context phrases or topics, or even to express conclusions only slightly related to an argument. In such a case, I would treat all parts and Layered Memories related to these disorders. Blocking of speech could be a part blocking communication, just as parts sometimes block finger responses. Look for parts or Layered Memories associated *with* Predispositions triggered by the receptive speech processes that cause the shift in topics. An Independent Behavior System, or System Fragments, could be running or altering the speech of the patient. A conscious speech process could also be involved.

2. Rate-of-speech symptoms

Mumbled speech—the patient is talking as though he or she has rocks in his or her mouth.

Staccato speech—the words are clipped and abrupt.

Scanning speech—words are stretched out and the speech has a slow and sliding cadence.

Rapid and pressured speech—continuous and intrusive speech; the person talks continuously, rapidly and seems pressured to talk.

Look for a trauma that may have caused these speech patterns. See if you can contact the patient's mother and inquire about birth or prebirth trauma or any other trauma that might account for the onset of this disorder. You could also ask the subconscious about these possible incidents. Parts may cause such idiosyncrasies as scanning speech or mumbling. The cause may be a structure problem such as an Independent Behavior System or System Fragments. The expressive speech process may be damaged. There may be some unusual collage of emotions in the Emotion System that may cause the rapid or slow speech.

3. Speech lacking meaning

Driveling speech—like double-talk, where the grammar and syntax are maintained but the words communicate no meaning.

Rambling speech—similar to tangential speech but shows loose-ness of association because the phrases are unrelated frag-ments, making the communication meaningless.

It may be difficult to establish rapport with this kind of patient. Look for a different kind of muscle response to communicate with the subconscious, like an eye blink or a sneer. Talk through to the subcon-scious to try to achieve rapport. Do a careful history with the patient's mother to find out when this condition started. Rule out organic brain damage. A damaged association process or composition process may be the cause of the lack of meaning. Also check for parts and Layered Memo-ries as a possible cause. Look for a conscious speech process that might be involved in these issues.

4. Repetitive patterns in speech

Perseveration—words and phrases appear repeatedly in the per-son's speech.

Verbigeration—the person repeats the word or words at the end of the thought several times.

Clang association—the patient organizes his or her speech by the sound of words rather than the meaning.

Look for parts or Layered Memories that like to echo words or phrases. Repeated patterns of speech could be caused by the composi-tion and editing processes. The expressive speech process might cause the clang associations. There could be a part that echoes words at the end of sentences in receptive speech so that the system thinks that speech is cor-rectly formed with clang associations. Look for parts or Layered Memo-ries creating clang associations.

5. Word distortions

Word approximations—the patient substitutes an incor-rect, but slightly related, word or words in a sentence, like the word "watcher" for "television."

Private language—use of words that have private meanings, such as "bicycle" used in place of "feelings."

Neologisms—new words like "tidgat" for "gadget."

Have the brain function medically assessed. If there is no trauma or organic basis for the issue, then assume that these disorders are caused by dysfunction in the composition or editing processes. Find out if parts, or some memory structure, are the cause of the word substitutions. Word substitution may involve Predispositions that may be causing the word substitutions or letter play. Perhaps receptive language processes caused distortions of meaning that resulted in the meaning of words to be novel.

Trauma may be associated with the correct word, word usage, or structure, thus leading to word avoidance by the substitution of approximations. It may also be caused by conscious assembly of distorted sentences.

In general, for these thought-process disorders, I would try to get a detailed history of the patient's trauma. This may give some clue to the origin and protective function of these forms of speech. Work closely with the subconscious to understand when the trauma happened and what caused the thought-process disorder. Always ask if trauma to Basic Neurostructure, Memory I, or Memory II contributes to the disorders. I would look for an automatic creation process. Determine whether an Independent Behavior System or fragmented Behavior Systems might be the source of the thought-process disorders.

10-6 Treating pervasive negative traits

Pervasive personality traits can cause some problems for people. These include mania, pervasive negative affect, and lack of relatedness. I have had the opportunity to treat some of these issues, but they have never been pervasive. In this section I am offering suggestions for treating pervasive negative traits. These are complex issues and would be interesting to problem-solve.

1. Manic behavior

Manic behavior is defined as overactive or underactive behavior. Flight of ideas, labile affect, hyperactivity, impulsiveness, talking incessantly, elation, and chronic irritability are all examples of overactive behavior. Hypoactivity is defined as underactive behavior such as slow movement or shyness. It is likely that these issues are all trauma based. Nevertheless, it is good to consult with the patient's doctor and rule out the possibility of some organic problem as the cause. This is especially important if the behavior started suddenly or recently.

I assume that the patient is a willing patient. After doing the usual procedure of installing the treatment method and treating parts, do the following:

   a. Ask for a fine-grained, detailed report of the onset of the issue in everyday experience. If it starts suddenly, a part might be the cause. If this has been continuing for many years, then suspect a more basic cause, which might involve the Basic Neurostructure and Memory I and II, or an Independent Behavior System or System Fragments.

b. Find when it was first noticed. If possible, ask both the patient and a parent of the patient for the historical detail. Look for a trauma that might have caused this condition or an unusual belief that could result in mania.

c. Work with the subconscious and explore the basis for the high or low motivation. Inquire about unusual collages or emotions in the Emotion System.

d. Ask the subconscious if intruding parts cause the behavior. Use the Sentence Procedure and the Structure Procedure, or simply have the subconscious tag the parts as they become active. Inquire about the automatic creation of parts or other memory structures.

e. Inquire about simple Predispositions or Predispositions that associate *with* or *to* other memory structures that cause the issue.

2. Personal affect

The affect of a person is defined as the emotional tone that underlies all of his or her behaviors. It can be sadness, happiness, anxiety, anger or rage, apathy, or euphoria.

a. Interview the patient to see if his affect is continuous or constant or if there is a shift in affect suddenly during the day. In the first case, I would expect Basic Neurostructure and Memory I and II. In the case of a sudden shift, I would expect parts, a complex memory, or system structures.

b. See if there is trauma or a protective function that causes the pervasive emotional tone of the person. If so, treat the trauma in the usual ways. See if the resulting normal affect would cause problems.

c. See if damage to the association process caused the affect issue.

d. Look for a trauma structure or problem in the Emotion System.

3. Constricted or labile affect

Constricted affect is when the person has a very narrow range of affect at some intensity. A person with a labile affect shows rapid mood shifts within a short period of time. In both of these cases, I would look for the following.

a. Determine if a trauma or an environment that demanded constricted or labile affect caused the affect issue. Tightly controlled affect may be a protective measure or a learned pattern of behavior.

b. Assess for trauma in the Emotion System.
c. Assess for trauma damage to the association and dissociation processes. The trauma could keep emotions out of the Active Experience to create the constricted affect.
d. Assess for trauma in the midbrain and the Basic Neurostructure.
e. Consult with the subconscious to find out if other neurostructures were involved (for example, the forebrain).

4. Lack of relatedness

The patient typically shows some robotic, emotionless behavior. He or she is cold and does not relate to, or bond with, people. This lack of relatedness can probably be treated unless it is caused by brain damage or a systemic problem. It is probably a severe form of attachment disorder. It may require many sessions and continuous problem-solving.

a. Look for a trauma or environmental influence, such as a family system or role model that may have caused this robotic behavior.
b. Very strong beliefs are often formed, which radically change a person's behavior.
c. Find out if the association or dissociation processes are protecting the conscious experience from being flooded by past trauma, or from being hurt by others.
d. Ask the subconscious if other memory or system structures, like Predispositions and complex parts, or problems in the Emotion System, are causing the lack of relatedness.
e. If any of the self-perpetuating behaviors are relevant (see Chapter 9-13), treat the basis for those behavioral patterns.

10-7 Treating delusions

Delusions are false or arbitrary beliefs that cannot be proven or disproven. Most of the delusions you will see are called secondary delusional ideas. These develop from hallucinations or altered moods, but they are real to the person experiencing them. Patients are not usually willing to reveal their delusions.

Delusions can be based on or related to a mood, such as "I am a terrible person," or by taking responsibility for deaths or abuse. Delusional thoughts, such as taking responsibility for being hurt, are often created in little children in abuse situations. When these delusional beliefs continue into adulthood they can become a problem. Usually they can be treated and eliminated. Be sensitive to the patient's attachment to delusions and, if necessary, reframe the interventions so as not to alienate the patient. Steps in the treatment of delusions include:

a. Treat parts, Layered Memories, and beliefs related to the delusions.

b. Treat all the negative emotion collages in the Emotion System motivating the delusions, and follow the associations back to the memory structure.

c. Look for delusions that get in the way of treatment. Try to use the Sentence Procedure with "I can be treated and live a healthy life" to activate delusional responses and other memory structures that can obstruct treatment.

d. As you notice delusional thoughts, treat them as you would treat a belief and have it replaced with a positive, self-empowering belief.

e. Teach the patient to recognize delusions and to ask the subconscious to treat them.

Primary delusional systems are widespread and well organized, and cause major impact on a person's life. These delusional systems are all-encompassing and may not be easy to work around. First try all the approaches suggested for secondary delusions. If you have no success, and if your patient allows you to contact the subconscious, and if communication is good, then ask for and take directions from the subconscious. I suggest the following:

a. Have the subconscious map the delusional structure into a private memory and look for a strategy to treat the delusional system. As a precautionary measure I would also determine if a structure was put in by some organization to control and use the person.

b. Assess for an Independent Behavior System and for System Fragments that could cause or contribute to the delusional system.

Examples:

1. Confusion and fear leading to a delusional belief about self

When this patient decompensated, she experienced fear, confusion, and ignorance of what to say, do, or how to be. She remembered having this experience from early in her childhood. Whenever the confusion was present, she would experience fear and ask if she said the wrong thing. Problem-solving revealed there was a Predisposition associated *to* the Emotion System, which evoked confusion and fear. Another Predisposition was associated *with* Layered Memories that cast doubt on what she last did or said. In this case, the association was connected to a memory that served an Active Experience independent of the primary Behavior System. Once I understood the problem, it was treated in this way:

a. The subconscious treated the Predispositions, and then the memories in the Independent Behavior System. The memory of the Independent Behavior System was joined with the Memory III in the Behavior System. In this case, the Independent Behavior System presented no barriers. I have had some Independent Behavior Systems that took weeks of searching for the correct reframe before we could finally progress and treat the system.

b. Many delusional beliefs were treated in Memory III. The Structure Procedure was used to treat many of these delusional beliefs. Delusional beliefs that appeared during our conversation were treated.

c. Teach the patient to recognize and treat the delusions.

This intervention appeared to stop the experience of confusion, fear, and doubt about her actions.

2. Delusional beliefs and thoughts can be easily formed

The patient had many delusional beliefs that she held as true. She appeared to overhear a statement or comment said in jest or out of context and then created a Belief Memory with that belief. These freshly created delusional beliefs were held to be true and were disruptive in her thinking and behavior. The process that easily creates delusional beliefs had to be treated. The easy creation process appeared to be triggered by confusion and resulted in any current statement or observation becoming "learned" as a delusional belief.

a. Treat any parts or memory structures that cause confusion in certain situations. See if the dissociation process has to be treated.

b. See if Predispositions are involved in the easy creation of delusions and look for any structure that is triggered by Predispositions. Treat the Predispositions and structures.

c. Treat the condition that causes the easy creation of delusions in the Basic Neurostructure, Memory I, II and III, and treat constellations of System Fragments.

d. Treat the barriers to clarifying comments overheard or read, and strengthen the behaviors clarifying comments.

e. Treat all introjected beliefs by treating the collages of emotions motivating the delusional beliefs and follow the emotions back to the memory structures and treat them.

The patient's thought process became clearer. She reported no longer becoming confused and had stopped creating delusions.

10-8 Treating psychosis

1. Delusional perception

People who believe in unverifiable plots against them or in the world hold delusional perceptions. They can feel controlled by electromagnetic fields (EMF) that are triggering them to lose time. Electromagnetic fields may be coming through the wall or from satellites. They can feel thought insertions or pain when they think about something or someone. They can feel implants in their heads or body and intertwine them in a conspiracy theory about who is monitoring or controlling them. They may present delusions about being snatched by people or aliens and being experimented with or programmed. They may talk about strange things happening at home or strange people entering the house at night and bothering them. While some of this is natural trauma-based delusional behavior obtained through natural childhood trauma, it is more likely that the person has a mind-control history caused by some organization (Ross, 2000). Consult with a therapist who has some familiarity with these types of "delusions." Whether the delusional perceptions are naturally trauma-based or the result of mind-control programming, I treat the symptoms without discounting the patient's delusional system.

With a well-organized natural trauma-based delusional system running the person's life, I would first try to use a reframe to get the patient to agree to have the system treated. Then I would treat it as a structure and have the subconscious transfer it into a private memory (see Chapter 6-14) and analyze the system to determine the best way to treat it. If many memory structures and Predispositions make up the system, I would attempt to use a Structure Procedure to treat the system without alerting it or confronting the patient. Treating the collages of emotions in the Emotion System and following associations to memory structures is another option. I would look for an Independent Behavior System or System Fragments as the basis for the delusional system. Careful interviewing and problem-solving will be necessary to discover an entry to dismantle the system.

To ascertain if the person is a ritual-abuse or mind-control survivor, I ask the subconscious:

T: **Subconscious, is there a large structure that was put in there on purpose by someone or some organization?**

When the patient wonders what I did, I say, "Oh, I was just curious about something."

When I get a "Yes," a dysfunctional family system or a normal trauma system of some kind has to be ruled out. I do not reveal any suspicions to the patient. I treat the large structure by communicating only with the subconscious. The intervention is beyond the scope of this book.

2. The experience of alienation

It is probable the patient has intrusive thoughts that cause the feelings of alienation. Identify those thoughts and look for evidence that the feelings of alienation are based on real experience. A patient with a ritual abuse or mind control history can also present with these symptoms. With these cases, I usually tend to believe that his or her perception is accurate, but that some memory-based process has distorted the patient's response. I would first ask about parts and Layered Memories. I would assess the Basic Neurostructure, Memory I, Memory II, and Predispositions. If necessary, I would further explore for System Fragments and for activity in Ego States or Tandem Memories. An Independent Behavior System might introduce distortion into the patient's perceptions.

3. Visual and auditory hallucinations

Visual and auditory hallucinations are typically found in dissociative patients and are routinely treated. Patients who have been diagnosed as schizophrenic because of other psychotic behavior can have many fields that block treating parts. If you find a treatment barrier that appears impossible to treat, check for a field. Either way, treat any parts that have to do with the hallucinations as follows:

Ask the subconscious to use the Structure Procedure to treat any parts or memory structures causing the hallucinations. Then, treat all memories, beliefs, and experiences that were caused by the parts that were just treated and do a Massive Change History. When you finish that, look for more parts related to hallucinations. Use a different procedure such as treating the emotion collages that motivate the hallucinations and follow associations back to memory structures. If the hallucinations continue, ask the subconscious if there are other structures causing the hallucinations or if hallucinations are still being easily created. Check Ego States and Tandem Memories for structures, Predispositions, parts, and Layered Memories. Check for System Fragments or an Independent Behavior System.

4. Intrusive thoughts and images

Whenever an intrusive event is mentioned, I assume that some aspect, perhaps an amnesic part, is responsible for the intrusive thought, sound, image, feeling, emotion, or muscle jerk. These intrusive responses are usually motivated by negative emotions. Keep in mind that all parts are healthy; namely, they learned their problem behavior in a sick, traumatic environment. So the goal is to get rid of these intrusions by treating the negative emotions. Assuming the subconscious has the treatment process, you work to set up rapport with the part that's giving the intrusion and obtain agreement to accept treatment. Start by asking, "Can I talk to that part that is (describe the intrusion)?" Sometimes you have to coax communication with the incentive of "more satisfaction and less pain." After you get communication, you simply educate and troubleshoot until you reach the goal—namely, to treat and integrate the intrusive parts. Intrusive responses are not usually challenging.

Intrusive thoughts and images can be triggered by a Predisposition associated *with* or *to* another memory structure in the Main Personality, the Tandem Memories, or Ego States. There may be trauma in the Basic Neurostructure or Memory I or II, or there may be Behavior System Fragments or a field causing the intrusion. You may have to get creative and extend the theory to solve the problem.

5. Thought injection and thought broadcasting

I was working with a young woman who experienced thought intrusions and thought broadcasting. She experienced the intrusions accompanied by a feeling of energy moving in or out of her body. I worked with her for several weeks when, for some reason, it occurred to me there might be some kinesthetic response that created the experience. I tested this hypothesis by having her create energy moving in and out of her knee. I found she could voluntarily create and stop the experience of energy entering and leaving her knee. I resolved this problem in the following way.

T: **Subconscious, is there a part in the Kinesthetic System that causes this energy feeling that associates with intrusive parts to give an energy sensation?**

S: **Yes.**

T: **Are there more than one of these parts?**

S: **Yes.**

T: **Can you treat these parts one after the other?**

S: **Yes.**

T: [Done] **Have you finished treating the parts in the Kinesthetic System?**

S: **Yes.**

T: **Is there anything else to do?**

S: **Yes.**

T: **Do you have to do the Massive Change History and everything?**

S: **Yes.**

T: **Please do it.**

The kinesthetic intrusions stopped. However, I had to return to the Kinesthetic System in one or two later sessions to completely stop the intrusive energy feelings again. After several sessions, the experience of thought intrusions and thought broadcasting were reduced to occasional events. It took several sessions to treat the parts providing the thoughts in thought insertion and broadcasting. The subconscious tagged the intrusions in between sessions.

10-9 Treating war trauma

With this patient, I first treated current bothersome intrusions and behaviors, such as hypersensitivity and intense emotions that were interfering with work and family. We also dealt with failures in many past jobs and relationships before we treated the war trauma. The army tour was treated in the following way:

1. We broke his tour of duty into defined segments. Then we asked the subconscious to treat each segment slowly and carefully to avoid any undue flood of emotions. The patient reviewed the memories for each segment of his experience and asked the subconscious to tag the emotional spots and treat them in the correct order. This reviewing was repeated until there were no more problematic emotional spots. These are the segments treated:

    a. Basic training

    b. Arrival in Vietnam and first several months

    c. Saigon for three months

    d. Other assignments, one at a time

    e. Duty in the United States and discrimination by the public

2. The patient was asked to scan through each segment again in fine grain, and to open his eyes when an emotion arose (Shapiro, 1985). The subconscious was asked to treat the issue and other tagged emotional memories. This process was repeated until the entire segment was neutral.

3. Look for atrocities. I try to "normalize" any war atrocities within the context of war by reframing war as a crazy-making environment. War puts soldiers into survival mode, and the intensity of war unleashes behaviors that we would not otherwise do, and so

forth. The subconscious is asked to treat and strengthen the re-frame. Treat guilt and shame.

4. We treated the issues associated with killing by breaking down the experience and treating it in parts such as just before the kill, thoughts, eye contact, thoughts, body and gore, grief and guilt.

5. Later, I had the patient tell me about his experience in the army from induction to discharge. I asked the subconscious to tag and treat any emotional experiences that arose during our conversation.

6. Occasionally, when treating war-induced trauma, I find obsessions with death or dying. In these cases I look for experiences or parts that trigger this obsession and I ask the subconscious to treat them. Use the Sentence Procedure for this issue.

7. We asked the subconscious to strengthen the beliefs and memories that could make the Vietnam memories as comfortable as possible.

8. Finally, positive beliefs were strengthened, such as "I can feel comfortable with my past and I do not have to have any painful memories."

10-10 Treating barriers to peak performance

Process Healing can be used to treat any barrier that gets in the way of a person's peak performance. Some barriers are caused by the lack of skills to reach their goal. Patients often need to be guided to a resource to get the necessary skills. The patient may need to role-play difficult or novel situations to become comfortable behaving in those situations. When role-playing, have the subconscious tag any negative emotions for treatment and continue the role-playing until the imagined behavior seems natural.

It is more common to have emotions get in the way of peak performance. Examples of this are anxiety in the golf game or stepping into the batter's box, or when speaking to relatives or strangers, taking a test, applying for a job, or when learning to use a computer. Have the person slowly go through the activity in which he or she wants to excel and treat any emotion that arises.

Have the patient write down all the issues, beliefs, or behaviors that get in the way of peak performance. For each barrier, write down the desired belief or behavior to replace the treated barrier. Set a score for each barrier to assess your treatments. Ask the subconscious to treat each barrier, one after the other and strengthen the desired belief or behavior to replace the treated barrier. Return to this list in following sessions to assess the effectiveness of your interventions.

Sometimes motivation for preparing or practicing can be a problem. Weaken the motivation collages in the emotions system for the incompatible and unwanted behavior, and follow the associations back to memory structures and treat them. Strengthen the collages of emotion for the desire to achieve the goal. Strengthen any related memory structures. If that does not work, try to clear any other barriers in the Main Personality, Ego States, and Tandem Memories that may be getting in the way of practicing to achieve the goal.

Look for self-limiting beliefs about the patient's potential for success or about his or her talents, and so forth. Parents, relatives, peers, teachers, or others could have taught the patient these self-limiting beliefs. Treat the unwanted beliefs, remove any barriers blocking the wanted, positive belief, and then strengthen the positive belief until it feels 100 percent true.

Before you see results, you may have to carry out most of the interventions required to achieve peak performance. It is also possible that other aspects or parts of the personality have some interest in blocking success. If you find a barrier like this, use the techniques described in this book to problem-solve the barrier. Use the Futurepace Intervention to transfer the changes in the office to the patient's performance in other settings.

Use this approach to treat procrastination, disorganization, failure to set priorities, and so forth. Some of these issues can be extremely complex, depending on the patient's trauma history and, I must say, generational history. Continued problem-solving and treatment may have to be undertaken. With one patient, I worked more than 95 sessions treating the presenting issue, "When I advance, I self-sabotage." This was one of my most difficult patients, but the one who taught me the most about this issue.

Physical Issues

10-11 Treating physical issues

When treating physical issues, know that only memory-related physical problems can be treated. On the other hand, all body, organ or brain functions are run by memories and, in theory, can be treated. Of course, if the physical or other issues are caused by physiological problems, then the interventions may not work. Always be sure the patient is under a doctor's care or has consulted with a doctor about the issue you want to treat.

There is no risk in using Process Healing as an adjunctive treatment while standard medical approaches treat physiological or medical issues. There may be no limit to what can be achieved, and the results can be surprising for many symptomatic problems. Having a clear medical understanding of the problem is vital for constructing interventions for physical issues. It is best to use anatomical descriptions as close as possible to the cause of the physical issue. Memories run the anatomical structures. Give the subconscious interventions in well-formed statements specifying exactly what has to be changed. This will facilitate a positive outcome. Work with the subconscious to get an acceptable, well-formed statement for the intervention. As long as you take the usual precautions and check with the subconscious to see if your suggested intervention is safe, you can try treating any physical or medical issue.

Joaquin Andrade, M.D., has been experimenting with healing-resistant physical symptoms. His unpublished results (personal communication, March 26, 2004) are encouraging. His tactic is simply to diagnose and then ask, "May I ask the part that's maintaining the symptom . . .?" and then to problem-solve and treat the involved parts and memory structures. Treating physical symptoms may take many sessions. I am encouraged by the results reported by others and in my own patients who are using the Process Healing Method to address physical issues.

Examples:

1. Muscle tension

Muscle tension is often easy to treat. Look for parts giving the muscle tension, or do the Sentence Procedure on the muscle tension. If you fail to get positive results, then ask the subconscious if the muscle memories themselves were in chronic tension. With a "Yes," treat the muscle memories causing the chronic tension. Active parts can also give muscle tension as symptoms when they are active. Remember to look for parts or other memory structures from trauma. Other complicated causes for muscle tension can be discovered through problem-solving and treatment.

2. Asthma

Asthma attacks are triggered by some environmental stimulus. An asthma attack is a physical response where the muscles that wrap around the airways in the lungs swell and constrict the airways. When this happens, the person experiences wheezing, shortness of breath and often chest tightness. Asthma attacks are triggered by allergies, cold air, or exercise. Have the patient list all the triggers that cause asthma attacks. The order of the following interventions can be changed. I treat the physiology last.

    a. Identify and treat any traumas related to the asthma.

    b. Treat from conception forward all beliefs, memories, and experiences related to asthma.

    c. Do the Sentence Procedure with "I no longer have asthma."

    d. Treat the parts that have asthma.

    e. Strengthen the motivation for not having asthma by strengthening the belief "I no longer want to have asthma."

    f. Treat memories of situations where asthma attacks have occurred. Talk about all the places where they are likely to occur, and have the subconscious tag and treat memory structures.

    g. Treat the structure of triggers that cause asthma attacks.

    h. Treat all the stress situations that trigger asthma. Use the Futurepace Intervention with all stress situations.

    i. Treat the memories and neurostructures involved with the lungs to normalize control.

    j. Treat the trauma of the memories causing the muscles to swell around the airways.

    k. Treat field phenomena that contribute to asthma.

3. Irritable bowel syndrome

This is how I treated a patient who had Irritable Bowel Syndrome. The patient had a pain in her stomach. I asked the subconscious if there were parts that caused the tension. With a "yes," I asked the subconscious to treat all the parts that wanted treatment, and then asked the subconscious if there were parts that did not want treatment. I resolved their issues and treated those parts, too. I then asked the subconscious to do the Sentence Procedure on "I have treated my IBS." This was a check for other memory structures that might be contributing to the issue. When the subconscious was done, I asked for a Massive Change History and everything. The patient said the pain in her stomach was gone. I asked the subconscious to tag any parts or memories related to IBS that emerged in the next week.

Results during the session looked promising, but I did not follow up.

4. Temporomandibular joint disorder (TMJ)

Here is the strategy I use to treat TMJ:

T: **Subconscious, is it OK to treat the TMJ now?**

S: **Yes.**

T: **Subconscious, can you treat the muscle memories that cause TMJ and any other muscles that have become affected?**
S: **Yes.**
T: **[Done] Please do a Massive Change History and everything.**
S: **Yes.**
T: **Are there any dreams that contribute to TMJ?**
S: **Yes.**
T: **Please treat any dreams that contribute to TMJ and in the future tag and treat any other dreams that become active.**

I treat the dreams as described in Chapter 9-7. Just to make sure there are no other contributions to TMJ, I ask the following:

T: **Subconscious, would it be good to do a Sentence Procedure to further treat the TMJ?**
S: **Yes.**
T: **Please do the Sentence Procedure with "I will never clench my teeth again in my sleep."**
S: **Yes.**
T: **Subconscious, are there parts and beliefs that cause the TMJ?**
S: **Yes.**
T: **Please treat the parts and beliefs in the correct order and compose and strengthen self-empowering beliefs to take the place of the treated beliefs.**
S: **Yes.**

If parts were involved, TMJ may reappear later and could require more problem-solving. It is worth inquiring about sources of stress that might be contributing to TMJ.

5. Chronic illness and pain

There is always the possibility that a chronic illness or pain is caused by medical problems rather than remembered pain. If there is organic or physical damage that causes the chronic symptoms, then it is unlikely the subconscious can treat it. Because of this, it is advisable that the person sees a doctor about the illness or pain before using Process Healing to control or remove that pain. Non-memory-related physiological damage needs medical attention first. In these cases, use Process Healing as a therapeutic adjunct to proper treatment.

Only the remembered pain and emotions connected to the illness or physical trauma can be treated by the subconscious. Remembered pain and emotions can add to the pain caused by organic or physical damage.

It does not hurt to try to treat any of the symptoms connected to chronic illness or pain. If it works, the patient will feel better.

Examples:
a. Treating belief barriers
Beliefs can get in the way of reducing intensity or eliminating symptoms. Ask the subconscious to tag all beliefs and memories that come into the Active Experience when you say, "I want to treat all the symptoms of my illness or source of pain." Then ask the subconscious to treat all those tagged memories and parts in the correct order. When the subconscious is done, ask if the Sentence Procedure should be done again. Repeat the statement until you get a "No." Try different statements like, "I want to be over this . . ." or "I want to get rid of this . . ." Different statements can elicit different memories, beliefs, or parts that can get in the way of treating the learned pain.

b. Treating symptoms
Write down all the symptoms the patient reveals. Make the list as complete as possible. Then ask the subconscious to treat each symptom, one at a time, or in any order or combination that will result in the emotions or pain being reduced as much as possible. If remembered pain is treated, then legitimate pain for the issue will remain but the total pain for the issue will be reduced.

Sometimes, the overall pain decreases, but after some period of time it returns. When this happens, you simply ask the subconscious again to treat the remembered pain. Experiment with treating at fixed intervals—for example, treating the pain every two hours. See if a routine can be developed to keep the pain at a comfortable level.

6. Chronic liver disorder
The patient weighed about 104 pounds because she had a chronic liver disorder. She said that her digestive enzymes flooded in "on her own" and that she had severe stomachaches. She had a difficult time eating because of this condition. She ate every three or four days. I tried to treat the digestive disorder in the following way.

T: **Subconscious, can you treat the memory that runs the liver?**
S: **Yes.**

T: **Can you do a Massive Change History and everything including the memory that runs the liver, and treat whatever needs to be treated to get it to work properly?**
S: **Yes.**

T: **Subconscious, can you do a Massive Change History and everything?**

S: **Yes.**

In the next session, she said she started eating two to three meals each day and was having fewer stomachaches. I asked the subconscious to repeat interventions used in the previous session. In retrospect, I could have started with a Sentence Procedure: "I don't have a digestive tract disorder," and then worked specifically with the memory running the liver.

Summary

Tactics for treating complex issues briefly summarized:

Always rule out medical causes for any issue with which you are working.

Do a careful examination of the details of history and experience of the complex issue. This often gives some clues to a direction to problem-solve and treat the issue.

Treat any related memory structures and system structures.

When you have a barrier or difficulty discovering how to treat the issue, be creative. Assemble and test a new, unique structure until the structure is accepted by the subconscious as the one contributing to or causing the issue.

A final word

The Process Healing Method offers a new way to think about memories and about how our memories relate to every aspect of our mental and physical well-being. Though the basic theory is relatively simple and easy to grasp, the implications are enormous. The theory offers hope for many who now struggle with the damage that trauma, great or small, brings to a person's life.

Appendices

Appendix I

Patient and Therapist Treatment Aids

How your personality works

This description of how your personality works is based on the theory of Process Healing. This theory is, and has been, under development for more than 13 years. It is not "truth," but a model with metaphors that will help you to work with your personality, brain, and body to improve your experience of life.

The subconscious starts forming shortly after conception because verbal stimulation transmitted through the mother's abdominal wall is learned. These memories eventually become a language with which we can communicate. Although the subconscious experiences sensory stimulation, it does not experience sensations and therefore cannot be damaged by pain. We all have a subconscious who can learn several ways to treat painful or bothersome issues.

As your personality develops, all behaviors are memories that amass in Memory III. Memory III is the primary memory of the personality and all behavior is mainly created from behaviors already learned. Memory III is the storage area for all memories related to our five senses, nurturance, air, food, water, pleasure, and pain. Memories are either dormant or active. When memories are active, they are in what is called the Active Experience and some of those active memories are selected to create our behavior. As our thoughts and situations change, active memories go dormant and dormant memories become active.

The Basic Neurostructure operates on the memory activity in the Active Experience to create the next most worthwhile memory and response—namely, to get more satisfaction or happiness and to have less pain. Emotion Memories are in a different memory system and associate with the memories causing our behavior to motivate them.

Our conscious and unconscious thoughts, behavior, and other processes are created from active Content and Emotion Memories in the Active Experience. A memory is a collage assembled by the Basic Neurostructure from the last response created and some of the active Emotion and Content Memories. When the memory is completed, the response occurs.

The dissociation and association processes are normally formed early in life to help with focusing attention and controlling intrusions. These can be used voluntarily to cause repression and involuntarily to hide painful experiences. A primary function of the dissociation process is that it creates the conscious and unconscious Active Experience. The dissociation process effectively removes unuseful activity in our conscious experience, as well as memories that have become useful skills that would be too cumbersome to have in our conscious experience.

With intense emotions and no previous experience to manage the traumatic situation, the rush of triggered memories pushes the Main Personality into dormancy. A new personality part is created during the trauma. These trauma parts are more or less amnesic from the Main Personality and can cause intrusions or run the body.

Activity in the Active Experience can elicit Predispositions from another memory. The Predispositions are like habits that can routinely distort the behavior created from the Active Experience. Predispositions can be treated.

The subconscious can treat all mental health issues painlessly and with little chance of emotional flooding. He or she can slowly and safely treat amnesic parts with enormous pain. You can use the subconscious to problem-solve complex issues and barriers to treatment.

A Flow Diagram of Process Healing

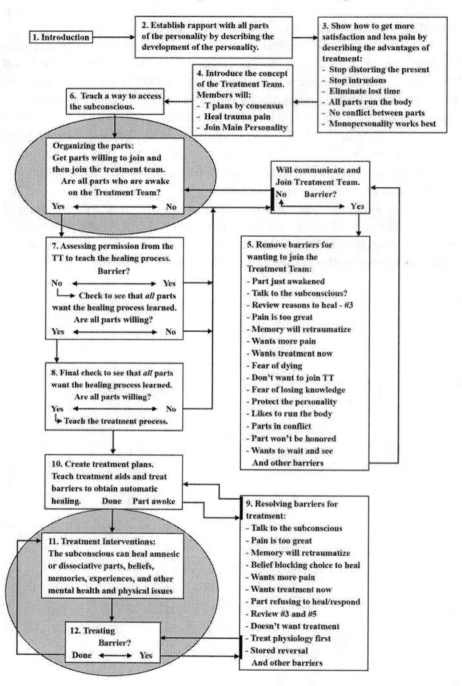

1. Introduction

2. Establish rapport with all parts of the personality by describing the development of the personality.

3. Show how to get more satisfaction and less pain by describing the advantages of treatment:
- Stop distorting the present
- Stop intrusions
- Eliminate lost time
- All parts run the body
- No conflict between parts
- Monopersonality works best

4. Introduce the concept of the Treatment Team. Members will:
- T plans by consensus
- Heal trauma pain
- Join Main Personality

6. Teach a way to access the subconscious.

Organizing the parts:
Get parts willing to join and then join the treatment team.
Are all parts who are awake on the Treatment Team?
Yes ◄─────► No

Will communicate and Join Treatment Team.
No   Barrier?
Yes

7. Assessing permission from the TT to teach the healing process.
Barrier?
No ◄─────► Yes
└─► Check to see that *all* parts want the healing process learned.
Are all parts willing?
Yes ◄─────► No

5. Remove barriers for wanting to join the Treatment Team:
- Part just awakened
- Talk to the subconscious?
- Review reasons to heal - #3
- Pain is too great
- Memory will retraumatize
- Wants more pain
- Wants treatment now
- Fear of dying
- Don't want to join TT
- Fear of losing knowledge
- Protect the personality
- Likes to run the body
- Parts in conflict
- Part won't be honored
- Wants to wait and see
  And other barriers

8. Final check to see that *all* parts want the healing process learned.
Are all parts willing?
Yes ◄─────► No
↳ Teach the treatment process.

10. Create treatment plans. Teach treatment aids and treat barriers to obtain automatic healing.   Done   Part awoke

9. Resolving barriers for treatment:
- Talk to the subconscious
- Pain is too great
- Memory will retraumatize
- Belief blocking choice to heal
- Wants more pain
- Wants treatment now
- Part refusing to heal/respond
- Review #3 and #5
- Doesn't want treatment
- Treat physiology first
- Stored reversal
  And other barriers

11. Treatment Interventions:
The subconscious can heal amnesic or dissociative parts, beliefs, memories, experiences, and other mental health and physical issues

12. Treating
Barrier?
Done ◄─────► Yes

Figure I-1 The Flow Diagram

An outline of the Process Healing Method

The Process Healing approach uses metaphors to describe the development of the personality, the subconscious, amnesic parts, dissociative parts, brain functions, and other constructs, all of which can be used to treat trauma-based issues. This treatment process has been used for 13 years and it works, because it appears to model the experience of the parts and the subconscious. It is also assumed that all brain functions and body activities are the effects of memory activity. All memories can be treated. The leverage for most treatment is that all parts want more satisfaction or happiness and less pain. If parts want less satisfaction and more pain, they can be changed easily.

The flow diagram of Process Healing (see Figure I-1) describes the steps for organizing the personality and engaging in the treatment process. Let me walk you through the flow by also referring to the more visual diagram of the treatment process, the one I draw while I am teaching patients the concepts (see Figure I-2). After the introduction (Figure I-1, box-1) rapport can be rapidly achieved by talking through the Main Personality (MP) to all parts or aspects that are active (I-1, box-2). As he or she talks, the therapist draws each of the figures to the left in Figure I-2, a to j, one at time. Each figure shows a different construct, including: the timeline of development of the Main Personality (Figure I-2, a), the formation of the subconscious (I-2, b), the Active Experience (AE) (I-2, c), the dissociative process (I-2, d), which causes the conscious and unconscious experience, and the association process (I-2, e). The time course of trauma is shown (I-2, f), resulting in the formation of an amnesic or trauma part

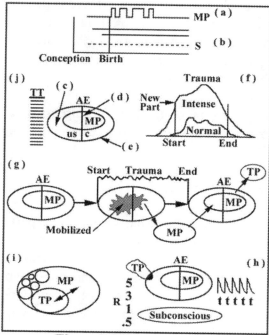

Figure I-2 Treatment Note

(I-2, g), the treatment of intense pain without abreaction (I-2, h), and the integration of parts (I-2, i). Embedded in this educational discussion are the reasons for healing (I-1, box-3) and the concept of forming a Treatment Team (I-2, j) (I-1, box-4). Then Communication is established with the subconscious (I-1, box-6). In the Education Process the therapist convinces parts to join the Treatment Team (I-2, j) by stressing the reasons for healing (I-1, box-3) and also by explaining away possible reasons for not receiving treatment or joining the Treatment Team (I-1, box-5).

Several checks are made to be sure that all the parts are on the Treatment Team and that they all want the therapist to teach the treatment process to the subconscious (I-1, box-7). When no part objects, the treatment process is taught by means of a simple metaphor that I have used with patients age 7 to 85 (I-1, box-8). This method of treatment is very respectful. Treatment plans are created for all members of the Treatment Team and barriers are removed to enable automatic and independent treatment by the subconscious. (I-1, box-10).

The treatment process (I-1, box-11) involves treating parts, painful memories, self-limiting beliefs, personality traits, and the cause of addictions. Although problem-solving is frequently needed to work with parts that awaken and don't know what is happening (I-1, box-9), nevertheless—if most of the parts are already on the Treatment Team—there is usually much less difficulty than is often encountered when treating dissociative or dissociative identity disordered patients. Usually within 90 minutes, a therapist can get the treatment process taught and demonstrated by treating, for example, one simple phobia (I-1, box-12). Treating amnesic parts can also be systematic and routine.

This is a very good method for treating difficult patients of all kinds. By using the subconscious and leading questions, barriers can be easily identified and treated. The model borrows concepts from learning and chaos theory, which provide a rich basis for Problem-solving—or even for creating new memory constructs that lead to successful treatment of problematic behavior or memory.

Parts, as used in this model, refer to amnesic parts, dissociative parts, active memories, or any aspect that has pain and needs to be treated. With all patients, there are usually some amnesic parts—formed *in utero*, at birth, in an accident, in a near-death experience, or during some other physical or sexual trauma. Some patients are extremely complex and others straightforward and routine. Either way, the methods of Process Healing work very well.

How to use Process Healing at home

The hardest part of treating yourself at home is remembering to do it. Find some way to remind yourself that your subconscious can treat most issues that arise during the day. In general, here is the way to treat parts and issues that you notice.

1. Identify the issue or emotion, then ask the subconscious: "Is it appropriate and safe to treat this issue now?"
2. If "Yes," then ask, "Are there any parts that have to be treated associated with this issue?"
3. If "Yes," ask, "Should these parts be treated first?" If "No," go to line 7, otherwise proceed to line 4.
4. If "Yes," ask, "Is it safe to treat the parts now, one after the other?"
5. With a "Yes," say, "Please treat these parts one after the other in the best order and treat the effects of each part from the time of its trauma to now."
6. After the parts are treated, skip to line 7 to treat the memory structures, otherwise go to line 8.
7. Please treat the memory structures associated with this issue one after the other in the best order. After the memory structure is treated, go to line 8.
8. Now treat the Main Personality. "Please do a Massive Change History and everything on the Main Personality and other memories that were influenced by the issue." If parts have not been treated, go to line 4.
9. Ask the subconscious if you have finished treating this issue. If "Yes," go on to the next issue. If "No," ask questions to problem-solve.

Problem-solving barriers to treating parts

- A part won't talk (no finger response): Ask if the part wants more satisfaction and less pain. If "Yes," ask if it wants to join the Treatment Team or receive treatment now.
- A part wants treatment now: Ask the subconscious if it is politically OK and safe to treat this part now.
- There is a conflict between parts: Ask the parts to resolve the conflict. Negotiate.
- A part awakened: Ask if he or she wants to join the Treatment Team (or be treated). If the part doesn't want to, ask if he or she is willing to get all the information from the subcon-

scious, so he or she has the information to make an informed decision. Follow up.

- Simply asking your subconscious to treat the issue can eliminate this nine-step treatment of an issue. While thinking about the issue, just say "Treat it," or "Fix it." Usually, this results in the treatment of the issue.

What to expect after a Process Healing session

This treatment process is usually safe, but there can be periods of discomfort caused by trauma symptoms or fleeting memories. During the treatment process, you may have memories or images pass through your conscious experience. Just let them come and go. If an image is scary, ask your subconscious if this is a memory that is being treated. If it isn't, ask your subconscious to treat it.

The treatment process can continue for hours or days. Since the subconscious is taught to treat negative emotions and is free to treat independently, you may feel the treatment process start any time of day or night. If you are not sure why you have that feeling or headache, ask the subconscious if the feeling is an active treatment process.

During the treatment, you may experience headaches or different brain sensations like numbness, flashes of pain, tingling feelings, lightness in your head, and so forth. You may even experience flu-like symptoms. If the processing gets too intense with a headache or extreme fatigue, ask your subconscious to treat more slowly.

While active processing is occurring, there is no danger in driving or operating equipment, but to be on the safe side, ask your subconscious to ensure your safety by not treating while you are cooking, operating equipment, or driving.

Summary of the Process Healing protocol

Reasons for treating parts:
- Get more satisfaction and less pain
- Stop intrusions
- Prevent the Main Personality from dissociating important information
- Allow all parts to run the body all of the time without conflict
- Monopersonality works best

Barriers to wanting treatment:
- The pain is too great to be treated
- The treated and integrated memory will retraumatize the personality
- Fear of dying
- Fear of losing knowledge, wisdom, and understanding
- Part will no longer be able to protect the personality
- Part likes to run the body
- Doesn't want to join the Treatment Team
- There will be more inner conflicts
- Weak little parts fear not being honored by big parts
- Part wants to wait and see
- Part wants treatment now
- Part wants more pain and less satisfaction
- Part just awakened.

Resolving barriers for treatment:
- Pain is too great
- The memory will retraumatize the Main Personality
- Parts are active
- Part doesn't want treatment
- Part wants more pain and less satisfaction
- Part demands to be treated now
- Part is talking for the subconscious
- A belief is blocking the choice for treatment
- Treat the physiology first
- Stored reversal
- A part is without eyes and ears
- A part's emotions are active but the other senses are dormant

Resolving barriers for treatment (cont.)

- Toxic substances are disorganizing the brain
- Drug trauma is blocking the treatment process
- A part refuses to be treated or to respond.
- A field is getting in the way
- Test to see if the subconscious can treat a phobia or negative belief
- Organize the Treatment Team — subconscious creates treatment plans
- Treat barriers to allow the subconscious to treat automatically
- Massive Change History to stop intrusions from Memory III
- Treat Predisposition barriers in Memory II

A list of basic interventions

These are reminders for the basic interventions. When a barrier persists after using these strategies, scan the chapter contents or index for other possible solutions.

Routine interventions:

- Check for independent and automatic treatment by the subconscious
- Strengthen positive coping skills with positive emotions before integrating
- Tag memory elements and treat between sessions
- Massive Change History and everything after every intervention
- Sentence Procedure
- Treat structures related to an issue
- Treat massive beliefs
- Treat fragile parts
- Treat issues or barriers caused by Predispositions
- Collages of negative emotions in Emotions System
- Ego States and Tandem Memories
- Treat and integrate the dissociative and associative parts
- Systems—Behavior System, Emotion System, Heart System
- The Basic Neurostructure
- Easily created structures
- Treat the easy creation of parts and other structures
- Treat and integrate subconscious fragments
- Treat constellations of System Fragments
- Treated System Fragments that fail to integrate
- Independent Behavior Systems

When everything fails:

- Treat parts without asking permission
- Ask for cues for the solution
- Use the non-question
- Establish a private line
- Move memory for problem-solving
- Ask if there is a field barrier

Barriers for automatic and independent treatment:

- Treat memories related to treatment
- Predispositions in Memory II triggered by negative emotions
- A massive belief barrier blocking treatment
- An active part blocking treatment
- A subconscious fragment
- Memory I structures floating in the Active Experience
- A subconscious surrogate

A protocol for treating addictions

This intervention assumes that the treatment process has been installed, that you have easy contact with the subconscious, and that the barriers for automatic treatment have been treated. If there are withdrawal symptoms, list all the symptoms and ask the subconscious for the order of treatment, and then treat the symptoms one after the other. If there are barriers, problem-solve and resolve the barriers.

Steps to treating addiction include:
1. As you talk to the patient, list the addictions and order them, from the first one to treat to the last one: for example, drugs, marijuana, drinking, smoking, food, sex, and so forth.
2. Start with the first addiction that the subconscious indicates.

T: **Subconscious, which addiction should I treat first?** [Offer to list them one by one and look for a "Yes" response.]

3. Treating parts.

T: **Subconscious, are there parts contributing to the addiction? Treat parts that want treatment.**

T: **Subconscious, are there any parts that don't want treatment?** [Reframe as needed and treat the parts.]

4. Do the Sentence Procedure.

T: **Subconscious, please do the Sentence Procedure starting with "I want to quit drinking." Please tag all beliefs, memories, experiences, and parts that are triggered. Please treat the tagged aspects in the correct order. Please repeat the process until you are done.**

5. Deal with motivation or lack of it.

T: **Subconscious, please do the Sentence Procedure and strengthen the belief "I want to quit drinking," or "I don't want to smoke."**

6. Talk with the patient about all the places where drinking is highly likely and enjoyed or not enjoyed.

T: [Give this instruction before talking.] **Subconscious, please tag and treat all of the positive and negative memories generated as we converse about the addiction. Treat the positive memories first and then treat the negative memories.**

T: [When done] **Subconscious, please repeat this intervention by generating statements to trigger into activity as many positive and negative beliefs, memories, and behaviors associated with this addiction.**

7. Do a Massive Change History.

T: **Subconscious, please do a Massive Change History and everything.**

8. Clear any barriers to being able to freely refuse the addictive substance.

T: **Subconscious, please do a Sentence Procedure starting with the statement, "No, thank you, I don't drink," and repeat it until you are done.**

9. Strengthen the protective assertive response.

T: [When done] **Subconscious, please strengthen the response, "No, thank you, I don't drink" until it is completely true.**

10. Then have the patient visualize several situations where the response, "No, thank you, I don't drink," is appropriate and imagine politely turning down the addictive substance.

T: **Subconscious, please treat all barriers and strengthen the response until it feels completely natural to say.**

11. Ask the patient to imagine holding a drink. What do you feel? Is there is a feeling that you want or need to take a drink? Use props to stimulate addictive urges.

T: **Subconscious, are there any parts, memory structures, or emotions that should be treated?** [Isolate and treat appropriately.]

12. Have the patient imagine that he or she is in a situation from the past where he or she has taken up the addiction again.

T: **Subconscious, please tag any belief, memory or part and treat it appropriately.**

13. Now treat the self-defeating beliefs that occur after breaking abstinence. You have held the belief "I don't drink at celebrations" and for some reason had a drink. Imagine you are at a party and you have a drink.

T: **Subconscious, please tag and treat any belief or memory that supports continued drinking, such as "I am addicted" or "I am a failure." Compose a positive self-empowering belief to take its place.**

14. Identify and treat the reasons for having the addiction.

Examples:

a. "I can't feel high energy unless I drink."

T: **Subconscious, please do a Sentence Procedure with "I can feel high energy without drinking," and strengthen, "If I eat and sleep well, I will have high energy." Also treat any sadness or feelings of loss.** [Grieving an addiction is normal.]

b. "I have to drink to have fun."

T: **Subconscious, do a Sentence Procedure with "I can have fun without drinking alcoholic beverages."**

15. Repeat the entire addiction procedure.

T: **Subconscious, please treat all the interconnections of the treatments done.**

16. Treat the other addictions and problem-solve as necessary.

T: **Subconscious, please repeat the above protocol to treat the next addiction on the list.**

Note: I often find field barriers associated with an addiction. Without removing the fields, addictions may be difficult or impossible to treat completely.

Appendix II

The Personality and Parts Phenomena

This appendix will clearly describe the development of the Behavior System in the emerging brain and body of the fetus. It will also describe constructs that I created to describe the Behavior System. Some descriptions of parts activity are given to help you in working with the personality and to aid in visualizing the parts activity with these constructs. These constructs are all clinically based and routinely used when problem-solving issues or barriers to treatment.

Shortly after conception, neural development occurs, leading to spontaneous neural activity in the brain and body. Figure II-1 illustrates

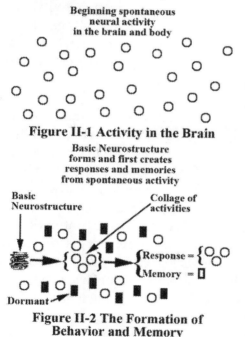

Figure II-1 Activity in the Brain

Figure II-2 The Formation of Behavior and Memory

this activity. This spontaneous neural activity (the little circles) is not organized — it is truly spontaneous. In a short time, when the neural activity becomes repetitive, a group of nerve cells associate and start working together to create memories and responses. I call this group of cells working together the *Basic Neurostructure* (see Figure II-2). The Basic Neurostructure selects activities from the spontaneous neural activity to create a collage of neural activities (in brackets)— a memory, which at the same time causes physiological activity called a response. The response occurs when the collage of the memory is created. Initially, the memories created become dormant after making a response (dark boxes). A response is a newly created memory. Thus it begins: collage, memory, and responses leading to more collages, memories, and responses.

Any brain activity triggers the Basic Neurostructure to create memories and responses. Each memory has a unique memory structure.

The common quality of the initial unique memory structures is simply neural activity. These memories accumulate between conception and birth to form Memory I. Memory I is a mass of memories that are only related to simple neural activity.

Later, when the dormant memories and spontaneous activity have content in common, the dormant memories are triggered into activity (see open boxes in Figure II-3) instead of the spontaneous repetitive neural activity. The

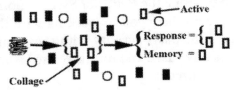

The Basic Neurostructure later creates a collage from active memories to form a memory and response

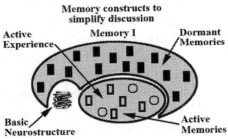

Figure II-3 The Creation of Behavior from Active Memories

Basic Neurostructure starts selecting both active memories and spontaneous activity to create memories and responses. This continues until the active memories triggered outnumber the spontaneous activity. From then on, the collages for responses (in brackets, left, Figure II-3) are primarily created from active memories.

Memory I and the *Active Experience* (shown as shaded enclosures in Figure II-4) are constructs to make it easier to talk about dormant and active

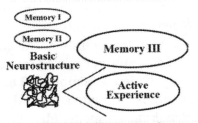

Figure II-4 The Constructs of the Active Experience

memories and the Active Experience. The Behavior System also includes constructs that I call Memory II and Memory III (see Figure II-5).

After Memory I is created, the Behavior System continues to develop. When sensory neural activity begins, a new memory is formed that is called *Memory II*. The memories in Memory II all have activity and primitive neural activity related to sensory experience as common properties. This memory starts amassing memories from before birth through about age four. This memory has the Protector-Con-

Figure II-5 The Behavior System

troller and Predispositions, which are habit-like responses that aid or distort our behavior. As memories are further amassed, responses are increasingly composed of memories from Memory II.

At some point before birth, sensory experience, basic needs, and reinforcement (reward or punishment) become significant factors in our behavior and are the common qualities that define the memories in *Memory III*. This memory amasses memories throughout our life. These memories in Memories I, II, and II are all dormant. The Basic Neurostructure, Memories I, II, and III, and the Active Experience are the primary constructs of the Behavior System (see Figure II-5, previous page).

To obtain the most fitting memories in the Active Experience, an *association process* is gradually learned (see Figure II-6). The asso-

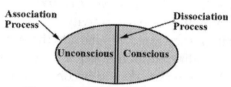

Figure II-6 Processes Managing the Active Experience

ciation process protects the Active Experience from triggering memories that are only slightly related to the triggers. As volitional behavior develops, the *dissociation process* develops to create a less complex con-

scious experience by causing irrelevant memories to be active in the unconscious (see Figure II-6). This simplifies the processing of information in the conscious experience. Our Active Experience includes both conscious and unconscious experiences.

All memories are associated *with* a Memory Structure. The *Main Personality* has a unique memory structure (see Figure II-7). Most people

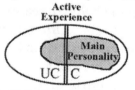

Figure II-7 The Main Personality

can remember back to age three or four. Usually, people who have no memories for periods of their childhood, have parts. These parts are really parts of the whole personality. Parts, as do all memories, have

unique memory structures. I will soon give some examples of parts.

When there are no memories in the Active Experience, the person is either asleep, in a meditative state, or in some state of hypnosis (see Figure II-8). Usually, our Active Experience is never completely

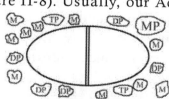

Figure II-8 Dormant Memories or Memories Under Hypnosis

empty because basic brain activity probably triggers memories into the Active Experience. When we dream, we create a meaningful story from intrusive current or past memories triggered into the conscious experience.

In our early years, we learn to compose speech, put in syntax, and edit our speech in our conscious mind to generate speech and thought.

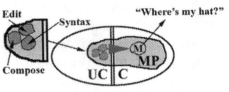

Figure II-9 Creation of
Speech and Thought

Over time, these behaviors are dissociated and become processes operating in the unconscious. Figure II-9 shows these dissociated processes like skills working together in the unconscious to create a response in the conscious experience. These skills are like *dissociative parts* operating in the unconscious. Now we will discuss parts activity.

When some parts are triggered, they rapidly enter into the Active Experience and push the Main Personality out of the Active Experience (see Figure II-10). This causes the Main Personality to become dormant

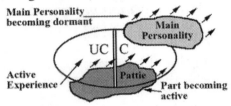

Figure II-10 A Part is Activating

and the intruding part takes over to run the body. A therapist can trigger parts into the Active Experience by simply asking to talk to the part causing some disruptive activity—or by name.

When an active part is running the body, the Main Personality is dormant. Figure II-11 shows a part running the body. In reality, it is not

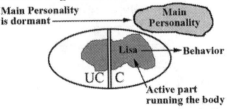

Figure II-11 A Part Running the Body

this simple. Often, many parts are active in the conscious or unconscious along with the Main Personality or any other part running the body. Not all of these parts are disruptive. Some dissociative and amnesic parts

give us adaptive skills that we use without knowing. Dissociative parts are dissociated skills or experiences and *amnesic parts* are created in severe trauma. Amnesic parts have executive function, which makes them similar to the Main Personality, but with less experience. They can run the body when the Main Personality is dormant, which causes blank periods in the Main Personality's experience.

When an amnesic part offers an intrusion to the Main Personality, the intrusion can be in the form of a verbal response (see Figure II-12).

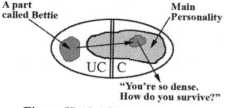

Figure II-12 A Vocal Intrusion

These verbal responses can be supportive of the patient or can provide punishing comments that severely disturb the Main Personality. Many people have annoying verbal intrusions and behavior. It is respectful to assume that the parts and memories are normal and are expressing appropriate behavior that was learned in order to deal with a very unhealthy, nasty situation. These intrusive parts and memories can be treated.

Emotional intrusions are frequently experienced (see Figure II-13). Often, these are not parts but simple memories from some experience,

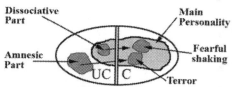

Figure II-13 Emotional Intrusions

which are triggered into the conscious experience. However, it is not unusual to have either dissociative or amnesic parts make emotional intrusions into the conscious experience.

Sometimes there is a community of parts that carry on conversations inside a person's thoughts (see Figure II-14). These parts can have

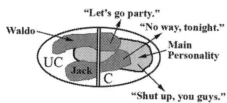

Figure II-14 Coconscious Parts Giving Intruding Comments

names and can be quite distracting when they get in a conflict. People have reported loud arguments that go on and on. By getting all the parts on the Treatment Team in the first session, a lot of time is saved by not having to deal with angry and disruptive parts.

Other unusual parts activity can occur and become quite disruptive to a person's experience. Figure II-15 (next page) shows an amnesic part running the body at the same time that the Main Personality is running the body. For example, such a part could run the mouth and say out-of-context comments, or take over the limbs to make body movements.

These are just a few examples of parts activity to give you an idea of the way they operate in the Active Experience. Other examples are given throughout the book. In most cases, parts are easy to treat and join

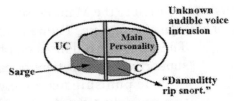

Figure II-15 Amnesic part activity

with the Main Personality. The difficult parts can challenge your problem-solving skills, but nevertheless always give you an opportunity to learn more about how the personality works.

Appendix III

Glossary — Alphabetical

This glossary gives definitions of the terms used in this book, which are either technical in nature or unique to Process Healing (some of the usages are idiosyncratic—Flint language). Words and phrases of this type, which can be problematic because of the specific use (for example, Basic Neurostructure, Active Experience and Main Personality), have been capitalized throughout the book.

Active Experience—a metaphor for the brain activity involved in creating behavior. It contains all active memories and neural activity of the brain and body. The Active Experience construct simplifies the brain activity and helps us talk about dormant, unconscious, and conscious active memories in a meaningful way. The active memories are those triggered from dormancy into the Active Experience. The triggers are active content or emotions in the Active Experience that are present in a dormant memory. Basic Neurostructure works on the Active Experience to create a collage from the Content and Emotion Memories, leading to a response and a memory of the response.

Active memories—memories that are active in the Active Experience. They are either unconscious or conscious active memories. Active memories are the memories that may be included in the creation of a collage of memories to run some brain or body activity

Active personality—a personality part with executive function that is active in the conscious and unconscious Active Experience in the present time. More than one personality part can be active at one time.

Amnesia—lack of awareness between two memories such as a trauma memory and an active personality part. The personality part does not know that the amnesic memory is there. The theory suggests the cause for the amnesia is that few or no neural connections exist between the memories. Some amnesic parts or memories can intrude into the Active Experience by causing some content or emotion in our Active Experience.

Amnesic parts—a personality part of which other personalities are more or less unaware. During severe trauma, for which there is no previous memory to create a response to manage the situation and when there are intense emotions independent of the Main Personality, memories rapidly activate with the intense emotions to handle the crisis. The Main

Personality goes dormant. This creates an amnesic part or memory. Amnesic parts with executive function can self-generate behavior and cause intrusions such as unknown voices, images in a person's thoughts, or unexplained emotion. See Appendix II for a description of parts activity. Amnesia between two parts can hide both parts from each other or operate in one direction only; namely one part knows what the other is doing but the other part is unaware of what the first part is doing.

   Associate *with* vs. *to* — all memories have a unique structure with which other memories associate. The memories associate *with* a structure to form a collage of memories (see Figure III-1). When the structure is active, the collage of memories creates a unique response in our brain or body. Memories associated *with* a structure are easy to change. On the other hand, when a memory associates *to*

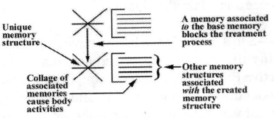

Figure III-1 Associated *with* vs. *to*

a memory structure, it is not possible to change the memories associated *with* the structure. The memory associated *to* the memory structure changes the neural plasticity. Until the memory associated *to* the structure is treated, the collage of memories associated *with* the structure cannot be treated. A memory associated *to* a structure is a barrier to treating memories causing unwanted behavior.

   Barrier — an active memory in the Active Experience that stops communication with the subconscious or parts, or stops treatment. A part, a belief, a memory structure problem, or a field, can cause a barrier in the Active Experience.

   Basic Neurostructure — a neurostructure that serves a specific function in our brain by creating collages causing activity and memory for the function or activity of systems, organs, brain functions, and so forth.

   Behavior System — consists of Basic Neurostructure, Memory I, Memory II, Memory III, the Active Experience, and other system related structures. The Behavior System has a unique Basic Neurostructure that assembles collages of Content and Emotion Memories from all related active memories and neural activity in the Active Experience to create behavior. Collages of memories, created by the Basic Neurostructure, create both responses and memories related to survival.

Change History of the Personality—the subconscious neutralizes the effects of negative trauma emotions associated with beliefs, memories, or responses from the creation of a past trauma emotion until now. At the same time, the subconscious can add positive emotions to desired responses. This is a treatment intervention taken from Neurolinguistic Programming. See Massive Change History.

Collage of memories—a collection of memory structures that work together to run neural activity to make a response. There are always many active memories in the Active Experience. Some of these active memories assemble into a collage to cause a response. This group of assembled memories, a collage of memories, works to create the necessary response. The collage of memories associates *with* the neural activity present to form another unique memory structure.

Conscious Active Experience—an awareness of emotions and behavior that we have in our conscious experience in contrast to the lack of awareness of activity in the unconscious experience. Behavior is created from the Active Experience in our conscious and unconscious experience and causes emotions and behavior in our awareness.

Constellation of fragments—a group of System Fragments that have a common origin such as a recurring trauma or traumatic situation. An early life trauma can cause the Behavior System to be able to split apart and form (behavior) System Fragments.

Content Memory—all sensory experiences: visual, auditory, touch, taste, and smell. It also includes basic needs such as air, food, and water and other neural activity, such as major neural pathways and brain and organ activity. Some of the active content (sensory experiences, needs, and so forth) makes up the content of the collage of a memory. It does not include emotions.

Dissociation—the process that causes the conscious and unconscious Active Experience. Dissociation is what we use voluntarily or spontaneously to hide memories that we don't want to remember, or to hide skills that run automatically. Examples of dissociated skills or memories are the mechanics of driving a car, composing and editing of speech or written prose. When you remember the details of a trauma that is very upsetting, and, later, you cannot remember the details, then the details have been dissociated. We call these memories dissociated memories. A dissociative process works to dissociate some or all of a memory. Dissociated memories can be active in the unconscious. Repression is voluntary dissociation.

Dissociative part—some skill or the memory of a painful experience moved to the unconscious where the skill is more efficient and the painful memory causes little or no pain. Dissociative parts can cause intrusive behaviors that are memory based but are not caused by executive function. Content or emotions can trigger dissociative parts into your Active Experience. Dissociated memories can cause intrusions such as hearing your name, a comment in another voice, or seeing an image. However, some skills with apparent executive function can be dissociated and perform a task, such as composing and editing verbal behavior.

Dissociative process—a part that associates *with* a memory in the collage to cause the content or emotions of the memory to be active in the unconscious. The dissociation process can associate *with* all or some of the memories in a collage. Though the dissociative process is like a learned part, I call it the dissociative process to distinguish it from dissociative parts. Trauma can change the role of the dissociative process. The dissociative process can associate *to* memory structures to cause barriers in the treatment process and personality problems by creating memory structures difficult to change.

Dormant Memories—memories that are not active in the Active Experience. The Active Experience consists of all active neural activity and memories that are used to create our behavior and experience. All dormant memories are available to be active, but most memories are not currently active. They remain dormant until they are triggered into the Active Experience. The triggers are active content or emotions in the Active Experience that are also present in a dormant memory.

Easily created Memory III—see Tandem Memory

Ego State—a system of memories dependent upon some specific situation. For example, a person may behave and feel different in a church as opposed to how they behave and feel in a police department. These Ego States are state-dependent memories within the Main Personality.

Emotional Freedom Techniques (EFT)—a therapy using techniques where the patient taps on twelve acupressure points to resolve mental health problems and physical problems. Emotional Freedom Techniques was developed by Gary Craig (1995, 2005). It does not involve diagnosis, which simplifies its use by the public (Flint, 2001) (see Appendix V).

Emotion Memory—a memory structure consisting of a collage of emotions that matches the present emotional experience. This Emotion Memory structure associates *with* the memory structure of the experience in the creation process. An Emotion Memory causes a positive or hurtful emotional experience. Emotions serve to motivate memory structures to be active and to cause behavior, a thought, or an intrusion.

Emotion System—a system consisting of Basic Neurostructure, an Active Experience, and a memory of emotions. The Basic Neurostructure of the Emotion System creates a collage of Emotion Memories to match the emotion experience in the Active Experience during the creation of behavior or experience.

Executive function—involves all aspects of the self-generation of behavior. This includes selecting information, planning, self-monitoring, self correcting, problem-solving, decision making, and controlling behavior.

Field—a word used to describe the experience of a patient when treating barriers not treatable by the usual treatment process. When an unorthodox method is used to treat the barrier, the patient feels a swoosh from his or her torso, chest, or some other part of his or her body.

Field barrier—a barrier that blocks communication or treatment that is treated by an unorthodox method that resolves the barrier.

Floating structures—structures active in the Active Experience formed after healing easily created systems. Trauma memory in Memory I prevents the structure from joining the Behavior System after treatment. By treating the memory in Memory I, the floating structures can be joined with the Behavior System. Floating structures stop the treatment process.

Healing—removal of pain. One can remove pain from an issue by treating the issue. This removal of pain is called healing the issue because issues treated with this method, as with TFT and EFT, seldom return. Healing, then, refers to the activity of treatment and the long-term outcome of the process of treatment.

Heart System—Basic Neurostructure operating on the Active Experience and heart memory to run heart activity.

Ideomotor responses—muscle responses, such as finger responses, used to communicate with the subconscious, parts or aspects of the brain and body system

Independent Behavior System—a behavior system created by intensely severe trauma leading to the splitting of the Basic Neurostructure. This behavior system operates independently of the main Behavior System. They both are motivated by the Emotion System. The Independent Behavior System can provide problematic intrusions to the Active Experience.

Integration—see Joining of parts.

Intrusion—memories or parts that become active and cause a behavior, a thought, an image, or an emotion in the conscious experience.

Issue—a mental problem or concern which requires a resolution. If the issue is not treated, then it will continue to be problematic for the patient.

Joining of parts—exchange of memories between parts until they associate *with* the same memories. More formally, the memory structures exchange associations until they have the same associations. After joining, all parts can create behavior without conflict. All integrated parts, namely the memory structures, remain unique and experience the same positive and negative experiences.

Kinesthetic System—Basic Neurostructure operating on the Active Experience and kinesthetic memory to run kinesthetic responses. The Kinesthetic System deals with feedback from our muscles, joints, and skin. Trauma to this system can give an "energy" experience in our brain or in different areas of our body. This energy experience validates thought intrusion or thought broadcasting in psychotic persons.

Layered Memory—a memory formed when another memory or part associates *to* a memory structure during its creation. A Layered Memory cannot be treated until the memory associated *to* the memory is treated. Trauma or unusual circumstances create Layered Memories. All people have some Layered Memories. Some beliefs or unwanted behaviors are Layered Memories.

Main Personality—the personality part with executive function who spends the most time running the body. The Main Personality starts forming at some point before birth or at birth. In people with extreme trauma history, a trauma part can become the most competent part and serves as the Main Personality for the longest time. Sometimes, the damage to the original Main Personality is so severe that it never learns enough skills to run the body. When this happens, other parts learn the skills to run the body.

Massive Change History—an intervention that involves the subconscious revising or updating of all memories in the brain and body distorted by a treated trauma memory. A Massive Change History always follows a treatment intervention. (See Change History of the Personality.)

Memory elements—memories of various structures associated with a structure of memories. The memory elements bind to the structure of memories because the emotions associated with the memory elements become associated in a structure.

Memory function—the neural activity (behavior, emotion, thought) created by the collage of memories associated *with* a memory structure.

Memory I—a memory that starts amassing shortly after conception and is state-dependent on neural activity. Shortly after conception, Basic Neurostructure creates a response and memory from activity in the Active Experience. Activity in the Active Experience is the common feature of all memories in Memory I at this time of development. Additional unique memory structures assemble over time to create Memory I as a state-dependent memory based on activity as the common property.

Memory II—a memory that starts amassing before birth and is state-dependent on both simple neural activity and primitive neural activity related to sensory experience. The Basic Neurostructure starts creating behavior and Memory II when the complexity of behavior includes neural activity related to sensory experience. Memory II continues to amass until age four. The Predispositions are in Memory II.

Memory III—a memory that starts amassing shortly before birth and is state-dependent on simple neural activity, the five sensory experiences, reward and punishment, and basic needs. Memory III includes all memory structures that primarily run the brain and body activities required for day-to-day survival.

Memory Structure—the basic building block of all memories. All memories have a unique memory structure (see Figure III-2). With the creation of each response, previously learned, active memory structures causing the response to associate *with* a new memory structure. Because neural activity is always chang-

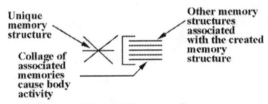

Figure III-2 A Memory Structure

ing, all memory structures in a changing environment are unique. The memory structures that run neural activity and that merge to cause the response are collectively called a collage. The collage activates neural activity to run brain or body activity. It is as if each memory collage has its own memory structure based on the complexion of neural activity in the brain when the structure was created.

Meridians—massive neural pathways related in some way to an organ. When stimulated by physical activity, endorphins are released in the cortex.

Motivation — positive or negative emotions associated *with* a memory that impels the memory to action. The more intense the emotions, the more motivated the memory, that is, the more likely it will become active. Intrusive thoughts, for example, are memories having emotions associated with them. When the emotions are replaced by neutral emotions in a treatment process, the memory is no longer motivated to intrude.

Neural — see Neurostructure

Neural pathways — see Neurostructure

Neurostructure — is a cooperative network of neurons in our brain and body that are capable of creating behavior and memories. Reference is made to neurostructure, neural activity and neural pathways because, basically, all of our behavior is caused by neural activity in our brain and body. There are interventions that operate directly on the neurostructure of a system. Being able to conceptualize some neural basis for the problem helps your understanding of the creation of behavior and more complex memory and system structures.

Part — a neural structure that has associated memories that can give intrusions into the conscious experience or run the body when triggered. A part is either an amnesic or dissociative part in Memory III that can independently run some of the activity of the brain. Dissociative parts are similar to skills or painful memories that are mostly active in the unconscious (see Dissociative part). Severe trauma creates amnesic parts with executive function in a way that results in few or no neural associations between the trauma part and the Main Personality. The absence of neural associations causes the amnesia between the part and the Main Personality. Parts can be created in the memory of other systems.

Predisposition — the tendency to respond to a situation in a predefined way. There are many Predispositions. Predispositions are usually parts or memories in Memory II.

Protector-Controller — a part formed in Memory II in the first four years of life. It provides the tendency to respond in a protecting or controlling way in particular situations. The Protector and Controller can be independent parts.

Reframe — a change in the experience of a negative situation or belief into a positive experience by giving an alternative explanation that has positive, self-empowering qualities. Reframes often cause positive therapeutic results in people. This is an intervention described in Neurolinguistic Programming.

Residual trauma—the after-effects of trauma early in life, when the *in utero* environment restricts the freedom of the fetus. Negative emotions caused by the restriction of movement results in pervasive trauma memory. After the brain develops, some of the trauma memories remain in areas of the brain that are relatively inactive. These trauma memories support shame.

Shadow Memories—memories induced or caused in the neural structures surrounding the primary neurological path of intense memory activity. After treating an intense traumatic symptom, to treat the symptom fully, it is often important to treat the Shadow Memory caused by the activity of the symptom.

Stacked parts—two or more parts associated *to* each other, caused when the intense pain continues to increase to cause another mobilization of memories "pushing" the active personality part dormant. This can result in a number of new parts associating *to* preceding parts. With continuing and increasing pain, many parts can be stacked in a pyramid-like structure that has to be treated by starting with the top part.

State-dependency—a group of memories, having some common features, that is necessary for inclusion in the state-dependent group. A memory with common features with a group of memories would be a state-dependent memory.

State-dependent personality—all Content and Emotion Memories that create our conscious and unconscious activity leading to behavior that is called the personality. Ego States are state-dependent memories in the personality that are only active in particular situations.

Structure—There are two kinds of structures.

1. a unique neural state *with* or *to* which other memory structures associate (see Figure III-1). The memory structures that associate *with* the unique memory structure form a collage that has active neural activity that altogether can run brain or body activity.

2. a structure caused by the neural association of a common content or emotion of the memories. The structure of memories is maintained by the emotions of the memories. The memories associated with the structure are called memory elements. When the emotions binding the memories together in the structure are treated, the structure falls apart.

Structure of memories—see Structure.

Subconscious—a pervasive primitive process that starts shortly after conception and is independent of Memories I, II, and III. The subconscious involves the entire brain. It doesn't store memories and is not conscious or unconscious activity. The subconscious has a language and

Behavior System involving the entire brain and body. It does not normally have sensory and emotional experiences but has access to the neural representation of all memory experiences in the body. The subconscious can access all active memories in the Active Experience. One can communicate with the subconscious. The subconscious can work with brain processes to change Basic Neurostructure, memory and behavior.

Sub-personality—consists of the Protector-Controller and other positive and negative tendencies called Predispositions. Sub-personality starts forming *in utero* and continues to develop through the first four years of life. A Predisposition, like a part, provides a predetermined response to situations by creating behavior in the Active Experience that handles intrusions or specific circumstances.

System—a Basic Neurostructure, an Active Experience, and memory working together to serve some function. A system runs every brain process, organ function, behavior, or body activity. The memory continues to amass as the Basic Neurostructure creates responses and memories from the activity in the Active Experience to run some brain or body activity, for example the Behavior, Emotion and Heart Systems.

System Fragment—a trauma can cause a System Fragment that runs in parallel with the Behavior System. Repeated early life trauma can cause the fragmenting of the Behavior System resulting in many fragmented systems running in parallel. Fragmented systems distort our experience with behavior or emotions. (See Constellation of fragments)

Tandem Memory— a memory caused by activity overload in the Active Experience that operates in tandem with Memory III. Early in life, if the Active Experience is overloaded for any reason, another memory and Active Experience is sometimes created. This results in creating one or more additional and parallel forms of Memory III, Tandem Memories, each serving another Active Experience. Tandem Memories can have significant differences from the Memory III. Most people have multiple Active Experiences, each with a unique Tandem Memory.

Tapas Acupressure Technique (TAT)—a technique of applying gentle pressure to three acupressure points on your nose and forehead while putting your other hand behind your head. The Tapas Acupressure Technique was developed by Tapas Fleming (1995, see also 2004). While this is an effective technique to treat mental health issues and allergies, I use it for treating obsessions (see Appendix VI).

Thought Field Therapy (TFT)—a therapy using a technique of tapping on diagnosed acupressure points to resolve mental health or physical problems. Thought Field Therapy was discovered and developed by Roger

Callahan (2001, see also 2005). Callahan developed algorithms to treat specific mental health issues like phobias, anxiety, depression, and so forth.

Trauma—a hurtful experience that creates a unique trauma memory structure with associated pain.

Trauma, residual—See Residual trauma.

Treatment by the subconscious—a method of working internally to eliminate the emotions caused by trauma. The results are similar to treatment by external stimulation, such as tapping on acupressure points or eye movement. The tapping, stimulating neural activity, causes a learning process in which the present neutral-to-positive emotional experience replaces the trauma-Emotion Memories associated with the trauma memory. The subconscious engages in treatment by creating the neural activity that is assumed to be similar to treatment obtained by physical tapping.

Treatment Team—an imagined team formed by aspects who want to heal, to have their positive beliefs and behaviors strengthened with positive emotions, to join with the Main Personality and to create treatment plans in consensus, namely with total agreement.

Unconscious Active Experience—active memories and behaviors created in the Active Experience that are not in conscious experience are said to be in the unconscious Active Experience. The normal process of dissociation causes this unconscious condition. When the dissociation process associates *with* all or selective qualities of the collage of memories in a new memory structure, those qualities become active in the unconscious activity of the new memory.

Appendix IV

Glossary of New Concepts

The Process Healing Method involves eight concepts that are different from the concepts people normally use to think about the brain and behavior. I have included them here in an organized way that will perhaps be helpful in learning this new way of thinking. Reading this Glossary of New Concepts will also prepare you to understand the theory presented in Chapter 5 and later chapters. This glossary is not alphabetical but presents an orderly description of each of the new concepts. Here is a list of the eight concepts and all of the components of each concept used in Process Healing. Though these terms are defined in the Glossary they are assembled here as part of the description of each concept.

    1. Memory—Structure, memory structure, memory function, collage of memories, associated *with* vs. *to*, Content Memory, Emotion Memory, memory intrusion, Shadow Memories

    2. Memory Activity—Dormant vs. active memory, Active Experience, conscious Active Experience, unconscious Active Experience, and subconscious

    3. State-Dependent—State-dependency, state-dependent personality, Memory I, Memory II, Memory III

    4. Personality—Part, active personality, Main Personality, Ego State, Tandem Memory, sub-personality, Protector-Controller, Predisposition, motivation

    5. Parts—Dissociation, dissociative process, dissociative parts, amnesia, amnesic parts, executive function, Stacked Parts

    6. Systems—System, Basic Neurostructure, Behavior System, Emotion System, Heart System, Kinesthetic System

    7. Treatment—Issue, treatment by the subconscious, ideomotor responses, Treatment Team, barrier, reframe, Massive Change History, joining of parts (integration), healing

    8. Fields—Field, field barrier

1. Memory—Structure, memory structure, memory function, collage of memories, associated with vs. to, Content Memory, Emotion Memory, memory intrusion, Shadow Memories

Structure—There are two kinds of structures.

1. a unique neural state *with* or *to* which other memory structures associate (see Figure IV-1). The memory structures that associate *with* the unique memory structure form a collage that has active neural activity that altogether can run brain or body activity.

2. a structure caused by the neural association of a common content or emotion of the memories. The structure of memories is maintained by the emotions of the memories. The memories associated *with* the structure are called memory elements. When the emotions binding the memories together in the structure are treated, the structure falls apart.

Memory Structure—the basic building block of all memories. All memories have a unique memory structure (see Figure IV-1). With the creation of each response, previously learned active memory structures causing the response to associate *with* a new memory structure. Because neural activity is always changing, all memory structures in a changing environment are unique. The

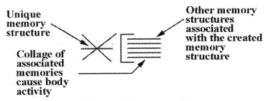

Figure IV-1 A Memory Structure

memory structures that merged to run neural activity and that cause the response are collectively called a collage. The collage activates neural activity to run brain or body activity. It is as if each memory collage has its own memory structure based on the complexion of neural activity in the brain when the structure was created.

Memory function—the neural activity (behavior, emotion, thought) created by the collage of memories associated with a memory structure.

Collage of memories—a collection of memory structures that work together to run neural activity to make a response. There are always many active memories in the Active Experience. Some of these active memories assemble into a collage to cause a response. This group of assembled memories, a collage of memories, works to create the necessary response. The collage of memories associates *with* the neural activity present to form another unique memory structure.

Associate *with* vs. *to*—all memories have a unique structure with which other memories associate. The memories associate *with* a structure to form a collage of memories (see Figure IV-2). When the structure is active, the collage of memories creates a unique response in our brain or body. Memories associated *with* a structure are easy to change. On the other hand, when a

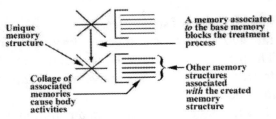

Unique memory structure

A memory associated *to* the base memory blocks the treatment process

Collage of associated memories cause body activities

Other memory structures associated *with* the created memory structure

Figure IV-2 Associated *with* vs *to*

memory associates *to* a memory structure, it is not possible to change the memories associated *with* the structure. The memory associated *to* the memory structure changes the neural plasticity. Until the memory associated *to* the structure is treated, the collage of memories associated *with* the structure cannot be treated. A memory associated *to* a structure is a barrier to treating memories causing unwanted behavior.

Content Memory—all sensory experiences: visual, auditory, touch, taste, and smell. It also includes basic needs such as air, food, and water and other neural activity, such as major neural pathways and brain and organ activity. Some of the active content (sensory experiences, needs, and so forth) makes up the content of the collage of a memory. It does not include emotions.

Emotion Memory—a memory structure consisting of a collage of emotions that matches the present emotional experience. This Emotion Memory structure associates *with* the memory structure of the experience in the creation process. An Emotion Memory causes a positive or hurtful emotional experience. Emotions serve to motivate memory structures to be active and to cause behavior, a thought, or an intrusion.

Memory intrusion—memories or parts that become active and cause a behavior, a thought, an image, or an emotion to come into the conscious experience.

Shadow Memories—memories induced or caused in the neural structures surrounding the primary neurological path of intense memory activity. After treating an intense traumatic symptom, to treat the symptom fully, it is often important to treat the Shadow Memory caused by the activity of the symptom.

2. Memory Activity — Dormant vs. active memories, Active Experience, conscious Active Experience, unconscious Active Experience, subconscious

Dormant Memories vs. Active Memories — dormant memories are memories that are not active in the Active Experience. Active memories are active in the Active Experience. The Active Experience consists of all active memories and neural activity that are used to create our behavior and experience. All dormant memories are available to be active, but most memories are not currently active until they are triggered into the Active Experience. The triggers are active content or Emotion Memories and neural activity in the Active Experience that are also present in a dormant memory.

Active Experience — a metaphor for the brain activity involved in creating behavior. It contains all active memories and neural activity of the brain and body. The Active Experience construct simplifies the brain activity and helps us talk about dormant, unconscious, and conscious memories in a meaningful way. The active memories are those triggered from dormancy into the Active Experience. The triggers are active content or emotions in the Active Experience that are present in a dormant memory. Basic Neurostructure works on the Active Experience to create a collage from the Content and Emotion Memories, leading to a response and a memory of the response.

Conscious Active Experience — an awareness of emotions and behavior that we have in our conscious experience in contrast to the lack of awareness of activity in the unconscious Active Experience. Behavior is created from the Active Experience in our conscious and unconscious experience and causes emotions and behavior in our awareness.

Unconscious Active Experience — active memories and behaviors created from the Active Experience that are not in conscious experience are said to be in the unconscious Active Experience. The normal process of dissociation causes this unconscious condition. When the dissociation process associates *with* all or selective qualities of the collage of memories in a forming memory structure, those qualities become active in the unconscious activity of the new memory.

Subconscious — a pervasive primitive process that starts shortly after conception and is independent of Memories I, II, and III. The subconscious involves the entire brain. It doesn't store memories and is not conscious or unconscious activity. The subconscious has a language and Behavior System involving the entire brain and body. It does not normally have sensory and emotional experiences but has access to the neural representation of all memory experiences in the body. The subconscious can access all active memories in the Active Experience. One can communicate with the subconscious. The subconscious can work with brain processes to change Basic Neurostructure, memory and behavior.

3. State-Dependent — State-dependency, state-dependent personality, Memory I, Memory II, Memory III

State-dependency — a group of memories, having some common features, that is necessary for inclusion in the state-dependent group. A memory with common features with a group of memories would be a state-dependent memory.

State-dependent personality — all Content and Emotion Memories that create our conscious and unconscious activity leading to behavior that is called the personality. Ego States are state-dependent memories in the personality that are only active in particular situations.

Memory I — a memory that starts amassing shortly after conception and is state-dependent on neural activity. Shortly after conception, Basic Neurostructure creates a response and memory from activity in the Active Experience. Activity in the Active Experience is the common feature of all memories in Memory I at this time of development. New memory structures assemble over time to create Memory I as a state-dependent memory based on activity as the common property.

Memory II — a memory that starts amassing before birth and is state-dependent on both simple neural activity and primitive neural activity related to sensory experience. The Basic Neurostructure starts creating behavior and Memory II when the complexity of behavior includes neural activity related to sensory experience. Memory II continues to amass until age four. The Predispositions are in Memory II.

Memory III — a memory that starts amassing shortly before birth and is state-dependent on simple neural activity, the five sensory experiences, reward and punishment, and basic needs. Memory III includes all memory structures that primarily run the brain and body activities required for day-to-day survival.

4. Personality — Part, active personality, Main Personality, Ego State, Tandem Memory, sub-personality, Protector Controller, Predisposition, residual trauma, motivation

Part — a neural structure that has associated memories that can give intrusions into the conscious experience or run the body when triggered. A part is either an amnesic or dissociative part in Memory III that can independently run some of the activity of the brain. Dissociative parts are similar to skills or painful memories that are mostly active in the unconscious (see Dissociative part). Severe trauma creates amnesic parts with executive function in a way that results in few or no neural associations between the trauma part and the Main Personality. The absence of neural associations causes the amnesia between the part and the Main Personality. Parts can be created in the memory of other systems.

Active personality — a personality part that is active in the conscious and unconscious Active Experience in the present time. More than one personality part can be active at one time.

Main Personality — the personality part with executive function who spends the most time running the body. The Main Personality starts forming at some point before birth or at birth. In people with extreme trauma history, a trauma part can become the most competent part and serves as the Main Personality for the longest time. Sometimes, the damage to the original Main Personality is so severe that it never learns enough skills to run the body. When this happens, other parts learn the skills to run the body.

Ego State — a system of memories dependent upon some specific situation. For example, a person may behave and feel different in a church as opposed to how they behave and feel in a police department. These Ego States are state-dependent memories within the Main Personality.

Tandem Memory — a memory caused by activity overload in the Active Experience that operates in tandem with Memory III. Early in life, if the Active Experience is overloaded for any reason, another memory and Active Experience is sometimes created. This results in creating one or more additional and parallel forms of Memory III, Tandem Memories, each serving another Active Experience. Tandem Memories can have significant differences from the Memory III. Most people have multiple Active Experiences, each with a unique Tandem Memory.

Sub-personality — consists of the Protector-Controller and other positive and negative tendencies called Predispositions. Sub-personality starts forming *in utero* and continues to develop through the first four years of life. A Predisposition, like a part, provides a predetermined response to situations by creating behavior in the Active Experience that handles intrusions or specific circumstances.

Protector-Controller—a part formed in Memory II in the first four years of life. It provides the tendency to respond in a protecting or controlling way in particular situations. The Protector and Controller can be independent parts.

Predisposition—the tendency to respond to a situation in a predefined way. There are many Predispositions. Predispositions are usually parts or memories in Memory II.

Residual trauma—the after-effects of trauma early in life, when the *in utero* environment restricts the freedom of the fetus. Negative emotions caused by the restriction of movement results in pervasive trauma memory. After the brain develops, some of the trauma memories remain in areas of the brain that are relatively inactive. These trauma memories support shame.

Motivation—positive or negative emotions associated *with* a memory that impels the memory to action. The more intense the emotions, the more motivated the memory, that is, the more likely it will become active. Intrusive thoughts, for example, are memories having emotions associated with them. When the emotions are replaced by neutral emotions in a treatment process, the memory is no longer motivated to intrude.

5. Parts—Dissociation, dissociative process, dissociative part, amnesia, amnesic parts, executive function, Stacked Parts

Dissociation—the process that causes the conscious and unconscious Active Experience. Dissociation is what we use voluntarily or spontaneously to hide memories that we don't want to remember, or to hide skills that run automatically. Examples of dissociated skills or memories are the mechanics of driving a car, composing and editing of speech or written prose. When you remember the details of a trauma that is very upsetting, and, later, you cannot remember the details, then the details have been dissociated. We call these memories dissociated memories. A dissociative process works to dissociate some or all of a memory. Dissociated memories can be active in the unconscious. Repression is voluntary dissociation.

Dissociative process—a part that associates *with* a memory in the collage to cause the content or emotions of the memory to be active in the unconscious. The dissociation process can associate *with* all or some of the memories in a collage. Though the dissociative process is like a learned part, I call it the dissociative process to distinguish it from dissociative parts. Trauma can change the role of the dissociative process. The dissociative process can associate *to* memory structures to cause barriers in the treatment process and personality problems by creating memory structures difficult to change.

Dissociative part—some skill or the memory of a painful experience moved to the unconscious where the skill is more efficient and the painful memory causes little or no pain. Dissociative parts can cause intrusive behaviors that are memory based but are not caused by executive function. Content or emotions can trigger dissociative parts into your Active Experience. Dissociated memories can cause intrusions such as hearing your name, a comment in another voice, or seeing an image. However, some skills with apparent executive function can be dissociated and perform a task, such as composing and editing verbal behavior.

Amnesia—lack of awareness between two memories such as a trauma memory and an active personality part. The personality part does not know that the amnesic memory is there. The theory suggests the cause for the amnesia is that few or no neural connections exist between the memories. Some amnesic parts or memories can intrude into the Active Experience by causing some content or emotion in our Active Experience.

Amnesic parts—a personality part of which other personalities are more or less unaware. During severe trauma, for which there is no previous memory to create a response to manage the situation and when there are intense emotions independent of the Main Personality, memories rapidly activate with the intense emotions to handle the crisis. The Main Personality goes dormant. This creates an amnesic part or memory. Amnesic parts with executive function can self-generate behavior and cause intrusions such as unknown voices, images in a person's thoughts, or unexplained emotion. See Appendix II for a description of parts activity. Amnesia between two parts can hide both parts from each other or operate in one direction only; namely one part knows what the other is doing but the other part is unaware of what the first part is doing.

Executive function—involves all aspects of the self-generation of behavior. This includes selecting information, planning, self-monitoring, self correcting, problem-solving, decision making, and controlling behavior.

Stacked parts—two or more parts associated *to* each other, caused when the intense pain continues to increase to cause multiple mobilizations of memories "pushing" the active personality part dormant. This can result in a number of new parts associating *to* preceding parts. With continuing and increasing pain, many parts can be stacked in a pyramid-like structure that has to be treated by starting with the top part.

6. Systems—System, Basic Neurostructure, Behavior System, Emotion System, Heart System, Kinesthetic System

System—a Basic Neurostructure, an Active Experience, and memory working together to serve some function. A system runs every brain process, organ function, behavior, or body activity. The memory continues to assemble as the Basic Neurostructure creates responses and memories from the activity in the Active Experience to run some brain or body activity, for example the Behavior, Emotion and Heart Systems.

Basic Neurostructure—a neurostructure that serves a specific function in our brain by creating collages causing activity and memory for the function or activity of systems, organs, brain functions, and so forth.

Behavior System—consists of Basic Neurostructure, Memory I, Memory II, Memory III, the Active Experience, and other system related structures. The Behavior System has a unique Basic Neurostructure that assembles collages of Content and Emotion Memories from all related active memories and neural activity in the Active Experience to create behavior. Collages of memories, created by the Basic Neurostructure, creates both responses and memories related to survival.

Emotion System—a system consisting of Basic Neurostructure, an Active Experience, and a memory of emotions. The Basic Neurostructure of the Emotion System creates a collage of Emotion Memories to match the emotion experience in the Active Experience during the creation of behavior or experience.

Heart System—Basic Neurostructure operating on the Active Experience and heart memory to run heart activity.

Kinesthetic System—Basic Neurostructure operating on the Active Experience and kinesthetic memory to run kinesthetic responses. The Kinesthetic System deals with feedback from our muscles, joints, and skin. Trauma to this system can give an "energy" experience in our brain or in different areas of our body. This energy experience validates thought intrusion or thought broadcasting in psychotic persons.

7. Treatment—Issue, treatment by the subconscious, ideomotor responses, Treatment Team, barrier, reframe, Massive Change History, joining of parts (integration), healing

Issue—a mental problem or concern which requires a resolution. If the issue is not treated, then it will continue to be problematic for the patient.

Treatment by the subconscious—a method of working internally to eliminate the emotions caused by trauma. The results are similar to treatment by external stimulation, such as tapping on acupressure points or eye movement. The tapping, stimulating neural activity, causes a learning process in which the present neutral-to-positive emotional experience replaces the trauma-Emotion Memories associated with the trauma memory. The subconscious engages in treatment by creating the neural activity that is assumed to be caused by treatment obtained by physical tapping.

Ideomotor responses—muscle responses, such as finger responses, used to communicate with the subconscious, parts or aspects of the brain and body system

Treatment Team—an imagined team formed by aspects who want to heal, to have their positive beliefs and behaviors strengthened with positive emotions, to join with the Main Personality and to create treatment plans in consensus, namely with total agreement.

Barrier—an active memory in the Active Experience that stops communication with the subconscious or parts, or stops treatment. A part, a belief, a memory structure problem, or a field, can cause a barrier in the Active Experience.

Reframe—a change in the experience of a negative situation or belief into a positive experience by giving an alternative explanation that has positive, self-empowering qualities. Reframes often cause positive therapeutic results in people. This is an intervention described in Neurolinguistic Programming.

Massive Change History—an intervention that involves the subconscious revising or updating of all memories in the brain and body distorted by a treated trauma memory. A Massive Change History and everything always follows a treatment intervention.

Joining of parts (integration)—exchange of memories between parts until they associate *with* the same memories. More formally, the memory structures exchange associations until they have the same associations. After joining, all parts can create behavior without conflict.

All integrated parts, namely the memory structures, remain unique and experience the same positive and negative experiences.

Healing—removal of pain. One can remove pain from an issue by treating the issue. This removal of pain is called healing the issue because issues treated with this method, as with TFT and EFT, seldom return. Healing, then, refers to the activity of treatment and the long-term outcome of the process of treatment.

8. Fields — Field, field barrier

Field—a word used to describe the experience of a patient when treating barriers not treatable by the usual treatment process. When an unorthodox method is used to treat the barrier, the patient feels a swoosh from his or her torso, chest, or some other part of his or her body.

Field barrier—a barrier that blocks communication or treatment. The barrier is treated by an unorthodox method that resolves the barrier.

Appendix V

Emotional Freedom Techniques— A Useful Resource

Emotional Freedom Techniques (EFT) is a powerful treatment technique. This treatment method is worth learning and adding to your skills because it is effective, safe, and simple to use. This description presents the basics of the EFT treatment procedure. The book *Emotional Freedom* (Flint, 2001) teaches EFT in detail, including how to resolve barriers and to problem-solve in a systematic procedure. As well, the developer of EFT, Gary Craig (1995), has a website (Craig, 2005) that offers many training CDs that are inexpensive. The website gives many examples of applications of EFT. Since 1995, Craig and his students have developed more refinements of the method that can be accessed through his website.

The presentation given here is intended to give just enough information to manage situations that might arise when doing Process Healing, particularly when emotional flooding interferes with the subconscious processing. I have only experienced this in cases where tearfulness was overwhelming the patient. In one case, I was treating a robbery issue. After we had seemingly treated the robbery issue and were reviewing the finer details of the issue by testing our work, similar emotions in the robbery issue triggered a rape memory. She was flooded with emotions. Process Healing appeared not to be working because the active emotional activity was thought to be a barrier to treatment. I immediately shifted to the EFT treatment and used several cycles of the EFT treatment to resolve the immediate emotions. After reducing the emotions to a comfortable level with EFT, I continued using the Process Healing Method. A six-month follow-up revealed that the robbery and rape intrusions had not reoccurred and that she was doing well working at the site of the robbery with no problems.

There are five steps in the EFT intervention: obtaining a sentence that describes the issue, identifying a phrase that triggers the issue, tapping on 12 acupressure points, doing what is called the 9-Gamut Procedure, and then repeating the tapping sequence (see Help Sheet next page). In emergencies with flooding emotions, you can skip the first two steps of EFT because the issue is already active in the Active Experience. The first

Help Sheet for EFT

Sample affirmation:

While rubbing the sore spot,

Say, " I accept myself even though I have this 'say your issue.'"

Treatment Sequence: Tap 5 times on each point – say your issue.

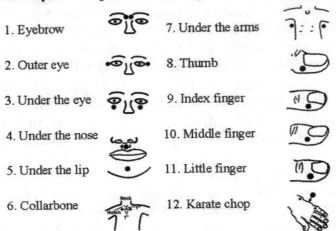

1. Eyebrow	7. Under the arms
2. Outer eye	8. Thumb
3. Under the eye	9. Index finger
4. Under the nose	10. Middle finger
5. Under the lip	11. Little finger
6. Collarbone	12. Karate chop

Do the 9-Gamut Procedure – While tapping on this spot on your hand:

1. Eyes closed	6. Rotate other way
2. Eyes open	7. Hum
3. Eyes down left	8. Count Say: "1, 2, 3, 4, 5"
4. Eyes down right	9. Hum
5. Rotate one way	

Repeat the Treatment Sequence: Tap 5 times on each point – say your issue.

step is to create a sentence that clearly describes the issue that one wants to treat—for example, "I am fearful whenever I think of the accident." A sentence like this will trigger the emotions associated with the issue. This allows the patient to assign a score ranging between 0 and 10 for the intensity of the emotions experienced (0 = no emotion, 10 = intense emotions). You will use this score to assess the change in emotions after each cycle of the EFT intervention. In the second step, you create an affirmation and a phrase that triggers the issue. The phrase is one or two words that elicit the emotions of the issue defined in step one—for example, "My fear" would serve as a phrase. When you create the affirmation, it is important to use an affirmation that states a positive self-belief such as, "I completely accept myself." The final part of this step is to complete the sentence by following the affirmation with the phrase for the issue you are treating: "I completely accept myself even though I have my (upset)." (Upset) is the phrase that identifies the issue and brings it into the Active Experience. You will, of course, replace the word "upset" with a phrase that describes the emotions of the issue that you are intending to treat, such as my anxiety, my fear, my phobia, my terror, and so forth. Now that you have the affirmation and phrase, when EFT is used in a normal treatment setting, you find the sore spot (see facing page), and while continuously rubbing on the sore spot, repeat the affirmation and phrase three times—"I accept myself even though I have this fear." Saying this statement while having a slightly painful experience caused by rubbing on the sore spot removes any barriers to treatment. The book *Emotional Freedom* (Flint, 2001) teaches these steps and gives many examples of sentences and phrases in its appendix.

In emergencies, one does steps three to five with only a brief introduction. Pat Cane (personal communication, April 16, 2002) provides group therapy to families in Latin America who have had enormous trauma. One example she shared with me was of a community meeting with 35 peasants who had family members or relatives who had been murdered and butchered. The meeting room had a feeling of gloom and the family members were numb and immobilized. Cane and her coworker started the meeting with many cycles of EFT and changed the experiences of the family members to the extent that there were many smiles, laughing and, in one case, an experience of spiritual awareness.

When working with a person who has flooding emotions, first identify the person's emotions either intuitively or by asking the person. Then guide them to start tapping on the acupressure points in the sequence described on the facing page. These are the points numbered

1 through 12 and they are defined as the treatment sequence. Coach the patient to tap five to seven times on each point at the location described in the figure, one point after the other. Model the tapping for them by doing it on yourself as they are doing it. Speak the phrase aloud at each tapping point, such as "My terror." By saying the phrase, you both keep the problem in their Active Experience and give the patient an interval (the time it takes to say the phrase) to gauge the number of taps on each point. When you finish the sequence, ask if the emotions have decreased. If the emotions have decreased, assess the score and then repeat the sequence again. Repeat assessing the score and treating until the painful emotions are reduced to zero. With some phobias like public speaking or fear of heights, the appropriate ending point of the treatment is when an anxiety level of one or two is reached.

When the emotions have not decreased after tapping on the points of the sequence, continue with the 9-Gamut Procedure (see preceding page). Help them localize the tapping point, one-half inch behind and between the knuckles of the little finger and ring finger of either hand. Ask the patient to tap on this spot repeatedly, like a woodpecker, while doing the nine exercises. While they are tapping, guide them through the nine exercises by saying, "I want you to close your eyes, open your eyes, look down to the left, look down to the right, rotate them one way in a big circle, rotate them the other way in a big circle, hum a tune (hum *"Happy birthday to you"*), count (say, 1, 2, 3, 4, 5) and then hum a tune again (continuing with *"Happy birthday to you"*). It is best that they hum and count out loud and with a tune, not a single note. If they don't count out loud, your humming and counting will have the same effect on the patient as if they were doing it. Now continue with the fifth step, which is doing the treatment sequence again.

Usually, the first cycle of EFT will lessen the emotions by 20 percent or more. Repeat the EFT procedure until the emotions decrease to little or no pain. Try to leave out the 9-Gamut Procedure to see if the emotions continue to decrease in intensity. If it works to leave it out, continue with just the treatment sequence. When the emotions do not decrease, put the 9-Gamut Procedure back into the treatment. When the emotions continue and don't decrease, have the patient rub on the sore spot on their chest and say, "I accept myself even though I **still** (emphasize still) continue to have **some** (emphasize some) of my 'upset.' " The words in bold seem to make a difference with the remaining barriers. Also, replace the phrase with "my remaining 'upset.' " Try the EFT treatment again.

There is some chance that this will not work with your patient. When it doesn't work, a barrier is stopping the treatment process. The book *Emotional Freedom* (Flint, 2001) gives a clear strategy to resolve barriers that arise when doing the EFT treatment. However, in most cases, the directions for the EFT procedure will work in a setting where the emotional flooding is blocking treatment with Process Healing. And for that matter, in most cases, you won't have to handle flooding emotions with the Process Healing Method.

Appendix VI

Tapas Acupressure Technique for Obsessions

The Tapas Acupressure Technique (TAT) is an effective treatment technique developed by Tapas Fleming (2003). She is a licensed acupressure practitioner who discovered this intervention when she was working with difficult patients. This is a useful and effective treatment method to learn. You can obtain more details about manuals and trainings for TAT from Tapas' website (Fleming, 2004). I am grateful to Tapas because my analysis of her treatment of allergies opened the door for me to understand and form a theory about other influences on human behavior that I otherwise would have probably rejected (Flint, n.d.).

While this technique is effective for most trauma-related disorders and allergies, I only use it for people who have obsessions. Obsessions are like intrusive memories. These memories have negative emotions associated with them. The negative emotions serve as motivation for the memories to intrude into the person's thoughts. By neutralizing or replacing the negative emotions associated with the intrusive thoughts, the obsessing thoughts stop. Without motivation, the thoughts remain dormant. In my experience, one can effectively treat a patient who obsesses about different topics by using the TAT intervention. It appears that TAT strips the negative emotions off the obsessive thoughts or neutralizes them.

I use the three-pose version developed by Jane Wakefield (2002). The three-pose version involves doing the pose with each hand and then a pose with both hands. The TAT pose involves putting the ring finger and thumb on the tear ducts next to your nose (see Figures VI-1 and VI-2) and then moving your fingers one-eighth of an inch out from the corner of the eye. Then put the tip of your middle finger on the center point between your eyebrows and about one-half inch above your eyebrows (see Figures VI-2, VI-3, and VI-4). Then put the other hand on the occipital bulge on the back of your head (see Figure VI-5). The patient does this pose first with one hand (for example, the right hand) in position on the front of the face (see Figures VI-3 and VI-4) and the other hand on the occipital bulge (see Figure VI-5). Then the patient is told to switch sides, placing the left hand in position on the front of the face, similar to Figures VI-3 and VI-4, but with the left hand, and the right hand on the occipital bulge. The third pose involves putting the thumbs of both hands under your ear lobe and your little finger or pinky on the center of your temple, and then radiating the other fingers around your ear (see Figures VI-6 and VI-7).

Tapas Acupressure Techniques: The Three-Pose Variation

The figure on the left shows the points for doing the pose (see Figure VI-1), showing the position for the thumb, middle finger and the

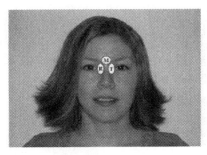

Figure VI-1 Points for Fingers   **Figure VI-2 Finger Placement**

index finger. With either hand, lightly touch the tip of the thumb to the area one-eighth inch out from the inner corner of your eye. Next, place the ring finger on the other side of the nose on the area about one-eighth inch out from the inner corner of the eye (see Figure VI-1). Then put the tip of your middle finger on the center point between your eyebrows and about one-half inch above the end of your eyebrows (see Figure VI-2).

Right Hand

Figures VI-3 and VI-4 show the positions of the thumb, ring finger and middle finger in the pose. Figure VI-3 shows the placement of

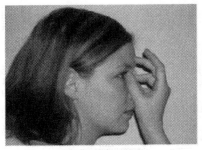
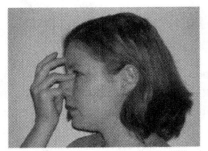

Figure VI-3 Right Thumb   **Figure VI-4 Ring Finger**

the thumb and Figure VI-4 shows the placement of the ring finger. Do the pose with your right hand. Now place the palm of your left hand on the back of your head covering the occipital bone with the thumb resting just above the hairline (see Figure VI-5).

Left Hand

Repeat the pose with your left hand in positions similar to Figures VI-3 and VI-4, which show the positions of the thumb, ring finger, and

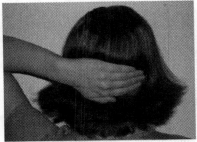

middle finger in the pose. Now place the palm of your left hand on the back of your head covering the occipital bone with the thumb resting just above the hairline (see Figure VI-5).

Figure VI-5 Back of Head

Both Hands

After you complete the poses with your left and right hand, you do the two-handed pose. Place the thumb of both hands under the ear

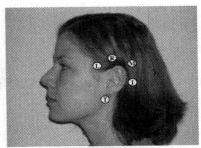

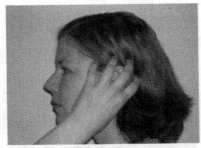

Figure VI-6 Points on Side   **Figure VI-7 Hands on Side**

lobes as shown in the Figures VI-6 and VI-7. Then put the little finger of both hands in the center of your temple. Radiate the other fingers around your ears as shown in the figure on the left.

Here is an example of treating an obsession:

T: **Do you have an obsession?**

P: **Yes. I am always thinking about the accident.**

T: **Subconscious, would it be safe to treat the obsession with the TAT pose?**

Sometimes, I show the pose to teach the subconscious what it is.

S: **Yes.**

T: **I want you to place your ring finger and thumb gently on the corner of your eye like this, and then move them out one-eighth of an inch. Then place your middle finger between your eyebrows like this. Then put your other hand behind your head on the knob on the back of your head with your thumb near your hairline.**

Sometimes, you have to correct finger placement by physically moving the patient's fingers.

T: **Now I want you to obsess on purpose by thinking about the accident. What you might feel are thoughts, images, or sounds streaming through your mind or you might feel some sensation in your brain. Do you feel either the sensations in your brain or thoughts streaming through your consciousness?**

P: **Yes, I feel my thoughts streaming through my mind.**

T: **I want you to hold that pose until the streaming thoughts or sensations stop. It may take two minutes or five minutes, but continue until the feeling completely stops. By the way, your subconscious can learn to do this treatment procedure without your active participation by maintaining the pose.**

I check in every minute or so to find out whether the processing is continuing. After doing the processing with the one hand, I repeat the process with the other hand. When that processing has completed, I continue with the following:

T: **Now I want you to do a pose with both hands.** [Model this as you explain the two-handed pose] **Place your thumb under your ears like this . . . then put your little finger on the center of your temple like this** [Correct the placement as needed] **and then radiate your fingers around your ear. Good. Now hold this pose until any sensations in your brain or your thoughts have finished.**

Again, check every few minutes. When the patient lowers her hands, I test the intervention by asking him or her to obsess on purpose to see if the obsessive thoughts are neutral or if they feel like obsessing. Usually, there is no pressure to obsess. When obsession occurs, I repeat the treatment. I also point out that he or she can use this procedure at home for other obsessions or for a racing mind when trying to sleep. I reveal that I often use the TAT procedure when I am going to sleep. I say to myself, "I want to treat the origin of all issues that might interfere with my sleep."

Examples using the TAT procedure:
1. An obsessing cult survivor

A woman was snatched by a cult that continued to abuse her for eight years. The abuse involved emotional and physical damage. Because of the abuse and her personal loses, when I first met her, she was an angry, hostile woman who continuously complained about her life to anyone she met. She expressed her anger about "losing her life" and the joys that should have been hers. I saw her for three 90-minute sessions in which she yelled for the entire time telling me about the details of her life and how wrong it was. In the fourth session, after 20 minutes, I told her to stop talking and then asked if I could put my hands on her head. She allowed me to do this and I carefully moved next to her on a separate chair and put the pose on her head. Then I asked her to tell me about her justified rage and anger about getting ripped off by that cult. She railed for about 20 minutes and then stopped. She sat there quietly. I took my hands down. She started talking about her living situation and decided to evict a room-mate who was taking advantage of her. In the two following sessions, she organized her life and planned a move back to the community where she had grown up.

2. Treating intrusive memories

I worked with a paranoid schizophrenic. Without going into the complex details of this patient, he appeared to have about 13,000+ parts or Layered Memories that gave intrusions that constantly reflected on his behavior and motivation with nasty comments. He heard other intrusions such as dogs barking, engines revving, footsteps around his house and people yelling. Although all of these intrusions were projected onto the world and led to paranoid thoughts, I called them internal intrusions. At that time, I thought they were amnesic parts. For many months, I worked with him weekly to clear these intrusions and to treat other serious issues. Finally, out of desperation, I suggested the three-pose TAT technique (Wakefield, 2002) to clear the memories that were intruding. The technique worked. From that point on, I decided to work with the subconscious, and at the start of each session inquired if we should do the poses. We usually did the poses. The patient soon became skilled at doing the poses—left, right and then both. After each set of poses, I would ask the subconscious how many parts we cleared with each pose. The subconscious would reply to the patient with numbers like 84, 92, and 40, and the patient repeated them to me. At one point, it appeared that parts rushed to be treated. This caused a crisis and he became paranoid and had to be admitted to a hospital. While in the hospital, he stabilized on a medication and returned to therapy. When he left the hospital, he was more even tempered but continued to have the intrusions. We continued this three-pose intervention week after week until after about 100 sessions there were no more intrusions. The patient was no longer paranoid and was better functioning by the end of the treatment. He continued to take the medication. We ended treatment and six months later, he returned to college but was later bothered by intrusions again. Clearly, I had not treated all the intrusive memories.

Though TAT can create a flooding of emotions, in general, the average patient or person who obsesses on something can be safely treated with the TAT procedure. This is especially true when the subconscious supports the intervention. Nevertheless, even after checking with the subconscious, if the patient feels some emotions stirring, then it is advisable to stop doing the TAT pose and do some problem-solving with the subconscious.

References

Andrade, J. & Feinstein, D. (2003). *Energy psychology: Theory, indications, evidence.* Retrieved December 26, 2005, from http://www.process-healing.com/report.htm

Andrade, J., Aalberse, M., Sutherland, C., & Ruden, R. (2006a). *In the hands of the patient: The science and art of brief multisensory activation for the treatment of anxiety, stress, unwanted emotions, and emotional components of physical complaints.* Retrieved April 15, 2006, from http://www.bsma-int.com/books.htm

Andrade, J., Aalberse, M., & Sutherland, C. (2006b). See website: www.bsma-int.com

Andrade, J. & Feinstein, D. (2003). *Energy psychology: theory, indications, evidence.* Retrieved December 26, 2005, from http://www.process-healing.com/report.htm

Blizard, R., Braude, S., Brown, R., Dell, P., Nijenhaus, E. R. S. (2005, November). *What is Dissociation?* Panel presentation at the annual meeting of the International Society for Traumatic Stress Studies. Toronto, ON.

Briere, J. (1991). Treating adult survivors of severe childhood abuse and neglect: Further development of an integrated model. In J. E. B. Myers, L. Berliner, J. Brier, C. D. Hendrix, & C. Jenny (Eds.). *The APSAC handbook on child maltreatment, 2nd Ed.* Newbury Park, CA: Sage Publications.

Callahan, R. J. (1985). *Five minute phobia cure.* Wilmington, DE: Enterprise Publishers.

Callahan, R. J. (1991). *Why do I eat when I'm not hungry?* NY, NY: Avon Books.

Callahan, R. J. (1993). *Diagnostic training in Thought Field Therapy.* Training presented in Indian Wells, CA: Author.

Callahan, R. J. (2001). *Tapping the healer within.* NY, NY: Contemporary Books/McGraw Hill.

Callahan, R. J. (2005). See website: http://www.tftrx.com

Cameron-Bandler, L. (1985). *Solutions: practical and effective antidotes for sexual and relationship problems.* San Rafael, CA: FuturePace Books.

Craig, G. & Fowlie, A. (1995). *Emotional freedom techniques: The manual.* Sea Ranch, CA: Author.

Craig, G. (2005). See website http://www.emofree.com

Diamond, J. (1995). *Your body doesn't lie.* NY, NY: Warner Books.

Dilts, R., Grinder, J., Bandler, R., & DeLozier, J. (1980). *Neuro-linguistic programming: Volume I The study of the structure of subjective experience.* Cupertino, CA: Meta Publications.

Erhard, W. (1976). Erhard Seminar Training. Training presented in San Francisco.

Feinstein, D. (2004). Energy psychology interactive CD. Retrieved December 26, 2005, from http://www.EnergypsychologyInteractive.com

Fleming, T. (2003). *You can heal now: The Tapas Acupressure Technique (TAT).* Redondo Beach, CA: TAT International.

Fleming, T. (2005). See website: http://www.tat-intl.com

Flint, G. A. (1968). *Unconditioned responses and bar holding in escape training.* Unpublished doctoral dissertation, Indiana University, Bloomington.

Flint, G. A. (1996). A chaos model of the brain applied to EMDR In B. Goertzel, M. Germine, & A. Combs (Eds.). *Mind in time: The dynamics of thought, reality, and consciousness.* Retrieved May 4, 2005, from http://www.goertzel.org/dynapsyc/1995/FLINT.html

Flint, G. A. (2001). *Emotional freedom: techniques for dealing with emotional and physical distress (Rev. ed.).* Vernon, British Columbia: NeoSolTerric Enterprises.

Flint, G. A. (2004). A chaos model of the brain applied to EMDR In B. Goertzel, M., Germine, & A., Combs (Eds). *Mind in time: the dynamics of thought, reality, and consciousness.* Cresskill, NJ: Hampton Press.

Flint, G. A. (2005). *The Process healing course.* Retrieved December 26, 2005, from http://www.process-healing.com

Flint, G. A. (n.d.). *A theory and treatment of your personal field: Another manual for change.* Vernon, British Columbia: NeoSolTerric Enterprises.

Flint, G. A. & Willems, Jo C. (2006). *A healing legend: Wisdom from the four directions.* Vernon, British Columbia: NeoSolTerric Enterprises.

Frankel, A. S. & O'Hearn, T. (1996). Similarities in responses to extreme and unremitting stress between eastern ghettos during World War II and DID patients: Cultures of communities under siege. *Psychotherapy: Theory, Research, Practice, Training.* 33, pp. 485-502.

Freeman, W. J. (1991). The physiology of perception. *Scientific American, 264,* pp. 78-85.

Krieger, D. (1993). *Accepting your power to heal: The personal practice of therapeutic touch.* Santa Fe, NM: Bear & Co. Publishing.

Millon, T. (1981). *Disorders of personality: DSM-III, Axis II.* NY, NY: John Wiley & Sons.

Ogden, P., Nijenhuis, E., & Steele, K. (2002). *Somatic resources for the treatment of dependency issues in complex PTSD.* Workshop presented at the ISSD 19th Annual Fall Conference, Baltimore, MD.

Oglevie, S. & Oglevie, L. (1997, 1999). *Working with cult and ritual abuse.* Workshops presented at the Elijah House, Mission, BC.

Pearson, P. (1998). *The heart's code.* NY, NY: Broadway Books.

Pulos, L. (1994). *Workshop on ideomotor questioning.* Workshop presented at the General Meeting of the Canadian Society of Clinical Hypnosis (British Columbia Division), Vancouver, BC.

Rice, J. & Caldwell, L. (1986). *Master programmer.* Trained and certified at The Neuro-Linguistic. Programming Center for Advanced Studies, Corte Madera, CA.

Ross, C. A. (1996). Millon Clinical Multiaxial Inventory-II follow-up of patients with dissociative identity disorder. *Psychological Reports,* 77, pp. 707-716.

Ross, C. A. (2000). *Bluebird: Deliberate creation of multiple personality by psychiatrists.* Richardson, TX: Manitou Communications.

Satir, V. (1972). *People making.* Palo Alto, CA: Science and Behavior Books.

Shapiro, F. (1991). *Eye movement desensitization and reprocessing: Level II.* Training held in Sunnyvale, CA.

Shapiro, F. (1995). *Eye movement desensitization and reprocessing: Basic principles, protocols, and procedures.* NY, NY: Guilford Press.

Skinner, B. F. (1953). *Science and human behavior.* NY, NY: MacMillan.

Skinner, B. F. (1957). *Verbal behavior.* NY, NY: Appleton-Century-Crofts.

Stone, H. & Stone, S. L. (1989). *Embracing our selves: The voice dialogue manual.* Novato, CA: Nataraj Publishing.

Taylor, M. A. (1981). *The neuropsychiatric mental status examination.* NY, NY: SP Medical and Scientific Books.

van de Kolk, B. A., Burbridge, J. A., & Suzuki, J. (1997). The psychobiology of traumatic memory: Clinical implications of neuroimaging studies. In R. Yehuda & A. C. McFarlane (Eds.), *Annals of the New York Academy of Sciences (Vol. 821): Psychobiology of Posttraumatic Stress Disorder* (pp. 99-113). NY, NY: Academy of Sciences

Wakefield, H. J. (2002). Multiple pose application of Tapas acupressure techniques with special populations. In F. Gallo (Ed.). *Energy psychology and psychotherapy.* NY, NY: Norton & Norton.

Index

A

Active Experience
  detailed 58
  overview 161–162
Active Personality 170–171
Addictions, treatment of 400–402
Amnesic parts
  creation of 61–63
  description 177–179
Andrade, Joaquin xi–xiv, 1–2, 348, 379
Association process 59–60
Automatic treatment by the subconscious
  possible barriers 192–195
  teaching 110–112

B

Barriers
  barriers for treatment
    barrier reframes 98–108
    caused by entire brain 189–190
    identifying barriers 187–189
    intent not to heal 195–196
    in the subconscious 190–192
    treating parts without permission 196–199
  communication
    get a private line 201
    the non-question 199–200
  field. *See* Field intrusions
    description 183–184
  first session 123–124
  Predisposition barrier 238–239
  treating floating fragments 281–282

About the Author

Garry A. Flint educated at Indiana University received a doctoral degree in experimental psychology specializing in learning (1968). For six years he worked with abused teens in Ukiah, California eventually becoming a staff psychologist at the county mental health outpatient clinic. Here, he continued to work with abused children and adults. It was at this time that he began his search for treatment techniques that worked faster than Behavior Modification. This included extensive training in hypnosis and Neurolinguistic Programming. Eventually, he became the program manager of a psychiatric health facility where he was able to work with severely disturbed persons. In private practice (1987—) he was further trained in Eye Movement Desensitization and Reprocessing (EMDR) and studied the diagnostic training for Thought Field Therapy™ (TFT) and Tapas Acupressure Technique.

It was to explain EMDR, and later TFT, that he developed a clinically based theory of brain processes and behavior. The theory is the basis for the Process Healing Method. This theory explains most of the phenomena in these and other therapies and accounts for the formation of the personality and complex mental issues. Flint current resides in Vernon, British Columbia, where he is a practicing clinical psychologist.

He and coauthor Jo C. Willems have published a book entitled *A Healing Legend: Wisdom From the Four Directions*. This little book provides the healing metaphor of the Process Healing Method to the reader's inner-self in a simple, easy-to-read way that is suitable for adults and children.

To Purchase

A Theory and Treatment of Your Personality:
   a manual for change
Purchase from:
- Website: http://www.neosolterric.com
- Amazon.com
- Bookstores through Ingram Books and Baker & Taylor

A Healing Legend:
   Wisdom From the Four Directions
Purchase from:
- Website: http://www.neosolterric.com
- Amazon.com
- Bookstores through Ingram Books and Baker & Taylor

Emotional Freedom: Techniques for dealing
   with emotional and physical issues
Purchase from:
- Amazon.com
- Bookstores through Ingram Books and Baker & Taylor

Book Clearing House:
- Telephone: 1-800-431-1579 (24-hour service)
- Web site: http://www.bookch.com/psych.htm#9512

CPSIA information can be obtained
at www.ICGtesting.com
Printed in the USA
BVHW042243261120
593996BV00012B/47

9 780968 519554